"The Diogenes of the Modern Corinthians without his Tub."

"Thomas Carlyle ('Men of the Day No. 12.')," cromolithograph
by Carlo Pellegrini, *Vanity Fair*, 22 October 1870
© National Portrait Gallery, London

THE COLLECTED LETTERS OF
THOMAS AND JANE WELSH CARLYLE

DUKE-EDINBURGH EDITION

IAN CAMPBELL
University of Edinburgh

AILEEN CHRISTIANSON
University of Edinburgh

DAVID SORENSEN
Saint Joseph's University

EDITORS

KATHERINE INGLIS
University of Edinburgh

BRENT KINSER
Western Carolina University

JANE ROBERTS
University of Edinburgh

LIZ SUTHERLAND
University of Edinburgh

VOLUME 47
May 1870–September 1871

DUKE UNIVERSITY PRESS
DURHAM AND LONDON
2019

NATIONAL
ENDOWMENT
FOR THE
HUMANITIES

The Collected Letters of Thomas and Jane Welsh Carlyle receives funding from the
Scholarly Editions program of the National Endowment for the Humanities.

For further information on the National Endowment for the Humanities, please
consult the website http://www.neh.gov/. Any views, findings, conclusions, or
recommendations expressed in this publication do not necessarily represent those
of the National Endowment for the Humanities.

Additional funding has been provided by

THE BINKS TRUST
and
THE BRITISH ACADEMY

THE
GLADYS KRIEBLE DELMAS
FOUNDATION

The electronic edition, *The Carlyle Letters Online*
http://www.carlyleletters.dukejournals.org/
is supported in part by the Gladys Krieble Delmas Foundation.

CONTENTS OF VOLUME 47

List of Illustrations
vii

Acknowledgments
xi

Introduction
xiii

Key to References
xxi

Letters to Thomas Carlyle
xxv

Chronology
May 1870–September 1871
xxxiii

Notes on the Text and Editorial Conventions
xxxix

Letters of Thomas Carlyle
May 1870–September 1871
1

Biographical Notes
229

Volumes of *The Collected Letters of Thomas and Jane Welsh Carlyle*
published to date
241

Index
243

ILLUSTRATIONS

Thomas Carlyle by Carlo Pellegrini
Frontispiece

Charles Dickens at Gad's Hill, 6 or 7 August 1866
29

Thomas Carlyle's notes to Dickens's carte de visite of Gad's Hill
30

Statue of Robert the Bruce, Stirling Castle
36

Statue of Robert the Bruce
37

Surrender at Sedan
58

Prussian guard of Louis Napoleon and Belgian charity to French soldiers
59

Hiram Rhodes Revels
69

Bombardment of Strasbourg
78

Fall of Strasbourg
79

French prisoners of war and wounded German soldiers
84

Proclamation of Wilhelm I as emperor of Germany
85

Scenes of the Paris siege
88

Maps of France, 12th to 16th century, and of Paris, 1789
92

Thomas Carlyle
115

The burial of French soldiers
120

Scenes of the siege at Versailles
132

The last oxen in Paris
138

Alexander Munro
144

Killing an elephant, Jardin des Plantes, Paris
146

Bois de Boulogne, Paris
147

The effects of bombardment on a single house
148

First floor plan of 5 Cheyne Row
172

"Dr Carlyle my Br*r*"
176

John A. Carlyle
177

Jane Welsh Carlyle's childhood chair
185

Presentation clock for Thomas Carlyle's 75th birthday
189

Presentation clock in its traveling case
190

Presentation clock (detail)
191

Alexander Carlyle, Alexander and Janet Carlyle's son
220

James Carlyle, Alexander and Janet Carlyle's son
221

ACKNOWLEDGMENTS

The editors are very grateful to the National Endowment for the Humanities, which has generously awarded the project a three-year grant (2018–21) under the auspices of its Scholarly Editions program, and to the Research Libraries Program of the Gladys Krieble Delmas Foundation, which has provided invaluable grant support for the Carlyle Letters Online. We are also grateful to the Binks Trust for its continuing financial contributions to the funding of the Edinburgh editorial team and office. The editors again express their gratitude to the British Academy, which made the Carlyle Letters a British Academy Research Project and continues to support us with an annual grant, and to the members of its Committee on Academy Research Projects and its assistant secretary, Ken Emond. The editors also express their gratitude to those private individuals who have made donations for the support of the Edinburgh Carlyle Letters office, to the University of Edinburgh Development Trust, and to Joyce Caplan and the Friends of Edinburgh University Library.

We remain extremely grateful for the advice of Paolo Mangiafico, Scholarly Communications Strategist, Duke University Library; and we continue to extend our thanks for early critiques of the electronic edition to David Chesnutt, formerly of the Model Editions Partnership at the University of South Carolina, and to Natalia Smith of the DocSouth project at the University of North Carolina. Brent E. Kinser serves as coordinating editor of *The Carlyle Letters Online* in addition to his editorial service to the print edition. DNC Data Systems of Mumbai, India, has electronically encoded volumes 1 through 45 of the Carlyle Letters. Colin Wilder and staff at University of South Carolina and their Center for Digital Humanities host the online edition.

We recognize a continued indebtedness and gratitude for help and permissions to the following institutions and their staffs: Jennie De Protani, archivist, Athenaeum Club; Rita Patteson, Melinda Creech, and Melvin Schuetz of the Armstrong Browning Library, Baylor University; the British Library and its Special Collections; the National Trust and Lin and Geff Skippings, curators of Carlyle's House, Chelsea; National Trust for Scotland and Carlyle's Birthplace, Ecclefechan; Michael Ryan, director, Tara C. Craig, reference services supervisor, and Jane R. Siegel, Rare Book and Manuscript Library, Columbia University in the City of New York, for their help with reproductions from the Thomas Carlyle Photograph Albums; Louisa Price, curator, Charles Dickens Museum, London; Duke University Library and librarians Andrew Armacost, Sara Seten Berghausen, Molly Bragg, Elizabeth Dunn, Andrea Loigman, and

Naomi Nelson; Jeremy Upton, director of library services, Edinburgh University Library, Joseph Marshall, director of the Centre for Research Collections, and Edinburgh University Library Special Collections; Richard Kuhta of the Folger Shakespeare Library, Washington, D.C.; the Houghton Library, Harvard University, and librarians Leslie Morris and Karen Nipps; Margaret Burri and John Buchtel, Special Collections Department, Eisenhower Library, Johns Hopkins University; Library of Congress manuscripts division and librarian Bruce Kirby; Marilyn Palmeri and the Morgan Library and Museum; the trustees and the librarian and chief executive, John Scally, of the National Library of Scotland, the Department of Manuscripts, and the Issue Desk; Elizabeth Denlinger, Carl H. Pforzheimer Collection, New York Public Library; Sir Roland Jackson, Frank A. J. L. James, and the Royal Institution, London; Christine Bunting, head of Special Collections and Archives, University Library, University of California, Santa Cruz, and Luisa Haddad; the Frederick W. Hilles Manuscript Collection, General Collection, Beinecke Rare Book and Manuscript Library, Yale University, and librarian Karen Nangle.

We wish to thank Steve Cohn, director of Duke University Press; and, also of the Press, Allison Belan, Jocelyn Dawson, Robert Dilworth, Cynthia Gurganus, Stacy Lavin, and Cason Lynley; the dean of arts and sciences, the provost, and the vice provost of Duke University. We also thank Dorothy Miell, head of the College of Humanities and Social Science, Jeremy Robbins, head of the School of Literatures, Languages, and Cultures, Andrew Taylor, head of English Literature, Greg Walker, English Literature, Janet Black, and Julie Robertson of the School, Neil Young, of LLC Computing Service, all of Edinburgh University; Neil Burns and the Edinburgh University Development Trust; Nathaniel Banfich, Anthony Burns, Kathy Chamberlain, Todd Endelman, Mark Engel, Bryan Homer, Travis Mullen, Terence Muzzell, Harrold Nuttall, Tom Raworth, Hilary Smith, Chris Stray, Greer Thomas, James Turner, Chris Vanden Bossche, and Joe Viscomi. We remain very grateful to members of the Carlyle family. Clare Cain continues to provide valuable research support at the Edinburgh office. We also thank David Southern, managing editor of the Carlyle Letters office at Duke University Press, and Laurel Ferejohn, proofreader.

INTRODUCTION

The letters in this volume cover May 1870 through September 1871; the volume includes 122 letters by Thomas Carlyle and his 1871 Will; many of these letters were dictated to his niece Mary Aitken, due to the developing weakness and palsy of TC's writing hand. By May 1870 his control of his right hand had deteriorated to such a degree that he could no longer write with a pen. Disability forced a change in writing practice: TC would dictate to Mary Aitken, occasionally correcting minor transcription errors, and usually signing the letter in his own hand. Those letters written in TC's own hand were written mostly in blue pencil rather than pen. The volume also includes 9 letters written by Mary Aitken at TC's request.

During this period TC was engaged in two endeavors: work towards the Chapman & Hall Library and People's editions of his collected works, and a statement of his views on the Franco-Prussian War, published as a letter in the London *Times* on 18 November 1870. In June 1871 he also gave James Anthony Froude the manuscript of *Reminiscences* and the edited collection of Jane Welsh Carlyle's letters that TC had worked on for several years after JWC's death (see vols. 43–46). He had already written an interim Will on 6 April 1871 (included in this volume), concerning the publication of JWC's letters and memorials, articulating his trust in Froude: "I solemnly request of him to do his best and wisest in the matter, as I feel assured he will." Shortly after he handed over the manuscripts, TC recorded a brief statement of gratitude: "The deepest thanks of my heart are due to you in regard to that MS" (TC to JAF, 7 July 1871). Froude considered them over the summer and concluded that the letters and the memoir should be published. They were then shown to John Forster, who told Froude he would advise TC that trouble might arise if TC's instructions for Froude were not stated clearly in his will (see 227–28 and Froude, *Carlyle* 4:408–15). These papers did prove controversial when they were published soon after TC's death (see 184), partly because of the ambiguity of TC's expression of his wishes, but also because of the public exposure of TC and JWC's relationship and their characters.

The period covered by this volume could not be called unproductive, but TC was deeply affected by the barrier his manual disability placed between his thoughts and the blank page; as he was no longer able to write with ease, TC began to think of himself as unable to work. Insomnia, loss of motivation, and dyspepsia exacerbated the problem. He also blamed his debility on, variously: railway whistles, the state of modern manufacturing, tradespeople, the weather, flatulence remedies, and specific foods (for example, mutton and grouse). Diverse tonics were suggested and tried, including riding, boat trips, and seclusion in the Highlands of Scotland. TC sometimes seemed reconciled to a less productive life but often castigated himself, as in a journal entry written after a three-month visit to Dumfries, when he complained: "Not a word written *here* or elsewhere barely; a three months shamefully empty; I think the *idlest*, and among the heaviest and silently meanest of all my life" (TC's journal, 20 Sept. 1870; privately owned; see 651). To correspondents, however, he continued to prescribe the imperative to work as the supreme duty and best comfort in life. TC's expressions of condolence to Meta Wellmer after the death of her mother combine sympathy with the exhortation "not to sit down in indolent despair"; TC reminded her of her "duty and obligation" to work: "This is a truth that I tell you not an idle figure of speech; and in fact it is the sum of all the advice and encouragement I have to give" (7 Dec. 1871). He resolved to escape from "basely quiescent torpor" (TC's journal, 8 Sept. 1870; see 56) and follow his own advice by writing by dictation: "I am much ashamed of myself. *Can* I 'turn over a new leaf'? Try it, try it ag*n*, in the vacancy of Chelsea. If a man had but an hour to live, he *ot* to employ that hour in some wise way,—in some *wiser* than this! To 'write by dictact*n*,' can*not* I learn that, then? Shame on me, shame!" (TC's journal, 10 Sept. 1870; see 63). The letters in this volume demonstrate that TC made considerable use of Mary Aitken as his amanuensis in order to keep up with correspondence, but he was never completely reconciled to this new method of composition. The loss of the use of his hand, he complained, "completely disfurnishes my life; makes real 'employ*t*' impossible in it" (TC to JAC, 15 May 1871). Ideas for subjects for essays punctuate his letters and journal entries, but the strength to research and compose was wanting. Yet intervals of activity could produce new compositions, some of a kind that TC found meaningful.

TC's work was enabled by his niece, Mary Aitken, who, in addition to her labor as amanuensis, managed the household, organized TC's travel, met with visitors in his absence, and cared for TC when he was sleeping particularly badly. After one bad night, Mary was "up three times in the hollow of the night ministering to me like a beneficent little Fairy" (TC to JAC, 25 March 1871). In January 1871, Mary Aitken took over responsibility for organizing a petition to William Gladstone to award a pension to Geraldine Jewsbury, whose health and sight were failing; when the petition was rejected, Mary Aitken enlisted Margaret Oliphant's support in an attempt to persuade Queen Victoria to consider Jewsbury's case. Mary Aitken was, by TC's account, an excellent amanuensis, but TC found the method of dictation interrupted the fluent expression of his ideas, and he was not satisfied that the text that was produced was of the same standard as that which he could produce with his own hand. To his sister Jean Carlyle Aitken, he apologized for his unusual verbosity, blaming the change of style on the method of composition: "excuse this long *clish maclaver*, which is due purely to the vice of dictating; had my own right hand been still mine I sh*d* have written in 5 lines what here occupies as many pages" (17 June 1871). With Mary Aitken's help, TC was able to remain in regular contact with his family in Scotland and in Canada: the letters in this volume record the customary exchanges of clothes, books, periodicals, medical recommendations, family news, holiday arrangements, and plans for extended visits. Mary Aitken's assistance as researcher and amanuensis was also essential for TC's letter on the Franco-Prussian War to the *Times* and the new editions of his collected works.

TC was often irascible in his correspondence with Chapman & Hall, the publishers of the Library and People's editions of his works, complaining of inaccuracies and failures to dispatch volumes to friends such as Ralph Waldo Emerson. Editorial work for the publishers consumed a significant portion of TC's time and energy, requiring him to work swiftly without sacrificing attention to detail. According to his brother John A. Carlyle, TC confined himself to correcting proofs, "making no alterations at all, only rectifying errors" (JAC to Charles Butler, 20 May 1871; MS: EUL; pbd: *CSA* 25:208). This assessment minimizes the labor involved in identifying mistakes and overseeing their correction. A letter to Frederick Anderson, the engraver tasked with preparing a woodcut of Oliver Cromwell's portrait, is indicative of the intensity with which TC worked; TC's tone is urgent, conveying the pressure of deadlines and importance of attaining historical accuracy, even in a matter as small as the location of Cromwell's wart, to which he devotes three paragraphs: "For Heaven's sake, *put* that wart right at last; and let me see a final Proof, *as soon* as possible, for the Printer is getting impat*t* now" (TC to FA, [2 or 9 May 1870]). Despite his continued dedication to the editions, he dismissed his contribution as "paltry bother" for a mere commercial enterprise (TC to R.W. Emerson, 4 June 1871).

TC expressed greater enthusiasm for the original work he composed with the aid of Mary Aitken, his letter to the *Times* on the Franco-Prussian War. The version of the letter reproduced in this volume is that which was published by the *Times* (TC to editor of the *Times*, 11 Nov. 1870). TC followed the progress of the war with growing elation, in hope and then certainty that Germany's conquest of France marked the beginning of her European ascendancy: "Germany *ought* to be President of Europe," he declared, and would be for "another 5 centuries or so"; he also recognized that the annexation of Alsace and Lorraine would prove critical, predicting that Germany would seize "what of Lorraine and Elsass is still German or can be expected to *re-become* such" (TC to JAF, 7 Sept. 1870). TC invested Germany's humiliation of France with geopolitical, moral, and cosmic significance: "magnanimous, pious, strong, and modest Germany is henceforth to be Queen of the Continent, instead of vain, vapouring, impious and mischievous France; which I take to be the most blessed event in European politics I have witnessed in my time" (TC to CAW, 20 Oct. 1870). He shared his enthusiasm for the German cause, which he claimed was the view of "all the intelligent in England," with his friend Thomas Wilson, who had long been living in Weimar (TC to TW, mid-Oct. 1870). Wilson passed TC's letter to the *Weimar Gazette*, and TC's note of "satisfaction" was duly reproduced in that newspaper and thereafter in British newspapers. TC's partisan enthusiasm for Germany's annexation of French territory was not in fact representative of a consensus of the English intelligentsia. Notably TC found himself at odds with John Ruskin's argument, published in the second of two letters to the *Daily Telegraph* of 7 and 8 October 1870, that Germany should give "unconditional armistice, and offer terms that France can accept with honour" (TC to JR, 10 Oct. 1870, n.6). Foreign correspondents and war artists working for British newspapers sent regular dispatches from France by telegraph and from besieged Paris by hot-air balloon, providing eyewitness accounts of military maneuvers and the lived experience of soldiers and non-combatants.[1] TC had been growing increasingly frustrated with English "maudlin wail about the Woes of France"; were it not for his hand, he would "write something on that monstrous ignorance of the English Nation about European History and the nature of Facts in this world" (TC to JAF, 2 Nov. 1870).

TC resolved to publish on the historical background of French-German conflict with Mary Aitken's assistance. Researching and writing the 3,770-word letter to the *Times* occupied a "terrible ten days": "Poor Mary had endless patience, endless assiduity, wrote like a little fairy, sharp as a needle, & all that could be expected of her, when it came to writing; and before that, there was such hauling down of old forgotten books, *Köhlers, Büschings Reichs-histories, Biographies* &c &c, in all which my little Helpmate was nimble and unwearied" (TC to JAC, 12 Nov. 1870). TC's letter appeared in the *Times* on 18 November 1870. Although it is typical of Carlyle's work in its distinctive style and historical detail, it is a markedly partisan misinterpretation of the historical record. It echoes Otto von Bismarck's notorious public statement of the objects of the Franco-Prussian war; in remarks that were reported in the *Standard* on 20 September 1870, Bismarck depicted the war as the twenty-fifth dispute between France and Germany in a century, in each of which France had been the aggressor, acting on "some pretext or another." Bismarck represented Germany's annexation of Strasbourg and Metz as an act of self-

---

1. See, for example, Henry Vizetelly, *Glances Back through Seventy Years: Autobiographical and Other Reminiscences* (London, 1893) 2:424–26, and R. J. Wilkinson-Latham, *From Our Special Correspondent: Victorian War Correspondents and their Campaigns* (London, 1979) 102–13.

defense intended only to establish an "improved frontier" and render France "harmless": "We do not want the territory as territory, but as a *glacis* between her and us."[2] TC extended Bismarck's analysis further back into the past, manipulating four hundred years of European conflicts into a simple and misleading story in which France was the eternal, irrational aggressor, and Germany—before she existed as a nation state—the perpetual victim. Viewing a long history of power struggles between distinct semi-autonomous regions, duchies, electorates, and city-states in terms of the contemporary conflict between modern states was an obvious distortion of history. Although the *Times* published TC's letter, it expressed strong reservations in a lengthy editorial statement printed alongside TC's piece (18 Nov. 1870). Affirming the importance of TC's past work, it warned its readers to approach his letter with "an intelligent independence," questioning the letter's conclusions and even "the method of its reasoning." The editorial disputed "the pertinency and value" of references to sixteenth-century conflicts to present-day dilemmas, and deplored TC's failure to consider "the relative worth of facts and of arguments." Recalling TC's challenge to pedantry in *Past and Present*, "dry rubbish shot here!" (Carlyle, *Works* 10:49), the editorial wondered: "Has he forgotten his own warning?" TC's tendency to anthropomorphize France and malign her as an unpleasant personality was also noted with concern: "'Franco' is not a terrestrial being," the editorial reminded its readers, and highlighted the danger of treating that mythic personality's "provinces as chattels and their inhabitants as vermin." TC's antipathy towards "Franco" enabled him to overlook and minimize the effect of the annexation of French territory on her inhabitants. The *Times* presented TC's letter as not only inaccurate, but even unethical historiography.

A preoccupation in TC's writing at this time in his letters is the issue of colonization. Where English-speaking migrants are praised and promoted, the indigenous inhabitants of lands settled by the migrants are minimized or absent entirely from TC's letters promoting state-sponsored emigration to British colonies. TC had expressed interest in emigration schemes since early 1870: he praised Arthur Helps's depiction of the subject in his novel *Casimir Maremma* (see 46:170), and he supported Sir George Grey's political campaign for imperial expansion and emigration (46:173, 179–80, 184, 185, 194). He continued to promote Grey after the failure of Grey's election campaign, attempting to convince the Australian politicians Sir Henry Parkes and Charles Gavan Duffy of the necessity of increasing the scale of migration from Britain to the colonies. With British support, TC told Parkes, Australia might have "as many hardy English Emigrants as you could gradually make room for, to the unspeakable advantage of us and of you!" (21 Septem-

2. "A Conversation with Count Bismarck," *Standard*, 20 Sept. 1870.

ber 1870). TC's enthusiasm for Edward Jenkins's satirical novel *Ginx's Baby* (1870) can be explained by its analysis of the root causes of and remedies for urban English poverty: surplus population, maintained by capitalists in order to keep wages down, could be alleviated by emigration to supposedly un-inhabited colonies (TC to CDB, 11 July 1870; Jenkins 156–57; 180–88). TC also praised Froude for his essay in *Fraser's Magazine*, "The Colonies Once More" ([Sept. 1870] 269–87) in which Froude used the Franco-Prussian War as cause to question the loyalty of the unpropertied masses in the event of a conflict in which Britain would have to fight. Froude argued that "the supply of human creatures is in excess of the demand as English society is now con-stituted" and called on the government to encourage the loyalty of the poor by establishing a "sustained and methodical emigration supported in part by the State" to British colonies, "where land is to be had for the asking" (Froude, "Colonies" 283, 278). TC congratulated Froude on fulfilling the writer's duty to the nation: "I can conceive no burden fitter for a writing Englishman than that of awakening this poor Country to the crisis for it which is now evidently nigh, and coming nigher every day" (7 Sept. 1870).

The effects of colonization on indigenous peoples were almost entirely absent from TC's writing on emigration, but an unguarded exchange with John Reuben Thompson revealed TC's attitude to the peoples of colonized lands, as well as underlining TC's continued prejudice against people of color. Thompson, an American poet and journalist who promoted the Confederate cause in Britain during the American Civil War, had sent TC a photograph of Hiram Rhodes Revels, the first African-American U.S. Senator. In his letter of thanks, TC commented negatively on Revels's physical appearance, denigrat-ing both his African and rumored Native American ancestry: "I yesterday re-ceived the announced Senatorial Nigger in the highest state of preservation, a very ugly figure indeed. He seems to have something of the wild Indian as well as of the d*o* [ditto] African; but no doubt knows on which side his bread is buttered; let us hope he may throw some light into the Senate of Mississippi" (TC to JRT, 22 Sept. 1870). This is as far as TC's sympathy for colonized and enslaved people extends; in TC's racist analysis, Revels shows himself capable of suppressing the supposed "wildness" of his Native American and African heritage in order to pursue a more profitable career in politics. Furthermore, TC told Thompson, he found Revels's image repulsive. He concluded: "To me he is so ugly that I have at once got him provided for in a safe Apartment where he will be seen only by the indifferent, or the well-affected." Revels's image was not entered in the later volumes of the Thomas Carlyle Photograph Albums; a contemporary photograph of the Senator is included in this vol-ume (see 69).

TC continued to be reluctant to make public statements on the issues of the day. With the notable exception of the Franco-Prussian War letter, TC seemed content with his absence from public life, expressing his views in private letters as he always had. Like his letters on emigration, TC's position on what he called "Female Emancipation" was not intended for wider circulation. In early 1871, a series of public meetings were held in Edinburgh to debate the question of whether to allow women medical students to obtain clinical experience at the Royal Infirmary of Edinburgh, which was a requirement of the University of Edinburgh's medical degree. This was the latest skirmish in the ongoing battle of the "Edinburgh Seven" (the pioneering women medical students led by Sophia Jex-Blake) to obtain qualifying medical degrees from the university. Following the "Surgeon's Hall Riot" of 18 November 1870, in which the women were abused by a mob when they entered the Hall to sit an extramural examination, and a live sheep was thrust into their lecture hall in an attempt to disrupt their exam, their supporters were attempting to organize and mobilize allies to challenge their opponents at the university. A Committee for Securing Complete Medical Education to Women in Edinburgh was formed in January 1871 and began to recruit supporters nationally.[3] Notable members of the committee included Frances Power Cobbe, Charles Darwin and Harriet Martineau.[4] As a former Rector of the University, TC's open support for or membership of the Committee might have helped to undermine the administrative maneuverings against the students by members of the university's professoriate. TC's friend David Masson, Chair of Rhetoric and English Literature at the University of Edinburgh, was an effective advocate for the Edinburgh Seven within the university (Jex-Blake; Roberts). John A. Carlyle was to send TC a copy of Masson's letter to the *Scotsman* in support of women's access to university education (see JAC to TC, 25 Dec. 1871 [vol. 48];); he had also met and liked Sophia Jex-Blake (see TC to RL, 9 Feb. 1871).

On 9 February 1871, TC wrote to Robert Lawson, an Edinburgh graduate, to express qualified support for women's entry to the medical profession, but in cautious terms that made no direct reference to the specific issue of the moment, access to the Royal Infirmary. He expressed great reluctance to touch the "subject of Female Emancipation," which he regarded as "one of the most afflicting proofs of the miserable Anarchy that prevails in human society," and insisted on the "strict condition that whatever I say shall be private." TC prefaced his defense of women's fitness for entry to medicine by affirming that "the true and noble function of a woman in this world was, is, and forever will be, that of being Wife and Helpmate to a worthy Man & discharging well the duties that devolve on her in consequence as mother of children, and mistress of a Household." But "if a Woman miss this destiny, or have

3. Sophia Jex-Blake, *Medical Women* (Edinburgh, 1872).
4. Shirley Roberts, *Sophia Jex-Blake: A Woman Pioneer in Nineteenth-Century Medical Reform* (1993) 101–8.

renounced it, she has every right, before God and man, to take up whatever honest employment she can find open to her in the world." "[P]rinting, tailoring, weaving, clerking" were likely to be suitable fields for women's work; so too medicine, which had until the recent professionalization of medicine, TC argued, been the province of women. He concluded that women had a right to study medicine, and "it might be profitable and serviceable to have facilities, or at least possibilities offered them for so doing." This statement sets TC against the most hardline opponents to women's medical education in Edinburgh. But TC's conclusion was less helpful to the women's cause: it seemed "obvious" to TC that women students should have "Female Teachers, or else an extremely select kind of Men"; TC may not have been aware that male lecturers were already instructing the Edinburgh Seven, albeit outside of the university. Furthermore, the notion that women might attend the same classes as men was "an incongruity of the first magnitude and shocking to think of to every pure and modest mind." Although women had first matriculated at the university in 1869, they were not permitted to attend mixed-sex classes within the university. They obtained instruction in extramural courses with male students, or, within the university, in small single-sex classes; because there were so few of them, they were required to pay higher fees than male students in order to make up the lecturer's salary (see TC to RL, 9 Feb. 1871). TC's prim affirmation of the importance of modesty in pedagogy would have been a useful statement of principle to the women's opponents, had it been made public. Lawson respected TC's request for privacy, and the letter was not published until 1907, after Lawson's death.

The period of TC's life covered in this volume is characterized by a declining power and interest in influencing public affairs. Running through the letters is a sense that TC's life's work is done and that he feels his end approaching, a feeling that was reinforced by the failing health of John Forster and the deaths of close friends and family, including his nephew James Aitken (Mary Aitken's brother), Charles Dickens, Anthony Sterling, and Thomas Spedding. TC wrote to Spedding's brother James: "We shall all soon follow Him, especially I soon must into that undiscovered country from which there is no return. . . . Telos, Telos! Our thoughts on it ought rather to be silent; but may well be sad solemn & even devout" (TC to JS, 27 Nov. 1870). The end of life and work was years away, but in this volume we see TC adjusting—sometimes with difficulty, sometimes with philosophical acceptance—to a life of retirement and rest.

Katherine Inglis

KEY TO REFERENCES

Allingham Diary. William Allingham, a Diary, ed. H. Allingham and D. Radford. London: Macmillan and Co., 1907.

Annals. Joseph Irving. *The Annals of Our Time*. London: Macmillan, 1890.

Armstrong Browning. Armstrong Browning Library, Baylor Univ.

Berg. Berg Collection, New York Public Library.

Blunt, *CCH*. Reginald Blunt. *The Carlyles' Chelsea Home*. London: George Bell and Sons, 1895.

Blunt, *Memoirs of Gerald Blunt*. Reginald Blunt. *Memoirs of Gerald Blunt of Chelsea, His Family and Forebears*. London: Truslove & Hanson, 1911.

A. Carlyle, *CB*. Alexander Carlyle, ed. "Correspondence between Carlyle and Browning." *Cornhill Magazine* n.s. 38 (1918): 642–69.

A. Carlyle, *CMSB*. Alexander Carlyle, ed. *Letters of Thomas Carlyle to John Stuart Mill, John Sterling, and Robert Browning*. London: T. Fisher Unwin, 1923.

A. Carlyle, *CS*. Alexander Carlyle, ed. "Thomas Carlyle and Thomas Spedding." *Cornhill Magazine* n.s. 50 (1921): 513–37, 742–68.

A. Carlyle, *NL*. Alexander Carlyle, ed. *New Letters of Thomas Carlyle*. 2 vols. London and New York: John Lane, 1904.

CA. Carlyle Annual: 10, Queens College, CUNY, NY, 1989.

Carlyle, *On Heroes*. Thomas Carlyle. *On Heroes, Hero-Worship, and the Heroic in History*. Ed. Michael K. Goldberg. Text established by Michael K. Goldberg, Joel J. Brattin, and Mark Engel. Strouse Edition. Berkeley, Los Angeles, and London: Univ. of California Press, 1993.

Carlyle, *Past and Present*. Thomas Carlyle. *Past and Present*. Ed. Chris R. Vanden Bossche. Text established by Chris R. Vanden Bossche, Joel J. Brattin, and D. J. Trela. Strouse Edition. Berkeley: Univ. of California Press, 2005.

Carlyle, *Reminiscences*. Thomas Carlyle. *Reminiscences*. Ed. K. J. Fielding and Ian Campbell. New and complete edn. Oxford and New York: Oxford Univ. Press, 1997.

Carlyle, *Sartor*. Thomas Carlyle. *Sartor Resartus*. Ed. Rodger L. Tarr. Text established by Mark Engel and Rodger L. Tarr. Strouse Edition. Berkeley, Los Angeles, and London: Univ. of California Press, 2000.

Carlyle, *Works*. Thomas Carlyle. *Works*. Ed. H. D. Traill. Centenary Edition. 30 vols. London: Chapman and Hall, 1896–99.

Carlyle's House. Illustrated Memorial Volume of the Carlyle's House Purchase Fund Committee, with Catalogue of Carlyle's Books Manuscripts Pictures and Furniture Exhibited Therein. Original edn., London: Carlyle's House Memorial Trust, 1895; facsimile edn., London: National Trust, 1995.

Cate. G. A. Cate, ed. *Correspondence of Thomas Carlyle and John Ruskin*. Stanford, Calif.: Stanford Univ. Press, 1982.

Columbia. Rare Book & Manuscript Library, Columbia Univ. in the City of New York.

Conway, *Carlyle*. Moncure Daniel Conway. *Thomas Carlyle*. New York: Harper, 1881.

Copeland. Charles Townsend Copeland, ed. *Letters of Thomas Carlyle to His Youngest Sister*. London: Chapman and Hall; Boston and New York: Houghton Mifflin, 1899.

Copeland, "Unpublished Letters." C. T. Copeland, ed. "Unpublished Letters of Carlyle. IV." *Atlantic Monthly* 82 (Dec. 1898): 785–92.

Cromwell. Oliver Cromwell's Letters and Speeches. Carlyle, *Works* 6–9.

CSA. Carlyle Studies Annual: 14–18, Dept. of English, Illinois State Univ., Illinois, 1994–98; 19–21, Dept. of English, Memorial Univ., Newfoundland, 1999–2004; 22–32, St. Joseph's Univ. Press, Philadelphia, 2006–17.

Davies, *John Forster*. J. A. Davies. *John Forster: A Literary Life*. Leicester: Leicester Univ. Press, 1983.

Duke. David M. Rubenstein Rare Book and Manuscript Library, Duke Univ. Library.

Dumfries Courier. Dumfries and Galloway Courier. Dumfries, 1809–84.

EUL. Edinburgh Univ. Library.

FC. Forster Collection, Victoria and Albert Museum.

Fitzgerald's Letters. The Letters of Edward Fitzgerald. Ed. A. M. Terhune and A. B. Terhune. 4 vols. Princeton: Princeton Univ. Press, 1980.

Ford. George H. Ford, "Stern Hebrews Who Laugh." *Carlyle Past and Present*. Ed. K. J. Fielding and Roger L. Tarr. London: Vision Press, 1976. 112–26.

Frederick. History of Friedrich II of Prussia, called Frederick the Great. Carlyle, *Works* 12–19.

Froude, *Carlyle*. J. A. Froude. *Thomas Carlyle: A History of the First Forty Years of His Life, 1795–1835; A History of His Life in London, 1834–1881*. 4 vols. London: Longmans, Green, 1882, 1884.

Froude, *LM*. J. A. Froude, ed. *Letters and Memorials of Jane Welsh Carlyle: Prepared for Publication by Thomas Carlyle*. 3 vols. London: Longmans, Green, 1883.

Froude, *My Relations*. J. A. Froude, *My Relations with Carlyle*. London: Longmans, Green, 1903.

GV. Gesamtverzeichnis des Deutschsprachigen Schrifttums, 1700–1910. Munich and London: Saur, 1979–87.

Hansard. Hansard's Parliamentary Debates. 3d ser. 356 vols. London: T. C. Hansard, 1830–91.

HCC. Harvard Carlyle Collection, Harvard Univ.

Hilles. Frederick W. Hilles Manuscript Collection, General Collection, Beinecke Rare Book and Manuscript Library, Yale Univ.

Holme. Thea Holme. *The Carlyles at Home*. Oxford: Oxford Univ. Press, 1979.

Hornel. Hornel Collection, Broughton House, Kirkcudbright, Dumfries and Galloway.

Houghton. Houghton Library, Harvard Univ.

JBW. Jane Baillie Welsh.

JWC. Jane Welsh Carlyle.

Kaplan. Fred Kaplan. *Thomas Carlyle*. Cambridge: Cambridge Univ. Press, 1983.

Last Words. *Last Words of Thomas Carlyle*. London: Longmans, Green, 1892.

LC. Library of Congress.

Marrs. Edwin W. Marrs Jr., ed. *The Letters of Thomas Carlyle to His Brother Alexander with Related Family Letters*. Cambridge, MA: Harvard Univ. Press, 1968.

Morgan. Morgan Library and Museum, New York.

MUL. McMaster Univ. Library.

NLI. National Library of Ireland.

NLS. National Library of Scotland.

Norton, *CE*. Charles Eliot Norton, ed. *The Correspondence of Thomas Carlyle and Ralph Waldo Emerson, 1834–1872*. 2 vols. London: Chatto and Windus, 1883. Boston and New York: Houghton Mifflin, 1894.

Norton's Letters. *Letters of Charles Eliot Norton*, ed. Sara Norton and M. A. DeWolfe Howe. Boston, Houghton Mifflin, 1913.

ODNB. *Oxford Dictionary of National Biography*. Ed. H. C. G. Matthew and Brian Harrison. 61 vols. Oxford: Oxford Univ. Press, 2004. Also available online.

Rusk. Ralph L. Rusk, ed. *The Letters of Ralph Waldo Emerson*. 6 vols. New York: Columbia Univ. Press, 1939.

Ruskin's Diaries. *The Diaries of John Ruskin*. Selected and ed. by Joan Evans and John Howard Whitehouse. 3 vols. Oxford: Clarendon Press, 1956–59.

Ruskin Lib. Collection. The Ruskin Library Collection, Ruskin Library, Lancaster Univ.

Ruskin's Works. *The Works of John Ruskin*. Ed. E. T. Cook and A. Wedderburn. 39 vols. London: G. Allen, 1903–12.

RWEMA. Ralph Waldo Emerson Memorial Association, Harvard Univ.

Sanders, "Carlyle's Letters to Ruskin." C. R. Sanders. "Carlyle's Letters to Ruskin: A Finding List with Some Unpublished Letters and Comments." *Bulletin of the John Rylands Library* 41 (1958–59): 208–38.

Sanders, *CB*. C. R. Sanders. "Some Lost and Unpublished Carlyle-Browning

Correspondence." *Journal of English and Germanic Philology* 62 (1963): 323–35.

Sanders, *CF*. C. R. Sanders. *Carlyle's Friendships and Other Studies*. Durham, NC: Duke Univ. Press, 1977.

Scritti. Giuseppe Mazzini, *Scritti editi ed indediti di Giuseppe Mazzini*. 94 vols. Imola: Cooperativa Tipografico-Editrice Paolo Galeati, 1902–43.

Shepherd, *Carlyle*. Richard Herne Shepherd, ed. *Memoirs of the Life and Writings of Thomas Carlyle*. 2 vols. London: W. H. Allen, 1881.

Slater, *CEC*. Joseph Slater, ed. *The Correspondence of Emerson and Carlyle*. New York: Columbia Univ. Press, 1964.

SND. Scottish National Dictionary. Ed. William Grant and David D. Murison. 10 vols. Edinburgh: Scottish National Dictionary Association, 1931–76.

Sotheby's (1932). *Catalogue of Printed Books, Autographs Letters, Literary Manuscripts, Oil Paintings, Drawings & Engravings, Works of Art, China, Furniture, &c. Formerly the Property of Thomas Carlyle, 1795–1881 and Now Sold by Order of the Executors of his Nephew, Alexander Carlyle* (1932).

Strouse. Norman and Charlotte Strouse Carlyle Collection, Univ. of California, Santa Cruz.

Surtees, *Ludovisi*. Virginia Surtees. *The Ludovisi Goddess*. Salisbury, U.K.: Michael Russell, 1984.

Symington. A. J. Symington, *Some Personal Reminiscences of Carlyle*. Paisley and London; Alexander Gardner, 1886.

Tarr. Rodger L. Tarr. *Thomas Carlyle: A Descriptive Bibliography*. Pittsburgh, PA: Univ. of Pittsburgh Press, 1989.

TC. Thomas Carlyle.

TLS. *Times Literary Supplement*.

Trinity. Trinity College Library, Cambridge.

Tyndall, "Personal Recollections." John Tyndall, "Personal Recollections of Thomas Carlyle," *Fortnightly Review* 47 (Jan. 1890): 5–32.

V & A. Victoria and Albert Museum.

Wellesley. Wellesley Index to Victorian Periodicals, 1824–1900. Ed. Walter E. Houghton et al. 5 vols. Toronto: Univ. of Toronto Press; London: Routledge and Kegan Paul, 1966–89.

Wilson, *Carlyle*. David Alec Wilson. *Carlyle*. 6 vols. London: Kegan Paul, Trench, Trubner; New York: E. P. Dutton, 1923–34. Vol. 6 (1934) was completed by David Wilson MacArthur.

Wylie. William Howie Wylie. *Thomas Carlyle: The Man and His Books*. London: Marshall Japp, 1881.

Yale. Yale Univ. Library; see also Hilles.

LETTERS TO THOMAS CARLYLE
May 1870–September 1871

From	Source	Date
Caroline Bromley	NLS 1769.195	[29 April 1870]
John A. Carlyle	NLS 1775D.190	1 May 1870
John A. Carlyle	NLS 1775D.191	3 May 1870
David Masson	NLS 1769.196	3 May 1870
Lady Airlie	NLS 1769.197	4 May 1870
William R. Shedden-Ralston	NLS Acc. 11388	7 May 1870
Lady Salisbury	NLS 1769.198	8 May 1870
John A. Carlyle	NLS 1775D.192	9 May 1870
John A. Carlyle	NLS 1775D.194	13 May 1870
Lady Alford	NLS 1769.199	14 May 1870
Edward Strachey	NLS 1775D.217	14 May 1870
Jean C. Aitken	NLS 1775D.196	15 May 1870
Ada Eyre	NLS 1769.200	16 May 1870
John A. Carlyle	NLS 1775D.199	22 May 1870
John A. Carlyle	NLS 1775D.201	23 May 1870
John A. Carlyle	NLS 1775D.208	[26 May 1870]
John A. Carlyle	NLS 1775D.203	29 May 1870
John A. Carlyle	NLS 1775D.205	30 May 1870
John A. Carlyle	NLS 1775D.211	1 June 1870
John A. Carlyle	NLS 1775D.210	1 [2] June 1870
Lady Salisbury	NLS 1769.202	4 June 1870
George A. Duncan	Froude, *Carlyle* 2:19–20	4 June 1870
Jean C. Aitken	NLS 1775D.214	5 June 1870
Syed Ahmed	NLS 1775D.215	5 June 1870
John A. Carlyle	NLS 1775D.219	9 June 1870
John A. Carlyle	NLS 1775D.221	12 June 1870
John A. Carlyle	NLS 1775D.223	13 June 1870
John A. Carlyle	NLS 1775D.224	15 June 1870
Jean C. Aitken	NLS 1775D.226	15 June 1870
Henry Parkes	NLS 1769.203	15 June 1870
John Forster	NLS 527.21	15 June 1870
Ferdinand Lüders	NLS 1775D.230	15 June 1870
Ralph Waldo Emerson	Slater 570–72	17 June 1870
John A. Carlyle	NLS 1775D.60	22 June 1870

From	Source	Date
John A. Carlyle	NLS 1775D.228	23 June 1870
Maggie Welsh	NLS 1769.205	23 June 1870
Georgina Hogarth	Pbd: see Ford 123	27 June 1870
Henry Cowper	NLS 666.95	1 July 1870
Ralph Drury Kerr	NLS 1769.210	[6 July 1870]
John Forster	Armstrong Browning	11 July 1870
Lord Lyttelton	NLS 1769.212	11 July 1870
Lord Lyttelton	NLS 1769.216	15 July 1870
John A. Carlyle	NLS 1775D.232	19 July 1870
Jean C. Aitken	NLS 1775D.233	19 July 1870
Lady Elcho	NLS 1769.219	21 July 1870
John Forster	Armstrong Browning	25 July 1870
John Gordon	NLS 1769.221	26 July 1870
George Hill	NLS 1775D.237	26 July 1870
Lady Ashburton	NLS Acc. 11388	26 & 27 July 1870
Baldwyn Leighton	NLS 1769.223	28 July 1870
Alexander Gillespie	NLS 1769.225	30 July 1870
Charles Robson	NLS 1769.227	30 July 1870
John Forster	Armstrong Browning	31 July 1870
John A. Carlyle	NLS 1775D.235	6 Aug. 1870
John A. Carlyle	NLS 1775D.239	12 Aug. 1870
Baldwyn Leighton	NLS 1769.228	15 Aug. 1870
Thomas Spedding	A. Carlyle, *CS* 766	23 Aug. 1870
John Forster	Armstrong Browning	29 Aug. 1870
David Masson	NLS 1769.230	30 Aug. 1870
James A. Froude	Mirehouse Lib.	1 Sept. 1870
Charles E. Norton	NLS 666.96	1 Sept. 1870
David Masson	NLS 1769.231	7 Sept. 1870
Ann Welsh	NLS 1773.356	13 Sept. 1870
John A. Carlyle	NLS 1775D.240	18 Sept. 1870
Frederick Foxton	NLS 1769.232	20 Sept. 1870
Betty Braid	NLS 3278.154	25 Sept. 1870
John A. Carlyle	NLS 1775D.241	25 Sept. 1870
John A. Carlyle	NLS 1775D.244	[27 Sept. 1870]
John Aitken	NLS 1775D.242	29 Sept. 1870
John Ruskin	NLS 555.42	[5 Oct. 1870]
John Ruskin	NLS 555.41	[7 Oct. 1870]
John Ruskin	NLS 555.40	[8 Oct. 1870]
Thomas Wilson	NLS 1769.234	8 Oct. 1870
John Ruskin	NLS 555.43	[12 Oct. 1870]
Ralph Waldo Emerson	Slater 574–76	15 Oct. 1870

From	Source	Date
Charles A. Ward	NLS 1769.239	18 Oct. 1870
Thomas Wilson	NLS 1769.237	19? Oct. 1870
John A. Carlyle	NLS 1775D.245	20 Oct. 1870
Charles A. Ward	NLS 1769.241	21 Oct. 1870
John A. Carlyle	NLS 1775D.246	23 Oct. 1870
Jean A. Carlyle	NLS 1775D.246	23 Oct. 1870
Edward FitzGerald	*Fitzgerald's Letters*	23 Oct. [1870]
John Forster	NLS 527.28	23 Oct. 1870
Baron d'Eichthal	NLS 1775D.250	24 Oct. 1870
Charles A. Ward	NLS 1769.245	25 Oct. 1870
John A. Carlyle	NLS 1775D.258	26 Oct. 1870
Ann Welsh	NLS 1769.247	[28 Oct. 1870]
John M. Naesmyth	NLS 1769.250	28 Oct. 1870
Jean C. Aitken	NLS 1775D.252	30 Oct. 1870
John A. Carlyle	NLS 1775D.256	[31 Oct. 1870]
Edward FitzGerald	*Fitzgerald's Letters*	[late Oct. 1870]
John Forster	Armstrong Browning	4 Nov. 1870
David Laing	NLS 1769.252	5 Nov. 1870
Jean C. Aitken	NLS 1775D.270	7 Nov. 1870
John A. Carlyle	NLS 1775D.254	8 Nov. 1870
John Forster	Armstrong Browning	8 Nov. 1870
G. F. M. Foxton	NLS 1769.256	8 Nov. 1870
G. O. Trevelyan	NLS 1769.257	9 Nov. 1870
Roderick Murchison	NLS 1769.261	13 Nov. 1870
John A. Carlyle	NLS 1775D.260	13 Nov. 1870
John A. Carlyle	NLS 1775D.262	18 Nov. 1870
George Marsland	NLS 1769.263	18 Nov. 1870
Jean C. Aitken	NLS 1775D.264	20 Nov. 1870
Arthur Laurenson	NLS 1775D.265	21 Nov. 1870
Catherine Foxton	NLS 1769.266	21 Nov. 1870
William Gomm	NLS 1769.268	21 Nov. 1870
John Forster	Armstrong Browning	22 Nov. 1870
John A. Carlyle	NLS 1775D.266	23 Nov. 1870
James Spedding	A. Carlyle, *CS* 765–66	ca. 23 Nov. 1870
William Bathgate	NLS 8992.145	24 Nov. 1870
Count Bernstorff	Bernstorff Papers 2:293	25 Nov. 1870
Frederic Chapman	NLS 1769.277	25 Nov. 1870
John A. Carlyle	NLS 1775D.267	27 Nov. 1870
Grant Duff	NLS 666.97	29 Nov. 1870
William Maccall	NLS 1769.278	30 Nov. 1870
William Allingham	NLS 1769.281	4 Dec. 1870

From	Source	Date
Duchess of Argyll	NLS 666.99	4 Dec. 1870
Duchess of Argyll	NLS 1769.282	5 Dec. 1870
Thomas Dixon	NLS 1769.283	6 Dec. 1870
John A. Carlyle	NLS 1775D.274	7 Dec. 1870
William Bathgate	Bathgate, *Worthies* 434–35	7 Dec. 1870
John A. Carlyle	NLS 1775D.276	9 Dec. 1870
W. H. Hereford	NLS 1769.285	11 Dec. 1870
John A. Carlyle	NLS 1775D.278	11 Dec. 1870
Jean C. Aitken	NLS 1775D.291	[11 Dec. 1870]
Catherine Foxton	NLS 1769.288	12 Dec. 1870
Ivan Turgenev	NLS 1769.290	16 Dec. 1870
William Benham	NLS 1769.292	17 Dec. 1870
John A. Carlyle	NLS 1775D.279	18 Dec. 1870
Edward FitzGerald	*Fitzgerald's Letters*	19 Dec. [1870]
Alfred Legge	NLS 1769.293	21 Dec. 1870
John A. Carlyle	NLS 1775D.282	21 Dec. 1870
John A. Carlyle	NLS 1775D.284	22 Dec. 1870
John Ruskin	NLS 555.46	23 Dec. 1871 [1870]
John A. Carlyle	NLS 1775D.285	25 Dec. 1870
Jean C. Aitken	NLS 1775D.286	25 Dec. 1870
Charles Neaves	NLS 666.98	26 Dec. 1870
John A. Carlyle	NLS 1775D.288	29 Dec. 1870
W. H. Hereford	NLS 1769.287	30 Dec. 1870
John A. Carlyle	NLS 1775D.290	30 Dec. 1870
John A. Carlyle	NLS 1775D.295	Wednesday [1870]
John Ruskin	NLS 555.56	[1870/1871]
John Ruskin	NLS 555.50	[Jan. 1871]
John Ruskin	NLS 555.57	[1871]
George A. Duncan	NLS 1770.1	4 Jan. 1871
John A. Carlyle	NLS 1775E.1	6 Jan. 1871
John A. Carlyle	NLS 1775E.2	10 Jan. 1871
Elizabeth Phipson	NLS 1770.3	10 Jan. 1871
J. Hawkins Simpson	NLS 1770.5	13 Jan. 1871
John A. Carlyle	NLS 1775E.3	17 Jan. 1871
John A. Carlyle	NLS 1775E.4	19 Jan. 1871
Gertrude Jacob	NLS 1770.7	20 Jan. 1871
John A. Carlyle	NLS 1775E.5	23 Jan. 1871
John A. Carlyle	NLS 1775E.12	27 Jan. 1871
Horrocks Cocks	NLS 1770.11	28 Jan. 1871
Gertrude Jacob	NLS 1770.14	31 Jan. 1871
John A. Carlyle	NLS 1775E.13	3 Feb. 1871

From	Source	Date
John A. Carlyle	NLS 1775E.15	5 Feb. 1871
John A. Carlyle	NLS 1775E.16	10 Feb. 1871
John A. Carlyle	NLS 1775E.17	12 Feb. 1871
John Tyndall	Royal Institution	20 Feb. 1871
Lady Stanley	NLS 1770.16	21 Feb. 1871
John A. Carlyle	NLS 1775E.19	23 Feb. 1871
John A. Carlyle	NLS 1775E.21	1 March 1871
Alexander Bain	NLS 1770.17	1 March 1871
John A. Carlyle	NLS 1775E.23	3 March 1871
John A. Carlyle	NLS 1775E.24	5 March 1871
John Forster	Armstrong Browning	7 March 1871
John A. Carlyle	NLS 1775E.26	9 March 1871
Martin J. Tupper	NLS 1770.19	11 March 1871
John A. Carlyle	NLS 1775E.27	12 March 1871
Jean C. Aitken	NLS 1775E.28	12 March 1871
John A. Carlyle	NLS 1775E.30	15 March 1871
Lyulph Stanley	NLS 1770.21	18 March 1871
John A. Carlyle	NLS 1775E.31	19 March 1871
John A. Carlyle	NLS 1775E.33	24 March 1871
Julia Sterling	NLS 1770.23	24 March 1871
Thomas Alexander	NLS 666.100	25 March 1871
John Forster	Armstrong Browning	26 March 1871
Maude Stanley	NLS 1770.24	29 March 1871
John A. Carlyle	NLS 1775E.35	31 March 1871
John A. Carlyle	NLS 1775E.37	4 April 1871
John A. Carlyle	NLS 1775E.39	6 April 1871
John Ruskin	NLS 555.45	[8 April 1871]
Ralph Waldo Emerson	Slater 577–79	10 April 1871
John A. Carlyle	NLS 1775E.40	12 April 1871
Jean C. Aitken	NLS 1775E.41	14 April 1871
Lady William Russell	NLS 1770.26	14 April 1871
John A. Carlyle	NLS 1775E.45	16 April 1871
Catherine Phillipps	NLS 666.101	18 April 1871
David Buchanan	NLS 1770.29	19 April 1871
Nathan Shepherd	NLS 1770.31	19 April 1871
John A. Carlyle	NLS 1775E.48	20 April 1871
Elizabeth de Bunsen	NLS 1770.33	20 April 1871
Lord Stratford	NLS 1770.35	21 April 1871
Jean C. Aitken	NLS 1775E.50	23 April 1871
John A. Carlyle	NLS 1775E.52	23 April 1871
John A. Carlyle	NLS 1775E.53	25 April 1871

From	Source	Date
George W. Reed	NLS 527.49	25 April 1871
John A. Carlyle	NLS 1775E.56	27 April 1871
John A. Carlyle	NLS 1775E.58	28 April 1871
Robert Koenig	NLS 1770.38	28 April 1871
Ivan Turgenev	NLS 666.102	29 April 1871
John Ruskin	NLS 555.52	1 May 1871
William Knight	NLS 1770.40	2 May 1871
Eliza T. Spottiswoode	NLS 1770.41	2 May 1871
Thomas Hedderwick	NLS 527.47	3 May 1871
John A. Carlyle	NLS 1775E.60	5 May 1871
Robert Waldmüller	NLS 1775E.62	7 May 1871
Augusta Stanley	NLS 1770.43	10 May 1871
John D. Ford	NLS 1770.45	13 May 1871
William D. Christie	NLS 1770.47	14 May 1871
John A. Carlyle	NLS 1775E.65	15 May 1871
John A. Carlyle	NLS 1775E.61	18 May 1871
John A. Carlyle	NLS 1775E.67	20 May 1871
Thomas Sadler	NLS 1770.49	22 May 1871
John A. Carlyle	NLS 1775E.68	24 May 1871
Thomas Hedderwick	NLS 1770.51	24 May 1871
Maggie Welsh	NLS 1770.53	26 May 1871
John A. Carlyle	NLS 1775E.70	28 May 1871
John A. Carlyle	NLS 1775E.72	31 May 1871
John A. Carlyle	NLS 1775E.73	2 June 1871
William Stanley	NLS 1770.57	8 June 1871
Baldwyn Leighton	NLS 1770.58	9 June 1871
James Marshall	NLS 1770.59	20 June 1871
David Laing	NLS 1770.61	23 June 1871
James Dodds	NLS 1770.63	29 June 1871
Ralph Waldo Emerson	Slater 581–83	30 June 1871
M. A. Hull	NLS 1773.262	30 June [1871?]
Ralph Waldo Emerson	Slater 584	3 July 1871
Frederic Harrison	NLS 1770.65	4 July 1871
G. Eichter	NLS 1770.66	6 July 1871
Mary C. Aitken	NLS 1775E.74	17 July 1871
K. Damman	NLS 1770.68	18 July 1871
Maude Stanley	NLS 1770.70	22 July 1871
John A. Carlyle	NLS 1775E.76	26 July 1871
Jean C. Aitken	NLS 527.53	30 July 1871
John A. Carlyle	NLS 1775E.78	1 Aug. 1871
John A. Carlyle	NLS 1775E.79	2 Aug. 1871

From	Source	Date
John A. Carlyle	NLS 1775E.80	7 Aug. 1871
John A. Carlyle	NLS 1775E.82	11 Aug. 1871
John Forster	Armstrong Browning	21 Aug. 1871
George Howard	NLS 1770.73	3 Sept. 1871
Ralph Waldo Emerson	Slater 584	4 Sept. 1871
C. Gavan Duffy	NLS 1770.75	6 Sept. 1871
John Forster	Armstrong Browning	24 Sept. 1871

May. TC writes to his nephew Thomas Carlyle in Canada to send good wishes to him and to his niece Jane (to whom he intends making a cash gift). He would gladly help both Thomas and his brother John in Canada with books or cash (4). He thanks his brother John A. Carlyle for news of Craigenputtoch and suggests other family matters where he could help. James Anthony Froude visits (10). Illustrations for *Frederick* are still being sought. TC receives several visitors, David Masson, Alexander Bain, Froude, and William Allingham (14). He thanks John MacFarlane for a biography of Dr. George Lawson (24). TC laments his loss of the power of handwriting; he tries dictation "but never with any success" (26). He proposes a gift of £1,000 to Canada for Thomas and Jane there. TC begins to think of a summer holiday, perhaps in Colvend in Kirkcudbrightshire. He writes to Ralph Waldo Emerson to acknowledge receipt of *Solitude and Society* (31).

June. TC draws back from his Colvend suggestion, but would still like a seaside holiday and asks John A. Carlyle to look around (1). He writes to his brother Alexander in Canada about his financial assistance to Alick's children Jane and Tom and sends £800 (having previously sent Tom £200): "My heart is with you, dear Bror" (3). He thanks James Fitzjames Stephen for his "interstg entertaining letters" from his travels (3). He writes to his sister Jean Aitken in Dumfries announcing his intention of holidaying there (rather than in The Gill, with railway noises too close) (8). Froude leaves for Ireland (9) and invites TC to accompany him (8), without success. A letter from George Duncan revives good memories of Ruthwell Manse, where a young Carlyle was once well treated by the Duncans (9). John has reported that there are no vacancies on the Galloway coast until August at earliest, but TC wants to leave London soon. He has had visitors from India, father and son (10). Charles Dickens dies (9) and TC tells John Forster that "no death since 1866 has fallen on me with such a stroke" [11]. The summer heat is making him "very weak and miserable"; he has had to refuse to visit Forster who is "very unwell too" (16). The new edition of *Cromwell* is published; TC is actively preparing to leave London for the country (20). He reassures Frederic Chapman (28) that he has no intention of changing his publishers. He congratulates William Christie on his memoir of Dryden [late June]. He leaves London for The Hill in Dumfries; after a successful railway journey, Mary Aitken reports to Lady Ashburton that they "have arrived all right" (29).

July. TC writes movingly to Georgina Hogarth to thank her for a memento of Charles Dickens (4). He declines an invitation from Sir John Naesmyth (4). Lord Lothian dies (4) and TC writes to Lord Ralph Kerr to thank him for his letter (10). He thanks Caroline Davenport Bromley for a "condition-of-England" novel. He sends a gift to Betty Braid to remember JWC's birthday (13). He writes to Forster from Craigenputtoch where he spends five days, with hopes that Forster's eye problems are improving (22). TC writes to Frederic Chapman about an incorrect reference in *Frederick*, about his accounts, and about Charles Robson's financial problems and the security of TC's stereotype plates (31).

August. TC thanks the Rev. Wallace for a sermon (1); he tells John he is "leading the idlest, most useless existence . . . *do* nothing but lazy dull reading, a little daily walking" (5). He tells Froude he will stay in Scotland until rain cools the summer heat in London (14); he writes to Forster, who is clearing up Dickens's affairs (26).

September. TC travels to Edinburgh (2–4), staying with the Massons, and visits Haddington (3) and Betty Braid (4), then returns to Dumfries. He writes to Froude congratulating him on his political journalism (7) and to Thomas Spedding acknowledging his "honest old friendliness" (8). He continues to choose illustrations for *Frederick* and asks Chapman to commission a photographic copy of the Frederic Watts portrait of TC. Back in London (16), he finds the city empty (17), and he thanks Margaret Duncan for her letter (20). He thanks Henry Parkes for a copy of his speech on Australian affairs (21), mentioning his own enthusiastic support to the proposals for emigration being made in Britain. He writes to Emerson to reassure him that his volumes of the new edition are in transit, but rules out any possible of visiting the United States (28).

October. TC writes to Alexander Carlyle in Canada, acknowledging letters and family news (6). He writes to John Ruskin (10) congratulating him on his letters to the press on the Franco-Prussian War. He tells John A. Carlyle that "Plenty of people come abt me, but few to my mind" (13). He reassures William Maccall that Chapman intends to employ him as a translator (17).

November. TC tells Forster he feels "heavy-laden, stupid, inarticulate, to a degree," and "much bothered with insignificant Letters," but with "Company enough." (2) After a difficult week of research and dictation to Mary, TC's letter to the *Times* on the Franco-Prussian War is dispatched (11) and published (18). Mary Aitken writes to Lady Ashburton to thank her for the present of game (19) and tells of letters of both support and criticism that TC has had for his *Times* letter; Charles Kingsley writes; TC replies with a friendly invitation to visit (22). Ivan Turgenev visits (25). TC tells John A. Carlyle that Forster is working on finding employment as a clerk for nephew John Aitken in London (26). TC writes (27) to James Spedding on the news of his brother Thomas Spedding's death.

December. Discussions have begun with Frederic Chapman about a popular edition of TC's works. TC thanks John A. Carlyle for clippings from the *Scotsman* and their good journalism about the Franco-Prussian quarrel; TC continues to receive a lot of mail about his *Times* letter (3). Discussions continue about the new edition of TC's *Works.* Though averse to all dinner invitations, TC accepts one from the duchess of Argyll (5). He thanks Thomas Dixon for "*two Hindoo Pamphlets*," and describes British society as "universal downbreak into slush and mud" (7); he thanks Samuel Hall for the gift of a book (8) and finds the Argyll dinner (9) unexpectedly pleasant. He writes formally to Von Foller in Germany about British attitudes to the Franco-Prussian War (10). Snow alternates with warm, wet rain (17). He is reading Anton Schindler's *Life of Beethoven,* and re-reading Goethe's *West-östlicher Divan.* His niece Mary Aitken visits friends in Regent's Park with the Reichenbachs for a few days. TC tells Jean Aitken that despite the cold he is venturing outdoors; on Forster's insistence, he and Mary will spend Christmas day dining there (24). He writes to Robert Waldmüller in Dresden to thank him for a book (27); he receives a gift of three partridges (30). He tells his brother John that "there can be nothing but a struggle till this fierce weather pass" and sends good wishes to all the family in Scotland (31).

January 1871. TC writes to Thomas H. Huxley to try to help a candidate who has applied too late for a position (5). He writes John A. Carlyle (5), who is visiting Edinburgh. TC has many visitors, including Turgenev, Froude, Reinhold Pauli (4), and a weekly visit from William Allingham, "really worth something." During the cold weather TC reads widely; he sends John pamphlets and papers. Mary Aitken has bought a good new reading lamp (13). Chapman visits to arrange a better engraving of Watts's portrait for the new people's edition of TC's *Works.* Mary is busy organizing signatures for a pension for Geraldine Jewsbury (21). TC writes to Robert Carruthers to sympathize on the death of Alexander Munro (25) and to Jean Aitken, describing a dinner at the Blunts' (28). He sends good wishes to JWC's relations in Edinburgh via John who is still there (30).

February. TC says farewell to Giuseppe Mazzini (7), who is leaving London for the last time (10). He writes to Robert Lawson on Female Emancipation "with reluctance" (9), specifically on the admission of women to medical studies which, with conditions attached, he approves. He complains to John A. Carlyle about sleeplessness and describes a visit from Lord Houghton and W. E. Forster (10). A new edition of TC's *Works* is advertised in the

Athenæum (11). TC visits Lady Derby ("last Sunday" [12]), J. A. Froude and Lord Stanhope are also there (TC's journal, 14 Feb. [TC to JAC, 18 Feb.]). He sends £10 to his sister Janet Hanning in Canada to "buy yourself something nice with" (13); he describes the decline of his handwriting facility and praises Mary Aitken as amanuensis. He praises Joseph Lawton's intention to read widely and his choice of books (14). He declines an invitation to tea from Lady Stanley at 5 p.m., though he and Mary would be glad to come at 4 p.m. (22). He admits to Jean Aitken that his sleep is slowly improving, though his digestion is not (25). TC and Mary have plenty of company, including visiting Lady Stanley for the surprise presentation of the clock to celebrate TC's 75th birthday (27). Anthony Sterling is dangerously ill (27). TC sends good wishes and offers copies of the new edition of his *Works* to his family in Canada (28).

March. TC is glad John A Carlyle is back in Dumfries; he hears of the deaths of Mme. Otthenin and of Anthony Sterling. The petition for a pension for Geraldine Jewsbury has failed (3). He acknowledges receipt of £350 in royalties from his publisher Chapman & Hall (6). Mary Aitken writes with condolences to Meta Wellmer (12). TC and Froude call on Lady Derby (12). TC acknowledges photographs of John A. Carlyle sent from Scotland (18). John Forster, ill all winter, has improved and gone traveling (18). Maggie Welsh arrives for a visit (23). TC and Lady Ashburton drive around Hampstead in the spring sunshine (25). He declines allowing his name to be associated with a German Association for Popular Education (29).

April. TC amends his Will (6). He thanks Arthur Helps for the dedication of his *Life of Hernando Cortes* (10). He thanks Margaret Oliphant for her help with the Jewsbury pension application and mentions the presentation of the clock: "it will give me great pleasure to see you here again" (11). He exchanges Ecclefechan memories with Jean Aitken (17), and thanks John A. Carlyle for his help with mutual friends and with money matters (22). He writes a long letter of reminiscences to Catherine Phillipps (23). He describes *Fors Clavigera*, Letter 5, to Ruskin as "incomparable; a quasi-sacred consolation to me" (30).

May. TC writes to John A. Carlyle from Melchet Court, where he is holidaying without any energy, but enjoys talking with Turgenev (13). Maggie Welsh leaves Chelsea after a successful visit. "Utterly idle," he praises Lady Ashburton's hospitality; he invites John A. Carlyle to consider coming to visit Chelsea (15), to which he returns from Melchet (22). Lady Ashburton invites him to join her on holiday in the Isle of Lewis (23). TC and Mary Aitken dine at the Forsters' (28), and TC is alarmed at Forster's ill-health (29).

June. TC writes a friendly letter to Emerson (4), and another to David Laing thanking him for his edition of David Lyndsay (10). TC contracts a bad cold and considers fleeing to Scotland to visit Jean Aitken in Dumfries, having given up waiting for Lady Ashburton's plans (17).

July. Froude writes to invite Carlyle on a holiday trip, but too late to prevent TC and John A. Carlyle from booking a cabin in the Aberdeen steamer (8); TC arrives in Lochluichart with John (who then, after a couple of weeks, goes to Strathpeffer); he writes to Betty Braid on JWC's birthday (14) and to Froude detailing his travel via Aberdeen, Inverness, Dingwall, to, finally, "this remote little paradise" (25).

August. Without Mary Aitken to write to his dictation, TC finds correspondence difficult. With the help of others, he asks after Forster's health and describes the entire peace and seclusion he feels in the Highlands (18); he writes to George Howard to thank him for a present of grouse sent to Cheyne Row: "No life has been quieter & more hospitably dealt with than mine among these solitudes" (23).

September. TC is staying with Jean Aitken and family in Dumfries, but Jean and Mary have to go to London after a serious accident to Mary's elder brother Jim (13), from which he dies (20). The funeral is on the 25th. TC stays a few days more in Scotland than he originally intended; he writes to Froude that he looks forward to seeing him in London after the "solitary Lotus-eating life of the Highlands" (25) and returns finally to London (late Sept.).

NOTES ON THE TEXT AND EDITORIAL CONVENTIONS

Within our editorial conventions we have tried to show as nearly as possible what the Carlyles actually wrote. Commas and periods in TC's letters have been regularized within quotation marks. In the letters, the square brackets that enclose any words indicate illegibility, areas that have been torn, or stains in the manuscript. Damage to manuscripts is normally noted in headnotes to the letters. Square brackets are also used to indicate glosses and translations and, in the headnotes, to indicate dates not given, or given incorrectly, by the Carlyles. In this volume, after 21 September 1870 (see 47:65), TC's letters were dictated to Mary Aitken and he generally signed them. Before this, it is noted if Mary Aitken has written them for TC; from this point we only note if TC added or corrected anything. All square brackets by TC or Mary Aitken are normalized to parentheses to avoid confusion with editorial square brackets.

TC sometimes put a line over a single "m" or "n" to indicate a double "m" or "n." He composed carefully, omissions of words and letters and occasional misspellings or other errors are normally indicated by notes. Sometimes he repeated words at the turn of a page; these repetitions have been noted and are not usually printed.

Where envelopes have survived, the address is given in the headnote; if there are postmarks, the first is given; subsequent postmarks are included only when they clarify the date of the letter or show the speed of the mail.

Titles cited frequently in the notes and elsewhere are abbreviated (see "Key to References"); others are listed with date and place of publication, with the exception of titles published in London, which give only the date. TC wrote his journal from 1 Aug. 1866; this is privately owned and the editors have had access to it and use it extensively; some sections are pbd. in Froude, *Carlyle*.

Where interesting information is available but not referred to in the texts of the letters, it is given in a footnote attached to the end of the nearest letter. For letters to TC that are quoted in the notes, the sources appear in "Letters to Thomas Carlyle" in the front of the volume.

THE COLLECTED LETTERS OF
THOMAS AND JANE WELSH CARLYLE

TC TO FREDERICK ANDERSON

[2 or 9 May 1870]

Dear Sir,

In my hurry at pres*t*, I see nothing *wrong* in the Mask except that extraordinary posit*n* of the *wart* (wh*h*, once for all, *must* be put WHERE the Model gives it you, —namely, *close* above the eyebrow, —and nowhere else, for any reason what*r*!) — In the rest of the Piece, I find nothing but success, and am well satisfied.[1]

For Heaven's sake, *put* that wart right at last; and let me see a final Proof, *as soon* as possible, —for the Printer[2] is getting impat*t* now.

If Mr Woolner (as I hope) get sight of the Proof, I much recom̄end you to listen to any hint of his, —EXCEPT (and ag*n* except!) on that of the *wart* only. For no reason must that be put in a place not its own!

In very great haste
T. Carlyle (Monday noon)[3]

TC TO THOMAS CARLYLE

Chelsea, 4 May, 1870 —

Dear Tom,

I had a Letter from you lately wh*h* gave me, and all y*r* kindred here, a great deal of satisfact*n*, and truly was fully of interest to us all. Indeed you have written us a good many Letters, and always (for I have read them all)

TC-FA, [2 or 9 May]. MS: Harry Ransom Center, Univ. of Texas at Austin. Pbd: F. Anderson, "The Mask of Cromwell," *English Illustrated Magazine* 14 (Nov. 1895): 118. Frederick Anderson (b. ca. 1833), wood engraver, 42 Warden Rd., Kentish Town. Dated "early in May" by Anderson.

1. Anderson had been approached by Thomas Woolner to do a woodcut of Cromwell's death mask for the library edn. of *Cromwell*; see 46:168–69. There had been some difficulty about the placing of Cromwell's wart, which TC insisted must be put in the correct position. Anderson had finished the wood cut, and an impression had been sent to TC for approval. Anderson later wrote: "I managed, with the kindly assistance of Mr. Woolner, to define the wart's position to Mr. Carlyle's satisfaction." Woolner wrote to Anderson, 17 May: "I think the print much improved" but suggested a few further corrections. The engraving was printed at the end of the appendix of vol. 5 of *Cromwell*, vol. 18 of the library edn. of TC's complete works.

2. Charles Robson.

3. David Masson, TC's friend from Edinburgh, was in London and invited himself for a visit, Sun. 1 May (28 April; MS: NLS 1769.194). TC wrote in his journal, 1 May: "Masson is coming (at 2½ p.m.)—I have hardly seen him for almost 2 years: a friendly ingenuous reasonable man" (TC's journal; privately owned). He visited twice; see TC to JAC, 14 May.

TC-TC, 4 May. MS: MUL. Pbd: Marrs 763–65. Thomas Carlyle, eldest son of TC's brother Alexander Carlyle, in Canada.

in an honest, clear, affectionate & practical form: just such Letters as one wants from dear relatives abroad; — so that the sight of yr handwriting on an envelope is, by this time, a hopeful sign so far. Continue to send us distinct news, the more in detail the better; — and let us all be devoutly thankful that the news you send have so often been *good*, when they might so easily have been other! — As to me, my old right hand[1] (and also my poor old heart) has grown weary of writing; and indeed, except with pencil, you see, I cannot do it: — very perverse that my right hand has got so *shaky*, while the left is still steady enough: a very great loss to me in many senses (laying me quite *idle*, for one thing); — tho' surely, were not I an UN*th*ankful creature, it is rather on the continuance of the left-hand that I sh*d* reflect, than on the decay of the right, after so many years of heavy service! — Meanwhile you perceive, I can still write, tho' in a slow, obstructed, uncomfortable manner: and there is one little private point, on wh*h* I want to quest*n* you a little; you, rather than yr Father who might not feel himself so free in answering ab*t* it. It is first and chiefly of yr sister Jane[2] that I wish for informat*n*; from whom I have had one or two pretty letters long ago; but nothing at all (I can well judge why) since the time of her troubles began. A gen*l* notice that now & then, that she is well in health, and holds out valiantly, while her poor husband is fallen quite a ruin:[3] this is nearly all I have, — and more of this from you in yr last Letter than from any other. On inquiry in Scotland, too, nobody can tell me what is now her Post-Office Address,[4] or even what is her *Name*.

The essential fact is, dear Tom, I privately intend to make her a little Gift, to satisfy many feelings in myself; and I much wish to know what*r* in her situat*n* and ways of life w*d* best enable to fix wisely the manner and amount of that. What details can be usefullest you can yrself consider and judge; all details will be welcome; — and (observe!) you are to keep the matter in the meanwhile perfectly a secret betw*n* you and me. Tell me her wedded *name*; how *far* her Farm (or Property) lies from you, and what it is *called*; what the extent & probably worth of it is; what children she has,[5] and of what outlook & character; whether you understand them & her to be *easy* as to money, or *not*? &c &c. Tell me what*r* you shall think *elucidative* of the matter in hand. If

1. TC's right hand had developed palsy in 1866; see 43:195. He wrote in his journal, 1 May: "Have been in a biliary cure of health for above 3 weeks past; and don't yet feel to have got 'improve*t*' by it as expected. Lamentablest of my *infirm*ty the *shaking* of my right-hand; condemns me as if to idleness, — wh*h* is an opening of the door to all kinds of dispi-rit*t* and weak useless misery. . . . 'Trading [Reading]' is latterly my main emply*t*; — *good* for absolutely nothing!" (TC's journal; privately owned).
2. Jane Welsh Sims, Alick's eldest da.
3. Jane's husband was Robert Sims; he had epilepsy; see TC to JAC, 31 Dec.
4. Robert and Jane Sims were registered in the Canadian Census, 1871, at Burford, South Brant, Ontario.
5. They had at least two children, Alexander and Thomas.

[2]

I had even a good *Photo*h of her, it w*d* have value:—she must be now ab*t* 40 years old (perhaps 39 or 38?)[6]—it is as an infant, as a wise little *child* to whom I have given lessons in reading,[7] that I still vividly remember her. "Good little *Jane*":—you know of *Whom* she is the *Namesake*; and how sad & strange and solemnly beautiful those recollect*ns* may have been to me now!—It is probable I shall write to y*r* Father directly after the arrival of y*r* report; to him (if you judge it useful) I do not forbid you speak in consultat*n*): but don't to any other person, especially not to Jane herself. And, in gen*l*, do y*r* best for me, what you judge best!—

I sh*d* also like to hear ab*t* y*r* Brother John, and what outlook towards settle*t* he has? Y*r* Father's last Letter shewed him as *carpentering* for some Neighb*r*;—and certainly the *wages* seemed to me to be small: but I guessed the acquisit*n* of the *talent* might be import*t* in his contemplated way of life.[8] Tell me what prospect you think he has of getting to a settle*t* of his own? and whether in y*r* neighb*d*, or farther away, perhaps in some more fertile, tho' as yet wilder and roomier territory? Let him walk wisely; stand wisely to himself, it seems to me he has essentially nothing to fear. In that wide and free element, where Labour is the one thing wanted,—how different from ours here where (madly and miserably) Lab*r* seems the one thing not wanted; and is getting at once ever *hungrier* and ever *falser*, in consequence, year by year!—

Finally, dear Tom, to tell me more and more ab*t* y*r*self will always be a welcome part of y*r* Letter. I cannot help you in many things; but I c*d* in some,—for example, in Books; if I knew any direct road to you, or indeed, except the Post-Office, any sure road at all. Tell me what is the best way *you* know. To "Boston Mass.," probably also to New York, I find I might have means of franking Parcels now & then: but what is y*r* Conveyance *thence*? Advise if you know anything *better*!——

As to health &c here, you are to report us not sensibly otherwise than usual, certainly not *worse*; except the weight of years & what that universally brings, I have no complaint as to health; *stomach* getting gradually weaker, *heart* & spirits d*o* do: for the rest, describable as "quite well." My lame hand, & the *idleness* it hitherto brings, is probably the worst feature of late;—and I cannot yet learn to *dictate* to little Niece Mary[9] (who is a most[10] swift and willing writer, if she c*d* fully understand!)—but I am often thinking I ought still to *try*.

Farewell, d*r* Tom; write so soon as you are fairly ready,—sooner the *better*

6. She was 38.

7. TC and JWC left Scotland, June 1834, before young Jane was three, so it was probably on later visits to Dumfriesshire that he read with her; he commented, 1838: "She is a clever lassie it seems with her book too" (10:79); Alick and his family emigrated to Canada, 1843.

8. Alick's second son, John, was working as a frame builder; see 46:195.

9. TC's niece Mary Aitken, who lived with him.

10. Word repeated with a line over it at turn of page.

I need not add! You will give my kind regards to yr Wife;[11] to my old and ever faithful Brother I have no words that wd express my feeling. Blessings on yu all.— Yr affecte Uncle T. Carlyle

TC TO JOHN A. CARLYLE

Chelsea, 10 May, 1870—

My dear Brother,— Saty last, by various inane hurries & interruptns, I was disappointed of writg to you; nor did yesterday, tho' I agn purposed well enough, prove kinder, but the reverse;— and now, this morng, comes yr kind and unusually interestg Letter;[1] on impulse of whh I *shove aside* all other things, and send a few words before we go farther. My poor right-hand, it does sadly lame me, and renders writing an affair like to running races in a sack: but I must not complain; let me be thankful rather that I can still, with whatr difficulty, write at all.

Yr acct of poor Craigk[2] is full of interest to me, and of manifold tender remembrance, impressive almost like prophecy, tho' it is (sacred) *his*tory only! Seems to grow ever sadder to me, if also ever more beautiful, more sacred. Such is one's wonderful path in this world. God is over all. Amen.

It is very agreable to me to hear that the poor Place is in good order, & Jamie farming it well.[3] I never saw a *Puttick*[4] myself; but Corson, at Dumfries 2 years ago,[5] told me he *had* pulled such out of certn holes in the Craig: it must have been an opulent enough hunting-ground for them, a 10,000 years

11. Margaret Carlyle.

TC-JAC, 10 May. Addr: The Hill / Dumfries / N.B. PM: London, 10 May 1870. MS: NLS 527.14. Hitherto unpbd. Letter addressed in another hand.

1. John A. Carlyle wrote, 9 May, that he, Jean, and James Aitken had been to Craigenputtoch the previous day, meeting Mary and James Austin there.

2. Craigenputtock; previously the Carlyles almost invariably used the spelling "Craigenputtoch" (which practice *CL* continues to follow); from 1865 TC changed mainly to the spelling "Craigenputtock"; see 41:220 and later.

3. Their nephew James Carlyle Jr. was the tenant of Craigenputtock; John wrote: "The day was very fine & we walked over most of the farm. It is all in excellent order. Eight or nine acres of the old woods have been replanted & fenced with very sufficient stone dykes. . . . The plantation at Stumpy is growing well, though the trees are still very small."

4. John A. Carlyle wrote: "James took us to a precipitous rock, promising to show us the hawks or *puttocks* from which the place has its name; & one hawk did fly out, probably from its nest, quite near us"; for TC's derivation of the name, see Carlyle, *Reminiscences* 80.

5. Rev. William Corson (1809–87), b. Craigenputtoch, son of Samuel Corson and Mary Dinwoodie; brother of the Carlyles' neighbors at Nether Craigenputtoch (see 5:360); minister of Girvan, Ayrshire, 1848–87. TC stayed with his sister Jean in Dumfries, 27 July–19 Sept. 1868, and visited Craigenputtoch ca. 25 Aug.; see 44:165; there is no mention of a meeting with Corson.

ago, when all that black moss was leafy hazel & birk, no doubt plentiful in birds! — I think we had no rabbits in our time; nor did I ever hear of Corbies. *Both* these sets of fellows it is clearly well to shoot![6] — (at this point, enter Edw*d* Strachey;[7] sits for an hour, — eating up all my *time*, sorrow on him![8])

I think you do well surely to be considering of Vichy,[9] or of something *better*, that you c*d* try by way of help to miserable "indigest*n*," while the summer is here. I know not whether Vichy is the advisablest; but *something* I hope you will get to consider before very long. Did you never seriously think of getting you a *good Horse*, and regularly riding it, all the fine season? I have the confid*t* persuas*n* you w*d* find it beneficial. To myself it *never* failed nor yet fails to do some perceptible good; — and of *nothing* else can I from experience say as much. Consider that, as *cert*n; and ask y*r*self. — When you want to investigate anything hereab*ts* (I can yet tell nothing ab*t* my own possibilities or likelihoods), — of course this Brother's House is always wide-open to you. And don't let either of us *miss fire* ag*n* this year! —

I did write last week to Alick's Tom a strict Letter of inquiry ab*t Jane* his sister. I tho*t* he might be *franker* than his Fath*r*. I wish I *had* got that poor matter settled.[10] (n.b. *Froude* came in *next*, top of last page; & still sits)[11]

It is well surely that you are to get Marg*t* of Ernh*t's* affairs settled at last.[12] I have not the smallest objec*tn* to go halves with you in the affair;[13] whate*r* pre-

---

6. John wrote: "[James Carlyle Jr.] has shot corbies & many rabbits. The corbies lie in wait for lambs just after birth. . . . The rabbits had become very numerous, & in winter time had eaten many of the newly-planted Scotch firs."

7. Sir Edward Strachey, son of Edward Strachey and Julia Strachey; the family had been friends of TC's since the 1820s; see Carlyle, *Reminiscences* 283–84.

8. One of TC's phrases; see 46:96.

9. Vichy, spa town in the Auvergne, central France, where JAC stayed May–June 1868; see 45:132.

10. TC asked John's advice in April (see 46:195–96) about sending money to Tom & Jane, suggesting £500 each; John replied that he too had thought of sending money but had not decided on a sum. John then wrote, 1 May: "I have thought more about the sums you spoke of sending to Tom & Jane, but cannot venture to give you any farther advice on the subject. In my own case I find the money saved & strictly economised for many years past has become an embarrassment to me, it being a most difficult matter to decide where & how it is likely to do real good, or the contrary."

11. James Anthony Froude; TC boxed this sentence in the space after "settled."

12. Their niece Margaret Stewart, whose husband, Thomas, d. April 1869; see 46:42; she was continuing to run their farm, Ernhirst (Ironhirst), about 5½ mi. (9 km.) SW of Dumfries.

13. Thomas Stewart had leased the farm jointly with his brother James, but Margaret wanted to take over as sole tenant; see 46:192. John A. Carlyle wrote, 9 May: "I hope to get Margaret's business at Ironhirst settled finally next week, for her brother-in-law Mr James Stewart has already by today's post formally resigned to her his share of the lease. . . . Some £328 is the sum her late husband had on loan from his brothers, & I mean to pay that next week. . . . It is not worth while to pester you with paying the half."

liminaries are needed for me, the same are for you, —or if none be needed (in yr opin*n*), wh*y* not ditto?—

Adieu dear Brother: I will write ag*n* str*t* way, —let me hope with more delibert*n* than now. My love to Jean & them all.

Ever yr affect*e* T. Carlyle

TC TO LADY ASHBURTON

[11 May 1870]

Dear Lady, —I cannot get to Ralston today:[1]—please you to *read* this, therefore; and if yr Ladyship's self or any Friend or Friends can stand another dose of Ralston, you see how much it will gratify the worthy man.[2] If nothing at all can be done, *burn* the affair, & let it go up the chimney safe!— In gr*t* haste,

Yrs ever, / T. Carlyle
(11 May, Noon)

TC TO JOHN A. CARLYLE

Chelsea, 14 May 1870

My dear Brother,

I have nothing to send you today in return for yr agreeable Note of this morn*g*. I have been much bothering ab*t* in that sorry "Print" bus*ss*, the *in*utility of wh*h*, and the large amount of dirty *fash*, provokes me often; but I am not n*r* thro' it, Fr*h* and all.[1] Only one Print now wanted for Fr*h* itself, —a cert*n* *Voltaire* (now getting hunted, not yet at all *caught!*) in *Paris* Printshops, since

TC-Lady A, 11 May. MS: NLS Acc. 11388. Hitherto unpbd. TC wrote on the back of a letter to himself from W. R. Shedden-Ralston.

1. William Ralston Shedden-Ralston (1828–89; *ODNB*), asst. librarian at the British Museum, translator from Russian, critic, and folklorist; see 45:114.

2. TC apparently attended Ralston's presentation of "last Wednesday," i.e., 4 May; *Pall-Mall Gazette* announced, 9 May: "Mr. RALSTON will tell RUSSIAN STORIES—a different set from those told last Wednesday—at ST. GEORGE'S HALL, Langham-place . . . May 11, at 4 P.M." Ralston wrote, 7 May: "You can scarcely realize, I think, the intense pleasure you gave me by honouring my story-telling the other day. There are moments, you know, when one seems to see one's former self plainly before one's eyes, and as you went up the Hall, I seemed to see myself as I was just after I left Cambridge, when I spent some months alone in Scotland, and I used to sit out on the Moors and read your books. And it was so strange to think that there was the Writer whom I used to look up to as someone quite out of my sphere, actually going to listen to me. . . . Allow me to . . . send you a Card for any friend of yours who may care to hear a new set of stories . . . next Wednesday."

TC-JAC, 14 May. MS: NLS 527.15. Quot: A. Carlyle, *NL* 2:266–67.

1. TC had been looking for illustrations for the library edn. of TC's works (1869–71), 30 vols.; see, for instance, 46:55 and 119 and 121.

there is nothing but a shadow of it in our own: —that curious *Sheet* of Portraits wh*h* you once bro*t* me from Geneva,[2] wh*h* w*d* have served rarely, has wandered away long since, and nothing like it known to the Printsellers here! I remember it well; but not with the least distinctn*ss* what became of it.

I have also had many people calling on me, few of whom give me much pleasure. Masson was here twice,[3] a welcome face tho' a very silent one. He went for Edin*r* Friday last (yesterday in fact). Bain also I saw twice; well enough, if you keep him off his "cerebrat*n*" balderdash,[4] wh*h* I did. Blackie I have not seen, nor wished to; but he sent me a Ticket to his 4 Lectures, and I ought to make an effort, on Tuesday next, towards his *last*;[5]—perhaps I shall break down nevertheless.— I am as before "the victim of indigest*n*," wh*h* naturally makes matters worse, *worse*.— Froude has been at Vienna for a 3 weeks, looking into Charles-V. despatches ab*t* Ann Boleyn;[6] & has come home illuminated on that matter. I have only seen him once, and had a large dose of that,—had it b*n* of use to me! He has got little Allingham to be "subeditor";[7] I suppose he will be off to Ireland ag*n* soon;[8] I always feel the want of

2. John A. Carlyle visited Geneva between July and Sept. 1835, and Sept.–Oct. 1836, and probably other times as well. TC wrote to him in Paris, 5 March 1829, asking him to look for a print of Voltaire; see 5:9. There are two portraits of Voltaire in *Frederick* vol. 5 (25:318 in the library edn.), neither of them with any attribution; for one of them, see Carlyle, *Works* 14:frontis. François-Marie Arouet, known as Voltaire (1694–1778), French writer and philosopher. See also TC to UC, [ca. 14 May].

3. The first visit was 1 May; see TC to FA, [2 or 9 May].

4. Alexander Bain (1808–1903; *ODNB*), philosopher and psychologist (see 45:145); he was interested in "cerebration," the way in which the nervous system influences information and feeling in the brain.

5. John Stuart Blackie delivered a series of four lectures at the Royal Institution on "The Principles of Moral and Political Philosophy," on Tuesdays, 26 April to 17 May. Blackie eventually saw TC, writing to his wife, Eliza, 3 June: "I knocked up Carlyle, a strange mixture of grey, weather-beaten solemnity and hilarity; full of sweeping denunciations as usual, but not at all bitter. I scribbled a note of him on my return: 'Carlyle is strong to arouse by a tremendous moral force, and to startle by vivid and striking pictures; but he has neither wisdom to guide those whom he has roused, nor sobriety to tone his pictures down to reality. He is always talking about veracity, but he habitually revels in exaggeration and one-sided presentation, which is more than a lie.' But we fraternised in a brotherly way and embraced on parting" (*The Letters of John Stuart Blackie to his Wife*, ed. Archibald Stodart Walker [Edinburgh and London, 1909] 191–92).

6. J. A. Froude was researching the trial and death of Anne Boleyn (ca. 1500–36; *ODNB*), for his *History of England*, the final two vols. of which (11 and 12), were pbd. 1870; he went to Vienna to look at the letters and papers of Eustace Chapuys (ca. 1490–1556), imperial ambassador to England 1529–45, for Charles V (1500–58), Holy Roman Emperor 1519–56, in the Austrian archives; see 46:194.

7. William Allingham worked in the Customs Service, 1846–70, but had long wanted to devote himself to literature; see 43:87–88. The post, 1870–79, as sub-editor of *Fraser's Magazine* (of which Froude was ed.) allowed him to move to London. He found rooms in Onslow Sq., near Cheyne Row, which he visited frequently, TC being very "friendly and en-

him when he is away (There *he* comes; I hear his knock! Alling*m* too follows: ah me, nothing more to be *done* then!)

I read with interest what you write ab*t* Marg*t* and Ernhirst:[9] inclosed is a little jotting of a not*n*[10] that struck me at breakfast;—read it.

Y*r* Cromwell Vol. will *not* go off *before* Tuesday next; arrive probably end of week. There will be inclosed a small vol for *John*, and a d*o* for John of Scots-brig.[11]

Adieu dear Brother; my blessings be upon you all. Will Jean write ag*n* soon?[12]

Y*rs* ever affect*e* / T. Carlyle

TC TO UNIDENTIFIED CORRESPONDENT

[ca. 14 May 1870]

[Commenting on an English engraving of Voltaire copied from a French one, of which the print-sellers have no more examples, and saying that he would welcome] a good clear copy [from Paris] fit for Photographing, and sent *soon*.

---

couraging" about his new prospects. Now too busy to keep his diary regularly, he did note: "Mary tells me she said to her Uncle—'People say Mr. Allingham is to be your Boswell,' and he replied, 'Well, let him try it. He's very accurate'" (*Allingham, Diary* 202). James Boswell (1740–95; *ODNB*), diarist and biographer of Samuel Johnson.

8. Froude and his family usually spent their summers in Ireland; see 46:75.

9. John A. Carlyle wrote, 13 May: "Margaret got receipt in her own name yesterday for Candlemas next, so that James Stewart is now by law out of her lease. Six years of it have still to run; & I become security for Stewart that no rent shall be demanded of him in that time."

10. Untraced.

11. John acknowledged, 23 May, the arrival of the four vols. of *Cromwell* and "certain other little books" for their nephews, John Aitken in Dumfries and John Carlyle at Scots-brig.

12. Jean Aitken wrote, 15 May: "the Dr has just handed me your letter. . . . I may as well write you a few lines, altho' I have nothing of moment to write about." She described their visit to Craigenputtoch (see TC to JAC, 10 May) and the circumstances of Mary Austin's da. (their niece) Grace Yeoward, living in some hardship (with only one cow) near Stratford, Ontario, Canada.

TC-UC, [ca. 14 May]. Pbd: John Wilson, New Yatt, Witney, Oxfordshire, booksellers catalog, nd. Dated around the time that TC told John A. Carlyle that "Paris Printshops" were being "hunted" for a Voltaire print; see TC to JAC, 14 May. The catalog described the note as "Autograph Note Signed with initials, written in blue crayon on 1 page 8vo (blank area torn away), annotated 'Thomas Carlyle 1870' in another hand."

TC TO JOHN MACFARLANE

5 Cheyne Row, Chelsea,
24 May 1870.

Dear Sir,

Your Biography of *Dr Lawson*[1] has interested me not a little, bringing present to me from afar much that it is good to be remin[d]ed of; strangely awakening many thoughts, many scenes & recollections of 40, of 60 years ago, —all now grown very sad to me, but also very beautiful and solemn.

I can perfectly remember reading *Sallust*[2] with the venerable Mr Johnstone[3] in that old Manse now vanished, and how completely he made me see into every fibre and wrinkle of the meaning; —65 years ago this was; a work of love on his part (for my Father's and Mother's sake), and to me the beginning of much benefit in the school way. Strange to reflect that Dr Lawson (what I did not know before) was also pupil of his; he the first[4] most probably, & I for certain the last! —

It seems to me I gather from your narrative and from his own Letters, a perfectly credible account of Dr Lawson's Character, course of life, and labour in the world; and the ref[l]exion rises in me that perhaps there was not in the British Island a more completely genuine, pious-minded, diligent and faithful man. Altogether original too; peculiar to Scotland, and so far as I can guess unique even there and then. England will never know him out of

TC-JM, 24 May. MS: NLS 518.50; initial draft in TC's hand, and final draft in Mary Aitken's hand with corrections by TC. Text: Mary Aitken's draft with TC's corrections; there is no signature. Pbd: William Graham, *Memoir of John MacFarlane* (Edinburgh and London, 1876) 31–32 inc. John MacFarlane (1807–85; *ODNB*), minister of the United Presbyterian Church, Clapham, S London, from 1862.

1. John MacFarlane, *The Life and Times of George Lawson, D.D. With Glimpses of Scottish Character From 1720 to 1820* (Edinburgh, 1862). George Lawson (1749–1820; *ODNB*), biblical scholar, prof. of theology in the Burgher Church of Scotland, 1787–1820; see 1:357.

2. Gaius Sallustius Crispus (ca. 86–ca. 35 B.C.), Roman historian; for TC's appreciation of him, see 1:332.

3. Rev. John Johnstone (1730–1812), secession minister in Ecclefechan; TC wrote about Johnstone, 1832, in his memoir of his father, James Carlyle: "He, in his last years, helped me well in my Latin (as he had done many); and otherwise procured me far higher benefits" (Carlyle, *Reminiscences* 30).

4. Lawson was taught by Johnstone while the latter was still a student; MacFarlane wrote: "The late Rev. John Johnstone, of Ecclefechan, was for a time classical tutor to George Lawson; and fortunate, indeed, for the future scholar was it that such a teacher was then at West Linton. . . . It is not the least creditable specimen of Mr. Carlyle's good sense and good feeling, that he still remembers the guide and instructor of his youth. We have heard that he has oftener than once declared, 'I have seen many capped and equipped bishops, and other episcopal dignitaries; but I have never seen one who more beautifully combined in himself the Christian and the Christian gentleman than did Mr Johnstone" (*The Life and Times of George Lawson* 27).

any Book, — or at least it would take the genius of a Shakespeare to make him known by that method; — but if England did, it might much and wholesomely astonish her. Seen in his intrinsic character; no simpler-minded more perfect Lover of Wisdom do I know of in that generation.

Professor Lawson, you may believe, was a great name in my boy circle; never spoken of but with reverence and thankfulness by those I loved best. In a dim but singularly conclusive way, I can still remember seeing him, and even hearing him preach (though of that latter, except the fact of it, I retain nothing); but of the figure, face, tone, dress I have a vivid impression (perhaps about my 12*th* year *i.e.* summer of 1807, '8): it seems to me he had even a better face than in your Frontispiece, more strength, sagacity, shrewdness, simplicity, a broader jaw, more hair of his own (I don't much remember any wig);[5]—altogether a most superlative steel-grey Scottish Peasant (and Scottish[6] Socrates of the Period) really as I now perceive, more like the Twin Brother of that Athen*n* Socrates, who went about, Supreme in Athens, in wooden shoes, than any man I have ever ocularly seen.[7]

Many other Figures in your narrative were by name or person familiar to my eyes or mind in that now far-off period of my life. You may believe me, I am much obliged by your bringing under my notice a Book which has had such singular interest to me, and indeed by your writing the Book itself which certainly was well worth doing.

With many thanks and good-wishes,

5. The frontis. was a drawing of Lawson (apparently wearing a wig), sitting in a chair with a book open on his lap, and a signature reproduced underneath: "I am yours affectionately / G. Lawson."

6. TC corrected Mary's "Scotch" to "Scottish."

7. TC had been reading a memoir of Sydney Smith as well as the biography of Lawson; he was more critical of MacFarlane's book, writing in his journal, 1 May: "Memoir of *Sydney Smith*, d*o* of *Dr Lawson* the Burgher Profess*r* of Divinity, my latest Books, — what a contrast bet*n* these two; each of them, to me, resuscitating so many buried recollect*ns*! Both ill-written, most incondite Books. Sydney rather sank in character, a Life passed in shallow haha-ing (shallowish all of it, tho' loud and hearty), in *un*heroic; perfectly faithful whiggery, terrene e[u]daimonism, e[u]pepticity &c &c, and very little that was bitter. — Poor old Lawson, on the contrary, tho' the Book on him is much the worse, has *risen* with me, almost into the essentially heroic. In his own dialect, veritably (a kind of *Old-Greek* Scotsman of our day; invincible, unconscious, devout, — Old-Greek and better. In my boyhood I once saw the Old Man; face & figure, tho' indistinct, become ag*n* curiously vivid to me. . . . Wherefore are these things *hid*? See my very *hand* now forbids! *Tant pis* [so much the worse] for me" (TC's journal; privately owned). Sydney Smith (1771–1845; *ODNB*), author, wit, and one of the founders of the *Edinburgh Review*; the memoir was by his da., Lady Holland, *A Memoir of the Reverend Sydney Smith . . . with a selection from his Letters, edited by Mrs.* [Sarah] *Austin*, 2 vols. (1855). TC knew Smith (see 8:189 and 11:88), probably through Francis Jeffrey (1773–1850; *ODNB*), another founder of the *Edinburgh Review* and old friend and supporter of the Carlyles.

TC TO JOHN A. CARLYLE

Chelsea, 26 May 1870

My dear Brother,—(I had got so far yesty; and was then interrupted by an influx, by two successive influxes, and obliged to stop. Try agn today, the first thing of the morng!)—

My correspondence, for the last two weeks, has been much stagnated, not altogr by want of the usual trifling things to have said; nor by the increase of the usual paltry interruptns & botheratns, but the hot weather, dyspeptic nausea, and total want of heart for anythg in the shape of exertn at all. Gloomy mournful musing, silent looking back on the unalterable, and forward on the inevitable and inexorable: that, I know well enough, is not a good employt; but it is too generally mine,—especially since I lost power of *penmanship*, and have properly no means of working a little at my old trade, the only one I have ever learned to *work* at. A great loss, this of my right hand's *steadiness*. "Dictatn" I try sometimes; but never with any success; & doubt now I shall never learn it. Courage, nevertheless; at least, silence in regard to all that!—

No ansr yet comes from Tom of Canada;[1] indeed it probably is not yet time. Can you tell me what sum of money it was we joined togr in giving *to Tom*, especially what part of it I gave?[2] My gifts to Jane & him ought to be *equalized*; poor little "Jane" never yet got anythg. If you can ansr the above questn, I think of making the joint amount £1,000; 500 for Niece, & for Nephw what is still *wanting* of that: I cd *immediately* direct the whole to Alick for distributn;[3] and so close and terminate this other little task pressing on me.

Yr treatt of the Ernhirst case is munificent and perfectly good; that *you* shd yrself distribute the "interest, if you get it," is completely the practical fulfilt of my notn—whh cd, by no other method, be other than a *crank* and dangers

TC-JAC, 26 May. MS: NLS 527.16. Quot: Froude, *Carlyle* 4:391; John Morrow, *Thomas Carlyle* (2006) 193.

1. Their nephew Thomas Carlyle; see TC to TC, 4 May.

2. John A. Carlyle replied, 29 May: "On the 13*th* Feb. 1868 I sent £100 to your namesake in Canada, & I think you sent £200 separately. In April 1869 I sent £45 more to him & £100 to Alick. This is all I can find in my cheque books." John wrote to TC, 13 Feb. 1868: "I have written to your namesake in Canada. . . . I have also sent him an order for £100 . . . to aid him in comfortably establishing himself, or in paying off the remainder of debt on his farm. I think he is a steady solid young man & may do well now that he has got a wife that he loves & esteems [Tom m. 31 Dec. 1867]" (MS: NLS 1775C.223). TC sent Alick £100 Oct. 1866; see 44:73. He and John both sent money to other relatives in Canada, 1869: their half-brother, John Carlyle (see 46:6–7), and their sister Jenny Hanning (see 46:38–39). TC and John had some discussion, March 1869, about possibly sending money to Alick (see 46:32), and Alick wrote to TC, 16 April 1869: "Please thank the good Dr. for his kind present which arrived safely a few days ago" (MS: NLS Acc. 9086).

3. See TC to JAC, 1 June.

theoretic kind of thing.[4] You say nothing of my running halves with you in that matter; wh*h* I am still perfectly willing for: but indeed it is of little or no consequence,[5]—as the whole property of both of us goes one & the same road.

My plans for the summer amount still only to the wish & determinat*n* to try something of the sea.[6] *Within 3 weeks* now, or less it ought *to be*,—and nothing at all is yet conclusively made out! Lady Ashburt*n* proposes "Loch Luichart"[7] and lone sea hamlets on the "Coast of Skye"; but I *don't* bite at that kind of bait, knowing well how aërial *it* is.[8] Mrs George Welsh[9] talked of a most enchanting *new* bathing-village "of 12 houses" at Colvend: did you ever hear of it,[10] c*d* any of you run down and look at it? I sometime think I sh*d* really like to possess a habitable cottage there; & fly out of these inane noises; into the divine solitudes and the great Ocean's "everlasting voice"[11] (assisted by some pony or cuddy to ride upon, &c &c)! All *moonshine*, I know: but I really wish the expert of you (James, Jean, Self) w*d* turn it over a little, and perhaps go down once and look?—

Mrs Russell's sad visitat*n* gave me a great shock; and I am much obliged by y*r* specific & punctual bulletins, wh*h* pray continue.[12] Things, this morn-

4. For Margaret Stewart's new lease for Ernhirst, see TC to JAC, 10 May; John wrote, 22 May: "I think it would not do at all to make any interest from the £328 payable to her mother or directly to her four unmarried sisters. The investment is of very uncertain issue in my opinion, & one can pay the interest, if one gets any, to the sisters & brother at the Gill; as I have generally done each year since I made the loan of £300 eight or nine years ago. On the whole I think it will be better to let the whole £628 take its chance, without any complications, as a simple loan from me without further details."

5. John replied: "the advancement of that sum puts me to no inconvenience & I can silently wait the result whatever comes of it."

6. Jean wrote, 15 May: "You have not resolved what is to be done as to holiday yet I suppose: I will be glad of the smallest word from you whither you can give a decision or not—only remember, *I dinna want an ill answer.*"

7. Kinlochluichart, Lady Ashburton's Highland estate, about 34½ mi. (60 km.) NW of Inverness.

8. Lady Ashburton was known for her tendency to change plans frequently.

9. Margaret Welsh, b. Kissock (1803–88), widow of JWC's paternal uncle George Welsh (1799–1835); she lived at 19 St. John's Grove, Richmond. JWC had been particularly friendly with her; see 43:213 and 280.

10. Colvend, hamlet on the Kirkcudbrightshire coast, about 15 mi. (24 km.) S of Dumfries. John replied, 29 May, that he had spoken to William M'Diarmid (in whose house in Colvend Mrs. Welsh had stayed), to ask about it: "Both Jean & I have been there & know the place well, & think it w*d* not suit you at all. Mrs Welsh obviously knew nothing about the realities of it, or she never w*d* have given you such a report of it. . . . [W]e know that the vulgarest people of Dumfries go there, that the houses they occupy are detestably bad & crowded together; & on Sundays great numbers of people go & spend the day there, starting between 7 & 8 in the morning & returning at 7½ p.m. by the Sunday Mail train." William Ritchie M'Diarmid (1819–95), ed. of the *Dumfries Courier*; see 42:109.

11. See Robert Southey, *Roderick, the Last of the Goths* (1814), part 1.

12. JWC's old friend Mary Russell (who lived at Holmhill, nr. Thornhill) was ill; her hus-

ing, do seem to be looking up: God grant it! In the whole world is no House whose sickness cd to me be more affectg; alas, alas! More than one Letter have I written in my mind to Dr Russell since I heard; but it was *better* that none of them cd come to paper, or add new bother to his grief & anxiety. You can, if you like, by some word or so, remind him of this fact, whh I shd hope he always knows.[13] — — Mrs George Wh told us farther of Elizabth's[14] being agn unwell, & Dr Hunter[15] attending &c: Mary wrote yesty to *ask*. — No more now, dear Brr; I intend to write agn *soon*. There are to go some triflg Books with the next Cromll volume. Lucky that the last have come all right. Orr as good as pleaded *guilty* poor soul.[16] — Yrs ever T. Carlyle

TC TO RALPH WALDO EMERSON

Chelsea, 31 May 1870 —

Dear Emerson, — In great *haste*, fruit of my miserable & scandalous indolence and dreamy waste of this fine last May morng, I do manage to announce, in one brief word to you, That the first copy of yr *Solitude & Society* has never

---

band, Dr. James Russell, wrote to John, 20 May: "I am sure you will be distressed when I tell you that about a week ago, Mrs Russell had a sudden seizure of a paralytic nature, and that now there is partial want of power in her left arm & leg. . . . Her speech is not affected . . . her mind is quite clear" (MS: NLS 1775D.198). John enclosed the letter, 22 May. He reported, 23 May: "Today I have been at Thornhill to see Mrs Russell. . . . I found Mrs R. in bed, but not nearly so ill as I had anticipated. . . . No distortion of the face, speech quite free as in perfect health. But in the left arm & leg there is some paralysis. In bed she can move both very freely, but cannot stand or walk without support, & cannot hold a fork firmly in carving any meat she gets. It is exactly a fortnight this evening since she had the seizure . . . & the want of power in arm & leg is about the same as it was at first. I should say one may have good hopes of her complete recovery. . . . Mrs R . . . desired to be most kindly remembered if I wrote to you."

13. James Russell wrote to John A. Carlyle, 6 June: "The message from your Brother was very grateful to Mrs R." (MS: NLS 1775D.218).

14. Elizabeth Welsh, JWC's aunt, living in Morningside, Edinburgh.

15. Both Grace (d. 1867) and Ann (d. 1877) Welsh's death certificates were signed Dr. J. D. Hunter; probably Dr. Jacob Dickson Hunter (ca. 1811–89), b. Bengal, East Indies; physician; studied at Edinburgh Univ. John A. Carlyle told TC, 5 March 1867: "The funeral letters were signed by *Dr Hunter* as 'cousin' of the deceased" (MS: NLS 1775C.97); he was therefore also related to JWC. Ann Welsh wrote to TC, 4 Feb. 1870: "Dr Hunter . . . has again been a blessing and comfort to us — What a pity he did not follow out his profession in Edinburgh he might have been almost at the top of the tree, by this time — seems to know his profession so well — and such a kindly manner" (MS: NLS 1775D.143). By 1881 Dr. J. D. Hunter was living at 18 Regent St., Portobello (1881 census).

16. William Somerville Orr (ca. 1801–73), working for Chapman & Hall (TC's publisher) and apparently very inefficient at sending out volumes; see 46:173.

TC-RWE, 31 May. MS: RWEMA. Pbd: Slater, *CEC* 569.

come to hand,[1] but that a *second* duly *has*,—three days ago, all safe & right; a much handsomer Copy, and better for my old eyes: wh*h* shall enjoy that in time coming, to exclusion of the other, perhaps to *benefiting* of some third party by the other. Thanks; double thanks for this double punctuality.

Some ten days ago, having fallen in with a brand new *Chapman's Homer* (2 voll. just out, *improved* or not),[2] and finding a bit of reference to yrself,[3] I bethot me that there was an older copy here, suffict & more for all my wants with it, and that I c*d* send *you* this new one. The *Piccadilly* Chapman people[4] got it accordingly, it was to go (infallibly, *these* Chapm*ns* said, but only the Pope is infallible!)[5] *along* with yr *4th vol of Cromwell*; and I hope it will,—if only as a punish*t* for yr praise of that monstrous *Homeric* Individ*l*; whom, after repeated trials, I have found that I cannot stand at all.[6] More like a *leprosy* of Homer than a new skin to him; the most intolerable of all the "translations" I have seen.

I hear of you lecturing at Harvard College,[7] with immense acceptance, *well*-merited, I do believe. Good speed, good speed!—My own days here are fallen weak and empty; seems as if the fewer days I had to live, the more inane they grew! Filled only with sombre solemn recollection, and d*o* d*o* dreamy contemplat*ns*; nothing of worth in them except the sorrowing *Love* wh*h* Time only strengthens, and (I think) only Death Eternal c*d* kill.

Adieu, dear Friend Yours ever as before T. Carlyle

---

1. Ralph Waldo Emerson, *Society and Solitude* (Boston, 1870). Emerson inscribed TC's copy, sent mid-March: "To the General in Chief from his Lieutenant, March 1870" (Slater, CEC 569); apparently TC had still not received it. He bought himself a copy, late March; see 46:177 and 190.

2. George Chapman (1559/60–1634; *ODNB*), poet, playwright; translator of *The Whole Works of Homer* (ca. 1616). TC presumably referred to *The Iliads of Homer . . . translated by George Chapman, with Introduction and notes by the Rev. Richard Hooper*, 2 vols. (2d revised edn. 1865); possibly there was a recent reprint.

3. Hooper quoted in his introduction (written 1857 for the 1st edn.; 2d edn. 1:xlix) Emerson's comment from *English Traits* (Boston, 1856): "We want the miraculous; the beauty which we can manufacture at no mill—can give no account of; the beauty of which Chaucer and Chapman had the secret" (*Collected Works of Ralph Waldo Emerson* [Cambridge, MA and London, 1994] 5:143–44).

4. Chapman & Hall's offices were at 193 Piccadilly.

5. The Vatican Council, Dec. 1869–Oct. 1870, was discussing the doctrine, soon to become dogma, of Papal Infallibility.

6. In his essay on "Books" in *Society and Solitude*, Emerson wrote: "Of Homer, George Chapman's is the heroic translation" (*Collected Works of Ralph Waldo Emerson* [Cambridge, MA and London, 2007] 7:99).

7. Emerson's series of lectures, Harvard, April–May 1870. He replied, 17 June: "the oppressive engagement of writing & reading 18 lectures on Philosophy to a class of graduates in the College, & these in six successive weeks, was a task a little more formidable in prospect & in practice than any foregoing one."

TC TO JOHN A. CARLYLE

Chelsea, 1 june, 1870—

My dear Brother,

Inclosed here is a Cheque for £800;[1] wh*h* sum I intend for Canada by y*r* help. Better to *finish* that, with*t* farther loitering, while time yet is! Of that, therefore, *first*. It appears I have sent Tom £200 already;[2] £300 more to him will be £500; to Jane the same, will make £800 as here. I intend to send it direct to Alick's charge, with*t* waiting or inquir*g* farther.[3] Please therefore take the thing at once to Adamson,[4] make him change it into the requisite *Canada* Document, and inclose to me, that I may send it off along with a little Note to Alick,[5] after wh*h* I can be at *peace* on the bus*ss*.

With regard to that other *domestic* thing,—I have evid*tly* thrown you all into quite an undue agitat*n* by that cursory hint I threw out in regard to Colvend, on very *loose* authority it w*d* seem! I had no deliberate intent*n* of going to Colvend in any case; I merely tho*t* of the clear sea-breezes, the silences solitudes there, and how pretty all that was, in contrast with the dusty empty tumults of London,—and how suitable it might be to *end* one's life in some such nook rather than here (a vague dream I sometimes have for moments, no settled intent*n* at any time): this was all the length I had gone, on the *Mrs George* Speculat*n*.[6]—

With regard to plans for this year also, I am still in a very crude state; hardly farther than the *wish* for some "spell of sea" this season, & the tho*t* or semi-design that something s*hd* be done by way of "effort" towards it: this is all the length I,—poor *lazy* I, not worth much trouble ab*t*, hope of 'improve*t*' being so near zero,—have yet gone. Add to wh*h*, the *weather* here is hitherto for me nearly perfect, breezy, fresh, *warm* with *grey skies*; so that I was not think*g* to quit it for a week or two yet; sensible (as *laziness* pleaded) that I really might go farther & fare worse. This is candidly how the matter stands.

Do *not*, therefore, my dear Br*r*, run off to Whithorn, Garlieston[7] &c on any

TC-JAC, 1 June. Addr: The Hill / Dumfries / N.B. PM: London, 1 June 1870. MS: NLS 527.17. Hitherto unpbd.

1. TC noted in his checkbook: "1 June 1870 / To Dr Carlyle (for Canada: Jane & Tom / (thro' Alex*r*) / £800 .. 0 .. 0" (TC's checkbook; MS: NLS 20753).

2. See TC to JAC, 26 May.

3. TC wrote, 15 June: "On the 2*d* of june, sent off that *Letter* to Alick with the £800 in it for his '*Tom*' (my Namesake and his '*Jane*' (who was Hers); £500 for *each* (for Tom at prest the *supplem*t to a *former* £200). May it do them *no ill*; to me it was devised as a solace*t* and benefit. '*Her* Namesake!' that was my tho*t*. Poor weak weary soul that I now am" (TC's journal; privately owned).

4. Samuel Adamson, of the British Linen Co. Bank in Dumfries.

5. See TC to AC, 3 June.

6. For Margaret (Mrs. George) Welsh's suggestion, see TC to JAC, 26 May.

7. Whithorn, village about 65 mi. (104.5 km.) SW of Dumfries; Garlieston, coastal vil-

quest specially *mine*; by no means! But withal if you have yrself the scheme that sea-side there or abt Colvend &c wd be the right thing for yrself as well, know that I will willingly *share* with you in any such adventure, and thus take *my* "spell of sea," *taliter qualiter* [for what it is worth], in comradeship beside you. In ten days time or so, I cd be completely ready to *join*. And as to habitatn, there is only one conditn *sine quâ non*, an absolutely quiet *sleeping-place*; all else will "suit" me just as it does *you*; & I shd like it well or like it ill just as you do. — The questn, then, is, What *you* want to do? I own rather to a wish it might *not* be Vichy.[8] This is perhaps unreasonable: nor indeed does it go far. But I always think (as you have heard me say) nothing cd be so *certain* to improve you as the steady *habit of Horse-exercise*; as the getting of a good steady Horse, and riding him daily! This is grounded on continl *experience*; the *sum* of all I cd make out in that importt province. I much wish I cd persuade *you* to what has all along done myself so much good. What a thing to find you well mounted when I joined you at the seaside!

In regard to *places* in that Galloway sea region,[9] I have little strength of preference, except that the nearer Dumfries & the Hill,[10] the better. By far the agreeablest bathg place I have in memory is *Kirk-Andrews*;[11] do you remember our bathing there, — abt 50 years ago, or more?[12] I have never seen it since; & it has become *ideal*. — — But now in regard to Jean's *report* tomorrow,[13] and the practical *corollary* to all I have been writing? This in brief it is: If *you* are for the thing, and find her report *good*, decide *for* it witht asking farther; & count on me aftds. If *you* are *not*, then let it *go* upon the winds; — I by myself being in no case to venture upon such an enterprise.

Yesty I sent you a little *posthumous* piece by Erskine,[14] not suffictly reflect-

---

lage about 60 mi. (96.5 km.) SW of Dumfries. John A. Carlyle wrote, 30 May: "This day has been wet, otherwise I might have gone to Garlieston & Whithorn. But I find one cannot go & return in one day."

8. John A. Carlyle had been thinking about going to Vichy again; see TC to JAC, 10 May.

9. Galloway, coastal region of SW Scotland.

10. Jean and James Aitken's house in Dumfries (which they had built and moved to in 1863), where John also stayed.

11. Kirkandrews, village about 33 mi. (53 km.) SW of Dumfries.

12. Visit untraced.

13. John wrote, 1 June: "In today's Courier . . . a house at Colvend is advertised to let for this month; & James & I have just been enquiring about it. . . . It stands far apart from other houses 'in a large garden,' & is about ten minutes walk from the sea. . . . Jean . . . has arranged to go . . . tomorrow. . . . You shall hear what she has to say about it." He wrote, 2 June: "it could not with any comfort or safety be ventured on. It is miserably small & low, beds without curtains or even room for them, ceiling of parlour bare whitewashed boards, of bedroom bare joists, & Mr M'Diarmid . . . who knows it well, says it is very damp in wet weather."

14. Thomas Erskine d. 20 March 1870; see 46:179, 180, and 192–93. TC probably re-

ing that most probably you already had it. In either case keep it carefully for me: it was[15] a soft & affectg kind of thing to me. Poor good Erskine; silent, silent now forever!— — With my best blessgs to one & all. Ever yr affect*e* T. Carlyle[16]

TC TO ALEXANDER CARLYLE

Chelsea, 3 june 1870—

My dear Brother,

Some time ago I wrote to Nephew Tom,[1]—as perhaps he may have told you (or perhaps *not*, for I left that optional with him): —my purpose privately was, to make some quiet inquiry after yr good "Little Jane" and her circ*s*, upon wh*h* I c*d* trust to Tom for more precise and fine details than I yet had. Dear little Jane; not "little" now, but grown big enough, and experienced in much toil and sorrow;—I often wonder what I sh*d* think of these Two Little Creatures now! They are the only Two of yr Bairns whom I have a clear idea of, and can vividly see:[2] Little Tom, with his white feet and grave steady face, stepping the Scotsbrig Burn for us with Letters, on a rainy morning, as I looked from the window there;[3] this must be 2 or 3 & 30 years ago or more, and I can see it now as if it had b*n* *this* morning! Little Jane I recollect from a still

---

ferred to the new rev. edn. of Erskine's *The Unconditional Freeness of the Gospel* (Edinburgh, 1870 [1828]).

15. "[W]as" repeated with a line over it at turn of page.

16. John Tyndall wrote to Mrs. McRaye (unidentified), 2 June: "I go down from time to time to Chelsea to see that grand old man Thomas Carlyle. When I was there [the] last two books of Emerson were on the table addressed 'With unchangeable affection to Thomas Carlyle.' It did my heart good to see this loyalty. Poor Mrs. Carlyle handed him over to my safe keeping when he went to Edinburgh to be installed as Rector of the University. She died while he was in Scotland. I afterwards went with him to Mentone. A few weeks ago I was with him in the country. It was a wild day and we got into a clearing in the middle of a wood, where we sat in calm while the storm rolled around us. I plucked a cushion of ferns for the old man, placed it on the stump of a tree, helped him to light his pipe, and there we talked of death, and the privilege of being released from the fear of it. I was so much pleased with Emerson's books and their superscription that I carried them away with me— They are here beside me" (MS [or transcription]: Joseph F. Cook papers, David M. Rubenstein Rare Book and Manuscript Library, Duke Univ.). For the inscription on vol. 1 of Emerson's *Prose Works*, 2 vols. (Boston, 1870), dated 30 Oct. 1869, see 46:138.

TC-AC, 3 June. MS: MUL. Pbd: Marrs 765–67.

1. See TC to TC, 4 May.

2. Although eight of Alick's children were born before he emigrated to Canada, 1843, TC remembered best the two eldest surviving children, born while he and JWC were still living in Scotland; see 46:144.

3. Presumably the occasion when Tom delivered letters to TC while he was staying at Scotsbrig, Aug. 1839; see 11:172.

earlier date; as an infant lying on yr knee *that* evg when you had recd *us* at Whinnyrig from London, with tears in the eyes of some of us:[4] ah me, ah me! What Time *brings*, and what Time *takes* from the transient Sons of Adam! My Father did not see that meeting; the "tears" of *other eyes* are now also wiped away.[5] God the Eternal look down in pity on us all. Amen, amen.——

Tom's ansr has not yet come, probably has not yet had time: but I have since been thinking that the secret little Purpose I had, behind those inquiries, cd be fulfilled at once and still more comfortably perhaps, *thro' you*; and being anxious that no delay or mistake shd occur in it, I have got ready, and now this day do it. (Alas, here enter intrusive person, "Visitors" whom I care little about; and I am *cut off* for today!)[6]

4. Whinnyrigg, village on the coast 1 mi. (1.5 km.) S of Annan; TC and JWC stayed there with Alick on their way home to Craigenputtoch, late March 1832, having spent the winter in London.

5. TC's father d. 22 Jan 1832, so this was the family's first meeting since; see 6:142 and Carlyle, *Reminiscences* 86.

6. TC was more sociable at this time than he acknowledged. He called on Lady Salisbury, 3 June; she wrote, 4 June: "I am very much vexed to have missed you again! My hours are rather less regular than they used to be. . . . If by chance you were disengaged tomorrow . . . about 5 o'clock you would find me, or on Tuesday next [7 June]. And I shd be most happy to see you." TC wrote on the letter: "Went, *twice*; a very amiable truthful Lady (Dowr now 2 years;—to be wedded to Ld Derby, '5 july' coming)." He recorded one of his visits, 15 June: "Yesty, walked to Uppr Grosvenor Street; called on Lady Salisbury (soon to be *Lady Derby*), a gentle, good and intelligt Lady, whom I wish well to, tho' our acquaintce is not yet of 3 years. Liked her late good old Marquis of Salisbury too, whom I saw but once: a physiognomy *à la Cecil* (I thot), 'a true Old-English face';—in some few months he died.— Mrs Lowe, the now great Robt Lowe's wife came in yesty while I was there; grown hugely chaotic & unwieldy; floundery still in her speech & manner: but has an unusual share of real sense and *veracity* of mind,—as yesterday I discovered by her mode of speaking abt the former Lady Ashburton ('*Harriet* Lady Ashburton') whom I knew so well! To my surprise, what poor Mrs Lowe said was, nearly altogr, as if spoken out of my own mind. A sketch *true* in every feature (I perceived), as painted on the mind of Mrs Lowe; nor was that a character quite simple to read: on the contrary, since Lady Ht. died, I never heard another that did so read it. Very strange to me yesty.— A *tragic* Lady Harriet; deeply so, tho' she veiled herself in smiles, in light gay humour & drawing-room wit, whh she had so much at command. Essentially a most *veracious* soul, too; noble and gifted by Nature,—had Fortune but granted any real career! She was the greatest Lady of Rank I ever saw; or rather the One Great Lady; with the soul of a Princess & *Captain*ess,—had there been any *career* possible to her but that 'Fashionable' one!— We spoke of Dickens too: 'Newsprs talking as if he were a *great man*, nearly equal to Shakespre!' &c to Mrs Lowe's astonishment. 'Newsprs speaking foolery & balderdash? Never mind it: 'tis their nature *to*!' ansd one. (n.b. '*Balderdash*,' I have long known, is Danish: 'Bag or Pocket (*Poke*ful) of Noise' in that language; equivt to German *Potter-Tasche*. Why do I write that here? No more today" (TC's journal; privately owned). Mary Catherine, dowager marchioness of Salisbury, widow of James Gascoyne-Cecil, 2d marquess of Salisbury; she was to m., 5 July 1870, Edward Henry Stanley, 15th earl of Derby. "Cecil . . . 'a true Old-English face'": probably either William Cecil, first Baron

june 4th (a baddish morng for me, compared with yest*y* (want of sleep &c &c); but I will finish, all the same, and by no means *lose the Post*, for wh*h* there is still time!)

Understand, then, dear Brother, that this inclosed £800 is a bit of *Gift to my Two Namesakes*, specially distinguishg them from all my other kindred,— to Tom who bears my own Name, and to his Sister who was named for AN- OTHER[7] not now in this world, but solemnly present to me at all hours, and for whom I seem as if acting in the matter;—and that the charge of cutting the money in two, and delivering it to the respective Parties is now laid upon you their Father, as the fittest person. Tom (I find on inquiry of the Dr) has had from me already (some years ago, on entering his Farm) £200; to this you will add £300; wh*h* will in all make £500 for him; and have for my dear "little Jane" an equal sum. *"Five Hundred Pounds for each,"* that is the sum of the affair: I wish you to draw the money at once, and at once hand it over to the respective parties (with their Uncle's love & blessing, you may safely say), each of them to be left *free* to dispose of it, invest it, lay it out, as he or she sees fittest. No doubt you will give them y*r paternal counsel* on that latter point (whether to put it in a Bank, to buy land with it, to buy better stock with it, to *lend* it on good security, &c &c); & I cannot doubt that they will be ready & thankful, in *this* as in all cases, to add their old Father's best wisdom to their own in forming a decis*n*! However, as this is a peculiar kind of Gift, and as they are both wise prudent hon*ble* kind of people, I do not wish them to be *bound* any *farther*. I myself have no knowledge what*r* ab*t* the ways of wisely using money in a Country so unknown to me. Do y*r best* for me, my good ever-helpful Alick,—y*r* best for me this once more,—and it will be well enough!— The money, I understand, you will get at once by slitting off the *2d* leaf of this & presenting it at any [bank];[8] nor, probably, will the rest of the Affair take up much time. *N.b.*, how*r*, it will be best for you to write at once, without any delay, so soon as the money comes, that *it* is safe and in y*r* hands: on other points there is no such hurry. Enough, then, enough.— My heart is with you, dear Bro*r*; my heart is all set melting by this Act I am ab*t*: but I write with great difficulty and will end till y*r* ans*r* come. With my best blessings on you all.

Y*r* ever-Affect*e* Br*r* / T. Carlyle

Burghley (1520/21–98; *ODNB*; see 39:1), royal minister, or his son Robert Cecil, first earl of Salisbury (1563–1612), politician and courtier, ancestors of the 2d marquess of Salisbury. Georgiana and Robert Lowe, both members of the Ashburton circle and liked by both Carlyles. Robert Lowe was Chancellor of the Exchequer, 1868–73.

7. JWC; for the check, see TC to JAC, 26 May.
8. TC omitted the word "bank."

TC TO JAMES FITZJAMES STEPHEN

Chelsea, 3 june, 1870—

Dear Stephen,

You have written me three of the most interstg entertaining letters,[1]—first of these from the Red Sea (where Pharaoh[2] fared so ill, & that ugly Abyssinian[3] was faring much too well!)—excellt offhand Letters, full of vigorous direct observatn and frank veracity; so that one can almost *see* along with you, and seeing believe everythg: Letters whh it does one good to read. If I cd hope that you wd go on writing such, so long as I live, witht articulate ansr, and only with *in*articulate thanks duly rendered,—most duly cd I render you these latter, and be glad to say nothing,—so disgustg is the act of writing grown to me, under these lamed conditns; so *slow*, so sad, a thing clearly to be avoided wherever avoidable! But I know well, with all yr tolerance, friendliness, & wealth of life, the hope is impossible; possible only for a time. Today, therefore, you shall have these few poor words *in pencil*; in token of the many I cd in other circs have sent you in pen and ink.

The news of yr lucky voyage, and then of yr dear Life-Partner's,[4] witht harm to either of yrselves or to any of yr household gods, was very gratifying to me and to everybody here. Indeed if you can but fairly *keep yr health* (whh I believe to *be* possible, with care), there seems to be no other anxiety on yr acct at all; and it is clearly the notion of every one who knows you that a right good stroke of work lies in this new Indn missionary[5] and that he, in all likelihood, will verily leave some stamp of himself on our confused interests out there,—to the *diminutn*, not to the increase, of said confusn, and to the benefit both of us and of those 100,000,000 poor sultry black brothers we have got to manage for! In whh case I can promise you, the "stamp of yrself," legible or not to mankind after 50 or 100 years, will absolutely *never* abolish itself, but continue a fact and an influence, "visible" enough to WHO has busss with it, so long as Time runs or longer. This is the first clause in my *Credo*; this I believe in as I do in arithmetic:—confess to yrself these are fine terms for

TC-JFS, 3 June. MS: Strouse. Hitherto unpbd. James Fitzjames Stephen; for TC's most recent meeting with him, see 46:97.

1. For one of these letters, see 46:131. Stephen traveled to India via Egypt, Nov.–Dec. 1869.

2. Cf. Exodus 14:26–28.

3. King Téwodros II (1818–68), emperor of Abyssinia 1855–69, who surrendered to British troops, 13 April 1868, and subsequently committed suicide; see 45:66 and 134.

4. Stephen arrived in Calcutta (Kolkata, W Bengal), 12 Dec. 1869; his wife, Mary, and their da. Rosamond arrived early March 1870.

5. Stephen was legal member of the council to the Indian viceroy, Richard Southwell Bourke (1822–72; *ODNB*), 6th earl of Mayo.

a Working man, in the Tropical Zone or elsewhere; and step stoutly along in *God's* name,—as men used to do!

Here at home we are in the old chaotic & to me rather scandalous way; not in any better or less unlovely. Gladstone, it seems, has just got his "Irish Land-Bill" 'thro' the House[6] with cheers': much good may it do him! Good to the Irish I have not yet expected it w*d* much do: the beging of all *good* there, I mournfully perceive, w*d* be the extirpat*n* of habit*l* murder; the complete "repale"[7] & extinct*n* forevermore of that astonishg Supreme Court of Irish Justice,[8] Court consisting of 5 or 6 truculent ragamuffins sitting in their Shebbeen House over whiskey & blunderbusses, *deciding* (now & for ages back) in regard to any & every Irish*n*, "Thou shalt die, Thou shalt live!"— But of this primary & preliminary Problem, I don't yet see any real attempt towards the solut*n*.— Sec*y* Bruce[9] is much disappointg me. A flagrant and most ugly murderer got sentence of the gallows lately; a couple of Drs reported, "He has a 'wen on his neck,' gallows will be painful beyond com̄on."[10] "Oh, then, we *can't* hang him," ans*d* Bruce,—and did not add, "I can at least hang myself!" Whereby we have got a new member of our "British Prytanaeum,"[11] thank— *Whom*?—Dizzy's *Novel*,[12] after all the noise ab*t* it, is not worth sixpence except in bad silver. Oh this People, and this "Peoples Will*m*"[13] & Co!——

Froude is ab*t* setting off for Kerry[14] ag*n*; to me a sensible loss for 5 months coming. I myself am not in worse health, and not in *joy*fuller spirits, than when you saw me last. *Externally* altog*r* idle; from day to day more indifft to being so.

With my kindest regards to Mrs S. & best wishes to you all

Ever truly T. Carlyle

6. The prime minister William E. Gladstone's Irish land reform bill passed its third reading in the House of Commons, 30 May.

7. TC's idea of the Irish pronunciation of "repeal."

8. Dublin Castle, seat of the British govt. in Ireland, as well as the higher law courts.

9. Henry Austin Bruce (1815–94; *ODNB*), home secretary 1868–73.

10. James Rutterford (b. ca. 1843), laborer, was sentenced to death for murdering James Hight, gamekeeper, 31 Dec. 1869, near Barton Mills in Suffolk. The *Times* reported, 9 April, that Henry Bruce, contacted by the prison authorities, sent a Govt. Inspector of Prisons to visit the convict, who reported: "owing to a malformation of the convict's throat . . . there might be great difficulty in executing the sentence of the law without risk of failure." The *Times* reported, 11 April: "Mr. Bruce, not having the power to give effect to the sentence by any but the ordinary means, and finding by the . . . report from a Board of medical gentlemen that the risk of a very revolting spectacle was imminent, had no alternative but to reprieve the convict." Rutterford's sentence was commuted to penal servitude for life.

11. The public hall of a Greek city or state.

12. Benjamin Disraeli, *Lothair* (1870), pbd. 2 May; the 1st edn. of 2,000 copies sold out in two days.

13. Gladstone's government; the nickname had been given to him by the *Daily Telegraph*; see 46:194.

14. See TC to JAC, 14 May.

TC TO JEAN CARLYLE AITKEN

Chelsea, 8 june 1870

Dear kind Sister,—It seems very stingy that I do not write to you, lamed as my hand is,—hand and heart alike lamed incurably! But the Truth is, I have no fixed resolut*n*, or import*t* outlook, ab*t* this or any future summer or season[1] I may have; or at least none that invites me to *speak* of it much, tho' *it* is forever pres*t* to me (as beseems), grand & sad & quiet, not unblessed either, or with*t* sacredness & hope! As God wills; as God shall have willed.— —

With regard to the days now passing, I have the gen*l* feeling that I will fly out of London, when they grow too hot; that Scotland sea-bathing & sea-air *might* do a little for me (a little, not much); that Scotland, with or with*t* this adjunct, is the likeliest, ultimate or primary direct*n* for me, in wh*h* case I am sure to land on y*r* premises, there being in fact no other feasible lodging-place for me, nor any other *place* at all where I have *more* than a most brief errand. The good Mary, my best of Hostesses I am shut out from, by that hideous railway and its tearing horrors;[2] no sleep for me well possible there! Not to add that the remembrances themselves that must & w*d* await one there are too painful far to front!— Really this is *all* I have got to say on what w*d* be the real interest to you of any Letter from me; and that is why I do not write. Courage: the weather tho' beautifully windy and cool up to this day is secretly growing warmer (as one feels today, for instance, when the wind still easterly has sunk lowish); and probably before many days I may write to you on the sudden: Coming, *practically* coming such a day!— For cert*n* there is nothing here to be much regretted when I go—Froude (I understand) is off for Irel*d* *tomorrow*: to utmost Kerry;—he invites me much, "whole Atlantic to bathe in, other side his garden-wall; bright silent moorlands, d*o* d*o* skies," &c &c; but alas it is 20 hours away,—and that is always my excuse for No. The other brightish creatures to me have, *friendly* all to help me, and in truth the bright-est going,—are alas fallen very dim to me, and form really not a solace to me, but rather the reverse, so dim & weary have I myself grown. *Weather* once hot enough I feel it actually probable I shall weigh anchor.

The Doctor, I conclude, found nothing of a feasible sea-lodging n*r* Kirk-cudbr*t*?[3] I myself consider there is probably none to be anywhere found;

TC-JCA, 8 June. MS: NLS 527.18. Hitherto unpbd.

1. Jean and their brother John were looking for a house for the summer for TC; see TC to JAC, 26 May and 1 June.

2. Their sister Mary Austin at The Gill; the railway passed very close to their farm; see 42:66.

3. John A. Carlyle wrote, 30 May, that there were three or four possible places in Kirk-cudbright: "I shall wait till you write again, & then be ready to go & see . . . any . . . you might have a liking for."

Lady Asb*n's* fine yacht speculat*n* seems extinct too (if it ever deserved to be called alive)—the sea probably [yet?] be con[sidered] unattainable. Well, well: like the jun*r* "Stewart Lewis," one can say, "I sometimes, when I can get it, induldulge in a cup of tea[4]

But it is 4 o'clock! adieu dear Sister: I must out & walk. Mary, the little mouse, is still at work downstairs.— Tomorrow I am to have a black Ind*n* Dignitary,[5] whom I w*d* much rather have avoided. As we have no language in common, it is likely he won't stay long. Read those 2 Notes & give them to John for whom I intend soon someth*g* more.

With my blessing on you all,

Yr affect*e* T. Carlyle

TC TO GEORGE A. DUNCAN

Chelsea: June 9, 1870.

Dear Sir,—You need no apology for addressing me;[1] your letter itself is of amiable ingenuous character; pleasant and interesting to me in no common degree. I am sorry only that I cannot set at rest, or settle into clearness, your doubts on that important subject.[2] What I myself practically, in a half-articulate way, believe on it I will try to express for you.

4. TC refers to the son of Stewart Lewis (ca. 1756–1818; *ODNB*), poet, from Ecclefechan; see 4:96. Lewis was apparently known for excessive drinking; see 1:53–54, so perhaps the phrase is humorous.

5. Syed Ahmed Khan (1817–98; *ODNB*), Indian Muslim leader, magistrate, administrator and educationist. He wrote, 5 June, enclosing Sir Edward Strachey's letter of introduction, and asking to visit "some day & hour." Sir Edward Strachey wrote, 14 May: "This note will introduce to you Syed Ahmed . . . an old friend of my Brother John, and a distinguished Indian Judge. Syed Ahmed is writing a life of Mahomed, and highly appreciates all that you have written on that Hero." John Strachey (1823–1907; *ODNB*), administrator in India; knighted 1872. The Stracheys were sons of TC's old friends Edward and Julia Strachey. For TC's lecture on Muhammed (Mahomet), see "The Hero as Prophet," Carlyle, *On Heroes* 37–66.

TC-GAD, 9 June. MS copies: NLS 8992.182 and Bodleian Lib. Pbd: Froude, *Carlyle* 2:21–22; Wilson, *Carlyle* 6:210–12 inc. Text from Froude. Quot: Sophy Hall, *Dr. Duncan of Ruthwell* (Edinburgh and London, 1910) 81. George Alexander Duncan (1850–1906), grandson of TC's old friend Henry Duncan (1774–1846; *ODNB*), minister, Ruthwell, Dumfriesshire; see 1:223.

1. Duncan wrote, 4 June: "I am a stranger to you, but my grandfather . . . was not, and it is a good deal on that ground that I rest my plea for addressing you."

2. Duncan continued: "when people are perplexed or in doubt, they go to their minister for counsel: you are my minister, my only minister, my honoured and trusted teacher, and to you I, having for more than a year back ceased to believe as my fathers believed in matters of religion, and being now an inquirer in that field, come for light on the subject of prayer." Duncan felt that to try and change the will of God by prayer was "in the last degree

First, then, as to your objection of setting up *our* poor wish or will in opposition to the will of the Eternal, I have not the least word to say in contradiction of it. And this seems to close, and does, in a sense though not perhaps in all senses, close the question of our prayers being *granted*, or what is called 'heard'; but that is not the whole question.

For, on the other hand, prayer is and remains always a native and deepest impulse of the soul of man; and correctly gone about, is of the very highest benefit (nay, one might say, indispensability) to every man aiming morally high in this world. No prayer no *religion*, or at least only a *dumb* and lamed one! Prayer is a turning of one's soul, in heroic reverence, in infinite desire and *endeavour*, towards the Highest, the All-Excellent, Omnipotent, Supreme. The modern Hero, therefore, ought *not* to give up praying, as he has latterly all but done.

Words of prayer, in this epoch, I know hardly any. But the act of prayer, in great moments, I believe to be still possible; and that one should gratefully accept such moments, and count them blest, when they come if come they do—which latter is a most rigorous preliminary question with us in all cases. '*Can* I *pray* in this moment!' (much as I may *wish* to do so)? 'if not, then NO!' I can at least stand silent, inquiring, and *not* blasphemously *lie* in this Presence!

On the whole, Silence is the one safe form of prayer known to me, in this poor sordid era—though there are ejaculatory words too which occasionally rise on one, with a felt propriety and veracity; words very welcome in such case! Prayer is the aspiration of our poor struggling heavy-laden soul towards its Eternal Father; and, with or without words, ought *not* to become impossible, nor, I persuade myself, need it ever. Loyal sons and subjects *can* approach the King's throne who have no 'request' to make there, except that they may continue loyal. Cannot they?

This is all I can say to you, my good young friend; and even this, on my part and on yours, is perhaps too much. Silence, silence! 'The Highest cannot be spoken of in words,' says Goethe.[3] Nothing so desecrates mankind as their continual babbling, both about the speakable and the unspeakable, in this bad time!

Your grandfather was the amiablest and kindliest of men; to me pretty much a *unique* in those young years, the one cultivated man whom I could feel myself permitted to call *friend* as well. Never can I forget that Ruthwell Manse, and the beautiful souls (your grandmother,[4] your grand-aunts,[5] and others) who then made it bright to me. All vanished now, all vanished!

---

absurd"; he asked: "Is it too much to hope that you will kindly write me a few lines throwing light on this subject? . . . Lest these remarks should seem to you intolerably shallow, I must inform you that I am only twenty."

3. See Goethe, *Faust* 3432, and Carlyle, *Reminiscences* 370 and 462.

4. Agnes, b. Craig (d. 1832), m., 1803, Henry Duncan.

5. The only grand-aunt traced is Mary Duncan (1784–1857).

Please tell me *whose* son you are—not George John's, I think, but Wallace's,[6] whom I can remember only as a grave boy? Also whether bonny little 'Barbara Duncan' is still living;[7] or indeed if she ever lived to be your aunt? I have some sad notion No. I will not trouble you about the Mitchell letters: I wrote many letters to the good Mitchell;[8] but I fear now they were all of a foolish type, fitter to burn than to read at present. Tell me also, if you like, a little more about yourself, your pursuits and endeavours, your intended course in the world.[9] You perceive I expect from you one more letter at least,[10] though it is doubtful whether I can *answer* any more, for *reasons* you may *see* sufficiently!

Believe me, dear Sir,

Yours with sincere good wishes,

T. CARLYLE.

TC TO JOHN A. CARLYLE

Chelsea, 10 june, 1870—

My dear Brother,—I was thinking to write a word to you today; and here has yr Letter just come in, reinforcing my already settled purpose. For the rest I am very useless today; under a kind of biliary crisis for some three days past, involving two "bad nights" (neither of them nearly *quite* sleepless, howr, and the former much the worse of the two);—this is a thing I am evid*tly* growing more liable to; but the dreadful *wake*fulness with its shivering miseries, has much left me since you were last here. Continual *nausea*; indifference, or

6. Henry Duncan had two sons, George John Duncan (1806-68; see 38:246), and William Wallace Duncan (1808-64), Free Kirk minister at Peebles, who m., 1842, Rachel Borthwick, b. Hill (d. 1879); George A. Duncan was Wallace and Rachel's son.

7. Their sister, Barbara Ann Duncan (1811-1901), m., 1843, Rev. James Dodds (1812-85; *ODNB*); see 12:29-30.

8. Duncan asked if TC was interested in reading "some letters written by you to Mr. Robert Mitchell when this old century was in its teens, and thus recall from your own beloved past a thousand persons, thoughts and scenes and schemes bygone?" These letters were now among Duncan family papers. Robert Mitchell (ca. 1795-1836; see 1:6), early friend of TC, tutored the family and boarders of Henry Duncan, Ruthwell Manse, 1814-21.

9. See also TC to MD, 20 Sept.

10. Duncan replied, 4 Jan. 1871: "In your most kind letter to me last summer you said: 'You perceive I expect from you one more letter at least, tho' it is doubtful whether I can answer any more'; in these words 'at least' & 'any more' I find my warrant for writing again to wish you a good New Year." He told TC that he had not taken the job he spoke of in his last letter as "the Master of the school convinced me that he was not a man I could work loyally under"; he was tutoring and studying further to become a better teacher. He concluded: "My Aunt Barbara & all the rest of us are well. She & my Uncle spent last week with us here."

TC-JAC, 10 June. MS: NLS 527.19. Quot: Wilson, *Carlyle* 6:207-8.

absolute repugnance to almost all kinds of food, and dining and even break-fast*g* as if by *force of* charac*tr*: this, ag*n* has visibly increased, and I expect will go on increasing. I get nothing, or less, out [of] medical attempts; once or so I have tried half a *blue pill*, wh*h* appeared to have some slight success, but not enough to encourage the risk of going into a *series* of that sort, on[1] no responsibility better than my own. Great weakness, darkness, lonesomeness of mind, &c &c are the nat*l* consequence; wh*h* ought not to surprise me, nor I think do or will, —tho' I w*d* fain enough these[2] symptoms (sympt*ms* of *Advancing* AGE), if I knew how! — — I sometimes feel as if this *shaking of the right hand* is in reality the worst evil of all: sentence "Not to do any work more, while thou livest!" In brighter hours I see still many things I might *write*, were the merely mechanical means still there: but *they aren't*;[3] and no attempts at "dictat*n*" have yet had the smallest real success, nor I doubt *will*. Well, well; be quiet any way! —

I duly got the £800; and next day (2 june I think) sent it away by the "U.S." course you advised; —giving poor Alick, on the other leaf, abund*t* direct*ns* how to dispose of it:[4] £500 to his *Jane*; £300 to *Tom* (wh*h* with the 200 before, w*d equalize* the sums): I was very *wae* in writing of the thing; but felt bound to have done with it while time still was. Alick was to give the Two their respective sums at once, —adding, of course, his own best advice ab*t* the disposal of it, but not insist*g* upon that. I hope it will do no *ill* to either of them, or to anybody: but that is gen*lly* all one can aspire to in such things; & one never is sure even ab*t* that.

Y*r* survey of the Galloway coast appears to be complete now, and the result is, *Nothing there till Aug*t *at soonest*.[5] That is one thing settled then. For y*r* own self, have you yet resolved on anything: *Vichy*, voyage *to Norway*, any *voyage*?[6] Let us not lose time, I beg; only 10 days hence will be the Longest Day. I am ready for anything of the *voyage* kind you c*d* fairly judge eligible; at least, I know I sh*d* strive to be; & the very *feeling* on tongue & palate at pres*t* ought to be an incite*t*! On arrival of the first torrid heat I believe I must at once take flight.— Froude is off, yest*y*, quite in a hurry; did not even take leave, had that been necess*y*. Lady A. is bent for Lochluichart,[7] with

1. Word repeated at turn of page.
2. Thus in MS; TC possibly omitted "ignore" or "cure" after "enough."
3. John A. Carlyle wrote, 9 June: "what you do write is clear & easy to read. If you could get a good pencil with longer handle, you might perhaps write more freely with it even at the outset."
4. See TC to AC, 3 June.
5. John A. Carlyle reported, 9 June, seeing "all the places on the shore between Gatehouse & Dundrennan," and none were "vacant that would be at all likely to suit. Every thing engaged long ago for the months of June & July." Some were still available in Aug.
6. See TC to JAC, 1 June.
7. See TC to JAC, 26 May.

Nairn as an "excell*t* Sea-village":[8] route is, to Edin*r* by Steamer, rail thence to Greenock,[9] and then Caledon*n* Canal,[10]—"before june end."

My two Hindoos yesterday, the Bahadur & his Son (a Cambridge Student),[11] were, apart from something of singularity, a *bore* and little else. They lasted above an hour, & (in my evil condit*n* of body & nerves) did me visible mischief. The Papa is a bulky, gloomily serious, heavy kind of man of European (i.e. Caucasian) features, and respectable express*n*; ab*t* fifty,—a *sincere* Mahometan (from Delhi)!—and what is worse, not able to speak three words of Engl*h*, hardly to understand above *two* or so if the chances are fav*ble*. He is writing a *Life of "Mohummed,"* has already printed 1 vol, wh*h* he gave me (done into Engl*h*, but unreadable, huge, chaotic, full of Arabic citat*ns*, of Egypt*n* sundry darkness gen*lly*), wh*h* I mean to pres*t* to the London Library as the only refuge for it.[12] The junior had a superficial knowledge of English, but a deep ignorance of all things European: had never heard of *Goethe*, c*d* hardly be made to understand what Silvestre de Sacy's *Article on Mahomt* was, or even what the *Biogr*ie *Universelle* when I showed it him.[13] They begged each a Photo*h* from; and the Senior, at going, not only bowed into quite parabolic shape, twice over, but twice *kissed* my hand in a sort. "Poor fellow, after all!"[14]—(a case really of that old kind!)—

Possibly you may get some interest out of the yg *Duncan* Letter, wh*h* I inclose;—or may even know the man? I wrote some ans*r* to him yesterday:— and expect to hear ag*n* from him *once*, if only *Whose Son he is.*

Adieu, it is striking 4; I must *out* direct;—have spent say thrice or *ten times* as many minutes in the act of *pen*manship (so to call it)[15] as you w*d* have

8. Nairn, town on S coast of the Moray Firth, 16 mi. (26 km.) NE of Inverness.

9. Greenock, port on the Firth of Clyde, 23 mi. (37 km.) NW of Glasgow.

10. Presumably Lady Ashburton planned to sail up the west coast to Fort William, and then through the Caledonian Canal to Inverness.

11. Syed Ahmed Khan (see TC to JCA, 8 June) and his son Syed Mahmood, who had been granted a scholarship to study law in England. "Bahadur" is a Hindi word for a distinguished person.

12. Syed Ahmed Khan, *A Series of Essays on the Life of Mohammed, and Subjects Subsidiary Thereto* (1870). TC apparently did present it as the *London Library Catalogue* (1913) listed "Ahmad Kha, *Sayid*, 'Series of essays on the life of Mohammed &c.' v. 1 [no more publ. Each essay has sep. tp. & pagin.] 1870." "[Syed Ahmed] had an interview with Carlyle, and the Chelsea Sage was unusually gracious to him. They talked long and earnestly over 'Heroes and Hero-Worship,' especially about Mohammed, of whom Carlyle expresses a very high opinion in that work; and also about Syed Ahmed's 'Essays on the Life of Mohammed,' then in the press" (George Farquhar Graham, *The Life and Work of Syed Ahmed Khan* [Edinburgh, 1885], 98–99).

13. A. I. Silvestre de Sacy and Henri d'Audiffret, "Mahomet," *Biographie Universelle, Ancienne et Moderne* (Paris, 1811–28) 26:186–213 (see also 44:209), one of TC's sources for his lecture on Muhammed (Mahomet) in "The Hero as Prophet"; Carlyle, *On Heroes* 37–66.

14. Coterie speech, an early phrase of John A. Carlyle's; see 1:211.

15. TC was writing in pencil.

needed: think of that. — —*Fortnightly Review* (now sent) is *not* "Dr Russell's Copy,"[16] but one for yrself, — an accidental *Duplicate*, wh*h* has 3 articles in it (perhaps *4*) worth a kind of glance from you.[17]

Adieu, dear Brother. Ever yr affect*e* / T. Carlyle

TC TO JOHN FORSTER

[11 June 1870]

Dear Forster, — I am profoundly sorry for *you*,[1] and indeed for myself & for us all. It is an event world-wide; a *unique* of Talents suddenly extinct; and has "eclipsed" (we too may say) "the harmless gaiety of Nations."[2] No death since 1866 has fallen on me with such a stroke; no Literary Man's hitherto ever did. The good, the gentle, ever friendly noble Dickens, — every inch of him an Honest Man!

I had[3] tho*t* to attend the Funeral[4] (this one Funeral of its kind); but now I suppose it will be impossible for me in my pres*t* feeble condit*n*. — God be with you all, you at Gad's Hill in these sad hours.

*Y*rs ever

T. Carlyle[5]

16. TC regularly sent the *Fortnightly Review* to Dr. James Russell; see 46:16.

17. John wrote: "Several of the articles are interesting . . . I have already read Mazzini's tho' it is cloudy & too long for effect." Joseph Mazzini, "A Letter to the Members of the Ecumenical Council," *Fortnightly Review* (June 1870: 725–51); among the other articles was one by Frederic Harrison (1831–1923; *ODNB*), "The Romance of the Peerage" (655–67), which quoted several times from TC's *French Revolution*.

TC-JF, [11 June]. Addr: Palace-Gate House / Kensington; delivered by hand; letter dated by Forster. MS: FC. Pbd: John Forster, *Life of Charles Dickens* (1872–74) 3:475 inc; Shepherd, *Carlyle* 2:292 inc; Wilson, *Carlyle* 6:209 inc.

1. Charles Dickens d., 9 June, at his home at Gad's Hill, Kent. John Forster, a particularly close friend of Dickens, as well as his literary adviser, was soon to begin his biography.

2. Phrase of Samuel Johnson (1709–84; *ODNB*), author and lexicographer, on the death of his friend David Garrick (1717–79; *ODNB*), actor and playwright, in "The Life of Edmund Smith," *Lives of the English Poets* (1781); Edmund Smith (1672–1710; *ODNB*), poet and playwright.

3. "I had" repeated at turn of page.

4. Dickens was buried, 14 June, in Westminster Abbey.

5. TC was sent a carte-de-visite of Dickens (see opp.) by Robert Hindry Mason (1824–85) of Mason & Co., Photographers, 28 Old Bond St., London; Mason had taken photographs of Dickens at Gad's Hill, 6 Aug. 1866; see *DL* 11:230. His letters to TC are untraced, but he presumably gave TC the date of the photograph, "6 or 7 Aug*t*," reproduced on the carte-de-visite and the information about the book Dickens was reading; for TC's notes on the reverse of the carte, see 30; carte and notes, pbd: K. J. Fielding, "Carlyle and Dickens or Dickens and Carlyle?" *The Dickensian* 69 (1973):113; Leon Litvack, "Dickens in the Eye of the Beholder: The photographs of Robert Hindry Mason," *Dickens Studies Annual* 47 (2016):190; the carte is owned by the Charles Dickens Museum, London.

Charles Dickens at Gad's Hill, 6 or 7 August 1866,
photograph by Robert Hindry Mason
Courtesy of Charles Dickens Museum, London

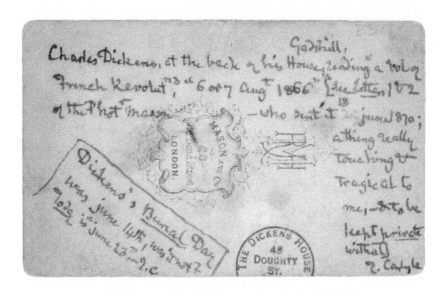

Thomas Carlyle's notes, 23 June 1870, on the reverse of the
carte de visite of Charles Dickens at Gad's Hill
Courtesy of Charles Dickens Museum, London

TC TO JOHN A. CARLYLE

Chelsea, 15 june, 1870

My dear Br*r*

You won't get much good of the Two Pamphl*ts*[1] I send you today: the Irish
one, especially I have not read at all; nor *acknowledged*; being too sick, from
the very starting, of the whole Gladstonian Irish "reconciliat*n*"[2] Futility, and
wishful only that the babble on it w*d end*. So soon as one Irish Assassin has
been fairly, by Govt*'s* declared industry & fixed resolut*n*, got hold of from
among the associating People, and hanged dead, under "*Irish* ideas,"—I will
begin to believe that some real result of "benefit" may be achievable in that
Country; till then not. The Greenock Pamphl*t* gives, in dull form, view of a
"Pauper" *Malebolge*, little short of y*r* Dante's,[3]—if you add to it the Parl*t* Pala-

TC-JAC, 15 June. MS: NLS 527.20. Quot: K. J. Fielding, "Carlyle and Dickens or Dickens
and Carlyle?" *The Dickensian* 69 (1973): 117.

1. Pamphlets (one Irish, the other pbd. in or about Greenock) unidentified further.

2. See TC to JFS, 3 June.

3. Greenock's position as a port on the S coast of the Firth of Clyde made it a major des-
tination for Irish emigrants; the majority were Catholic and most were desperately poor;
only the most menial work was available to them. Malebolge is the eighth circle of hell in
Dante's *Inferno*.

[30]

ver and idle universal official Nescience of such phenom*a* among "practical" men of high "statesmanship"; accord*g* to the Brit*h* standard. *Pfui*!

But I wanted to tell you in a word, that y*r* last Mrs Arbuckle-Kirkandrews speculat*n*[4] seems to me by far the likeliest yet started, indeed the only fairly *possible* one; and I wish you to let it stand, for me and for y*rself*, as the one that shall be tried, if any be found triable at all. My kindest comp*ts* and remembrances, to Mrs Arbuckle therefore, while you announce the above fact; and let said fact be our final one on that head just now. Our weather in the last 3 days is growing very hot, my poor stomach ever more like ceasing altog*r:* — it seems to me we shall not now be many days here.

I am very glad to hear the news from Holm-Hill;[5] it w*d* be very miserable to me that anything sh*d* befal *there* in my time. — Mary wrote to Birm*m* yesterday, inviting Jamie[6] for a few days, "while the Season is at its wonderfullest & maddest." But for you I sh*d* not have known Jamie was there.

Blunt the Rector[7] has come in; eaten away all my time; sorrow on it!

Poor Dickens, poor Dickens: Forster called yest*y* morning, had just been laying him (*quite* private Funeral) in West*r* Abbey: —was weeping every word.[8]

Adieu, d*r* Brr— *Yrs* ever T. Carlyle

4. Anna Maria Arbuckle, widow of John A. Carlyle's old friend Dr. Robert Arbuckle (1802–62), living with their five children at Auchenhay, about 20 mi. (32 km.) SW of Dumfries; see 38:274. John visited her 3–10 June. John wrote, 12 June: "Mrs Arbuckle [took] me to Knockbreck & Kirk Andrews, which I was glad to see again. No bathing quarters that would suit us at either place.... The house at Auchenhay is large & Mrs Arbuckle would like much to have us there.... The house is very dry & good & the situation excellent. Three bedrooms vacant, & Jean invited too or any of her daughters. The offer valid for any part of the summer.'" Knockbreck and Kirk Andrews, villages on the Kirkcudbright coast.

5. John A. Carlyle had visited Holmhill; he wrote, 13 June: "Mrs Russell was very glad to see me, & insisted on my staying all day. She has not yet got quite free of disease, but has walked once or twice into the dining room without help, & is making progress. She sleeps unusually well, has a good appetite for all her meals, & looks cheerful. In a day or two she hopes to get out for a drive."

6. Their brother James Carlyle, visiting his da., Jenny Scott and her husband, William, in Birmingham.

7. Rev. Gerald Blunt, of St. Luke's, Chelsea.

8. TC noted in his journal, 14 June: "Dickens *laid in West*r* Abbey* this morn*g*, a quite private Funeral, not intended to be there, but the little quiet Country Churchy*d* (I suppose) being found *in*accessible (shut by Act of Parl*t*), and *this* having offered itself. Forster called (I still loitering over breakfast), on his way home, from Gad's Hill and the sad solemnity at Westm*r*. Poor F. was overwhelmed with misery, c*dn't* speak with*t* burst*g* into tears: has been running ab*t* bet*n* Gadshill & London (very unwell too) ever since he was summoned home from Cornwall by telegram, on Thursday night last. / I myself did not hear of the Event till, accidentally, on Friday night, 24 hours after the *end*, 48 hours after the *stroke*, wh*h* from the first was reckoned fatal. To me also an Event wh*h* felt sad and heavy, in a singular degree, and has been much in my thots ever since. For the first time in reference

TC TO JOHN A. CARLYLE

Chelsea 16 june [1870]
3 p.m.

This is literally *nothing*; only to say (my *Proofs*[1] being done) that yr Letter has come, — & that one can keep these *Norwayers* as a kind of second string,[2] tho' still rather hold by the first.[3] My state of utter *dyspepsia* renders me exceedingly tremulous, in fact very weak & miserable ("crisis" not gone yet, &c &c): *sleep* howr is far beyond hope.

Jamie has yet sent no ansr from Birmm: perhaps he is off homewards? We shall see in a day or two. Thank Jean for her Letter.[4]

We refused Forster last night; *possibly* enough will have to do so Sunday too, — it depends.[5] Poor fellow, very unwell too. I am just bound *thither*.

T.C.

TC TO JEAN CARLYLE AITKEN

Chelsea, 18 june 1870

Dear Jean, —I have not a single word of news; but will send as I have done almost daily for this *one* week, a symbol of salutatn. New Proofsheets came

---

to any 'Literary Brr,' I wished to have been of the Funeral; but 'no stranger whatr' being the rub, I was forbidden that poor bit of symbolism—wh*h* w*d* have been sincere enough towards the Deceased" (TC's journal; privately owned).

TC-JAC, 16 June. Addr: The Hill / Dumfries / N.B. PM: London, 16 June 1870. MS: NLS 527.21. Hitherto unpbd. Written on reverse of Forster's letter to TC, 15 June.

1. Presumably proofsheets of the library edn. of *Frederick*; see TC to JCA, 18 June.

2. John A. Carlyle wrote, 15 June, that there were new steamer routes to Norway and Sweden from London, as well as steamers to Orkney and Shetland from Aberdeen: "If one went with any of them one would at least get the free air of the sea, though one might have to submit to some inconveniences. A little later in the season they will all be crowded . . . . I shall be ready at once if you wish to have a voyage in any of them."

3. Presumably TC meant he would rather go and stay with Anna Maria Arbuckle; see TC to JAC, 15 June.

4. Jean wrote, 15 June: "Jamie . . . is still at Birmingham. Mrs Scott [Jenny] has had an addition to her family since her father went to B-ham. He was taking home their little boy who had been staying at Scotsbrig for some time." John James Carlyle Scott was 5. Their 2d da., b. in June, was Jessie Beattie Scott.

5. Forster wrote, 15 June: "The good Elwin has come suddenly up to town—and I should much like that you and Mary would come and [dine] with him here tomorrow (Thursday) at punctual seven. Of course *only ourselves*. If however you cannot, this is not to interfere with Sunday." Whitwell Elwin (1816–1900; *ODNB*), Church of England clergyman and journal editor, friend of Forster.

TC-JCA, 18 June. MS: NLS 1763.312. Hitherto unpbd.

[32]

to me (the *beginning* of *Fried*h vol. IV, only 7 volumes now to print!)¹—and after reading Proofs there is still a small minute left.

The "Jenny Corrie" whom you are to go & see,² is vividly in my remembrance! She is Niece of Jenny Lockhart,³ sure enough, Daughter (base-born) of *Jean* Lockht and a Hash Corrie, kind of dissolute Drover⁴ (one of 3, whom I also remembr—fie on them!) This Jenny was always a *fait* well-doing wench, & had grown to be a tight handsome very decent Dressmaker; living quietly with her Aunty Jenny. These "Bells,"⁵ I suppose, are grandchildrn of another Aunt "Aggie" married to a Davy Bell⁶ in Dumfries, & who was always reckoned a kind of *Leddy* in comparison.— Jamie Beattie & the Jenny you are to see had long been expected (and expect*ing*) to marry; and had done so not long before our "Comely Bank" (ah me!)—at least they were in Dumfries wedded, when Craig*h* began;—I rem*ber* seeing Jamie on Wed*y* at the mid-steeple,⁷ and *avoiding* to speak with him. I heard he was a cruel husband to Jenny; a cleverish cunning enough shifty kind of fellow, but very selfish & hard-tempered. He died as *Tailor of Haddington*⁸ (esteemed in that capacity),—heard of him *last*, you well guess from *Whom*!⁹

By all means go & see this poor of Contemporary of mine; tell her sparingly of the above, only how well I remember her from beyond above 60 years;— and (privately) inform yrself a little ab*t* her actual condit*n* Poor old Soul!——

Adieu, dear Sister. T.C.

1. TC was presumably working on proofs of *Frederick* for vol. 23 of the library edn.; vols. 21–23 were pbd. 1870; the final 7 vols., 24–30, were pbd. 1871.

2. Jean Aitken wrote, 15 June: "I hear that the widow of James Beattie (both from Ecclefechan long ago *her* name I believe to be "Jenny Corrie" niece to Jenny Lockhart (?). What I shd have begun with *is*, this old woman now 84, is on a visit to W*m* Bells Irish Street & wants me to go & see her w*h* I intend to do one of these days." Jenny Beattie, b. Corrie (b. ca. 1786), m., ca. 1826, Jamie Beattie (b. ca. 1791), possibly the son of James Beattie, an Ecclefechan weaver whom TC met in 1802; see 1:364.

3. Jenny (Janet) Lockhart (1771–1840), m. TC's paternal uncle John Carlyle (1754–1801); for her death, see 12:358 and 363–64. A pencil note (not in TC's hand) has been added: "Wife (2nd) of C's Uncle John; lived in the Arched House, Ecclefechan."

4. Jean Lockhart, presumably Jenny Lockhart's sister. "Hash" Corrie unidentified further; probably related to Andrew Corry; see 19:231. "Hash" is a person who makes a mess of things, thoughtless, careless, thriftless.

5. William Bell and family living in Irish St., Dumfries (possibly a bacon curer [1878 Dumfries directory]), unidentified further.

6. Aggie Bell, b. Lockhart, and Davy Bell, unidentified further.

7. Presumably at the Wednesday weekly market, held around the Mid-Steeple in Dumfries; see also 36:252–53.

8. Jamie Beattie was listed as a tailor in the Haddington census, 1841; he was then listed, 1850, as the keeper of Haddington Prison, and his wife, Jennie, was also listed, 1854, as keeper and matron.

9. JWC.

TC TO JOHN A. CARLYLE

It is becoming evid*t*, dear Br*r*, that I ought to get away out of this place: the weather is grown burning hot, all grass grown brown; and my poor faculty of *swallowing* anything (except "cold spring water," could I get it), much more digest*g* anyth*g*, verging more and more towards *zero!*

If you have, for y*r*self or me, any outlook upon those *Northern Steamers*[1] (at wh*h*, as at everyth*g* else, I myself cowardlike shudder), it will be good that you come up in person & fly-off with me! If on the contrary it is to be Dumfries & Kirkcudbr*t* only[2] (at wh*h* also I shudder, but *not so much*), send me at once *Note of the best train*,[3] that I may work my own passage (with help of poor Mary) before things quite take fire! — This is *the needful*; & shall be *all*, in such hurry.

Y*r* Cromwell vol.[4] ought to come this week; we had ours yest*y*. Forster is much better; "only some addit*l* *Liver*-attack produced by agitat*n* & want of sleep." We are to "dine" (so-to speak) with him tomorrow.

Please reduce that Hamburg stuff to interpretability for me,[5] — or if you are too busy, *don't*, but merely shove it back to me. It has come this moment; and from my remembrance of the Figure (2 Figures, both schoolmasterish)[6] I half-guess it may not need much ans*r* from me. — Adieu, dear Brother

Y*r* affecte T. Carlyle

TC-JAC, 20 June. MS: NLS 527.23. Hitherto unpbd.

1. See TC to JAC, 16 June.

2. John A. Carlyle wrote, 22 June: "Every thing is ready for you here whenever you resolve to move; & John tells us Jean & you 'might have the upper rooms at Scotsbrig quite free at any time.'" Their nephew John Carlyle who lived at Scotsbrig with his wife, Margaret, and father, James.

3. John A. Carlyle wrote, 23 June: "The train for Dumfries is the same that you came by last time, & is by far the best that starts from Euston Square. It generally has a 'through-carriage' for Dumfries, starts from *Euston Square at 10 a.m.*, has few stoppages, & goes steadily & quietly.... Arrives at Dumfries 7.19 p.m. & is generally punctual except on Tuesdays. You would require to be at the Station ten minutes before 10 a.m. at latest, in order to get started comfortably. Last time Mary & you had a compartment to yourselves all the way—perhaps in consequence of a trifle to the Guard given at starting."

4. Presumably the 5th and last vol. of the library edn. (vol. 18 of that edn.) of *Cromwell*; for the first four vols., see TC to JAC, 14 May.

5. Dr. Ferdinand Lüders (1824–1915), philologist, author, and senior lecturer at the Johanneum, 1864–69, wrote from Hamburg, 15 June, requesting permission to print TC's essays on Voltaire and Diderot. John wrote, 23 June, returning the German letter copied: "I daresay you will send two words to D*r* Lüders, granting permission to print the Essays on Voltaire & Diderot.... He remembers having seen you in 1858!" TC visited various places in Germany, Aug.–Sept. 1858, starting in Hamburg; see 34:155.

6. The 2d figure was possibly Johannes Classen (1805–91), rector of the Johanneum from 1864 to 1874.

TC TO FERDINAND LÜDERS

24 June 1870

The Johanneum[1] is a place I always regard with a kind of veneration for the excellent old Huebner's sake, who was Rector there 150 years ago and has taught me so many things in so masterly a manner.[2] It seems to me that no man has treated any enormous mass of labour more herioically than he his.[3]

TC TO CHARLES ROGERS

25 June 1870

[TC expressed his willingness to subscribe his] bit of contribution [to a Bruce Monument at Stirling.] Dr. Gregory's Inscription[1] is very good, but besides mentioning the year of Bannockburn it surely would be an obvious improvement to give the *day* of the *month* (and even of the week,[2] if that latter is indubitably known. . . . sincere wishes [for the success of the plan] *un*troubled in this instance.[3]

TC-FL, 24 June. Quot: Edmund Kelter, *Hamburg und sein Johanneum im Wandel der Jahrhunderte, 1529–1929* (Hamburg, 1928) 66.

1. The Johanneum: grammar school in Hamburg, founded 1529 by Johannes Bugenhagen (1485–1558), teaching particularly Greek and Latin, and the works of the protestant reformers.

2. Johann Hübner (1668–1731), German geographer, scholar, and author, rector of the Johanneum 1711–31; TC used Hübner's *Genealogische Tabellen* (Leipzig, 1725–28) in *Frederick*, referring to it as "A Book of rare excellence in its kind" (see 27:129 and Carlyle, *Works* 12:61); for TC's copy, see HCC.

3. Presumably TC also gave Lüders permission to publish his essays; see TC to JAC, 20 June.

TC-CR, 25 June. Quot: Wylie 288 inc. Rev. Charles Rogers (1825–90; *ODNB*), Church of Scotland minister and historian; garrison chaplain, Stirling Castle, 1855–mid-Aug. 1863; he was proposing the building of a monument on Stirling Castle esplanade to Robert the Bruce (1274–1329; *ODNB*), king of Scotland 1306–29.

1. Dr. James Gregory (1753–1821; *ODNB*), Edinburgh physician; from 1799 "first physician to the king in Scotland." Gregory wrote more than one Latin inscription to Bruce. One included the description: "prudent, just, mild, pious, prosperous; the restorer and ornament, the avenger, and the father of his country" (letter from 'Medicus,' *Stirling Journal*, 15 July 1830: 81).

2. The statue of Robert the Bruce, first proposed 1869 and sculpted by Andrew Currie (1812–91), sculptor and antiquarian, was erected 1877. The front of Bruce's statue, with a shield bearing the lion rampant sculpted on the plinth beneath, looked towards the battle site 2½ mi. (4 km.) SSE of Stirling; see 36. The date of the Battle of Bannockburn (when Bruce and the Scots defeated the English), 24 June 1314, was inscribed on the W side of the plinth under "King Robert the Bruce"; see 37.

3. TC was peripherally involved with Rogers's previous venture, the commissioning and

Robert the Bruce (front view), by Andrew Currie
Courtesy of Aileen Christianson

Robert the Bruce, by Andrew Currie
Courtesy of Aileen Christianson

TC TO FREDERIC CHAPMAN

Chelsea, 28 June 1870

Dear Sir,

To yourself I believe it is perfectly well known, and you can make it known to any person interested, that I have not at present the least thought of changing my Publishing House, which has comfortably served me in that capacity for near thirty years past[1]—

Of course no Author can make *a marriage contract* with his Publishers, or tie himself from changing whenever he finds that unpleasant step advisable: but, sure enough, the state of facts is quietly as above, at this date

Yr. truly always / *T. Carlyle*

TC TO JOHN FORSTER

Chelsea, 28 june 1870

Dear Forster,

Mr Chapman, for a reason wh*h* he will explain to you, wishes me to write and sign something like the inclosed.[1] Naturally I feel it altog*r* fit that *you*, in the first place, sh*d* know & control.[2] With*t* y*r* sanct*n* I will not write even that on the matter; but if (as I anticipate) you find the Inclosed what is suitable enough,—by all means *forward it* at once.

In deep botherat*n* of *packing*[3] (but hoping better news *from* & *to* before long)

Y*rs* ever truly T. Carlyle

---

building of the Wallace Monument; see 38:164. This project and Rogers were criticized at the time. According to *ODNB*, Rogers's financial transactions for his various projects could be questionable and he "left Scotland [spring 1864] under a cloud indistinguishable from blazing notoriety."

TC-[FC], 28 June. MS copy: Johns Hopkins Univ. Libraries. Hitherto unpbd. The paper was headed "193 Piccadilly," the address of Chapman & Hall's offices. Presumably Frederic Chapman asked TC for the letter confirming Chapman & Hall was his publisher, possibly because there was a rumor that he might be changing publishers. TC sent the note for Forster's approval; see TC to JF, 28 June.
1. Chapman & Hall pbd. TC's works from Feb. 1842; see 14:46–47.

TC-JF, 28 June. Addr: Palace-Gate House / Kensington. MS: FC. Hitherto unpbd.
1. See TC to [FC], 28 June.
2. Forster was TC's literary advisor.
3. TC and Mary Aitken left for Dumfries the next day; Mary wrote to Lady Ashburton, Wed. evening [29 June]: "We have arrived all right—only half an hour ago— He was very well and did not at all complain of weariness, said he had never had a journey with fewer inconveniences in it & slept for ab*t* half an hour & at Preston enjoyed his dinner very much. . . . When we came in sight of Burnswark—the strange Roman Hill quite close to his Father's house, he fairly broke down & was very sad after that" (MS: NLS Acc. 11388).

[38]

TC TO WILLIAM DOUGAL CHRISTIE

[June 1870]

Dear Christie,—My hand is very unwilling, mutinous even, but I compel it to act,—in pencil. I have lately read a life of Dryden which seemed to me done with rigorous fidelity.[1] Yours always, T.C.

TC TO GEORGINA HOGARTH

The Hill, Dumfries, 4 july / 1870

Dear Miss Hogarth,

I accept with a mournful gratitude, and many sad and tender feelings, that little memorial of the Loved Friend who has suddenly departed;[1]—*gone* the way wh*h* is that of us also, and "of all the Earth, from the beging of things!—

It is almost thirty years since my acquaintance with him began;[2] and on my side, I may say every new meeting ripened it into more and more clear discern*t* (quite apart from his unique *talent*) of his rare and great worth as a brother man. A most correct, precise, clear-sighted, quietly decisive, just and loving man;—till at length he had grown to such a recognit*n* with me as I have rarely had for any man of my time.[3] This I can tell you then, for it is true, and will be welcome to you: to others less concerned I had as soon *not* speak on such a subject.

Poor Mrs Collins, poor Miss Dickens,[4]—deep, deep is my pity for them,

TC-WDC, [late June]. Pbd: Wylie 213. Letter probably dated around the time of the *Athenaeum* review, 25 June, of William Dougal Christie's *Poetical Works of Dryden*.

1. W. D. Christie, "Memoir of Dryden," *The Poetical Works of Dryden*, ed. W. D. Christie (London, 1870) xv-lxxxvii. Christie had been working on the book for some years (see 43: 130); presumably he sent TC a copy.

TC-GH, 4 July. MS: Berg. Addr: Gad's Hill / London. PM: Dumfries, 4 July 1870. Pbd: John Forster, *Life of Charles Dickens* (1872-74) 3:475 inc; Shepherd, *Carlyle* 2:291-92 inc; Wilson, *Carlyle* 6:209 inc; George H. Ford, "Stern Hebrews Who Laugh," *Carlyle Past and Present* (1976) 123-24. Georgina Hogarth (1827-1917; *ODNB*), sister-in-law, friend, and companion of Charles Dickens.

1. Georgina Hogarth wrote, 27 June: "I have the charge under my dearest Brother-in-law's Will of distributing the "familiar objects" belonging to him amongst the friends who loved him. . . . Mr. Forster assures me that I may venture to offer you one of the walking sticks which he constantly used—and that you will value it as a Memorial of your lost friend."

2. TC first met Dickens at a dinner party, 1840; see 12:80-81.

3. Georgina wrote: "You did not meet very often of late years—but there was *no one* for whom he had a higher reverence and admiration besides a sincere personal affection than for yourself."

4. Georgina wrote: "The two poor girls join me in sending respectful love to you." Dickens's two surviving das., Catherine (Kate), b. Dickens (1839-1929), m., 1860, Charles Allston Collins (1828-73; *ODNB*), artist and writer, and Mary (Mamie) Dickens (1838-96).

dear young souls; but what word can I say that will not awaken new tears! God bless you, all Three;—I will say that & no more.

Yrs with many thanks & sympathies / T. Carlyle

TC TO SIR JOHN MURRAY NAESMYTH

The Hill, Dumfries,
4 July 1870.

Dear Sir John,

You are very kind and obliging; and certainly I owe you and yours many thanks for such friendly feelings. Certainly too your hospitable offer awakens in me something of hope as well as pleasure; nor will I quite give it up as *im-possible*! But the sad fact is, I am grown mostly as good as incapable of making visits: such incapacity of sleeping, such nicety of management in diet &c &c (in brief, the most dyspeptic of all my contemporaries),—and such a horror of railwaying to begin with!— This little place of my Sister's, perfect for me in all particulars (*except* the unblessed railway whistle[1] now and then) I consider as my "Convalescent Hospital"; and here I must lie, shrunk into the uttermost attainable seclusion, the heat and broil of London, cower out of it as I might, having so ruined me of late. These are the literal facts.

If I do travel in Scotland, and come at all within reach of your benefi-cent and quiet circle,[2] I shall not need farther temptation to announce myself there. There, or when some of you perhaps visits London:—let us still hope to make a little acquaintance by and by!

Yrs with many thanks & regards / T. Carlyle

TC-Sir JMN, 4 July. MS: NLS 7197; in Mary Aitken's hand, with last line and signature added by TC. Hitherto unpbd. Sir John Murray Naesmyth (1803-76), 4th bart. of Dawyck and Posso, Peebleshire; see 45:25 and 155.

1. Mary Aitken wrote to Lady Ashburton, [9 July]: "He has not been sleeping at all well since he came—the railway whistles drive him almost mad at nights; but for them he likes being here very much—and confesses that even with his bad sleeping, he feels much better in health than he did at Chelsea" (MS: NLS Acc. 11388).

2. Since the address line was from Dumfries, presumably Naesmyth knew that TC was in Scotland.

TC TO LORD RALPH DRURY KERR

The Hill / Dumfries
10 July 1870

Dear L*d* Ralph,

The news of Lord Lothian's death[1] fell sad & heavy news on us here the more so as it was altogether unexpected too. I had seen him at Carlton Terrace in May:[2] found nothing changed in his fine gracefully intelligent talk & always kindly & perfect ways—except, transiently once or twice, a something in the look of his eyes, which I spoke of to Froude as we came away, who then & afterwards assured me it was nothing. Twice three times, after this, I attempted another visit, & once has actually set out for Clapham Park[3] under Froude's Escort who had promised me there; but something peremptory turned us elsewhither that time:—and in brief I was to behold that loved & always beautiful & interesting Fellow-Man no more. He honourably rests now, and all his heavy & continual sorrows are done.—

I am much obliged by this Note you have written me, I feel it an honor to have had something of friendship from so bright a spirit & to be counted among his friends.[4] Seldom was there a more tragic destiny, a crueller shutting of the road upon a brave young Soul & all his noble prospects & purposes in this world, & nobody could have borne it with a gentler finer heroism than he seemd constantly to do.[5]

Thanks also for your little word about poor L*y* Lothian.[6] Alas, I can well conceive her sorrowful *bereaved* feelings her tender fruitless retrospect—her mournful & loving heart! To her I will not presume to say anything—except what she knows well already, nothing could be said. If at a calmer time, she

TC-Lord K, 10 July. MS copy: Gordon N. Ray Collection, Morgan. Hitherto unpbd. Lord Ralph Drury Kerr (1837–1916), brother of William Schomberg Robert Kerr (1832–70; see 45:227), 8th marquess of Lothian. The letter is written on headed notepaper of Newbattle Abbey (the family seat, Midlothian), so is presumably a copy by him or one of his family; for TC's visit to the Lothians there, Aug. 1865, see 42:210–11.

1. Lord Kerr wrote, [6 July]: "It is with great sorrow that I announce to you the death of my poor Brother Lothian—after 15 years of weariness he has at length found rest." Lord Lothian d. 4 July. TC wrote on the back of his letter: "L*d* Ralph Kerr (death of L*d* Lothian 6 july 1870)."

2. There is no mention in TC's letters of this visit; the Lothians were staying at 4 Carlton Terr. earlier in 1870.

3. Lord Lothian d. at his home in Clarence Rd., Clapham Park.

4. The Carlyles were friendly with the Lothians by 1862; see 38:120–21.

5. Lord Lothian was an invalid for much of his life.

6. Lady Constance Harriet Mahonesa, b. Chetwynd-Talbot (1836–1901; see 45:227); Lord Kerr wrote: "His poor wife is bearing the blow with great courage—but I fear she will only find it heavier as time goes on. Lothian died peacefully in her arms—and—as the doctors tell me quite painless."

could ever think of writing to me, any bit of news from her, I need not say how welcome it would be. You yourself, too, were to have called on me, —twice over; & you never did.[7] That was not well—

With my blessing on you all / Yours truly

(Signed) T. Carlyle[8]

TC TO CAROLINE DAVENPORT BROMLEY

The Hill: July 11.

Ginx's Baby[1] is capital in its way, and has given great satisfaction here. The writing man is rather of penny-a-liner habits and kind, but he slashes along swift and fearless, sketching at arm's length, as with a burnt stick on a cottage wall, and sketches and paints for us some real likeness of the sickening and indeed horrible anarchy and godless negligence and stupor that pervades British society, especially the lowest, largest, and most neglected class; no legislator, people's William[2] or official person, ever casting an eye in that direction, but preferring to beat the wind instead. God mend it! I perceive it will have to try mending *itself* in altogether terrible and unexpected ways before long, if everybody takes the course of the people's William upon it. This poor penny-a-liner is evidently sincere in his denunciation and delineation, and, one hopes, may awaken here and there some torpid soul, dilettante M.P. or the like, to serious reflection on what *is* the one thing needful at this day, in Parliament and out of it, if he were wise to discern.

Alas! it is above thirty years since I started the Condition of England question as well worthy of considering,[3] but was met with nothing but angry howls and Radical Ha, ha's! And here the said question still is, untouched and ten times more unmanageable than then. Well, well! I return you Ginx, and shut up my lamentations.

7. For an earlier meeting with Lord Ralph Kerr, see 33:70.

8. The copyist was presumably indicating that TC signed the original letter, Mary Aitken having written it.

TC-CDB, 11 July. Pbd: Froude, *Carlyle* 4:398–99 inc; Wilson, *Carlyle* 6:213 inc.

1. [John Edward Jenkins], *Ginx's Baby: His Birth and Other Misfortunes* (1870), a satirical novel on the struggle of rival sectarians for the religious education of an abandoned child. John Edward Jenkins (1838–1910; *ODNB*), lawyer, social reformer, and satirist; the book was pbd. anonymously.

2. William Gladstone.

3. The phrase "Condition of England" was coined by TC, 1839; it was the title of the first chapter of *Chartism*; see Carlyle, *Works* 29:118–204.

TC TO BETTY BRAID

The Hill, Dumfries
13 july 1870

Dear Betty,—Tomorrow,[1] when you receive this, is a memorable Day to both of us; to me especially it may well be the memorablest and most sacred of the Year: Birthday of Her you used to call "your Bairn"! For the sake of Her who loved you so well, accept this little Gift from me;[2] it will be a kind of solace to me to think that you have bo*t* with it some article of clothing, or otherwise of use or convenience, wh*h* you might like to have, the sight of wh*h* might be a kind of mute message both from Her and from me to you. My poor blessing (if that c*d* be of any value), you well know is not wanting to it.

Do not trouble y*r*self with writing any Ans*r* to this;—merely a few words to say How you are, and so indicate that the thing has come:—a couple of words will do; but these I do want, news from you now being *rarer* than before. Good Mr Erskine is gone;[3] cannot any more drive out, as he was duly wont, for our sake and y*r* own, and send me word how you are! Our Loved Ones go fast; are now almost all Gone;—and in a short sum of days we also shall have gone, and be where They are. At God's good time. Amen.

If I come to Edin*r*, as seems possible, I will not fail to show myself at Green End[4] once more. I am at my Sister's here for a fortnight past: not worse in health than formerly, but getting very languid, sad of heart as ever, and more useless than ever.

God's blessing be on you, dear Betty.

Y*rs* affec*tely* / T. Carlyle

MARY AITKEN TO FREDERIC CHAPMAN

The Hill, Dumfries,
15 July 1870

Dear Sir,

My Uncle bids me write to ask if you will be so kind as send him a specimen of the Portrait of Ziethen Seidlitz Keith—which the Cundalls[1] were going to

---

TC-BB, 13 July. MS: NLS 3278.152. Hitherto unpbd.

1. JWC's birthday, 14 July.

2. Mary Aitken recorded in TC's checkbook: "14 July 1870 / For Betty / £5 .. o .. o" (TC's checkbook; MS: NLS 20753).

3. Thomas Erskine d. 20 March; he had regularly visited Betty Braid; see 46:43 and 192.

4. Area of S Edinburgh where Betty Braid lived; see 35:206 and 37:157.

MA-FC, 15 July. MS copy: Morgan. Hitherto unpbd. Written to TC's instructions.

1. Joseph Cundall (1818–95; *ODNB*), publisher and photographer, partner in Cundall & Fleming (1865–71), photographers, 168 New Bond St.; see 46:119.

do for *Friedrich*[2]—also of the Portrait of Cromwell's Wife[3] and the others which he says he told you of. He would also like to have a note of his account up till the 22nd of June.

He has not been doing very well here. It is cool and pleasant, but we are rather near to the railway & he has been sleeping badly most of the time— He is going up to Craigenputtock on Monday for a few days.

Yours truly / Mary Carlyle Aitken[4]

P.s. After Monday the address for him will be

Craigenputtock / Corsock / Dalbeattie / N.B.

TC TO JOHN FORSTER

Craigenputtock, 22 july, 1870

Dear Forster,—I trust and hope you are recov*g* rapidly from that miserable accid*t* wh*h* shocked us all so much! it was the brutallest of events, an un-mixed bit of human-diabolic ugliness on the part of that poor simple fellow-creature;—from wh*h* surely the officers of the establish*t are* blameable not to have secured all visitors, especially you?[1] Don't forgive them quite; leave them what will be a reminiscence; that is a duty you owe, to everybody, them-selves included!— For the rest, happily, I can believe in Quain's prognosis ab*t*

2. The library edn. of *Frederick* reproduced these prints: "Cavalry General von Ziethen / Facsimile of a common German Print," *Frederick*, vol. 8 (1870, library edn. 28:281); "Cavalry General Friedrich Wilhelm von Seidlitz," *Frederick*, vol. 9 (1870, library edn. 29:330); and "Feldmarschall Jakob Keith / Reduced Facsimile of Menzel's Woodcut, Berlin, 1857," *Frederick*, vol. 6 (1870, library edn. 26:221). Hans Joachim von Ziethen (1699–1786; see 35:31 and 40:194), cavalry general, Prussian army. Friedrich Wilhelm von Seydlitz (or Seidlitz) (1721–73; see 35:31), cavalry general, Prussian army; TC had requested a print of Seydlitz (among many others) in 1859; see 35:31; for TC on Seydlitz, see 33:192. James Francis Edward Keith (1696–1758; see 45:174, 176), field marshal, Prussian army.

3. Elizabeth Cromwell, b. Bourchier (1598–1665); the library edn. of *Cromwell* had just been pbd. (see TC to JAC, 20 June); there are no pictures of her in it.

4. There was apparently a print of von Ziethen originally attached to this letter, on which TC wrote: "Inscript*n*, all but the first two lines, to be erased. The rest will do. / T.C." The first two lines of the portrait's subheading gave von Ziethen's name, birth, and death details; the whole of the inscription was reproduced in the library edn. (28:281).

TC-JF, 22 July. MS: FC. Quot: *CSA* (2015–16): 57.

1. Forster wrote, 11 July: "[T]he assault was made upon me, by one of a very dangerous class of men—an insane Indian soldier whose delusion was that I had ordered his food to be poisoned. I had reason to complain of the authorities & attendants of the Asylum—but the terrible suddenness of the frenzy was some excuse. . . .[T]here is now no external mark of the injury"; he was still suffering from "the sense as of a film or veil passing continually over the left eye (the opposite side to that on which the blows were struck)" and all his engagements had had to be abandoned. The soldier is not further identified. Forster was presumably attending the asylum as a commissioner of the Lunacy Commission.

the muscles of the eye;[2] and almost hope you are already quit of that and all remains of the affair. If not yet altog*r*, only *festina lente* [make haste slowly] (mind!), and you soon will.

No doubt this date of place surprises you, and it even does myself. I fled up hither monday last, to escape from the railway whistles,[3] wh*h* were threaten*g* at last to drive me sleepless utterly, and to become a torment unendurable. My Nephew,[4] the Tenant here, bro*t* me up at a tearing pace thro' the beautiful old vallies, now so *preternat*l to me; landed me at the old door, 10 miles from any pres*t* or future railway; in the centre of the solitudes,—a silence to soul & to ear, wh*h* I may well liken to that of *the grave*. It is in fact the *Forecourt of the Grave*, this where I have been living, and thrice mournfully musing for the last four days: a scene comparable to no other under the sky; *sad* to me as the Sepulchre at Jerusalem;[5] *sacred* too as that, and with a nobleness that is eternal and belongs to Heaven. Yea, verily, *yea*. And so, in this Sky-domed "Cathedral" (what is my one consolat*n*) I *do* a kind of *worship* withal, and with my whole sad soul can ans*r* from the deeps. Amen, Amen.— — Forgive all this, dear Friend; you know it well enough with*t* any telling. But I leave this tomorrow morn*g*; run across, 40 miles, to Annandale; & shall not probably be here ag*n*, or write another Letter hence. Dumfries is still the cert*n* Address.

That "Dickens sale" made even the Newspapers beautiful to me, and was surely a most successful & well-managed thing.[6] May the 2*d* at Gads Hill[7] be equally so,—for the sake of those poor bereaved ones whom it will benefit, tho' to Him it is of no acc*t* thro' all Eternity now. How strange, how sad, and full of mystery and solemnity, to think of our bright, high-gifted, ever-friendly Dickens, lying there in his silent final rest!

Adieu, dear Forster; let me have a word from you very soon. The good Mrs[8] knows already what I think of her, how welcome *her* news always is. Yrs ever truly.—T. Carlyle

2. Dr. Richard Quain; Forster wrote: "Quain assures me there is no injury to the eye itself, but that it will be some weeks before the discomfort passes away."

3. See TC to Sir JMN, 4 July.

4. James Carlyle Jr.

5. The site of the tomb of Christ in the Old City of Jerusalem on which several churches have been built and which became an important place of Christian pilgrimage.

6. Forster and Georgina Hogarth were the executors. The auction in London by Christie, Manson, and Wood of Dickens's paintings, art objects, and curiosities, 9 July, was widely reported in the newspapers. Forster wrote, 11 July, on its "success far beyond the most exaggerated expectation. I should have thought 5000£ a fair, even a great, result: and we have obtained £9410— The pictures all went for prices far beyond their value; but the other smaller things brought prices even more disproportionate; bits of china obtainable for 10s. or 20s. going for 20 and 30 guineas!"

7. The second sale was of Gad's Hill house, 5 Aug., and of its remaining contents, particularly furniture, 10–13 Aug. For the sale of the house, see TC to JF, 26 Aug.

8. Eliza Forster.

TC TO LADY ASHBURTON

[29 July 1870]

None of yr kind words, that I cd clearly make out, *reached* me here, O benefict Lady,—tho' it seems to me some indistinct echo of them sometimes did![1]—

I have had, and have, a continual *Fight for Sleep*; this, and gloomy musings not *always* impious, have been the No-Hist*y* of my existence since you last saw me. *Except*g sleep, the elem*t* here is perfect for me: seclusion as if in La Trappe or even Hades, clear transparent skies, beautiful green Mother earth, pure air, and (except those accursed railways) a silence wh*h* is salutary to one's very soul. Good Books, too; and lie on sofas to read them,—within double[2] doors, sh*d* a wandering hour of sleep (as does happen now & then) chance to fall on me there. *Am* probably a little better since arriving here.[3] Dare not think of Strathpeffer[4] thro' such steam-engining and clashings & smashings;—glad too that you are well loose of the Kinloch for this season.[5]

From Castle Ashby,[6] I sh*d* think your directest and finest road is by Dumfries, up beautiful Nithsdale (Drumlanrig, Sanquhar, Clydesdale &c) to Glasgow.[7] You have seldom seen a prettier town and region than Dumfries; bright,

TC-Lady A, [29 July]. MS: NLS Acc. 11388. Hitherto unpbd. Dated with reference to Lady Ashburton's (26, 27 July) and Mary Aitken's (29 July) letters (see below).

1. Lady Ashburton wrote, 26 and 27 July, explaining that although she had not written recently, "so many unspoken words have gone out of my soul to yours, that I believe some of them must have reached you."

2. Word repeated with a line over it at turn of page.

3. Mary Aitken wrote to Lady Ashburton, 29 July, at TC's request and enclosed: "the little scrap he has been able to write to you with any little news of him that I can tell. / He was in despair at the noise of the railway whistles and rushed off to Craigenputtock (about 18 miles off) where two of my Cousins, who are married to each other, live. I was to join him the next week if he could sleep—but he came back here after four days worse than ever. He said it was as bad as living in one's grave to attempt to live there again. He sometimes speaks of taking a house near this & out of the reach of railway whistles where he could come & spend every summer; but the speculations have never taken any practical form as yet. We hope he may be able however to weave the railway whistles into his dreams as he has been complaining of them much seldomer latterly. My Uncle John [A. Carlyle] is in Ireland at present—at Portrush; & I think he [TC] feels much more at home here when he [JAC] is away" (MS: NLS Acc. 11388).

4. Lady Ashburton wrote that she had "taken a wee place close by Strathpeffer where the Doctors urge me to go for the Waters." She wrote: "I shall have a quiet room for you—& a highland welcome if later on it smiles on you." Strathpeffer, spa town 25 mi. (40 km.) NW of Inverness.

5. Kinlochluichart, Lady Ashburton's highland estate, which was let for the season; see also 46:78.

6. Castle Ashby, Northamptonshire, seat of Charles Douglas-Compton (1816–77), 3d marquess of Northampton; Lady Ashburton wrote: "I have promised poor dear sick Northampton that I will go for a visit"; she had given up a planned visit there in Jan. (see 46:148).

7. Drumlanrig Castle, seat of the dukes of Buccleuch, about 19 mi. (31 km.) NW of Dum-

fruitful, suiting the environment;—and close westward, black *Galloway* piling itself up in subdued Highland form,—with "Galloway House" in it, too, accessible enough, if you were not an unnatural Daughter of the same![8]— At all events, mount the "Mid Steeple"[9] ab*t* sunset, and look round you. A little kiss of[10] Marygold.[11]

Yrs ever truly,— T. Carlyle.[12]

TC TO FREDERIC CHAPMAN

The Hill, Dumfries, 31 july 1870

Dear Sir,—In vol IV of the 7 voll. *Fr*h,[1] wh*h* Mr Robson is now using as *Copy*, there is one of the stupidest and grossest *errors* I ever saw,—in respect of the Principal *Map* given there!— Send for that vol. IV, and *look* there at bottom of pp. 16, 119, 245, 257 (all *referring* punctually to a "map" wh*h* doesn't seem to exist,—but wh*h* does stand quietly "facing," and *lithog*rd "to face, *p. 116*,"—where *it* neither has nor ever had any conceivable reason to be!— —

---

fries; Sanquhar, town on the river Nith about 10 mi. (16.5 km.) NW of Drumlanrig; Clydesdale, area between Sanquhar and Glasgow.

8. TC meant that Lady Ashburton was "unnatural" in not wanting to see the land of her forefathers. Galloway Hills, part of the Southern Uplands of Scotland; Galloway House, Garlieston, on Wigtown Bay, Dumfries and Galloway, about 62 mi. (99 km.) SW of Dumfries, seat of the earls of Galloway. Lady Ashburton's paternal great-grandfather was Alexander Stewart (1694–1773), 6th earl of Galloway.

9. The Mid-Steeple, Dumfries, townhouse with steeple, built in 1705; Robert Burns's body lay in the courtroom of the Mid-Steeple before his funeral on 25 July 1796; the townhouse was used variously as a council chamber, courthouse, and prison; see 36:252–53.

10. Thus in MS, presumably for "to."

11. Mary Florence, Lady Ashburton's da. Lady Ashburton wrote: "Mary is quite well, & so happy in this monotonous, quiet life—I hope *your* Mary is well—give Mrs Aitken & Mary my love." Mary Aitken wrote: "My Mother & myself are much obliged for yr kind remembrance of us" (MS: NLS Acc. 11388).

12. Lady Ashburton wrote: "Will you be *very* good? & send me 2 autographs." One was for a friend of her friend Margaret Coutts Trotter (ca. 1811–82; see 45:102); "The other, for the most delightful man the gardener of the Duke of Rutland—who tells me his guide & text Book has been 'Sartor'—& who nearly went down before your Bust—a *delightful* specimen of a highly educated earnest working man—the desire of his soul is a bit of your writing." Mary enclosed the autographs, saying: "He was much pleased with your kind Letter this morning & I am to say how much pleasure it gives him to be able to do you the smallest service. It took him a long time to write what looks so little or he sh*d* have written a Letter to you" (MS: NLS Acc. 11388). Charles Cecil John Manners (1815–88; *ODNB*), 6th duke of Rutland; his family seat was Belvoir Castle in Leicestershire; gardener unidentified further.

TC-FC, 31 July. MS: Berg. Hitherto unpbd.

1. Vol. 20 of *Frederick*, uniform (cheap) edn. of TC's *Collected Works* (1864–69), vols. 17–23.

For Heaven's sake, rectify that at once, and avoid the like in future![2] I have bid Rn call on you, and see it done, for that poor vol. IV from this day henceforth & forever! It has quite given me a shock, — least there be *others* like it: I heard of it only by accid*t*, and never myself had the least charge of such points.[3]

A week or fortnight ago my Niece was bidden write to you, and wrote, concerning our *Acc*ts, of 22 june ult.,[4]—I suppose the papers are not yet ready, but getting fast ready? "Short Acc*t*s make long friends"![5]—

This morning, I hear with real sorrow of Mr Rn's new disaster.[6] Seldom have I known a man as dilig*t* skilful and deserving so monstrously unlucky!— He seems greatly afflicted ab*t* the *Stereo Boxes*, & the careful Order Mr Fr has given on that matter.[7] Nothing that Mr Fr settles as proper can or will I contradict: but I have given Rn leave to *plead* with him, & and if Rn *can* convince him & you that *leaving* of the stereos there *is* quite safe for me, I sh*d* be glad. For the rest my own knowledge of the thing is *nothing*, and Mr F. always, he and not I, *decides*,—in all points.[8]

If yr weather had grown *cool* ag*n*, I w*d* return to Chelsea,—for quiet's sake!

Yrs always truly / T. Carlyle

2. The map, titled "For the First and Second Silesian Wars," comes at the end of bk. 14, which in the first edn. of *Frederick* was the end of vol. 3; however in the uniform (cheap) edn. bks. 14, 15, and 16 are in the same vol., thus the map, at the end of bk. 14, comes opp. p. 116, but the asterisked notes on the pages TC mentions read: "See Map, before Index in this Volume." In the library edn., vol. 5 of *Frederick* contains bks. 13, 14, and 15, and the map has been placed at end of the volume.

3. For TC's comments while proofreading *Frederick* for the uniform (cheap) edn., see 45:68.

4. See MA to FC, 15 July.

5. Anthony Trollope, *Rachel Ray* (1863) vol. 2, chap. 30.

6. Charles Robson had been involved in bankruptcy proceedings in 1864 (see 40:6), but had recovered and was now in business with his sons. He wrote, 30 July: "I did not intend to trouble you with my misfortunes, but am left no choice. I have lost so much money in various ways within the last 2 or 3 years as to be now obliged to have my affairs put 'in liquidation.'"

7. Robson wrote: "Mr Forster has desired Mr Chapman to have the whole of your Stereo Plates removed from my premises, fearing, I suppose, that they would be in danger of being seized by my creditors. But, as they are not my property, but are simply in my custody as yours, it is plain common sense that *my* creditors have nothing to do with them." The stereotype plates (see 45:10 and 113) were signed over to TC by Robson in April 1869; see 46:45.

8. Forster wrote, 31 July: "I have just heard of this miserable affair of Robson. . . . *Have no anxiety about it, and do not disturb or worry yourself in any way* . . . I have taken all necessary steps to render everything *quite* secure. If it be essential to remove the stereotype plates at once, they will be moved tomorrow. I do not myself think it will. If everything is paid in connection with the last that were stereotyped . . . there can be no danger."

TC TO JARDINE WALLACE

The Hill, Dumfries / 1 August 1870

Reverend Sir,

Accept my thanks for your politeness. I have read your Sermon with satisfaction and assent; composition, tone, tendency, all seem to me to be good.[1]

With many thanks, I remain,

Yrs truly / T. Carlyle

TC TO JOHN A. CARLYLE

Dumfries, 5 Aug*t* (Friday) 1870

Dear Brother,—I got yr Letter, night before yesterday; we are all well-pleased, as natural, to hear of yr Irish Tour having prospered; that you enjoy the fine sea-bathing &c of Kilrush,[1] and best of all, that you sleep better, and feel yr health sensibly improving. That is right, that is right!

I wd have written to you sooner; but you got otherwise what gen*l* news we had; and of my own I had no news, still less any that c*d* specially be called good. I am leading the idlest, most useless existence, of complete *inanity*,— *do* nothing but lazy dull reading, a little daily walking, and much ineffectual endeavr after *sleep*, abt wh*h* there is no temptat*n* to speak or to write. I don't really feel worse since I left Chelsea; rather *clearer* perhaps, and intrinsically *better*: so I lazily endure my allot*t* here (where everybody is so unweariedly kind to me); and hope only that the *weather* will cool before long, and solitary Chelsea be habitable ag*n*. No scheme of return, or route (by Edin*r* &c, or otherwise has *yet* shaped itself. Never mind me; you cannot help me, nobody can,—except *myself perhaps*, a very little!— — Yesternight, after days of stewing fog, & dusty heat ill to endure, we had a beautiful day of thunder & rain wh*h* has brightened up everyt*h*g into the liveliest breezy beauty: a gr*t* improv*t* for the time being. I have also just done my Six Proofsheets; and go off direct for the walking due.—— — Robson, poor fellow, has fallen utterly

---

TC-JW, 1 Aug. MS: NLS 7179.103; in Mary Aitken's hand, with TC's signature. Quot: *Border Magazine* 12 (1907): 75. Rev. Jardine Wallace (1834–1910), minister of Traquair, Peeblesshire, from 1859.

1. Wallace presumably sent TC a copy of his sermon, "Christendom: Its Unity in Diversity," delivered to the Synod of Lothian and Tweeddale, Edinburgh, 3 May. In it he argued: "There is no reason to prevent the most cordial co-operation at present on the part of sister Churches, but rather every argument for it. . . . There is a wide field for their united energies at home and abroad—a world of sin, ignorance, and misery" (15–16).

TC-JAC, 5 Aug. MS: NLS 527.24. Hitherto unpbd.

1. John A. Carlyle was traveling in the north of Ireland; Portrush, town on the N coast. TC presumably wrote "Kilrush" in error as it is on the SW coast of Ireland.

bankup[2] ag*n* (4/ in the £; was lost by that "Periodical" of his,[3] &c); but he seems to go on with "6 sheets weekly" all the same. Poor Forster is suffering a little still from that Accid*t* in the Madhouse.[4] Lady Ashb*n* is off (or sh*d* be) by Aberdeen Steamer for the Highl*ds*[5] I had *to refuse* accompanying.— I enclose L*d* George's Letter,[6] of 10 or 14 days ago; and will add no more of this dreary stuff. Ever y*r* affect*e* Br*r* T. Carlyle

TC TO J. A. FROUDE

The Hill, Dumfries
14 August 1870

Dear Froude,

I am glad to hear of you again; had not my *fingers* been unwilling you would have heard from me before this, and more at large: these long silences are not proper, especially at this epoch, when another kind of *Silence* is coming on so near!—

I fled out hither, urged by little Mary, and the burning weather, in the last days of june; & have been all but immovable ever since (all voyaging "to Norway" to &c, impossible to one so ticklish about *sleep*, in a world so full of uproar): and am quietly waiting till the *Lammas* rains quench Chelsea into habitability again, that I may creep back to my sad old den there. I am certainly not worse in health since I left; nor am I sensibly *better*,—perhaps never shall be; oftenest don't much *care*. My life here is encircled as if in Cotton (such the unwearied kindness and loving patience of all this Household to me); for the rest, a life utterly secluded, of silence almost complete; and outwardly as idle and as vacant as man can lead. Outwardly mere *zero*, reading &c without aim except to avoid the utterly stupid & *un*readable; tho' inwardly, as you guess, it is perhaps full enough, or too well filled with sombre meditations, recollections, unfathomable musings on the inexorable & inevitable. Three or four weeks ago, my Brother fled off to Gweedore, the Giants Causeway, Port Rush &c; and has not yet returned,—just got across to Galloway again,

2. See TC to FC, 31 July. TC wrote "bankup" for "bankrupt."

3. Robson's periodical untraced.

4. See TC to JF, 22 July.

5. Lady Ashburton's original plan was to sail up the W coast; see TC to JAC, 10 June; she apparently traveled overland to Strathpeffer; see TC to Lady A, [29 July].

6. Lord George Hill (1801–79), Irish "improving" landowner, whom TC first met Aug. 1849; see 24:73 and 176–77; see also 46:71. Lord Hill wrote to TC, 26 July, thanking him for introducing John, who had visited him at Ballyare, Ramelton, part of his Gweedore estate in County Donegal in N Ireland.

TC-JAF, 14 Aug. Pbd: Waldo H. Dunn, "Carlyle's Last Letters to Froude: II," *Twentieth Century* 159 (March, 1956): 255–56. Quot: Froude, *Carlyle* 4:398 and 397.

& still doing some small visits there. I have a small Errand to Edinburgh for one day; another ditto to native Annandale (only 16 miles off, where I have not yet been): nothing else of travel till I return. *This* (excepting railway whistles only!) is the most perfect lodging I have been able to discover in the world for myself since 1866.— But now for your little queries.

The Popular Edition[1] is welcome news to me; make it *cheap* enough, it is sure of an immense public. In regard to the Freeman & similar criticisms & calumnies,[2] my impression is very clear that, beyond recognizing their existence & their despicability, you will get no good by speaking at all. "The Public" is an idle fool, not worth appealing to to[3] whom all "appeal" is *degrading*,— as from a Plaintiff thrice in earnest to judge full of levity and of darkness; and interested only to see a fight rise! I think I would *not* repeat that Wager of Battle; or perhaps only *cite* it (in the way of mockery), from the Pall Mall Gazette,[4] as a thing that could come to no result, anymore than a cartel addressed to the jackdaws. Say little, above all, *little*; with the *minimum* of anger, visible or supposable, & the *maximum* of mild contempts—that seems to be the rule.

1. Froude's 12 vol. *History of England* was being pbd. in a "cabinet edn.," described as a "cheap and small edition. Clearly printed and bound in the sober school style, they form a desirable addition to the book-shelves of those whose means will not allow the larger and more expensive edition" (*Examiner*, 9 July); Froude's U.S. publisher, Charles Scribner and Son, New York, was publishing a similarly less expensive edn., marketing it as the "Popular Edition of Froude's History of England."

2. Edward Augustus Freeman (1823–92; *ODNB*), historian, who from 1864 onward had repeatedly criticized Froude's work for its alleged inaccuracies. In a two-part review (*Saturday Review*, 16 and 23 July), Freeman assessed Froude's two-part "Fresh Evidence About Anne Boleyn" (*Fraser's Magazine*, June and July). In these, Froude reconsidered Anne Boleyn's reputation in light of his recent discovery of an archive in Vienna containing the correspondence of Eustace Chapuys; see TC to JAC, 14 May. Froude had been unaware of this source when he was earlier writing *History of England*; it changed his previous estimatation of Anne Boleyn: "Chapuys's account, though it leaves the question of Anne's guilt still uncertain, yet reveals a mass of intrigue, political and personal, in Henry's court, which made it seem possible, for the first time to me, that the poor Queen might have been innocent, yet that the King and Parliament might have honestly believed her guilty" (Froude, *Carlyle* 4:397). Henry VIII (1491–1547; *ODNB*), king of England and Ireland. Freeman acknowledged that Froude "has learned something during the fourteen years which have passed since his first two volumes [of the *History of England*] appeared," concluding: "Mr. Froude deserves credit for the zeal with which he has sought out Chapuys' evidence which goes so far to upset his own former story. He has, in short, brought the hatchet to his own argument."

3. The printed text omitted the comma between "to" and "to."

4. Freeman wrote a scathing review of Froude's *History of England* (*Saturday Review*, 5 and 12 Feb.), to which Froude had responded, in a letter pbd. in the *Pall Mall Gazette*, 15 Feb., issuing a challenge to the editor of the *Saturday Review* [Philip Harwood (1811–87; *ODNB*)], that he subject any pages of the work to independent expert scrutiny; it appears that nothing came of this challenge.

As to Anne Boleyn, I find still a considerable want of perfect clearness;—and withal that the nearest approach I made to clearness about her was in the Dialogue we had, one day BEFORE *Chapuys* came out. *Chapuys* rather sent me to sea again, and dimmed the matter. I did not quite gather from him, what I did from you the then frantic, fanatical, rabid & *preter*natural state of "public opinion": this I had found to be quite the illuminative lamp of the transaction, both as to *her* conduct and to every one's. And such in fact it still continues, on the faith of what you said; and inclines me to *believe*, on all the prob[ab]ilities[5] I have that those adulterous abomination (even the Caitiff Lute player's part[6]) are most likely altogether *lies* upon the poor Lady. *Ohe, Ohe!*—

Did you read the Edinburgh *Life of Bergenroth?*[7] What a wild Buccanier kind of fellow, with such an appetite for believing everybod[y][8] a consummate rascal, and himself a man of piercing intellect and not of violent temper merely. He never explains to L. Romilly,[9] How if everybody was such a rotten Scoundrel his Lordship and mankind were likely to benefit by having *his* putrid and merely poisonous memory dug up again at Simancas or elsewhere.

With many regards to Madam & all the Household

Yours ever / T. Carlyle

TC TO JOHN FORSTER

The Hill, Dumfries / 26 Aug*t* 1870

Dear Forster,

I am wearying very much to have a word from you ag*n*,—first of all, to know to know[1] certainly how both of you are. That unlucky *eyelid*[2] I always hope is doing well; but y*r* own word upon it w*d* be the valuable thing. Where are you, Madam & you; how are you? Answer me all that, the more minutely

5. Thus in printed source; probably because TC omitted in MS.

6. Mark Smeaton (ca. 1512–36), musician at the court of Henry VIII, one of the people with whom Anne Boleyn was accused of committing adultery.

7. William Cornwallis Cartwright, *Gustave Bergenroth: A Memorial Sketch* (Edinburgh, 1870). Gustav Adolph Bergenroth (1813–69; *ODNB*), German historian, friend or colleague of Froude's; see 44:22 and 24.

8. Thus in printed source; probably because TC omitted in MS.

9. Much of the book consisted of letters written by Bergenroth, from the Spanish archives in Simancas, to John Romilly (1802–74; *ODNB*), 1st Baron Romilly, judge, master of the rolls 1851–73; he appointed Bergenroth as the official editor of the Spanish state papers, 1861.

TC-JF, 26 Aug. Addr: Palace-Gate House / Kensington / London. PM: Dumfries, 26 Aug. 1870. MS: FC. Hitherto unpbd.

1. Words repeated in MS.

2. See TC to JF, 22 July.

the better.[3] Since Robson's miserable downbreak I have heard nothing from you;[4] and various things since that have come and gone on wh*h* I am all in the dark. The sale & settle*ts* at Gad's Hill,[5] for example, —this enormous War,[6] filling all the Newspapers to overflow, has cut me off from any details about that; ab*t* wh*h* you were so interested, and I withal. Poor loved Dickens, how sad and strange to think that we shall never see his blithe face more. One other N*o* of that *Edwin Drood*;[7] and then no more, no more forever! The figure of him, with a strange impressiveness in it, often visits me, among the Shadows of my other Loved Ones that are gone. All vanished, gone;—yet, of a surety, all "with God," even as we are: Silence, silence; we have no word more to say.

My life here is retire*t* itself; nob*y* can be more silent, *withdrawn* altog*r* from the world; but, alas, dwelling mainly otherwise in the vague, in the cloudy and (to practical purposes) mournful and inane. I read 3 or 4 hours daily, goodish Books in my brother's Collect*n* here; that is the only pleasantish or *quiet* part of my time, —tho' of what *use* it is ever to be, I c*d* not the least explain to myself or another. All writing, r*t* right[8] hand still forbidding, is more and more a horror to me, avoided utterly except on the plainest compulsion otherwise. In all my days I have never been so idle and so lazy; no courage left in me that w*d* furnish out the heart of a sparrow. Is not this enough from me under the head of "news"!— I have begun latterly to think of coming home ag*n*; the sooner the better, now that the weather is grown cool ag*n*: but am too inert to form even that resolut*n"* —*proh pudor* [for shame].

The Copper Capt*n* Emperor of the French[9] has led himself a pretty dance:

3. Forster replied, 29 Aug.: "It has been a great comfort to hear from you, dear Carlyle. We are both *very grateful* to you for having written." He then gave TC a detailed account of his own and his wife's health.

4. Robson's bankruptcy; see TC to FC, 31 July; Forster replied that he had taken legal advice about TC's stereotype plates, and "there being no doubt or question in the matter at all . . . I am permitting the further impressions needed to be taken for the present by Robson. The folly of the poor man . . . is very sad. I know nothing yet of what the issue is to be, or whether another chance is to be afforded to him by his creditors."

5. See TC to JF, 22 July. Forster replied, telling TC about the sale of Dickens's house and estate; they were bought by Dickens's son Charles (1837–96; *ODNB*), who, not realizing that the executors (of whom Forster was one) had set a reserve price, believed, "from the slow and comparatively small offers at first made, . . . that the property was about to be sacrificed," bid against them.

6. France declared war on Prussia, 19 July, having been maneuvered into the declaration by Bismarck, who believed a war was the best way to get the German states to unite under the Prussian king.

7. *The Mystery of Edwin Drood* (1870), Dickens's final novel, left unfinished at his death; five instalments were pbd., April–Aug.; the last was due Sept. 1870.

8. Word in full repeated at turn of page.

9. Napoleon III, emperor of France 1852–70. "Copper captain" means someone who assumes a title without any right to it. TC had long disliked him; see, for example, 35:109 and

it is the one thing in the world Political that is not ugly to me just now. Adieu, dear F.— *Yrs* ever T. Carlyle

TC TO JOHN A. CARLYLE

Haddington, 2 p.m.
Saty 3 Septr 1870

Dear Brother,—I got a beautiful cart to Edinr, carriage all to myself &c; and found Masson waiting, who carried [me][1] to a place full of *home* qualities,[2] where I passed the evg rather tolerably (so truly *kind* and hearty to me everybody): but alas, the my[3] good fortune *paused*, & still pauses! I had not a wink of sleep: the railway whistles,[4] and *invincible*. I came out hither abt 11¾; I am just come in from the place I went to see;[5]—ah me, ah me:—I have *walked* too much during & since; and am very *tired*. Good Mrs Dodds[6] is waiting while I write.

155, and 36:119. By mid-Aug. the French had lost several battles; they lost the biggest battle of the war, 18 Aug., at Gravelotte, a village in Lorraine near the French-German frontier.

TC-JAC, 3 Sept. MS: NLS 527.25. Hitherto unpbd.
1. Word omitted.
2. David Masson moved to 10 Regent Terr., Edinburgh, late 1869.
3. Thus in MS.
4. Archibald Geikie wrote: "I [formed] one of a quiet dinner party at Professor Masson's house, to meet Thomas Carlyle who was his guest at the time. The sage was in excellent form, except when the scream of the railway whistle from the valley below reached his ear. He would then launch forth a torrent of vituperation on the noises that made life unendurable in a city" (Archibald Geikie, *A Long Life's Work* [1924] 140). TC wrote, 8 Sept.: "The railway whistles at Edinr had not permitted a moment's sleep the previous night [2 Sept.]; the road from Edinr was one clash and shriek of base confusions and intrusions: I returned hither (on Monday [to Dumfries, 5 Sept.]) with scarcely above 7 hours of sleep (in added pieces for all the three nights" (TC's journal; privately owned). Regent Terr. is above the entrance to the Calton Tunnel, through which the railway passes before reaching Waverley Station. Not everyone found it so upsetting; Rosaline Masson, Masson's da., remembered: "[T]he railway trains proved an endless source of interest. They flashed into view with so much strength of purpose, such puffing out of steam and rattle of carriages, and then, with a long shrill whistle, they dived into the tunnel—and were never seen again" (Rosaline Masson, *Poets, Patriots, and Lovers; Sketches and Memories of Famous People* [1933] 184).
5. JWC's grave in St. Mary's Church, Haddington. TC wrote, 8 Sept.: "Went, Friday last to Edinr, on an errand, wh*h* I did next day *at Haddington*, Saty 3 Septr: sight of my Dear One's Grave once more, with these eyes. An hour solitary in the Abbey Kirk; standing or kneeling by that sacred spot, three times over, or wandering abt the Churchyd in the intervals: beautiful and sadly noble, divine as Eternity, all that;—but *begirt* with the miserablest *environts*; & now figuring to me almost a *jewel set in*, let me not say what!" (TC's journal; privately owned). For the position of JWC's grave in the choir of St. Mary's Church (the Abbey Kirk), see 43:241.
6. Jane Dods, b. Wilkie (ca. 1809-85); her husband, William Dods (1795-1873), an old

I intend firmly to be home on monday,—w*d* it were this day!

My love to Jean and every one of them. Mary's packing was *correct* altogr,—you may tell her.

Ever y*r* affect*e* / T. Carlyle[7]

TC TO DAVID MASSON

[6 Sept. 1870]

Dear Masson, This morning I find (a sharp shower reminding me) that the indispensable *mackintosh* is still hanging amid its kindred miscellanea in y*r* Hall![1] Brown-paper Parcel (unpaid) by Caledon*n* railway; that is the clear remedy; one other bit of trouble I had still to add to the big kindness already accumulated *there*. Nothing else of harm was in the journey yest*y*; wh*h* I happily got transacted, after Abington Station,[2] in perfect solitude, in mute dialogue with the misty mountains, and *their* sad and great unfathomable preachings and prophesyings to me. . . .[3]

Of one thing I have, and shall retain, a right glad and thankful memory, the warmly human way in wh*h* you all rec*d* me, and wrapt my infirmities and me in soft down, in sympathy and ministrat*n* of your best. Not even the rail-

---

friend of JWC's, helped organize JWC's funeral; TC stayed with them at the time; see 43: 216 and 249-50.

7. Masson recalled: "[TC] was . . . passing through Edinburgh from Dumfriesshire on one of his periodical visits to his wife's grave in Haddington; and through the three or four days of his stay,—which he wanted to be as private as possible,—he was my guest in Regent's Terrace, where my house then was. . . . [One evening] we went out together, rather late, for a stroll through the streets. At the latish hour, in that season of the year, few persons were about; and I do not think that any one we met recognised Carlyle, though his venerable and feebly stooping figure, in his usual brownish dress, with his broad felt hat, and a pair of easy shoes . . . did attract some attention" (David Masson, *Carlyle Personally and in His Writings* [1885] 116-17). See frontis. for the cartoon of TC, looking very like Masson's description, by Carlo Pellegrini (1839-89; *ODNB*), caricaturist; no. 12 of the series "Men of the Day" (*Vanity Fair* 22 Oct. 166), it was probably made early Oct. after TC's return to London. TC sent a copy of the issue to John A. Carlyle, who gave it to Jean Aitken "as you suggest" (JAC to TC, 26 Oct.).

TC-DM, [6 Sept.]. Pbd: Rosaline Masson, *Poets, Patriots, and Lovers; Sketches and Memories of Famous People* (1933) 185-86 inc. Rosaline Masson, youngest da. of David and Emily Masson, introduced the letter: "A little sheet of paper lies before me, with a very narrow black border, covered all four sides, with small handwriting in almost indecipherable blue pencil. It seems to have been written from Dumfries, just after a visit" (R. Masson 185). Dated Sept. 1870 by context and Masson's reply.

1. Masson replied, 7 Sept.: "Your mackintosh is sent off to the Railway Station, in a parcel addressed to you. It had escaped notice, till your note came this Morning."

2. Abington station, 41 mi. (66 km.) SW of Edinburgh.

3. Ellipses in printed source.

way whistles and other *infernalia* of the case deprive me of that, or indeed do other than enhance all that.

But my journey, I find, was radically wrong-schemed. It was of the nature of a relig*s* Pilgrimage (truly such to me in this now wholly irrelig*s* world); I sh*d* have made direct for Hadd*n* and back, communicat*g* with no mortal; then w*d* there have been nothing that was not sacred that was *not* sacred, that was mundane, basely miserable and profane.[4] As it is, the hour I had in the Abbey Kirk,[5] that half hour interview with noble old Betty,[6] and the gen*l* element thro'out in Regent Terrace;[7] those do remain with me like jewels set in—I will not say what.

Thanks and kindest regards to you all, ye friendly ministering souls. . . .[8]

Yours ever, T. CARLYLE.[9]

TC TO J. A. FROUDE

The Hill, Dumfries
7 September 1870

Dear Froude,

Your Colonial Article came duly on the 1st of the Month;[1] and was read

4. TC wrote, 8 Sept.: "*Three* items of noble nature, one of them *divine*; embedded wholly in an element of tempestuous contradictories, and *sordido-infernalia*. Out of wh*h* I am still only struggling. A *sacred* Pilgrimage thoroughly wrong-schemed; wh*h* I ought to have kept *secret* from everybody, and rashly did not" (TC's journal; privately owned).

5. For the Abbey Kirk, see TC to JAC, 3 Sept.

6. TC recorded his visit to Betty Braid in his journal, 8 Sept.: "Sunday I had . . . half an hour of visit to old Betty, one of the venerablest and even noblest-looking old women I ever saw; clothed in endless, settled, piously stoical sorrow, and yearning (almost as myself) towards that Tomb in the Abbey Kirk,—Tomb to *me* of all that was beautifullest in my life, no shrine now so *sacred* to me in all the earth" (TC's journal; privately owned).

7. Masson himself, his wife, Emily Rosaline Masson, and family. TC recorded, 8 Sept.: "The Masons, at Edin*r*, also were the kindest and most pati*t* of hosts, tho' to them, healthy of soul & body, my sufferings from railway sonameries [sonanceries: sounds], & Edin*r* in- trus*ns* and incongruities, must nat*lly* have been inconceivable" (TC's journal; privately owned).

8. Ellipsis in printed source.

9. TC concluded his 8 Sept. journal entry: "The week before, I made my other pilgrim- age (of like kind) to Father, Mother, Sister Marg*t* and my kindred's resting place at Ecclef*n*; but the 'contradictories' to that, tho' not wanting either were infinitely less. / One thing at least I have perhaps gained by all this noble and ignoble sorrow & pain of mind & body: that it may have *awakened* me out of the basely quiescent *torpor* of the last 7 or 8 weeks, to the tho*t* that I must *get home* straight*y*, and there ACTUALLY '*try* to do better.' Hold by that; don't drop that;—don't" (TC's journal; privately owned).

TC-JAF, 7 Sept. Pbd: Waldo H. Dunn, "Carlyle's Last Letters to Froude II," *Twentieth Century* 159 (March, 1956): 257–58. Quot: Froude, *Carlyle* 4:400–401.

1. Froude's essay, "The Colonies Once More," *Fraser's Magazine* 82 (Sept. 1870): 269–87,

eagerly by me, and afterwards by all the house,—with unanimous approval, with mine emphatically hearty, to begin with. I agree with every word, every word is as if *aus meinem Sinn gesprochen* [as if spoken from my mind], could I but have spoken it so calmly and well! Paltry Goschen[2] will be better for what he has got; if not, he must get more & still sharper, People's Wm & he, and all the parties to so unspeakable a plan of "management" and state of things.[3] To me it is unendurable to think of; and terpid gluttonous sooty, swoln-and-squalid England is grown a phenomenon which fills me with disgust, and apprehension almost desperate so far as *it* is concerned. What a base pot-bellied blockhead this once heroic Nation has become; sunk in its own dirty fat and offal, and of a stupidity defying the very gods!— Do not you grow desperate of it, you who have still a hoping heart and "a *right hand* that does not shake"! I can conceive no burden fitter for a writing Englishman than that of awakening this poor Country to the crisis for it which is now evidently nigh, and rapidly coming nigher every day.

I have been to Edinburgh, on a small, most sad and sacred errand; and got a great deal of mischief from the railway whistles, and other botherations, of the 3 nights spent there. For things *sacred* it is pity when there is not a *Church*, or barrier of exclusion to things secular, profane and even infernal; but there is not in our poor time, except to things sham-sacred. Husht, husht.

I am now about lifting anchor for Chelsea again; heat having gone, and *Tellus* [earth] become habitable there again. It will likely be a 10 days yet, I suppose, before the actual exodus can manage itself; but I must not let my former *utter laziness* return upon me, either,—tho' my horror of all locomotion is extreme.

Of outward events the War does interest me, as it does the whole world: no war so wonderful did I ever even read of; and the results of it I reckon to be salutary, grand and hopeful beyond any such that have occurred in my time.

---

argued that because the British population was growing so fast with so many people suffering from acute poverty, everyone would benefit if the British government instituted a comprehensive policy of organized and, if necessary, subsidized emigration to its colonies; it would be better if the emigrants went to British colonies thus continuing to benefit the home country, rather than, like the majority of Irish emigrants, going to the U.S.

2. George Joachim Goschen (1831–1907; *ODNB*), liberal unionist M.P. for the City of London, 1863–80; president of the Poor Law Board, 1868–71; in his article Froude reported Goschen's argument made in a speech in the House of Commons, 17 June: "no case had been made out for Government interference. The supposed distress had been exaggerated. . . . Trade was fast reviving. The prosperity of the working classes was returning, and as an infallible index of improvement he stated . . . that they were consuming increasing quantities of beer, gin, and tobacco" (*Fraser's Magazine* 82:277).

3. William Gladstone; see TC to JFS, 3 June. Gladstone thought that the colonies should eventually be given independence, while others, including TC and Froude, thought they should remain under direct British rule; see 46:179.

The Surrender at Sedan
Illustrated London News, 17 September 1870

[58]

Prussian guard of Louis Napoleon; Belgian charity to French soldiers
Illustrated London News, 24 September 1870

Paris City must be a wonderful place today! I believe the Prussians will certainly keep, for Germany, what of Lorraine and of Elsass[4] is still German or can be expected to *re-become* such;[5] and withal that the whole world *cannot* forbid them to do it, —and that Heaven will not (nor I). Alone of Nations Prussia still seems to understand something of the art of governing, and of *fighting enemies* to said art: Germany from of old has been the peaceablest, most pious, and in the end most valiant and terriblest of Nations; Germany *ought* to be President of Europe, —and will again, it seems, be tried with that office (for another 5 centuries or so?).—

Adieu, dear Froude; I ought to be out walking, instead of here. Tell Allingham I liked very well indeed his bit of Irish History (in *Fraser* last but one),[6] and consider it of good *omen* to him. My kindest regards to Mrs. F. and all her Household. Thank Stephen also for that pleasant letter (and for 2 others I have had).[7]

Yours ever truly
T. Carlyle

TC TO THOMAS STORY SPEDDING

The Hill, Dumfries
8 Septr 1870—

Dear Spedding,

Yr Letter is very welcome to me; the voice of *your* honest old friendliness, in this new invitatn[1] awakens many thoughts, very beautiful, tho' also very

---

4. "Elsass": German for Alsace.

5. The Battle of Sedan, 1–2 Sept., resulted in the decisive defeat of the French; Napoleon III surrendered and was taken prisoner, and the French Second Empire collapsed; see 58 and 59. The territory known as Alsace-Lorraine, on the border of France and Germany, had been disputed for centuries; under French control since the 17th century, the Prussians annexed it in 1871; it was returned to France in 1919. TC wrote in his journal, 10 Sept.: "The sudden great French Prussn War interests all persons,—even me, as no other public thing for long has done.... Masson met me [3 Sept.] ... with news that 'the Emperor' so-called was prisr of War, and my 'scandals Copper Captn' quite done for and ended,—to pity almost even of me! ... and Paris is—an anarchy such as never was in the world before!" (TC's journal; privately owned).

6. William Allingham, "Seven Hundred Years Ago. An Historic Sketch," *Fraser's Magazine* 82 (Aug. 1870): 135–58. See also TC to JAC, 14 May.

7. James Fitzjames Stephen; he was currently in India; see TC to JFS, 3 June.

TC-TSS, 8 Sept. MS: John Spedding. Pbd: A. Carlyle, *CS* 767–69 inc. Quot: K. J. Fielding, "Carlyle and the Speddings—New Letters II," *Carlyle Newsletter* 8 (Spring 1987) 64.

1. Thomas Story Spedding wrote from his home in Cumbria, 23 Aug.: "Will this find you again in N.B. [North Britain]? and if so is there any chance of catching you in your flight Southwards?"

mournful, very solemn! It is now, or ought to be, altogether plain to me that I can make no more visits: — incapable even of *sleep* in strange places; good for nothing, or little, except suffering unknown miseries, among my hospitable fellow creatures, when awake; in fact such a piece of frail humanity as nobody not absolutely bound to it ought to be troubled with handling! That is the veritable state of the case.

You I expect to see ag*n* in London,[2] and still ag*n*; for you are not to conclude that in essentials I am weaker than men at my age, but the contrary rather; troubled with no *disease* what*r*, except a gradually increasing *dyspepsia* of fifty-three years standing, and d*o* d*o* thinness of skin, —*un*manageable now out of my own shop. L*d* Bacon[3] now seldom or never comes to me; but you, I calculate, are still up to such things; and neither of you, I know well, has ever forgotten me, or will till the end. Amen, Amen! —

This Pruss*n* War, this with France and the former with Austria are the two Sacred Wars of my time;[4] this latter especially, and as it were, miraculous to boot! Never in Human History before was Diabolus so rid by Sir Michael,[5] — and sent home ag*n* all in shards, within the month. *Gloria in excelsis*, think I, but say nothing; and privately discern that this ag*n* is the *"voice of God"* speaking from the whirlwind,[6] — true and awful as in earliest days! —

The case of Eng*d* ag*n*, if I think of it at all, lies on me like a dark nightmare; insoluble to me what Eng*d* with its pres*t* tendencies and established courses *can* do, except rot rapidly in its own dirty grave and go down to the Bottomless Pool! — Let me recommend to you the first Article in Sept*r* Fraser.[7] Here also is a Letter from the Author wh*h* you need not take the trouble of returning.

With many hearty regards to Madam[8] and all of you young and old, —Yrs ever T. Carlyle

I return to Chelsea so soon as I can get the anchor up; *i.e.* probably in about 10 days.

2. TC saw Spedding in April when they walked in Hyde Park; see 46:198.

3. Spedding's brother, James, known as "Lord Bacon" as he had been working on his 14 vol. edn. of *The Letters and The Life of Francis Bacon* (1857–74) since the early 1840s; see 38:77–78.

4. For the Franco-Prussian War, see TC to JAF, 7 Sept.; for the earlier Austro-Prussian War, or Seven Weeks' War, June–July 1866, resulting in the establishment of a federation of North German States under Prussian leadership, see 44:34 and 42.

5. TC wrote in his journal, 10 Sept.: "Never saw, or heard of such a war, —mirac*s* smashing down of the risen *Satan* by his appropriate *Michael*, day after day, with huge uninterrupted stroke after stroke, till, in a month's time, *Sat*n is in shards, and almost low enough!" TC presumably means St. Michael; see Rev. 12:7–10.

6. Cf. Job 38:1.

7. J. A. Froude's essay, "The Colonies Once More"; see TC to JAF, 7 Sept.

8. Frances Elizabeth Spedding.

TC TO FREDERIC CHAPMAN

Dear Sir,

Both these Prints of the *Great Elector* go into vol I, —only *one page* apart from one another.¹— I send you the Inscript*ns* needed at the bottom; but cannot *here* mark for you what the *pages* are. How*r*, that latter will be a very brief affair (an hour's work for y*r* Engraver²) after I am got to Chelsea, where I hope to be before next week end.

Cundall³ has sent me nothing since you went to Scotland. I wish you bid him go up to Mr Forster's (*before* Mr F quite go!⁴), and with his best skill consider whether *he* cannot make a Photo*h* of that *Watts Picture*, I am very anxious he sh*d*, the other being so mad and hideous.⁵

The *Sterling Portrait* (in last Vol) fatally *wants* Painter's name, Engraver's do & *date*;⁶ all of wh*h* I delivered to you with my own hand sev*l* months ago! *Look*, and I think you may still find them. From me the Painter's name & the date are both gone ag*n*; and I had to dig them out *twice* (as it happened) before they got to you. Pooh, pooh!— The last *Fortnightly* has never come by whose blame I do not know.⁷ I hope you profited by your Scotch excursion;⁸ I don't seem to have made very much of mine.

Yours sincerely / T. Carlyle⁹

The Hill, Dumfries
9 Sep 1870

TC-FC, 9 Sept. MS: Huntington Lib. Hitherto unpbd.

1. Friedrich Wilhelm (1620–88), elector of Brandenburg. The two prints of him in vol. 1 of the library edn. of *Frederick* have the inscriptions: "The Great Elector, / Friedrich Wilhelm of Brandenburg, aetat 27. / Reduced Facsimile of a Contemporaneous Dutch Print" (opp. p. 360); he is on a horse, with hunters chasing a deer in the background; and "The Great Elector, Friedrich Wilhelm of Brandenburg, aetat 63. / Reduced Facsimile of a Contemporaneous Dutch Print" (opp. p. 362); this is a full-face head and shoulders portrait.

2. Probably Joseph Brown (1809–87), photo-engraver.

3. Joseph Cundall; see MA to FC, 15 July.

4. Forster was due to go on holiday towards the end of Sept.

5. George Frederic Watts; see 46:119–20. For TC's opinion of the portrait, see 46:86–87.

6. The portrait of John Sterling was painted by Benjamin Delacour (ca. 1795–1843) in 1830, and engraved by Joseph Brown; see Carlyle, *Works* 11 (frontis.) and 46:99–100.

7. *The Fortnightly Review* was pbd. by Chapman & Hall.

8. Forster wrote to TC, 29 Aug., telling him that Chapman had returned from Scotland, 25 Aug., "covered with boils and blotches, on his face, his neck, his feet, everywhere. . . . I have since heard that he is 'laid up'. . . the eruption is attributed to insect-stings—a very superficial explanation of what seemed to me to go much deeper!"

9. TC wrote in his journal, 10 Sept.: "Yesty was ag*n* involved in inactivities, & futile miseries,—by want of *sleep* &c &c woe's me! Today too late for getting to Sister Mary's, and knitting up one other of those final thrums; preparatory to departure, which must now be within a week hence. Not in my life have I had so utterly inane a time. Silent, solitary, sorrowful of soul; concerning only with any Loved Ones that are gone. Except for the railway

TC TO JOHN A. CARLYLE

Chelsea, 17 Septr 1870

My dear Br*r*,—I meant to write more at large, tho' in ill case for writing; but Anth*y* Sterling[1] staggered in full of *asthmas*, fruitless *yacht*ings &c and quite prevented me.

You know already we got hither duly; one of the quietest & least *troublesome* journey to Lond*n* from Scotland (or *vice versa*) I ever made; except the complex*n* of my tho*ts* wh*h* was not to be helped,[2] nothing wrong at all. Unfortunately I took for supper egg-in-teacup (having *dined* on a *good slice of roast-beef*), & lost a good part of my sleep (had to wake poor Mary ab*t* 4 a.m., &c &c); and am still only *expectg* "a good sleep." But do expect to be right in that point soon. House is all clean as a new shill*g*, and was never quieter. In fact London seems empty to wonder, everybody gone his ways.

Tom's *Canada*[3] Letter was one of a big heap; it and Jenny's Newsp*r* cover[4] I designed for you last night,—& counted on *writing* with more effect than I now can! Note T.'s mode of conveying Books, and tell me what or how is the mode. He means sending Books *from* BOSTON,[5] doesn't he?—

Except my sorrowful love to Jean & her James and EVERY ONE *of you*, not a word more.

T.C.

---

whistles & continual scarcity (sometimes absolute want) of *sleep*, I have been physically well off, too; I am much ashamed of myself. *Can* I 'turn over a new leaf'? Try it, try it ag*n*, in the vacancy of Chelsea! If a man had but an hour to live, he o*t* to employ that hour in some wise way,—in some *wiser* that this! To 'write by dictat*n*,' *cannot* I learn that, then? Shame on me, shame!" (TC's journal; privately owned).

TC-JAC, 17 Sept. MS: NLS 527.26. Hitherto unpbd.

1. Sir Anthony Coningham Sterling.

2. John A. Carlyle wrote, 18 Sept.: "I was very glad to see your little note this morning, & hear that you & Mary had got back to Chelsea easily & safely. . . . I felt very sad after your departure, & lonely in my upper room here."

3. Their nephew Thomas Carlyle in Canada; TC and John had recently sent money for him and his sister Jane; see TC to JAC, 1 June.

4. Their sister Janet Hanning; the Carlyles sent newspapers (free of charge) to indicate all was well.

5. John replied: "The 'American Express Co' I never heard of before, but John [Aitken] tells me it has an office in Liverpool as well as Boston, & Jim [Aitken Jr.] knows the Liverpool manager of it; so John will write to him today & ask him to send you particulars direct from Liverpool."

TC TO MARGARET DUNCAN

Chelsea, 20 September, 1870.

Dear Madam—Having been in Scotland for a good while, it was not till yesterday that I got sight of your Letter. I feel much grieved at your anxieties about your Brother;[1] but am rather confident, withal, that your affection considerably exaggerates the matter. He seemed to me a very honest-minded, clear and pious-hearted man; and if it *be* his genuine *Love of Truth* (as I take it to be) that has led him into these embarrassments and miserable anxieties, you are to be patient, and also hopeful, in a very high degree, in reference to that high quality,—the highest that can dwell in man!

For the rest, if he have any value for my advice, I authorize you to inform him, with all emphasis, that nobody can less approve than I do his throwing off of practical employment, and exchanging his firm land there for a sea of dubitations, to which I know too well there is neither Shore nor Bottom. Tell him, my first commandment to all men is, To find their work and do it; that except in *Work*, I have long since discovered, and do steadily believe, there is no deliverance possible from Doubt. Indeed, if he has been reading *me*, this I think is the main precept he will find, That the chief end of man is to work in a faithful manner; that Thinking which does not lean upon Work is an effort thrown away; and if he plead uncertainty about his Work, and cannot find what his real duty in regard to Work is, this is an excellent precept:

"Do the duty that lies nearest thee;[2] DO *it*; thy second duty (thy second bit of Work) will already have become clearer to thee."[3]

This is all I have to say at present,—except to recommend, which probably is not necessary, a kind and hopeful attitude towards your dear Brother, of whom I yet have not the least despair.

Believe me, dear Madam, Yours, with many good wishes,

T. CARLYLE.[4]

TC-MD, 20 Sept. Pbd: A. Carlyle, *NL* 2:267–69. Margaret Ann Borthwick Duncan (b. 1842), sister of George Alexander Duncan; see TC to GAD, 9 June.

1. George Alexander Duncan; see TC to GAD, 9 June; Margaret Duncan's letter untraced.

2. Cf. Goethe, "Wilhelm Meister's Apprenticeship" (Carlyle, *Works* 24:2), and Carlyle, *Sartor* 145.

3. Apparently on the advice of TC, Duncan went to Berlin to study history after graduating from the Univ. of Edinburgh in 1870. An obituary notice in *The Academy*, 29 Dec. 1906, reported that Duncan was "for a time fairly successful, and besides teaching and translation work he assisted the Berlin correspondent of the *Standard*. Latterly he had an appointment in the Staff College. Through all Duncan's mental vicissitudes Thomas Carlyle remained his hero, and all his views and conduct of life were reduced to the standard of the Sage of Chelsea" (649).

4. TC wrote in his journal, 20 Sept.: "Been in Dumfries for nr 3 months; got back on

P.S.—I received in Dumfries, a pleasant and very kind Letter from your worthy Uncle, the Rev. Mr. Dodds of Dunbar,[5] to which I fear there went, contrary to my intention, no answer. My right hand shakes and I have great difficulty and great unwillingness to write. Have the goodness to make my apologies to Mr. Dodds; to say that I remember him worthily as an old correspondent,[6] and regret to have yielded to my many impediments in that matter. My kind regards also to his Wife, whom I well remember as pretty little Barbara-Ann of long ago.[7]

TC TO HENRY PARKES

5 Cheyne Row, Chelsea
21 September 1870.

Dear Sir,

Your Letter came to me in Scotland; and since my return last week, I have

---

fri*day* night last [16 Sept.]. Not a word written *here* or elsewhere hardly; a three months shamefully empty; I think the *idlest*, and among the heaviest and silently meanest of all my life. Nothing in them but gloomy musings, and private,—that was their one merit or excuse! Hope of 'improving health' proved utterly futile,—health will never 'improve,' how can it? Sea-voyaging, sea-bathing (with Brr John) proved all impossible; nor w*d* they, I guess, have done me any good. I read some Books, not quite bad; I 'saw' nobody, or nobody I was not bound to. Boundless kindness, d*o* patience, from Sister & kindred;—*loss* (my worst) of ab*t* ⅓ of my sleep, from 'railway noises,' that was the *Hack-beast* of my rusticat*n*, not to be helped. For one week (5 days it proved) I desperately fled to Craigenp*h* [late July] seeking '*silence*'; found it indeed, but such a plunge of nameless grief and misery withal as I never had before, unforgettable 5 days!— I made 2 pilgrimages, one to my poor Birthplace & the Kirkyard ('God's Field') there [late Aug.]; one to Haddington and *Her* Grave [3 Sept.]. Wrong planned that latter, and begirt with such environ*t* (3 sleepless nights at the kind Masson's, for one thing)! These were my *sacred* places; these, with a visit to poor old Betty [4 Sept.]; *grand* old Betty, were all I got of heavenly or eternal from my misery of 3 months. *Jewels* as of Heaven, especially that Haddingt*n* one, and of a sorrow that was high as well as painful: *jewels* set in such a *floor*,—don't think of it!— And try *now* to *do* a little better, if thou canst,—if thou by any means *canst*!" (TC's journal; privately owned).

5. Rev. James Dodds was Margaret's uncle by marriage; see TC to GAD, 9 June.

6. TC replied, 5 Feb. 1840 (*CL* 12:29–31), to the Rev. James Dodds's original letter to TC about his cousin James Dodds (1813–74; see *CL* 12:29–30), lawyer, lecturer, and poet. Dodds published TC's first letter to him and TC's four subsequent letters to his cousin in his "Memoir," attached to *Lays of the Covenanters by James Dodds* (Edinburgh, 1880), 44–47 (*CL* 12:20–30), 48–49 (*CL* 13:58–59), 58–60 (*CL* 16:175–76), 61 (*CL* 18:34), and 62–64 (*CL* 18:120–21).

7. Barbara Ann Dodds; see TC to GAD, 9 June.

TC-HP, 21 Sept. MS: Mitchell Lib., Sydney, Australia. From this point, TC's letters were written by Mary Aitken and signed by him; this is no longer noted unless TC wrote more than just his signature. Pbd: Henry Parkes, *Fifty Years in the Making of Australian History* (1892) 1:201–3. Henry Parkes (1815–96; *ODNB*), Australian politician and journalist; see 45:228.

read carefully your Speech on the Education Question.[1] You are very kind to remember me so steadily, and always from time to time to send me some interesting notice of what you are about.

I am greatly pleased with your calm, quiet, lucid and honest Speech, and with all the useful and manful labour you have so successfully gone through for one of the most sacred interests in human affairs. The Speech, though studiously inoffensive, gives[2] clear indication of the much opposition you have had to confront in achieving such a bit of calm and impartial Legislation, surrounded by so many difficulties and contradictions. I well enough understand the clamours of dark sectaries, Protestant and Catholic; especially of your Irish Priests,—the worst section of that miserable category; but I own myself much surprised that you should have incurred the estrangement of C. G. Duffy[3] in the adventure. You give no details of that little personal matter. My judgment of C. G. Duffy, and of the thing you have been advocating, and accomplishing, leads me to believe that this little rub will only be temporary.

At all events, I can congratulate you on having laid down a plan, judicious, clear, impartial; probably the only sound plan practicable in your Colony;—which plan is already in vigorous practice there, and will be a blessing to millions on millions of your Colonial Countrymen, and indeed more or less a benefit to all men long after we are gone. Well done, Well done.

There is at present among us a considerable stir about Emigration,[4] a grow-

1. Parkes wrote, 15 June: "I have sent to your address by this mail a copy of our last report on Education. If you can spare time to look over it I hope you may find matter to interest you." Parkes introduced the Public Schools Act 1866, New South Wales (see 45:54), which established non-sectarian schools, and trained teachers. Parkes wrote: "In 1869, having consented to open a new public school at Dundas, a village near Parramatta [suburb of Sydney], I made the occasion serve for an address of some length, expository of the new system and its successful working. . . . I sent a copy of it to Mr. Carlyle, and received the following letter from him. . . . The letter has an additional interest, as it also expresses his views on emigration as a question of British policy" (Parkes, *Fifty Years* 1:201).

2. Word repeated with a line over it at turn of page.

3. Charles Gavan Duffy; Parkes wrote: "I appear to have lost the friendship of Mr Gavan Duffy in consequence of the course I have taken over the School question." As an Irish Catholic, Duffy suffered as a child from laws preventing the education of Catholics, and supported denominational public education. In 1867 he led the opposition to a plan in Victoria to abolish denominational schools and replace them with "a new system established under which something described as religion without dogma would be taught, and at which the attendance of children would be compulsory." In justifying his campaign, Duffy used the example of TC: "Education supplies a more stringent control of character than natural endowments, and often contends successfully with the philosophy and experience of manhood. Thomas Carlyle, in the acme of his intellectual force and scornful indifference to thrones and conventions, was to the end of his life, in many of his prejudices, a Scotch Calvinist" (Duffy, *My Life in Two Hemispheres* [1898] 2:292).

4. See TC to JAF, 7 Sept. The *Times* reported, 6 Oct.: "The work of the Emigration Com-

ing desire that the Government would take some charge of cooperating with the Colonies in this great interest of ours; which I hope the Government, in spite of its lazy reluctances, will gradually be compelled to do. By a little human arrangement between Mother Country and her Daughters, you and Sydney for example might have as many hardy English Emigrants as you could gradually make room for, to the unspeakable advantage of us and of you! A thousand by the year, or two thousand, if you liked. But there needs co-operation, a mutual stretching out of hands on both sides of the Ocean; and, alas, on our side the one thing we are sure of is not a practical putting forth of hands in any kind of Work or Government; but a plentiful wagging of tongues in Parliament & elsewhere. If to you, on your side of the water, any opportunity occur, I charge you not to neglect it. The Government is deaf at this time, and will continue so I know not how long; but there are various private Associations already of magnitude, and vigorously growing;—I specially mention Sir George Grey,[5] formerly a Governor among you, as the leading man in this Movement here, who might be the properest of all to consult in the first instance, if you had occasion.

Believe me,

Yours, with many good wishes and regards, / T. Carlyle
The Hon*ble* / Henry Parkes / &c &c

TC TO J. R. THOMPSON

5 Cheyne Row, Chelsea
22 September 1870

Dear Sir,

Your Letter was lying here for me on my return from the Country some days ago. I yesterday received the announced Senatorial Nigger in the highest state of preservation,—a very ugly figure indeed![1] He seems to have some-

mission during the past year has been exceedingly important and extensive ... with the exception of 1854, the number was the largest that ever left the United Kingdom in a single year. According to the statistics just published 258,027 persons emigrated in 1869 ... [of whom] 203,001 went to the United States, 33,891 to British North America, 14,901 to Australia and New Zealand."

5. Sir George Grey (1812–98; *ODNB*), governor of various colonies 1841–68, governor of South Australia 1841–45; see 46:179–80.

TC-JRT, 22 Sept. MS: New York Public Lib. Hitherto unpbd. John Reuben Thompson (1823–73), from Virginia, U.S., poet and journalist; he met TC while in Britain, 1864–66, to promote the Confederate States of America cause; see 44:55.

1. Thompson apparently sent TC a photograph of Hiram Rhodes Revels (1827–1901), U.S. minister and politician; born free in Fayetteville, N.C., he became the first African-American U.S. Senator; he took his seat as a Republican for the Mississippi State Senate,

thing of the wild Indian as well as of the do African;[2] but no doubt knows on which side his bread is buttered; let us hope he may throw some light into the Senate of Mississippi; which, I have no doubt, needs it, like very many other Senates. To me he is so ugly that I have at once got him provided for in a safe Apartment where he will be seen only by the indifferent or the well-affected.[3]

I am much obliged by this new remembrance of me; and wish you had told me something more specific of your own history since we last met.[4] The gift of Virginia Tobacco, and of Virginia Pipes came safe to hand; nor, I can hope, did Alfred Tennyson want his due share.[5] Except once transiently about four months ago, I have not seen Alfred since you left us; but his share of the Tobacco was twice over demanded from me by an insolent Moxonite fellow (who wanted something quite other with me, but didn't get that; with whom Alfred, I think, is now at Law);[6] and to him, on the second demand, I liberally made over the Alfred Tobacco, and happily never saw him at all. Many thanks also f[or] that mark of your attention whic[h I][7] still remember with pleasure.

I am not in bad health beyond what is naturally to be expected at my time of life. Perhaps my worse physical misfortune is that of my right Hand; which has latterly become very shaky and unwilling to write. A nimble little Niece, who puts this on paper, would be the best of Amanuenses, if I had only learnt to *dictate*, which I fear I never shall.

Believe me,

    Yours, with many kind wishes,

    and mournfully pleasant remembrances,

                    T. Carlyle

J. R. Thompson Esq

    &c &c

1869, and was then chosen as a senator for the U.S. Senate, Jan. 1870. For a photograph of Revels taken about 1870 (possibly identical to the one sent by Thompson), see opp.

2. Revels was rumored to be of mixed African, Scottish, and Native American lineage.

3. Revels's photograph is not included in the Thomas Carlyle Photograph Albums.

4. Their last recorded meeting was 4 Sept. 1866; see 44:55.

5. When Thompson returned to the U.S. he arranged to send tobacco from Virginia to TC; presumably he also sent some for Alfred Tennyson. TC last saw Tennyson in April; see 46:187.

6. Presumably James Bertrand Payne (1833–98), employee of Tennyson's publisher, Edward Moxon (1801–58; *ODNB*) & Co.; after Moxon's death Payne continued to manage the business on behalf of Moxon's family; however the business lost money, Tennyson and Payne disagreed; Tennyson moved to a different publisher, 1868, but was still in dispute with Payne over monies owed to him.

7. Letters obscured.

Hiram Rhodes Revels
Courtesy of the Library of Congress

TC TO RALPH WALDO EMERSON

5 Cheyne Row Chelsea
28 September, 1870

Dear Emerson,

Your Letter, dated 15*th* June, never got to me till about ten days ago; when my little Niece and I returned out of Scotland, and a long, rather empty Visit there! It had missed me here only by two or three days; and my highly *infe-licitous* Selectress of Letters to be forwarded[1] had left *it* carefully aside as undeserving that honour,—good faithful old Woman, one hopes she is greatly stronger on some sides than in this literary-selective one. Certainly no Letter was forwarded that had the hundredth part of the right to be so; certainly, of all the Letters that came to me, or were left waiting here, this was, in comparison, the one which might *not* with propriety have been left to be stranded forever or to wander on the wind[2] forever!—

One of my first journeys was to Chapman, with vehement *rebuke* of this inconceivable "Cincinnati-Massachusetts" business.[3] *Stupiditas-stupiditatum* [stupidity of stupidities];[4] I never in my life, not even in that unpunctual House, fell in with anything that equalled it. Instant amendment was at once undertaken for, nay it seems had been already in part performed: "Ten voll., following the nine you already had, were dispatched in Field & Co's box above two months ago,"[5] so Chapman solemnly said and asserverated to me; so that by this time you ought actually to have in hand 19 voll.; and the 20*th* (first of *Friedrich*), which came out ten days ago, is to go in Field & Co's Box this week, and ought, not many days after the arrival of this Letter, to be in Boston waiting for you there. The *Chapman's Homer* (2 volumes)[6] had gone

TC-RWE, 28 Sept. MS: RWEMA. Pbd. Norton, *CE* 2:330–34; Slater, *CEC* 572–74.

1. Sarah Warren, TC's housekeeper.
2. Word repeated and pluralized at turn of page.
3. Emerson wrote, 15 June: "I received duly, as I wrote you in a former letter 9 volumes . . . these books oddly addressed to my name, but at CINCINNATI, Mass*tts*. Whether they went to Ohio, & came back to Boston, I know not."
4. TC was possibly parodying "vanity of vanities"; Eccles. 1:2.
5. Field, Osgood, & Co., Boston, U.S. publishers; their London office was at 76 Mark Lane. Emerson wrote, 15 Oct.: "Already many days before your letter came, Fields sent me a package from you, which he said he had found a little late. . . . Unhappily, Vol. 2d of Cromwell is wanting, and there is a duplicated of Vol. 5th instead of it." He also mentioned that he had previously received a duplicate copy of *Sartor* instead of vol.1 of the *French Revolution*: "I proposed to Fields to send back to Chapman these two duplicates. But he said, 'No, it will cost as much as the price of the books.'"
6. See TC to RWE, 31 May; Emerson wrote, 15 Oct.: "Now, two days ago came your letter, & tells me that the good old gods have also inspired you to send me Chapman's Homer! & that it came—heroes with heroes—in the same enchanted box. / I went to Fields yesterday & demanded the book. He . . . [suggested] that it must be that all these came in a box of

with that first Field Packet; and would be handed to you along with the ten volls which were overdue. All this was solemnly declared to me as on Affidavit; Chapman also took extract of the Massachusetts passage in your Letter, in order to pour it like ice-cold water on the head of his stupid old Chief-Clerk,[7] the instant the poor creature got back from his rustication: alas, I am by no means certain that it will make a new man of him, nor, in fact, that the whole of this amendatory programme will get itself performed to equal satisfaction! But you must write to me at once if it is not so; & done it shall be in spite of human stupidity itself. Note, withal, these things: Chapman sends no Books to America *except* through Field & Co; he does not regularly send a Box at the middle of the month; but he does "almost monthly send one Box"; so that if your monthly Volume do not start from London about the 15*th*, it is due by the very *next* Chapman-Field d*o*; and if it at any time don't come, I beg of you very much to make instant complaint through Field & Co, or what would be still more effectual, direct to myself. My malison on all Blockheadisms and torpid stupidities and infidelities; of which this world is full! —

Your Letter had been anxiously enough waited for, a month before my departure; but we will not mention the delay in presence of what you were engaged with then.[8] *Faustum sit* [Good luck to it]; that truly was and will be a Work worth doing your best upon; and I, if alive, can promise you at least one reader that will do his best upon your Work. I myself often think of the Philosophies precisely in that manner. To say truth, they do not otherwise rise in esteem with me at all, but rather sink. The last thing I read of that kind was a piece by Hegel, in an excellent Translation by Stirling;[9] — right well translated, I could see, for every bit of it was intelligible to me; — but my feeling at the end of it was; — "Good Heavens, I have walked this road before many a good time; but never with a Cannon-ball at each ankle before!" Science also, Science falsely so-called, is—— But I will not enter upon that with you just now.

The Visit to America, alas, alas, is pure Moonshine. Never had I, in late years, the least shadow of intention to undertake that adventure;[10] and I am

---

sheets of Dickens from Chapman, which was sent to the Stereotypers at Cambridge [MA]; and the box shall be instantly explored."

7. Unidentified further.

8. Emerson had been busy "writing & reading 18 lectures" at Harvard; see TC to RWE, 31 May.

9. Probably James Hutchison Stirling (1820–1909; *ODNB*), "The Symbolism of the Sublime (from Hegel's Aesthetic)," *Macmillan's Magazine* (Oct. 1867); see 45:47. Stirling had also pbd. *The Secret of Hegel*, 2 vols. (1865). Georg Wilhelm Friedrich Hegel (1770–1831), German philosopher.

10. Emerson wrote, 17 June: "But what do I read in our Boston Newspapers twice in the last 3 days? that 'Thomas Carlyle is coming to America,'—& the tidings cordially greeted by the Editors."

quite at a loss to understand how the rumour originated. One Boston Gentleman (a kind of universal Undertaker, or Lion's Provider of Lecturers,[11] I think) informed me that *"The Cable"* had told him; and I had to remark "And who the devil told the Cable?"[12] Alas, no, I fear I shall never dare to undertake that big Voyage; which has so much of romance and of reality behind it to me; *zu spät, zu spät* [too late, too late]. I do sometimes talk dreamily of a long Sea-Voyage, and the good the Sea has often done me,—in times when good was still possible. It may have been some vague folly of that kind that originated this rumour; for rumours are like dandelion-seeds; and *the Cable*, I dare say, welcomes them all that have a guinea in their pocket. n.l.[13] Thank you for blocking up that Harvard matter, provided it *don't* go into the Newspapers, all is right.[14] Thank you a thousand times for that thrice-kind potential welcome, and flinging wide open of your doors and your hearts to me at Concord.[15] The gleam of it is like sunshine in a subterranean place. Ah me, Ah me! May God be with you all, dear Emerson.

Yours ever / T. Carlyle

R. Waldo Emerson Esq.
&c &c

TC TO JOHN TYNDALL

5 Cheyne Row Chelsea
28 Sep. 1870

Dear Tyndall,

Your Letter, the solitary Snipe, *not* without its bill (Der einzige Schnepfe hat doch einen Schnabel) [the solitary snipe has yet its beak] was very welcome to me, especially when bringing, withal, the prospect of soon seeing you

11. Not further identified.

12. Slater noted that the "Boston *Daily Evening Transcript* announced, on the authority of the 'British Cable': 'Thomas Carlyle will soon sail for the United States'" (Slater, *CEC* 571). "British Cable" or *The Cable* unidentified.

13. TC inserted "n.l." to indicate a new paragraph should start.

14. TC had asked Emerson in April not to publicize his gift of books to Harvard; see 46: 190; Emerson wrote, 17 June: "Though I could see no harm in making known the bequest of books to Cambridge—no harm, but sincere pleasure, & honor of the donor from all good men, yet on receipt of your letter touching that, I went back to President Eliot,—& told him your opinion on newspapers. He said it was necessarily communicated to the seven persons composing the Corporation, but otherwise, he had been very cautious, & it would not go into print." Charles William Eliot (1834–1926), president of Harvard.

15. Emerson wrote, 17 June: "This house entreats you earnestly & lovingly to come & dwell in it. My Wife & Ellen & Edward E. are thoroughly acquainted with your greatness & your loveliness. And it is but ten days of healthy sea to pass."

TC-JT, 28 Sept. MS: Royal Institution RI MS JT/1/C/15. Hitherto unpbd.

in person again.[1] I heard repeatedly of your new discourses at the Scientific Association;[2] but did not anywhere see it, nor a readable report of it: furthermore the Copy of it did not accompany your Letter yesterday, nor has come today; so that I am still left in the dark, though not without my curiosities upon the matter. If you have by you another copy, please dispatch it at once.[3]

I warmly agree with all you say about this War. It is such an instance of Michael *versus* Satan as I have never read in all History before. Satan getting himself smashed to impalpable pulp in one month's time. Bismarck, I suppose, will insist upon his Alsace and Lorraine; nor can all the world hinder him if that is his determination.[4] To poor France it is the frightfullest Lesson she ever had; and unless she can learn by it, which is doubtful, may be the beginning of incalculable downbreak *quod Deus avertat* [may God forbid].

Return winged; and let us see you light at Chelsea at 9 p.m. the first night you have to yourself

Believe me / Yours always
T. Carlyle

TC TO [THOMAS WILSON]

[early Oct. 1870]

Your anxieties about the war must have been of short duration; in fact, they must after the first few days' practical experience have been changed into

1. Tyndall was often away during the summer, returning in time for his autumn lectures. Snipe are winter visitors to parts of Britain.

2. Tyndall's lecture, "On the Scientific Use of the Imagination," was delivered to the British Association at Liverpool, 16 Sept. Tyndall concluded the lecture with one of TC's favorite quotations: "'Two things,' said Immanuel Kant, 'fill me with awe: the starry heavens and the sense of moral responsibility in man'" (John Tyndall, *Essays on the Use and Limit of the Imagination in Science* [1870] 51). The *Times* reported, 17 Sept.: "The great event of today [16 Sept.] was Professor Tyndall's Lecture on the scientific use of the imagination, delivered to a crowded audience at the Philharmonic-hall." TC read Tyndall's first lecture on the subject, "On the Scientific Limit of the Imagination," delivered to the British Association at Norwich, 19 Aug. 1868, and wrote to Tyndall that he was looking forward to the sequel; see 46:35–36.

3. Presumably Tyndall promised to send TC a copy of the lecture which was pbd. immediately, price 7 shillings and 6 pence.

4. See TC to JAF, 7 Sept.

TC-[TW], [early Oct.]. Pbd: *Weimar Gazette*, mid-Oct. inc; *Times*, 25 Oct. inc; *Pall Mall Gazette*, 26 Oct. inc; *Glasgow Herald*, 27 Oct. inc; *Newcastle Courant*, 28 Oct. inc; Shepherd, *Carlyle* 2:293–94 inc; Wilson, *Carlyle* 6:218–19 inc. Text: *Times*, introduced: "The *Weimar Gazette* publishes a few extracts from a letter written by Mr. Thomas Carlyle, with references to the war." Recipient identified as Thomas Wilson (b. 1811; see 22:xiii and 26:304), old friend of TC's, living in Weimar; see also 40:235. TC wrote early Oct. as Wilson

bright hope, into a hope increasing in rapid geometrical progression till it obtained its present dimensions. So far as my reading goes there never was such a war, never such a collapse of shameless human vanity, of menacing, long-continued arrogance, into contemptible nothingness. Blow has followed blow as if from the hammer of Thor,[1] till it lies like a shapeless heap of ruins, whining to itself, 'In the name of all the gods and all the devils, what is to become of us?' . . .

All Germany may now look forward to happier days in a political sense than it has seen since the Emperor Barbarossa[2] left it. My individual satisfaction in all this is great, and all England, I can say all the intelligent in England, heartily wish good fortune to brave old Germany in what it has accomplished—a real transformation into one nation, no longer the chaotic jumble which invited the intrusion of every ill-disposed neighbour, especially of that ill-disposed France which has inflicted on it such interminable mischief during the last 400 years—wars heaped upon wars without real cause except insatiable French ambition. All that, through God's grace, is now at an end. I have, in my time, seen nothing in Europe which has so much delighted me. . . . 'A brave people,' as your Goethe calls them, and as I believe a peaceful and a virtuous one. I only hope that Heaven will send them the wisdom, patience, and pious discretion to turn to a right use all that has been achieved.

TC TO ALEXANDER CARLYLE

5 Cheyne Row Chelsea
6 October 1870

My dear Brother,

Since your Letter in June, which punctually gave fortunate account of that Bank Paper for your Jane's & Tom's behoof,[1] which I was glad to see & much thanked you for, there have come addressed to the Dr, but for benefit of us all, Two Letters from you,—the last only four or five days ago, forwarded

---

replied, 8 Oct.: "It is long indeed since the post brought us any thing so welcome and so gratifying as your letter." He wrote again, 19 Oct., ending his letter saying: "I have taken the liberty to read to two or three worthy listeners your grand and exhaustive appreciation of the war . . . but I do not intend to send them to our Papers without permission." Presumably TC gave such permission.

1. The symbolic hammer of the Norse god Thor came from his association with thunder.
2. Frederick I (1122–90), Holy Roman Emperor, 1155–90, known as Frederick Barbarossa, one of the greatest of medieval rulers.

TC-AC, 6 Oct. MS copy: MUL inc; copy apparently by one of Alexander's children; note on MS: "Letter from Uncle to our Father. . . . copied 1884." Pbd: A. Carlyle, NL 2:269–71 inc; Marrs 767–70. Quot: Kaplan 504. Text from Marrs.
1. Alexander's children; see TC to AC, 3 June.

hither from Dumfries.² I have also had a Letter from Tom, which, you can tell him, I have read with pleasure. We are all right glad & thankful to hear of your continued welfare, and that nothing of notable misfortune hitherto occurs to disturb the current of your days. Old age, indeed is of itself sad, and ought naturally to be, as it is with you, serious & even solemn, not "joyful" any more; but we have all of us great reason to acknowledge with gratitude to Providence that extraordinary misfortune has visited us so rarely, & that so many of us, brothers & sisters, have all lived peaceably to be old men & old women. All grown or growing old, and *two* of us (I myself well a-head) already past the Psalmist's limit of three score & ten.³ Many a time I remember the old pious Annandale phrase, which every sinful man may well apply to himself, "A Monument of Mercy!"⁴—

In the end of June, as doubtless you have heard from John, we came to Dumfries (Niece Mary & I); staid there till the middle of September. A silent, quiescent, very empty, dreary kind of life to me, cheered only by the great affection patience & kindness of every one about me. The air was was pure & excellent; the solitude not unbeneficial; but the railway whistles, which are near that excellent House of Jean's were a sore misery to me (tho' to no one else of the smallest inconvenience); & I lost, often in a very wretched way, on the whole, about a third part of my natural sleep; which of course was much in the way of the salutary influences there. So that I know not at this time if my health got any improvement or not; though of course the change itself was something,—the turning of a poor sick creature from one side to another. I feel, at least, no worse; am gradually recovering my sleep here, & hope sometimes to do a little better this winter than last. My worst inconvenience in these years is the refusal of my right hand to write for me. The left hand is yet quite steady; but the right shakes so as to render writing, if not impossible, at least intolerably slow and unsatisfactory; literally enough, the breaking of my work arm, & cutting me off from any real employment I may still be fit for. In these weeks, however, I am trying to write by dictation (as you see here), and Mary, who is both swift & willing, eagerly helps & encourages; so that perhaps something may come of it. Let us hope! The⁵ noises during my first month at Dumfries, drove me to Craigenputtock for shelter for one week (properly for five days),—how inexpressibly sad I need not describe to you. Silent, empty, sorrowful and mournful as death & the grave. Not in my life have I passed

2. John A. Carlyle wrote, [27 Sept.]: "Both these letters from Canada have just arrived tonight (8¼ p.m.) & I send them on at once to you."

3. See Ps. 90:10.

4. An expression of TC's mother; see *Early Letters of Thomas Carlyle*, ed. C. E. Norton (1886) 2:242.

5. A figure "2" (underlined), written above "The," was presumably to indicate a new paragraph.

five more heavy-laden days. Your old stone dyke, the fence to the Cow Field which you built for us the year we were in London,[6] that was still standing, firm every stone of it, a Memorial of affection still alive for me; *all* else was of affection now in the death-realms, gone, gone, and only a sorrow & a love for it left in me which exceeds all others. The place is all, I believe, in substantially superior order; immensities of grass upon it this season, effectually drained and a great deal of money laid into it. "Young Jamie," who is a kindly active & clever young fellow, standing in a far flowerier element than yours and mine was there. Well, well, how much better so, than if it had been the reverse way! I was twice at The Gill and back,—no where else on *visit*. I made two Pilgrimages, one to Ecclefechan (was some hours at Scotsbrig), another to Haddington; on what errand each of them you may conjecture. The Ecclefechan one did my heart a solemn kind of *good*; the other Pilgrimage was wrong planned, *it* involved three sleepless nights in Edinburgh,—and the blessing in it was encircled by a great deal of mean wretchedness. This & the day's railwaying hither, which soon followed, was all the journeying I did.

The D*r*, I suppose, gives you precise accounts of all the little Annandale history, & the doings & conditions of our kindred there; so that I need not enter upon that head. Outwardly, they seem to me to be all prospering. Old age not crushed down with any burdens except its own. Sister Mary at The Gill is as loving-hearted as ever, not specially in ill-health either, so far as I could notice though looking worn & old, as she well may.

Jamie, I fear, suffers a great deal from want of health mid his economic prosperity,—sleeps very badly, eats very badly, and, I fear, has nobody at Scotsbrig to do well for him what is still do-able by way of cheering his now lonely home for him.[7] His Son John is said to be less sympathetic with him than Jamie is; and John's Wife is, hitherto, tho' a very amiable looking, innocent creature, extremely helpless in domestic matters. Daughter Jenny was with him during part of our time. He seems to spend a good portion of every summer at Birmingham on visit to her Husband & her; and, at other seasons pretty frequently comes & goes to Craigenputtock for a week or two at a time. He makes no complaint to any of us; is a hardy, steel-grey little fellow, and as emphatic of speech and as decided of conduct as ever he was.

Dear Brother, I doubt you have abundantly enough of this; and, at any rate, my own time is up. If you would write me similar details about yourself and Bield, it would be right welcome to me, and I could write in a similar strain as copiously once more. Pray tell me about poor old John, our half-brother.[8]

6. TC and JWC lived at Craigenputtoch, 1828–34, but stayed in London, Sept. 1831–March 1832.

7. Jamie's wife, Isabella, d. June 1859.

8. See 46:6–7 and 40.

I often think inquiringly about him & what is becoming of him in his lonely old age. Some rumour was going among us that he was to come over to Bield to spend some of the dark months with you. Was that true or not? Give my affectionate regards to him, and to every one of yo[urs,] down to the youngest; especially to Tom & Jane, whom I personally know.[9] [May Go]d's blessing be on you and yours. Dear Brother, Ever affectionat[el]y T. C[arlyle].[10]

TC TO JOHN RUSKIN

5 Cheyne Row, Chelsea,
10 October 1870.

Dear Ruskin,

On Saturday morning, on my first sally out into the open air, I noticed on a Newsvendor's Placard that there was a "Letter from Mr Ruskin,"[1] which it would be necessary for me to see. Not having the copper penny in my pocket, I took the necessary steps immediately on my return home; and, along with my Coffee, comfortably swallowed the *Ruskin Letter* accordingly;—*more* comfortably than I did my Coffee, for which, alas, as for all other material things (tho' *not* for things spiritual, thank God), there is now a clearly decaying appetite.[2]

In the course of the day I learnt that there had been another *Letter*, which somehow must be attained here; and, by our last post, came your beneficent announcement that both *Letters* had been duly put underway by you. By you duly; but not by the Postoffice Authorities, who did not, till our second post *this* day, forward your two *Daily Telegraphs*[3] at all;—and now further, to my confusion, I discover that they are BOTH Copies of the Saturday's *Telegraph*, which I had already possessed, and given away several copies of, before the week ended! Letter First,[4] therefore, still stands as a lonely *Desideratum* in that waste howling Wilderness of human mismanagement, disloyalties and infidelities!— You see, then, what is at once to be done. Pray clip out Letter

9. See TC to TC, 4 May.
10. Marrs's brackets.

TC-JR, 10 Oct. MS: Yale. Pbd: Cate 155–56.
1. *The Daily Telegraph* pbd. two letters on the Franco-Prussian War by John Ruskin, 7 and 8 Oct.
2. Ruskin replied, [12 Oct.]: "You must not cease enjoying your coffee— All your work is grandly done—and it is just time for coffee, & pipe—and peace."
3. Ruskin wrote, [8 Oct.]: "I send two daily Telegraphs with a word or two which you may care to glance at."
4. Ruskin commented in his first letter, 7 Oct., on the news that the painter Édouard Frère (1819–86), whose work he admired, and his fellow artist Rosa Bonheur (1822–99), were allowed to escape through the Prussian lines during the siege of Paris.

Bombardment of Strasbourg
Illustrated London News, 24 September 1870

First for me, and dispatch it *quàm primùm* [as soon as possible].— Your Second Letter, full of holy indignation was as if it came from my own heart;[5] at the end, however, I think you do the Germans wrong. My notion is; Bismarck knows very well what he is aiming at; & I find withal that it is a perfectly just thing; likewise that all the World cannot prevent him from getting it; and that

5. Ruskin wrote about the destruction of much of Strasbourg (French spelling) / Strasburg (German spelling) in letter two, 8 Oct.: "At Strasburg the Picture Gallery—with the pictures in it?—the Library—with the books in it?—and the Theatre, with certainly two hundred persons in it, have been burnt to the ground." He then discussed "the actual question of the war," which he defined as "a simple and testing struggle between pure Republicanism on the one side, expressed in the most exquisite, finished, and exemplary anarchy . . . and one of the truest Monarchies and schools of honour and obedience yet organized under heaven" (*Ruskin's Works* 34:500–501). He also cited Carlyle's *Frederick*: "for all the wars of the Great Friedrich would have passed away resultless—as great wars usually do— had it not been for this pregnant fact at the end of them: 'all his artillery horses are parted into plough-teams, and given to those who otherwise can get none'. . . that 21st book on the repair of Prussia being of extant literature the most important piece for us to read and digest in these days of 'raising the poor without gifts'—never asking who first let them fall" (*Ruskin's Works* 34:501–2); see also Carlyle, *Works* 19:10. For the bombardment and fall of Strasburg as depicted in the *Illustrated London News*, see above and opp.

The Fall of Strasbourg
Illustrated London News, 22 October 1870

he is calmly taking all the necessary steps for coercing an inarticulate mad and furious Wasps' nest of thirty five million delirious Mountebanks to quietly grant it him, —with the *minimum* of *Sulphur* applied. He seems to me at this moment to have power to cut France into thongs, and, in a few days, to convert Paris, if he liked, into a red hot Cinder; but is far from intending anything beyond the strictly necessary for his objects.[6]

I am reading Bitzius, with astonishment at the dull gritty strength of him; also at his cruelty, limitation, dimness, narrowness:[7] but there is the charm in him of a rugged Veracity; strange "Dutch Picture," as you say;[8] of an object curious to me and unknown to me. With great pleasure my little Niece will be of your party to the Theatre[9] whenever you see good. Whether her poor old Uncle, who also would *like* much, can accompany or not will depend on the complexion of the Nervous System for that evening;—the willing mind for many things is still partially here; but the Man is way-worn, weary, and rigorously ordered to be aware of that fact.

Send me the Newspaper Clipping, dear Ruskin; and believe me.

Ever yours, T. Carlyle[10]

6. In his conclusion, Ruskin criticized Germany for "pressing her victory too far—dangerously far, as uselessly. The Nemesis of battle may indeed be near her; greater glory she cannot win by the taking of Paris, nor overrunning of the provinces—she only prolongs suffering, redoubles death, extends loss, incalculable and irremediable. But let her now give unconditional armistice, and offer terms that France can accept with honour, and she will bear such rank among the nations as never yet shone on Christian history."

7. Albrecht Bitzius (1797–1854), Swiss pastor and novelist; he wrote under the pseudonym "Jeremias Gotthelf." Ruskin replied, [12 Oct.]: "why [do] you call Bitzius 'cruel'—he seems to me an entirely sweet and loving person."

8. Ruskin wrote, [7 Oct.]: "I send you another—perhaps a little too long—study of Gotthelfs—study—for it is hardly a story in any sense—but as you will instantly see . . . a most finished piece of Dutch painting of two persons only." Ruskin sent the first vol. of Gotthelf's *Oeuvres choisies* (Paris, Genève, and Neuchâtel, 1859). TC recorded, 11 Oct.: "*Jeremias Gotthelf* (i.e. Bitzius, a revd Swiss of strange type) is ag*n* my reading for this last day or two. Not worth *much* to me; indeed, except as he is original (*like* no other writing mortal) and *veredical*, worth nothing" (TC's journal; privately owned).

9. Ruskin wrote, [7 Oct,]: "Would you care to come with me by ourselves or with Joan only sometimes to a private box—to see anything absurd enough to be interesting," and then wrote, [8 Oct.]: "I've been in a misery of provocation against myself ever since the note to you yesterday was sent off—for the stupidity of its wording, as if I meant Joan only to come with us, & not your niece—it would be so nice for us to go altogether. . . . But even if you won't come, I want your niece to come with me & Joanna." Joan Agnew, Ruskin's cousin.

10. TC attempted a visit to Ruskin, 5 Oct.; he wrote, 11 Oct.: "Did not find Ruskin; but had a *scenic* kind of ride home by London Bridge. . . . Ruskin came to me next evg: friendly to a degree, and more serious and instructive than usual. . . . R's age is now 51" (TC's journal; privately owned).

TC TO JOHN A. CARLYLE

My dear Brother,—I have hardly any time; but must send you a word. Mary is gone to a little mild *luncheon* &c—party at the Ruskins'[1] (*express* came yesterday upon it): so that I have no writing resource but my own poor pencil and disobed*t* right-hand.

Mr Harding's Letter to John,[2] wh*h* we saw yesterday, appeared to me frank, sincere and abund*tly* kind: so that my feeling was, and is, there was still possible (or even *probable*) a *good* result there; *provided* John will vigorously bestir himself. With*t* that proviso it is evid*tly* up!—and indeed ought to be.[3]

My impress*n* is (tho' I don't like to advise on a thing still obscure to me) that John ought instantly to set ab*t* fairly *learning* what*r* is mysterious to him in "Book-k*g* by double Entry," and never rest at all till he is able to report himself ready for performing it![4] I sh*d* think that might be achieved with*t* struggle by a head and hand like John's.— It is true, or likely, he w*d* have to *give up* his pres*t* post as a preliminary; but ought not that too to be resolved upon & *done*? With*t* this of "Double Entry" at his fingers ends, he can never, as appears, get into any kind of Clerkship except his pres*t* kind, & is condemned to

TC-JAC, 13 Oct. MS: NLS 527.27. Hitherto unpbd.

1. Mary Aitken wrote to Lady Ashburton, 14 [Oct.]: "I spent the day at Denmark Hill yesterday and Mr Ruskin took his Cousin, a beautiful Irish girl and myself to the Theatre at night—I enjoyed it very much. They were all so kind and Ruskin shewed us his minerals and pictures in the afternoon" (MS: NLS Acc. 11388); Joan Agnew, Ruskin's cousin, and Constance Hilliard (1852–1915), the Irish girl; see 43:195.

2. Robert Palmer Harding, head of a prominent London accounting firm, Harding, Pullein, Whinney, & Gibbons. TC had been asking help from Frederic Chapman to find a position for his nephew John Aitken; presumably Chapman suggested the approach to Harding as he m., autumn 1870, Harding's da. Annie Marion (b. 1848). John A. Carlyle wrote, [27 Sept.]: "Chapman's letter with remarks on it arrived by our morning mail, & was at once given to John. . . . Tomorrow evening he hopes to send off to Mr Harding an answer to all the queries Chapman gives."

3. John Aitken wrote, 29 Sept., thanking TC for his help, and sending a copy of his letter of 28 Sept. to Harding; on that letter TC wrote: "absurd Letter altog*r*,—as by a person only half-awake" (MS: NLS 1775D.243), and on John Aitken's letter to himself, he wrote: "John Ait*kn's first* shot:—*a*ltog*r* a miss!"

4. John A. Carlyle sent, 20 Oct., a copy of John's second letter to Harding, in which he wrote: "I know the *theory* of B. by D. [balancing by double] Entry quite well; & even should I not at once be competent for a situation in your office, I w*d* gladly give up my situation here & devote a few weeks of my time to practicing B. by D. E. & I have not the least doubt but that I sh*d* then be able to undertake what work w*d* be required of me. . . . I am most anxious for a change of work, & sh*d* be very glad if you w*d* give me a trial for a few months in your office; & if you still thought me unsuited for my work . . . my prospects would not be at all injured by the trial" (MS: NLS 1775D.261). TC wrote on John A. Carlyle's letter: "John An's *second* shot (*to R* Harding): *better!*"

that for life!⁵ To *cut* with base Gordon & it,⁶ seems to me a thing not lamentable. — But Mary wrote all this & more to him yest*y*; I need not *repeat* it on
pres*t* terms. All I had to say was, that if he will *pull* heartily, some *tracing*
might still be in my power; & I calculate he w*d* or c*d get over the brae.* —

I am sleeping tolerably well here; but my *digestive* faculty, and consequ*tly*
my "spirits" &c &c do not improve. Y*r recipe* for "flatulence" was taken to the
Drugg*t*, and one *go* of it sucked up, some nights ago; but any relief it gave
seemed to be outweighed by its pain & derang*t* to the miserable ghost of a
"stomach": so that I durst not ag*n* try.⁷ — Plenty of people come ab*t* me, but
few to my mind.⁸ Thank Jean for writ*g*. Good be ever with you all.

Y*r* affect*e* — T. Carlyle

TC TO WILLIAM MACCALL

5 Cheyne Row, Chelsea
17 October 1870.

Dear Maccall,

I saw Chapman yesterday; he has in nothing changed his ideas about employing you in translation; but professes to have been held back not only by a
bad fit of Rheumatism &c, but also by the provoking fact that certain Woodcuts, indispensable for the Book you are to translate, lie at the moment unattainable in Paris across the Prussian line!¹ He certainly seemed to me to
intend and wish employing you in translation; but you must not be surprized
to find him now & then, so many are the Irons he has in the fire, a considerably unpunctual man of business. For the rest, he told me yesterday that his
common outlay for Translation is latterly almost £500 a year (suppose it were

5. John Aitken had been a clerk at the Commercial Bank in Dumfries for more than six
years.

6. Probably James Gordon (1809–84), listed in 1871 census as "Banker / Writer. J.P. and
Sheriff Substitute."

7. John replied, 20 Oct.: "I dont now take that acid mixture after meals, but in smaller
7 drop doses just before meals, & I find it does me good. After meals it made the bowels
sometimes very sore in doses of 15 drops." Druggist probably Charles Rowett Quiller
(1829–71), pharmacist, 15 Sloane Sq., Chelsea.

8. Mary Aitken wrote to Lady Ashburton, 14 [Oct.]: "[TC] sleeps very well and is in
good spirits about the victories of his own Prussians (He is *so* proud of them!); but he often
talks very sadly of the loneliness of his life, and he frets a good deal because his right hand
wont write for him any more. However I feel sure you would be satisfied that he is very
well, could you but look at him through a magic glass. The Froudes are still in Ireland; but
Woolner, Tyndall and Ruskin have been here since we came back — and little Mr Allingham
comes to walk with him about four times a week" (MS: NLS Acc. 11388).

TC-WM, 17 Oct. MS: Yale. Hitherto unpbd.

1. Paris was under siege by the Prussians from Sept. 1870 until Jan. 1871.

arithmetically but the half of that sum!); and I do believe he is convinced that *you* can do that Work for him probably better than any other man he has on his pay. My advice is, therefore: Patience and shuffle the Cards.

That message of Tait's[2] is surely a beautiful bit of munificence of some noble-hearted Friend who wishes, like Heaven, to do good in absolute silence that there be no danger of human admixture with it.

Believe me / Yours always sincerely, / T. Carlyle

TC TO CHARLES A. WARD

5 Cheyne Row, Chelsea,
20 October 1870

Dear Sir,

Accept many thanks from me for your beautiful Autumnal Gift,[1] which reminds me kindly of Pomona[2] in her Southern opulences; and has many grateful and pathetic meanings to me. As a mark of your continued regard, in the midst of such interruptions and long-continued absences, I greatly prize it: thankful to find that, amid this loud swift whirl, of personal business and public event, you still keep me in mind; — that is certainly a precious fact! —

It is long months, almost years, since I have personally seen you,[3] though you have once or twice left a card. No doubt your modest reserve is much to be applauded; but I regret withal that it issues in this manner. Cannot you, at present, while Countinghouse operations are slack, come, some day, and let us have a walk once more together?[4] I go out daily with that object at, or rather before 3 p.m.; and seldom have company (if, as is rather the exceptional case, I have company at all) which I should prefer to yours. — —

You seem to me, if you will allow me to say so, much in error in regard to King William and his Germans. I believe King William to be a just and pious as well as valiant man, and that his "Prayers to God" are not a thing of Cant, but of profound Sincerity[5] — in a word, that he is one of the few living Euro-

---

2. Presumably Robert Scott Tait; message untraced.

TC-CAW, 20 Oct. MS: NLS Acc. 9086. Hitherto unpbd.
1. Charles Augustus Ward wrote, 18 Oct.: "Kindly accept a box of Elva plums." Ward regularly sent TC gifts of autumn fruit; see 46:113.
2. Pomona, Roman goddess of fruit trees and orchards.
3. They probably last met Sept. 1867; see 45:48.
4. Ward replied, 21 Oct.: "Your kind letter gives me much pleasure. I do not know however whether your walk takes place on Sundays but at any rate I shall *perhaps* next Sunday look in upon you at 2.30. . . . I can come no day but Sunday at the *hour* specified. The Counting House with me makes inexorable demands on attention."
5. Ward wrote, 18 Oct.: "This French War touches the wine business. However that is not much matter when men's hearths are trampled on to gratify the lust of Kings & their

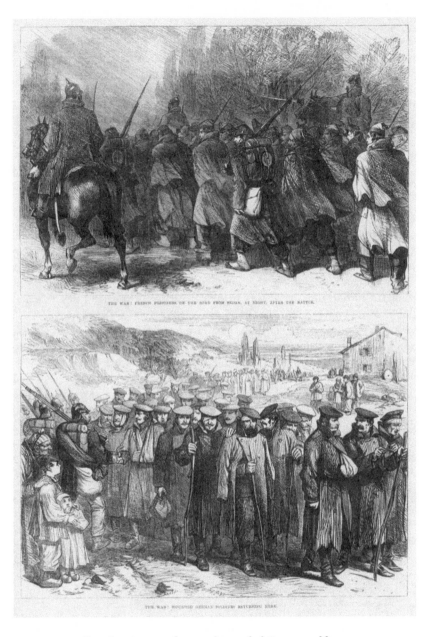

French prisoners of war and wounded German soldiers
Illustrated London News, 1 October 1870

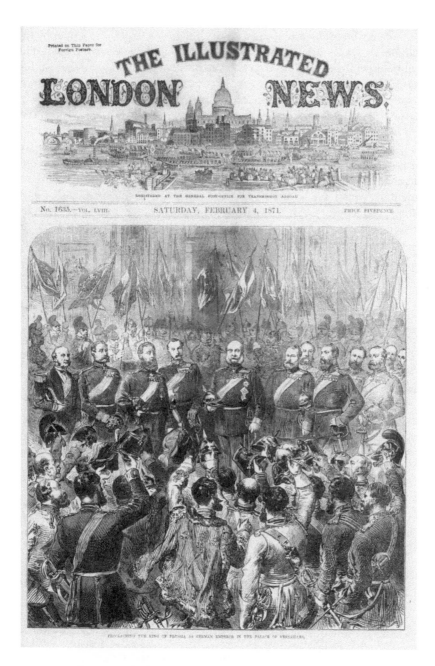

Proclamation of Wilhelm I as emperor of Germany, 18 January 1871
Illustrated London News, 4 February 1871

pean men who retain a real *capacity* of "praying to God"; other men by the million, in all Countries, I should rather recommend to cease that operation. I also differ altogether as to the probable results of French "National Enthusiasm" in defending Paris &c &c.[6] No 'Enthusiasm' except that of bitterly *irritated* VANITY,—terribly wounded and irritated, and justly deserving to be so,—is visible to me among these poor mountebank French; who surely are behaving, at this moment, in as mad a way, or a madder, than any Nation ever did. This "praying" King William has actually his foot upon the throat of France, and can if he please, in spite of all Europe, as matters now stand, slit anarchic France to ribbons, and reduce Paris to a Cinder, if such were his intention, which it is far from being. In brief, I believe magnanimous, pious, strong, and modest Germany is henceforth to be Queen of the Continent, instead of vain, vapouring, impious and mischievous France;[7] which I take to be the most blessed event in European politics I have witnessed in my time.[8]

Come and let us talk about these things, and others.

Yours ever truly,
T. Carlyle

TC TO JOHN A. CARLYLE

5 Cheyne Row, Chelsea
28 October 1870

Dear Brother,

Late last night came the enclosed Letter from one whom you knew well,[1] and will be interested to hear of at first hand again. Poor fellow, his helpless

---

Viziers. That psalm-singing old William full of prayer & gratitude is amusing in his familiar intimacy with the Secret Immensity who made him & the Universe. [His] god however is Moloch a god of slush & abattoirs." Wilhelm (William) Friedrich Ludwig von Hohenzollern (1797–1888), king of Prussia, 1861–88, and 1st German Emperor, 1871–88.

6. Following the defeat of the French army at Sedan, 2 Sept., popular pressure forced the creation of a provisional Republican government in Paris on 4 Sept. The Prussians laid siege to Paris from 18 Sept., but Parisians refused to accept that the war had been lost, and the authorities were reluctant to negotiate peace terms. See also TC to JAF, 7 Sept.

7. The *Illustrated London News* included contrasting post-Sedan pictures of lines of French prisoners of war and lines of wounded German soldiers; see 84.

8. See also TC to the editor of the *Times*, 11 Nov. For Wilhelm's proclamation in Versailles, 18 Jan. 1871, as emperor of a united Germany, see 85.

TC-JAC, 28 Oct. MS: NLS 527.29. Hitherto unpbd.

1. Baron Charles d'Eichthal, with whom John A. Carlyle had stayed in 1827–28; see 5:134 and 277. D'Eichthal wrote, 24 Oct.: "It is, I know, a great liberty I take in taking into my hand the pen to molest you for a few moments. . . . I had the great satisfaction to be introduced to you (in Chelsea) by your excellent brother who had been my friend for many years. It was in 1834 I was introduced to you . . . I have not forgotten your & Mrs Carlyle's

English, his eager strng-feelings[2] go quite into my heart & awaken many sad, beautifully sad & tender recollectns of what will return no more. His '1834' I think must be an error for 1835 or '6:[3] tell me if he is not the D'Eichtal whom Ann Cook used to introduce by the name of "*Dushty*"?[4] Ah me, Ah me!

Pray answer him, after good study, & in the very kindest terms you can. Tell him all that you think can be interesting to him about me, and what has come to me & gone from me;[5] to yourself also he will be a pathetic phenomenon. If my right hand were still my own I would send him a line direct,[6]— Poor good soul, do you think that blotch over the mention of his only Son 'near of Paris'[7] is the stain of a tear or not. It has repeated itself twice in the folds of the Letter, & you have it as we had it.

Not a word more; I have had six Proofs to correct, and am tired and belated.

Yours ever[8]

---

very kind hospitality,—I have since that remote period very frequently been reading in your books & admiring the . . . genius of the man who has always been sympathizing with German literature and with the spirit of our dear Country land." D'Eichthal wrote that he had read TC's letter in the *Weimar Gazette* (see TC to [TW], early Oct.) in which TC expressed his "sympathy for the German cause & for our welfare in coming times. . . . I thought that an old friend, a very old admirer of your person and of your works, & old friend of your brother might be permitted to transit to you the expression of his true feelings of the highest esteem." D'Eichthal's last recorded contact with TC was Nov. 1860; see 37:44.

2. Thus in MS.

3. D'Eichthal first visited Cheyne Row late 1835 or early 1836 (see 8:277), and again June 1851 (see 26:91–92).

4. Ann Cook from Annandale, the Carlyles' servant Oct. 1835–June 1837 (see 8:228), had coined the nickname "Dushtie." John A. Carlyle replied, [31 Oct.]: "No doubt he is the 'Dushty' of old times, He was always very kind & warm-hearted towards me when staying at Munich."

5. John replied: "I sent him a long answer in the kindest possible terms. . . . I asked him to write again."

6. Word repeated with a line over it at turn of page.

7. D'Eichthal wrote: "My only son [Karl] an Officer in the Bavarian 1st cavalry regiment . . . is now standing near of Paris. May God protect him." John replied: "Those stains . . . I too think, are from tears shed when he came to mention his only son." For illustrations in relation to the Prussian army's siege of Paris, *Illustrated London News* supplement, 3 Dec., see 88.

8. Signature cut away.

THE SIEGE OF PARIS: PRUSSIAN TROOPS AT VILLE D'AVRAY HASTENING TO RESIST A SORTIE.

THE SIEGE OF PARIS: THE 50TH PRUSSIAN REGIMENT RETURNING FROM THE FIGHT.

Scenes of the Paris siege
Illustrated London News, 3 December 1870

TC TO JOHN FORSTER

5 Cheyne Row Chelsea
2 Novr 1870.

Dear Forster,

We had a pleasant word from you not long ago[1] and are beginning to long much to hear of you again. If it is not increase of Cough or other ill-luck that delays you?[2] That would indeed be bad; but I hope it is only the miserable weather; or perhaps, which would be luckiest of all, increased application to the pious *Task*[3] you mentioned. In any case, pray send us a little world;—and especially say when you are coming home.

I myself have, as it were, no history at all since you left. I *sleep* pretty well, indeed almost like a common fellow-creature; but the dark muddy weather presses heavy on me in the multitudinous uproar of this London element; which has grown to have so little, or so altogether sad a meaning to me: I feel heavy-laden, stupid, inarticulate, to a degree. I am much bothered with insignificant Letters (which I mostly burn unanswered) about the German-French quarrel &c; and altogether as much disgusted as yourself at this maudlin wail about the woes of France,—a Country that to me more resembles a *Cartouche* upon the Gallows[4] than a Christ upon Calvary. If I were not so dark and stupid, nay, perhaps, if I still had my own *right hand*, I should write something on that monstrous ignorance of the English Nation about European history and the nature of Facts in this world; but perhaps it is better not. I all along calculate Bismarck will do his own way; and I calculate he can do it in spite, not of poor broken-backed France alone, but of all Europe combined at this particular juncture.[5]

TC-JF, 2 Nov. MS: FC. Hitherto unpbd.

1. Forster wrote from Steyne Hotel, Worthing, Sussex, 23 Oct.; both he and Eliza had been ill, but "things are a little better with us now. . . . And the first thought we have, with our more cheerful outlook, is of the dear good Carlyle and the kind little Mary."

2. Forster replied, 4 Nov.: "I have a hard struggle with my cough, notwithstanding the kindly south and west winds . . . on the whole I have got on fairly well here. . . . So well, that I do not think we will turn homeward till the holiday is fairly out—which will be exactly three weeks from today."

3. Forster was "at intervals turning to the inexpressively sorrowful task of looking over poor Dickens's letters. Whether anything will come of it I do not know" (23 Oct.). He was to publish *The Life of Charles Dickens* in 1872–74.

4. Forster wrote, 23 Oct.: "What a wonderful line the papers are taking about the poor . . . martyr France—as if another Calvary were come." "Cartouche" was the nickname of Louis Dominique Garthausen (1693–1721), French bandit and highwayman, eventually executed in Paris.

5. John A. Carlyle wrote, 23 Oct.: "a few clear & faithful words from you, who know the subject so thoroughly, might do much good"; Jean Aitken also wrote, 23 Oct., urging TC to write on the Franco-Prussian War: "It could not fail to do good." Forster replied, 4 Nov.,

There are plenty of people returning to Town. I myself have, or might have, Company enough; in general it avails me little, and Silence ever gloomy is about as good. The other day Browning[6] came athwart me in the Green Park; fresh from France and two months in Normandy; looking very brisk; and, I fear, getting nothing but damage out of my loud Germanism and me till our road parted. Froude professes to be coming home immediately; & to be, for the last ten days, stormstaid in Kerry where the winds have risen, and the waters are out.[7] Gladstone's grand Article in the *Edinr Review*[8] has not yet come in my way; perhaps I could not read it if it did; but might at least, as a matter of conscience, try,

Adieu dear Forster. Thank that wise Lady for discovering that I am not without Religion,[9] which truly is not a common outfit among human creatures at this time; nor capable of being recognised in others by those who have none of their own. Tell me that She is well and that you are well, and come soon home to us both of you. Mary salutes withal in her choicest manner.

Yours ever affectionately

T. Carlyle

---

that Mary Aitken's clear handwriting was "more than recompense for temporary loss of your own—above all what an inducement to turn off, in so choice a hand, that paper I very earnestly would have you put forth on what is now going forward in the world!" TC wrote a long letter to the *Times* on the war (pbd. 18 Nov.); see TC to ed. of *Times*, 11 Nov. Mary Aitken wrote to Lady Ashburton, [19 Nov.]: "He was busy writing the Letter to *The Times* or he would have gone to you at Stanhope St on Friday [11 Nov.] (I wrote it to dictation—his hand being so troublesome to him). He is very well just now and says he is so glad to have relieved his conscience by writing this Letter" (MS: NLS Acc. 11388).

6. Robert Browning.

7. Froude and family spent the summer in Kerry, SW Ireland; see TC to JAC, 14 May. The *Times* reported, 24 Oct., from Dublin, 21 Oct.: "A fierce gale has blown along the eastern coast since Tuesday night, and its effects have been felt with great severity in the Irish Channel."

8. William Gladstone, "Germany, France, and England; A Review of Emile de Laveleye's *La Prusse et l'Autriche depuis Sadowa* (Paris, 1870) and *Correspondence respecting the Negotiations Preliminary to the War* . . . (1870)," *Edinburgh Review* 132 (Oct. 1870): 554–93. Forster sent the article, 4 Nov., writing at length and highly satirically about it.

9. Eliza Forster had "been reading certain books here without intermission, and makes a discovery which *I* (in confidence) could have communicated to her before—that 'Mr Carlyle is the most religious of writers'" (JF to TC, 23 Oct.).

Sir,—It is probably an amiable trait of human nature, this cheap pity and newspaper lamentation over fallen and afflicted France;[1] but it seems to me a very idle, dangerous, and misguided feeling, as applied to the cession of Alsace and Lorraine by France to her German conquerors, and argues, on the part of England, a most profound ignorance as to the mutual history of France and Germany, and the conduct of France towards that country, for long centuries back.[2] The question for the Germans, in this crisis, is not one of "magnanimity," of "heroic pity and forgiveness to a fallen foe," but of solid prudence and practical consideration what the fallen foe will, in all likelihood, do when once on his feet again. Written on her memory, in a dismally instructive manner, Germany has an experience of 400 years on this point; of which on the English memory, if it ever was recorded there, there is now little or no trace visible.

TC-editor of the *Times*, 11 Nov. Pbd: *Times*, 18 Nov., headed "MR. CARLYLE ON THE WAR"; "Thomas Carlyle über den Krieg," *Beilage zur Allgemeinen Zeitung* (Augsburg), 23 Nov. inc; *Letters on the War between Germany and France* (Trübner & Co., 1871) 115–30; Carlyle, *Critical and Miscellaneous Essays* (people's edn.) (1872) 12:242–51; Carlyle, Works 30:49–59; for later publications, see Tarr 434. Text: *Times*.

1. TC presumably referred mainly to reports and commentary in print newspapers. The *Times* editorial discussing TC's letter was itself thoughtfully critical (see below). The *Illustrated London News*, summer 1870–spring 1871, published many illustrations of the war. As France lost, they possibly became more sympathetic to France than to Prussia; pictures of French prisoners of war were balanced by pictures of wounded Prussian soldiers (see 84); they showed the bombardment of Strasbourg (see 78 and 79). In Jan. 1871 they illustrated a burial of French soldiers (see 120), and, showing the privations late in the siege of Paris, the Bois de Boulogne with all its trees cut (see 147), the last oxen in Paris (see 138), a market for cats' and dogs' flesh (see *ILN*, 28 Jan. 1871), and the killing of an elephant for food (see 146). Henry Richard Vizetelly (1820–94; *ODNB*) and his son Ernest Alfred Vizetelly (1853–1922) became war correspondents for the *Illustrated London News* during the siege of Paris, sending sketches and reports by balloon post.

2. TC is somewhat disingenuous in equating France and Germany; France had been a nation state for seven hundred years, but the German-speaking part of Europe was still a loose federation of semi-autonomous states. At the death of Louis the Pious (778–840), son of Charlemagne (742–814), who had ruled most of Europe, his territory was divided, by the Treaty of Verdun (843), between his three surviving sons, Lothair (795–855), Louis (ca. 804–76), and Charles (823–77); the central area was given to Lothar, and thus known as Lotharingia (which was to become Lothringen, German name for Lorraine). This area has been fought over by its independent rulers, the dukes of Burgundy, the kings of France, and the Holy Roman Emperors and their German successors, many times since. Alsace was part of the Holy Roman Empire until annexed by France in 1639; Lorraine was more or less independent, although occupied by France 1641–48, 1670–97, and then from 1766; both were annexed, 1871, after being captured by Bismarck's Prussian forces, 1870. For maps of France and of Alsace and Lorraine, 12th to 16th centuries, see 92.

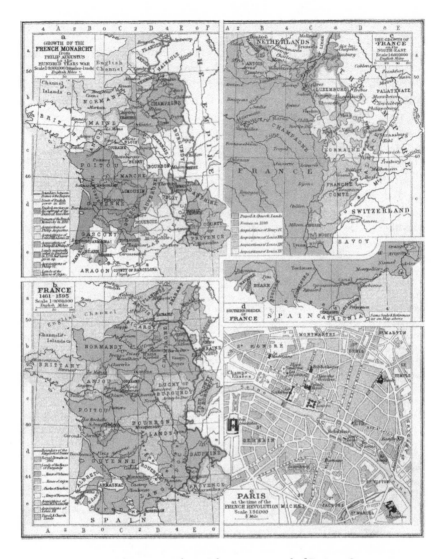

Maps of France, 12th to 16th centuries, and of Paris, 1789
Ramsay Muir, *A New School Atlas of Modern History* (1921)

Does any of us know, for instance, with the least precision, or in fact know at all, the reciprocal procedures, the mutual history, as we call it, of Louis XI. and Kaiser Max?[3] Max in his old age put down, in chivalrous, allegorical, or emblematic style, a wonderful record of these things, the *Weisse König* ("White King," as he called himself; "Red King," or perhaps "Black," being Louis's adumbrative title), adding many fine engravings by the best artist of his time:[4] for the sake of these prints, here and there an English collector may possess a copy of the book; but I doubt if any Englishman has ever read it, or could, for want of other reading on the subject, understand any part of it. Old Louis's quarrel with the Chief of Germany at that time was not unlike this last one of a younger Louis: "You accursed Head of Germany, you have been prospering in the world lately, and I not; have at you, then, with fire and sword!"[5] But it ended more successfully for old Louis and his French than I hope the present quarrel will. The end, at that time, was that opulent, noble Burgundy did not get re-united to her old Teutonic mother, but to France, her grasping step-mother, and remains French to this day.[6]

Max's grandson and successor, Charles V.,[7] was hardly luckier than Max in his road-companion and contemporary French King. Francis I.,[8] not content with France for a kingdom, began by trying to be elected German Kaiser as well,[9] and never could completely digest his disappointment in that fine enterprise. He smoothed his young face, however, swore eternal friendship

3. Louis XI (1423–83), king of France, 1461–83, called Louis the Prudent, and Maximilian I (1459–1519), King of the Romans, 1486–1519, Holy Roman Emperor, 1508–19.

4. Maximilian I, *Der Weisskunig* [the White King], a thinly disguised biography in the form of a chivalric novel, written partly by Maximilian and partly by his secretary, Marx Treitzsauerwein (d. 1527), 1506–16; it was not intended for commercial publication but finally pbd. Vienna, 1775. The French king is called the Blue King in the work. It was illustrated with 251 woodcuts by Hans Burgkmair (1473–1531) and Leonhard Beck (ca. 1480–1542), Augsburg, 1514–16. See also 46:178.

5. Louis Napoleon, president of France, 1848–52, Emperor Napoleon III, 1852–70; after the defeat at Sedan, he lost all power and was known as Louis Napoleon. TC attributed to Louis Napoleon words that were very similar to Bismarck's remarks in his speech, 30 Sept. 1862: "Prussia must concentrate its strength . . . our frontiers have been ill-designed for a healthy body politic. It is not by speeches and votes of the majority that the great questions of our period will be settled . . . but by iron and blood."

6. Burgundy, an area originally comprising the southern half of Lotharingia, by the 16th century was an independent duchy covering large and scattered territories, some, such as the Low Countries, within the Holy Roman Empire, and some owing allegiance to France.

7. Charles V (1500–58), duke of Burgundy, 1506–56, king of Spain, 1516–56, king of Sicily, 1516–56, king of Naples, 1516–54, and Holy Roman Emperor, 1519–56.

8. Francis I (1494–1547), king of France, 1515–47.

9. The position of Holy Roman Emperor was an elected one; when Maximilian I died in 1519 there were three contenders: Charles, duke of Burgundy, lord of the Netherlands, and king of Spain; Francis I, king of France; and Henry VIII, king of England.

with the young Charles who had beaten him; and, a few months after, had egged on the poor little Duke of Bouillon,[10] the Reich's and Charles's vassal, to refuse homage in that quarter, and was in hot war with Charles. The rest of his earthly existence was a perpetual haggle of broken treaties, and ever-recurring war and injury with Charles V.—a series, withal, of intrusive interferences with Germany, and every German trouble that arose, to the worsening and widening of them all, not to the closing or healing of any one. A terrible journey these two had together, and a terrible time they made out for Germany between them, and for France too, though not by any means in a like degree. The exact deserts of his most Christian Majesty Francis I. in covenanting with Sultan Soliman[11]—that is to say, in letting loose the then quasi-infernal roaring-lion of a Turk (*then* in the height of his sanguinary fury and fanaticism, not sunk to *caput mortuum* [worthless remains] and a torpid nuisance as now) upon Christiandom and the German Empire, I do not pretend to state. It seems to me, no modern imagination can conceive this atrocity of the most Christian King, or how it harassed and haunted with incessant terror the Christian nations for the two centuries ensuing.[12] Richelieu's[13] trade again was twofold: first, what everybody must acknowledge was a great and legitimate one, that of coercing and drilling into obedience to their own Sovereign the vassals of the Crown of France; and secondly, that of plundering, weakening, thwarting, and in all ways tormenting the German Empire.[14] "He protected Protestantism there." Yes, and steadily persecuted his own Huguenots, bombarded his own Rochelle,[15] and in Germany kept up a 30-years' war,

10. The control of the duchy of Bouillon (in present-day Belgium) was apparently disputed between brothers Erard de la Marck (1472–1538), prince-bishop of Liège, 1506–38, and Robert II de la Marck (1465–1536); the duchy was part of the Holy Roman Empire, owing allegiance to Charles V, but at various times allied itself with France.

11. Sulieman (1494–1566), known as Sulieman the Magnificent, sultan of the Ottoman Empire, 1520–66.

12. France was the first country in Europe to establish formal relations with the Ottoman Empire; seen at the time as sacrilegious, the pact lasted intermittently until 1798. The Ottoman Empire and the Holy Roman Empire continually fought over areas of eastern Europe, particularly Hungary.

13. Armand Jean du Plessis (1585–1642), duc de Richelieu and Fronsac, French cleric and politician; cardinal from 1622, chief minister of state from 1624.

14. TC's "German Empire" was the Holy Roman Empire. Richelieu's domestic policy was to restrain the power of the nobility and make France into a strong and centralized state; his foreign policy was to resist the power of the Habsburg dynasty, which ruled most of the rest of Europe (including the Holy Roman Empire).

15. Protestants in France (Huguenots) had been granted religious toleration by the Edict of Nantes, 1598, and had become an increasingly powerful faction in French politics; Richelieu ordered the army to lay siege to their stronghold of La Rochelle; and despite the help of Charles I (1600–49; *ODNB*), king of England, Scotland, and Ireland, 1625–49, the city fell, 1628; religious toleration continued, but their political rights were withdrawn.

cherishing diligently the last embers of it till Germany were burnt to utter ruin;[16] no nation ever nearer absolute ruin than unhappy Germany then was. An unblessed Richelieu for Germany; nor a blessed for France either, if we look to the ulterior issues, and distinguish the solid from the specious in the fortune of the nations. No French ruler, not even Napoleon I.,[17] was a feller or crueller enemy to Germany, or half so pernicious to it (to its very *soul* as well as to its body); and Germany had done him no injury that I know of, except that of existing beside him.

Of Louis XIV.'s four grand plunderings and incendiarisms of Europe[18]— for no real reason but his own ambition and desire to snatch his neighbour's goods—of all this we of this age have now, if any, an altogether faint and placid remembrance, and our feelings on it differ greatly from those that animated our poor forefathers in the time of William III. and Queen Anne.[19] Of Bellisle and Louis XV.'s fine scheme to cut Germany into four little kingdoms, and have them dance and fence to the piping of Versailles,[20] I do not speak; for to France herself this latter fine scheme brought its own reward: loss of America, loss of India,[21] disgrace and discomfiture in all quarters of the

---

16. The Thirty-Years' War (1618–48) in the rest of Europe was already under way when Richelieu came to power. Initially a war between the various Protestant and Catholic states within the Holy Roman Empire, sparked off by the Emperor's attempts to impose Catholicism on all his domains, it gradually embraced most of Europe, resulting in catastrophic destruction, famine, and disease, and about eight million deaths.

17. Napoleon Bonaparte (1769–1821), 1st consul, 1799, emperor of France, 1804–14 and 1815.

18. Louis XIV (1638–1715), king of France, 1641–1715; his main wars were the War of Devolution, 1667–68, the Franco-Dutch War, 1672–78, the War of the League of Augsburg, 1688–97, and the War of the Spanish Succession, 1701–14; see Carlyle, *Works* 12: 288, 295, and 307.

19. William III (1650–1702; *ODNB*), prince of Orange, 1650–1702, king of England, Scotland, and Ireland, 1689–1702, known as William of Orange; Anne (1665–1714; *ODNB*), queen of England, Scotland, and Ireland, 1702–7, queen of Great Britain and Ireland, 1702–14.

20. Charles Louis Auguste Fouquet (1684–1761), duc de Belle-Isle, French general and statesman; Louis XV (1710–74), king of France, 1715–74. Belle-Isle was sent to Germany, 1741, on a diplomatic mission to assist in the election of the next emperor, and the political reorganization of the empire; see Carlyle, *Works* 15:66–71. Versailles was the chief residence of the French kings and representative of their political power; as such the proclamation of Wilhelm I (see below) as emperor of Germany there (18 Jan. 1871; see 85) was particularly pointed.

21. France claimed huge territories in America, but had few colonists; the French and Indian War, 1754–63, against the British, resulted in the dissolution of New France, with Canada going to Britain and Louisiana to Spain. The French East India Company established various ports in India during the 17th century but were involved in regular wars with the British and the Dutch and were left with little territory by the end of the 18th century.

world—Advent, in fine, of the FRENCH REVOLUTION, embarcation on the shoreless chaos on which ill-fated France still drifts and tumbles.[22]

The Revolution and Napoleon I., and their treatment of Germany, are still in the memory of men and newspapers; but that was not by any means, as idle men and newspapers seem to think, the first of Germany's sufferings from France; it was the last of a very long series of such—*the last but one*, let us rather say; and hope that *this* now going on as "Siege of Paris,"[23] as widespread empire of bloodshed, anarchy, delirium, and mendacity, the fruit of France's latest *"marche à Berlin"*[24] may be the last! No nation ever had so bad a neighbour as Germany has had in France for the last 400 years; bad in all manner of ways; insolent, rapacious, insatiable, unappeasable, continually aggressive.

And now, furthermore, in all history there is no insolent, unjust neighbour that ever got so complete, instantaneous, and ignominious a smashing down as France has now got from Germany. Germany, after 400 years of ill-usage, and generally ill-fortune, from that neighbour, has had at last the great happiness to see its enemy fairly down in this manner; and Germany, I do clearly believe, would be a foolish nation not to think of raising up some secure boundary-fence between herself and such a neighbour now that she has the chance.

There is no law of nature that I know of, no Heaven's Act of Parliament, whereby France, alone of terrestrial beings, shall not restore any portion of her plundered goods when the owners they were wrenched from have an opportunity upon them. To nobody, except to France herself for the moment, can it be credible that there is such a law of nature. Alsace and Lorraine were not got, either of them, in so divine a manner as to render that a probability. The cunning of Richelieu, the grandiose long-sword of Louis XIV., these are the only titles of France to those German countries. Richelieu screwed them loose (and, by happy accident, there was a Turenne,[25] as General, got screwed along with them;—Turenne, I think, was mainly German by blood and temper, had not Francis I. egged on his ancestor, the little Duke of Bouillon, in

22. French Revolution, 1789–95; since then France had had seven different types of government: The French Directory, 1795–99, French Consulate (Republic), 1799–1804, and First French Empire, 1804–14, both under Napoleon; restoration of the Bourbon monarchy, 1814–30; July revolution and installation of Orleans monarchy, 1830–48; Second French Republic, 1848–51, and Second French Empire, 1851–70, both under Louis Napoleon.

23. Siege of Paris, 19 Sept. 1870–28 Jan. 1871; see TC to WM, 17 Oct.; for further illustrations connected to the siege, see 88, 138, and 146.

24. Napoleon took Berlin, 1806, during the War of the Fourth Coalition, 1806–7.

25. Henri de La Tour d'Auvergne (1611–75), vicomte de Turenne, French marshal general.

the way we saw, and gradually *made* him French);[26] Louis le Grand, with his Turenne as supreme of modern Generals, managed the rest of the operation, except indeed, I should say, the burning of the Palatinate, from Heidelberg Palace steadily downwards, into black ruin; which Turenne would not do sufficiently, and which Louis had to get done by another.[27] There was also a good deal of extortionate law-practice, what we may fairly call violently sharp Attorneyism, put in use. The great Louis's *"Chambres de Réunion,"* Metz Chamber, Brissac Chamber,[28] were once of high infamy, and much complained of, here in England, and everywhere else beyond the Rhine. The Grand Louis, except by sublime gesture, ironically polite, made no answer. He styled himself on his very coins (écu of 1687, say the Medallists), *Excelsus super omnes Gentes Dominus* [God is above all people], but it is certain attorneyism of the worst sort was one of his instruments in this conquest of Alsace. Nay, as to Strasburg, it was not even attorneyism, much less a long-sword, that did the feat; it was a housebreaker's *jemmy* [short crowbar] on the part of the *Grand Monarque.* Strasburg was got in time of profound peace by bribing the magistrates to do treason, on his part, and admit his garrison one night.[29] Nor as to Metz la Pucelle, nor any of these Three Bishoprics,[30] was it force of war that brought them over to France; rather it was force of fraudulent pawnbroking. King Henry II. (year 1552) got these places—Protestants. applying to him in their extreme need—as we may say, in the way of pledge. Henri entered there with banners spread and drums beating, "solely in defence of German lib-

26. Turenne was the second son of Henri de La Tour d'Auvergne (1555–1623), vicomte de Turenne and duc de Bouillon (through his first wife, Charlotte de La Marck), marshal of France, and his second wife Elisabeth (1577–1642), countess of Orange-Nassau; they were a prominent French Huguenot family.

27. The Palatinate, an electorate of the Holy Roman Emperor adjacent to Alsace and Lorraine (see 92 [top right of map]); Turenne had implemented Louis' policies, and devastated the Palatinate countryside, 1674. In 1689 Louis again instituted a scorched-earth policy in the Palatinate, including the burning of Heidelberg; by this time Turenne was dead, so it was carried out by René de Froulay (1648–1725), Comte de Tessé, soldier and diplomat.

28. "Chambres de Réunion" were French courts established by Louis XIV in the early 1680s to legitimize his annexing of territories that he claimed were originally French. Metz, the original capital of Lotharingia, had been absorbed as a free independent city into the Holy Roman Empire, annexed by France, 1552. Brissac [Breisach], city on the Rhine in the Holy Roman Empire, occupied by France, 1648, returned to the Empire 1697, retaken by France 1703, given back to the Empire 1714. For Metz and Brissac's positions, see 92 (top right of map).

29. Strasbourg, a free independent city in the Holy Roman Empire; peacefully annexed by Louis XIV's forces after negotiation with the citizens, 30 Sept. 1681.

30. Metz was known as Metz la Pucelle [the maiden], because it had fought so often to retain its freedom, and was regarded as impregnable. Under France it became capital of the Three Bishoprics, Metz, Toul, and Verdun; see Carlyle, *Works* 12:215–17.

erty, as God shall witness;"[31] did nothing for Protestantism or German liberty (German liberty managing rapidly to help itself in this instance); and then, like a brazen-faced, unjust pawnbroker, refused to give the places back,— had ancient rights over them, extremely indubitable to him, and could not give them back. And never yet, by any pressure or persuasion, would. The great Charles V., Protestantism itself now supporting, endeavoured, with his utmost energy and to the very cracking of his heart, to compel him, but could not.[32] The present Hohenzollern King,[33] a modest and pacific man in comparison, could and has. I believe it to be perfectly just, rational, and wise that Germany should take these countries home with her from her unexampled campaign, and, by well fortifying her own old *Wasgau* ("Vosges"), Hundsrück (*Dog's-back*),[34] Three Bishoprics, and other military strengths, secure herself in time coming against French visits.

The French complain dreadfully of threatened "loss of honour;" and lamentable bystanders plead earnestly, "Don't dishonour France; leave poor France's honour bright." But will it save the *honour* of France to refuse paying for the glass she has voluntarily broken in her neighbour's windows? The attack upon the windows was her dishonour. Signally disgraceful to any nation was her late assault on Germany; equally signal has been the ignominy of its execution on the part of France. The honour of France can be saved only by the deep repentance of France, and by the serious determination never to do so again—to do the reverse of so for ever henceforth. In that way may the honour of France again gradually brighten to the height of its old splendour, far beyond the *First* Napoleonic, much more the *Third*, or any recent sort, and offer again to our voluntary love and grateful estimation all the fine and graceful qualities Nature has implanted in the French. For the present, I must say, France looks more and more delirious, miserable, blamable, pitiable, and even contemptible. She refuses to see the facts that are lying palpable before her face, and the penalties she has brought upon herself. A France scattered into anarchic ruin, without recognizable head;[35] *head*, or chief, indistinguishable from *feet*, or rabble; Ministers flying up in balloons[36] ballasted with noth-

31. Henri II (1519–59), king of France, 1547–59; he had joined with Protestant princes within the Empire fighting for religious freedom against the Emperor Charles V's imposition of Catholicism, and was given the Three Bishoprics in the Treaty of Chambord, 1552.

32. By the Peace of Augsburg, 1555, Charles V accepted that the individual rulers of each state within the Empire could choose Catholicism or Lutheranism (no other form of Protestantism was permitted); he then tried to reclaim the Three Bishoprics, but failed.

33. Wilhelm, king of Prussia, 1861–88; proclaimed emperor of Germany at Versailles, 18 Jan. 1871.

34. Wasgau / Vosges and Hunsrück are low mountain ranges in the Rhineland-Palatinate.

35. Napoleon III (Louis Napoleon) lost power after being taken prisoner, Sept. 1870; see TC to JAF, 7 Sept. and above.

36. Léon Gambetta (1838–82), French statesman, minister of the interior in the Govern-

ing but outrageous public lies, proclamations of victories that were creatures of the fancy; a Government subsisting altogether on mendacity, willing that horrid bloodshed should continue and increase rather than that *they*, beautiful Republican creatures, should cease to have the guidance of it: I know not when or where there was seen a nation so covering itself with *dis*honour. If, among this multitude of sympathetic bystanders, France have any true friend, his advice to France would be,—To abandon all that, and never to resume it more. France really ought to know that "refuges of lies" were long ago discovered to lead down only to the Gates of Death Eternal,[37] and to be forbidden to all creatures!—that the one hope for France is to recognize the facts which have come to her, and that they came withal by invitation of her own: how she—a mass of gilded, proudly varnished anarchy—has wilfully insulted and defied to mortal duel a neighbour not anarchic, but still in a quietly human, sober, and governed state, and has prospered accordingly. Prospered as an array of sanguinary mountebanks *versus* a Macedonian phalanx[38] must needs do;—and now lies smitten down into hideous wreck and impotence, testifying to gods and men what extent of rottenness, anarchy, and hidden vileness lay in her. That the inexorable fact is, she has left herself without resource or power of resisting the victorious Germans; and that her wisdom will be to take that fact into her astonished mind; to know that, howsoever hateful, said fact is inexorable, and will have to be complied with,—the *sooner* at the cheaper rate. It is a hard lesson to vainglorious France; but France, we hope, has still in it veracity and probity enough to accept fact as an evidently adamantine entity, which will not brook resistance without penalty, and is unalterable by the very gods.

The quantity of conscious mendacity that France, official and other, has perpetrated latterly, especially since July last,[39] is something wonderful and fearful. And, alas, perhaps even that is small compared to the self-delusion and *un*conscious mendacity long prevalent among the French; which is of still feller and more poisonous quality, though unrecognized for poison. To me, at times, the mournfullest symptom in France is the figure its "men of genius," its highest literary speakers, who should be prophets and seers to it, make at present, and, indeed, for a generation back have been making. It is evidently their belief that new celestial wisdom is radiating out of France upon all the other overshadowed nations; that France is the new Mount Zion of the uni-

---

ment of National Defence; he flew in a balloon over the German lines to Tours, Oct. 1870, to organize army recruitment. Balloons were also used for communications during the siege of Paris; the *Illustrated London News* noted when their sketches were sent by balloon post.

37. See Isa. 28:17–18.

38. A Macedonian phalanx was an infantry formation devised by Philip II (382–336 BCE), king of Macedon; the Prussian army used similar tactics.

39. France declared war on Prussia, July 1870; see TC to JF, 26 Aug.

verse; and that all this sad, sordid, semi-delirious, and, in good part, *infernal* stuff which French Literature has been preaching to us for the last 50 years is a veritable new Gospel out of Heaven, pregnant with blessedness for all the sons of men. Alas, one does understand that France made her Great Revolution; uttered her tremendous doom's voice against a world of human shams, proclaiming, as with the great Last Trumpet,[40] that shams should be no more. I often call that a celestial-infernal phenomenon—the most memorable in our world for a thousand years; on the whole, a transcendant revolt against the Devil and his works (since shams are *all* and sundry of the Devil, and poisonous and unendurable to man). For that we all infinitely love and honour France. And truly all nations are now busy enough copying France in regard to that! From side to side of the civilized world there is, in a manner, nothing noticeable but the whole world in deep and dismally chaotic Insurrection against Shams, determination to have done with shams *coûte qu'il coûte* [cost what it may]. Indispensable that battle, however ugly. Well done, we may say to all that; for it is the preliminary to everything; but, alas, all that is not yet victory; it is but half the battle, and the much easier half. The infinitely harder half, which is the equally or the still more indispensable, is that of achieving, instead of the abolished shams which were of the Devil, the practicable realities which should be veritable and of God. That *first* half of the battle, I rejoice to see, is now safe, can now never cease except in victory; but the further stage of it, I also see, must be under better presidency than that of France, or *it* will for ever prove impossible. The German race, not the Gaelic [possibly in error for Gallic], are now to be protagonist in that immense world-drama; and from them I expect better issues. Worse we cannot well have. France, with a deadlift effort, now of 81 years,[41] has accomplished under this head, for herself or for the world, nothing, or even less,—in strict arithmetic, *zero* with *minus* quantities. Her prophets prophesy a vain thing; her people rove in darkness and have wandered far astray.

Such prophets and such a people;—who in the way of deception and self-deception have carried it far! "Given up to strong delusion," as the Scripture says; till, at last, the lie seems to them the very truth.[42] And now, in their strangling crisis and extreme need, they appear to have no resource but self-deception still, and quasi-heroic gasconade. They do believe it to be heroic. They believe that they are the "Christ of Nations;"[43] an innocent godlike people, suffering for the sins of all nations, with an eye to redeem us

40. See 1 Cor. 15:52.

41. The French Revolution began in 1789.

42. See 2 Thess. 2:11; see also Carlyle, *Works* 5:241, where TC uses the phrase about Napoleon.

43. "Christ of Nations"; phrase sometimes used of republican France.

all:—let us hope that this of the "Christ of Nations! is the *non plus ultra* of the thing. I wish they would inquire whether there might not be a "*Cartouche*[44] of Nations," fully as likely as a "Christ of Nations" in our time! Cartouche had many gallant qualities, was much admired, and much pitied in his sufferings, and had many fine ladies begging locks of his hair while the inexorable, indispensable gibbet was preparing. But in the end there was no salvation for Cartouche. Better he should obey the heavy-handed Teutsch police-officer, who has him by the windpipe in such frightful manner; give up part of his stolen goods; altogether cease to be a Cartouche, and try to become again a Chevalier Bayard[45] under improved conditions, and a blessing and beautiful benefit to all his neighbours, instead of too much the reverse, as now! Clear it is, at any rate, singular as it may seem to France, all Europe does *not* come to the rescue, in gratitude for the heavenly "illumination" it is getting from France: nor could all Europe, if it did, at this moment prevent that awful Chancellor[46] from having his own way. Metz and the boundary-fence, I reckon, will be dreadfully hard to get out of that Chancellor's hands again.

A hundred years ago there was in England the liveliest desire, and at one time an actual effort and hope, to recover Alsace and Lorraine from the French. Lord Carteret, called afterwards Lord Granville[47] (no ancestor, in any sense, of his now honourable synonym),[48] thought by some to be, with the one exception of Lord Chatham,[49] the wisest Foreign Secretary we ever had, and especially the "one Secretary that ever spoke German or understood German matters at all," had set his heart on this very object, and had fair prospects of achieving it, had not our poor dear Duke of Newcastle suddenly peddled him out of it, and even out of office altogether,[50] into sullen disgust

44. "Cartouche" was the nickname of the French highwayman Louis Dominique Garthausen; see TC to JF, 2 Nov.

45. Pierre Terrail (ca. 1473–1524), seigneur de Bayard, French soldier known as "le chevalier sans peur et sans reproche" or "le bon chevalier"; the epitome of chivalry. His entire life was spent in military service for France.

46. Bismarck; TC uses "awful" in its original sense of "full of awe."

47. John Carteret (1690–1763; *ODNB*), 2d Baron Carteret, 2d Earl Granville (peerage of Great Britain [i.e., until 1800]), diplomat and politician. During the War of the Austrian Succession 1740–48, Britain was allied with Austria against Prussia and France; Carteret wanted to make peace with Prussia and ally all Europe against France, but the British parliament would not agree, and Carteret resigned as Secretary of State, 1744; see Carlyle, *Works* 15:439–42.

48. George Leveson-Gower (1815–91; *ODNB*), 2d Earl Granville (U.K. peerage [i.e., after the act of union of the United Kingdom of Great Britain and Ireland, 1 Jan. 1801]), politician; foreign sec., 1870–74.

49. William Pitt (1708–78; *ODNB*), 1st earl of Chatham, known as Pitt the elder, politician.

50. Thomas Pelham-Holles (1693–1768; *ODNB*), duke of Newcastle, politician; foreign

(and too much of *wine* withal, says Walpole[51]), and into total oblivion by his nation, which, except Chatham, has none such to remember. That Bismark, and Germany along with him, should now at this propitious juncture make a like demand is no surprise to me. After such provocation, and after such a victory, the resolution does seem rational, just, and even modest. And considering all that has occurred since that memorable cataclysm at Sedan,[52] I could reckon it creditable to the sense and moderation of Count Bismark that he stands steadily by this; demanding nothing more, resolute to take nothing less, and advancing with a slow calmness towards it by the eligiblest roads. The "Siege of Paris," which looks like the hugest and most hideous farce-tragedy ever played under this sun, Bismark evidently hopes will never need to come to uttermost bombardment, to million-fold death by hunger, or the kindling of Paris and its carpentries and asphalt streets by shells and red-hot balls into a sea of fire. Diligent, day by day, seem those Prussians, never resting nor too much hasting; well knowing the proverb, "Slow fire makes sweet malt." I believe Bismark will get his Alsace and what he wants of Lorraine; and likewise that it will do him, and us, and all the world, and even France itself by and by, a great deal of good. Anarchic France gets her first stern lesson there (a terribly drastic dose of physic to sick France!); and well will it be for her if she can learn her lesson honestly. If she cannot, she will get another, and ever another; learnt the lesson must be.

Considerable misconception as to Herr von Bismark is still prevalent in England. The English newspapers, nearly all of them, seem to me to be only getting towards a true knowledge of Bismarck,[53] but not yet got to it. The standing likeness, circulating everywhere ten years ago, of demented Bismark and his ditto King to Strafford and Charles I. *versus* our Long Parliament[54] (*as* like as Macedon to Monmouth,[55] and not liker) has now vanished from the

minister, 1730–39, defense minister, 1739–48, foreign minister, 1748–54, prime minister, 1754–56. He believed, rightly, that during the War of the Austrian Succession Prussia would maintain her alliance with France.

51. Horace Walpole (1717–97), 4th earl of Orford, author and politician. In his *Memoires of the Last Ten Years of the Reign of George II*, 2 vols. (1822) he wrote: "It is difficult to say whether [Carteret] was oftener intoxicated by wine or ambition: in fits of the former, he showed contempt for every body; in rants of the latter, for truth" (*Memoires* 1:146).

52. Battle of Sedan; see TC to JAF, 7 Sept.

53. Thus in text; otherwise the *Times* used the spelling "Bismark" throughout.

54. In 1862 the Prussian Diet refused to authorize increased funding for the army. Bismarck first found a legal loophole allowing the 1861 budget to continue, and then in 1863 King Wilhelm dissolved the Diet. Thomas Wentworth (1593–1641; *ODNB*), 1st earl of Strafford, chief minister to Charles I. The English Long Parliament, called in 1640 to raise money for troops, not only refused Charles money, it passed death warrants for Charles's advisors, including Strafford, and passed laws saying it could only be dissolved by its own members.

55. See *Henry V* 4.7. The character Fluellen draws a comparison between Monmouth

earth, no whisper of it ever to be heard more. That pathetic Niobe of Denmark, reft violently of her children[56] (which were stolen children, and were dreadfully ill-nursed by Niobe Denmark), is also nearly gone, and will go altogether so soon as knowledge of the matter is had. Bismark, as I read him, is not a person of "Napoleonic" ideas, but of ideas quite superior to Napoleonic; shows no invincible "lust of territory," nor is tormented with "vulgar ambition," &c; but has aims very far beyond that sphere; and in fact seems to me to be striving with strong faculty, by patient, grand, and successful steps, towards an object beneficial to Germans and to all other men. That noble, patient, deep, pious, and solid Germany should be at length welded into a nation and become Queen of the Continent, instead of vapouring, vainglorious, gesticulating, quarrelsome, restless, and over-sensitive France, seems to me the hopefullest public fact that has occurred in my time.

I remain, Sir, yours truly,

Chelsea, Nov. 11.   T. CARLYLE[57]

TC TO JOHN A. CARLYLE

5 Cheyne Row Chelsea
12 November 1870.

My dear Brother,

Thanks for your several Notes, punctually sent me as if there had been no deficiency of answer on my part. I return poor Alick's Letter: his response to

---

(Wales), birthplace of Henry V (1386–1422; *ODNB*), king of England, and Macedon (Greece), birthplace of Alexander the Great (356–323 BCE), because both have rivers, with salmon in them; and between Henry and Alexander as both being great war leaders who betrayed their best friends; the phrase had come to be used to mock unlikely comparisons; e.g., the *Times*, 10 Oct. 1861.

56. Niobe, character in Greek mythology whose children were taken from her; the duchies of Schleswig and Holstein, which had been mainly under Danish overlordship, were annexed by Prussia in the second Schleswig-Holstein war, 1864.

57. The *Times*'s editorial, printed on the same page as TC's letter, praised TC's past record as a historian: "He has illuminated the course of the past. His genius has brought home to the intelligence of the dullest the movements of nations. With an amount of labour that would have killed the energy of a mind of less vitality he has set forth the real life of many leaders of men." TC was "qualified by natural power and past study" to comment on the current "struggle between France and Germany." But, the editorial warned, his letter "should be read with an intelligent independence. We cannot dishonor a master by forgetting his spirit in accepting his words. We must add our conviction . . . that when the letter has been read, and read again, the last judgement of the sincere student will be a repudiation of its conclusions; we may even add, a protest against the method of its reasoning." It continued with a detailed critical analysis of the content of TC's letter; see *Times*, 18 Nov.

TC-JAC, 12 Nov. MS: NLS 527.30. Quot: Froude, *Carlyle* 4:404.

yr gift[1] is of rugged type; but honourably well meant, indeed does him credit, poor fellow, & you must not be checked by it in any future generosities to him or his. Far otherwise! His word about the poor Child's death,[2] "Dinna haud your puir wee boy's hands," is pungently affecting. *Sunt lachrymae rerum* [There are tears for things].[3] — D'Eichtal's Letter I also return.[4] Poor good *Dushty*, laden with many recollections, many sorrows & anxieties, was really interesting to me. If you ever again do want a real German Tour, it is evident, München would be the place for you. I also enclose a Letter from Emerson;[5] which you will return.

Poor Mary and I have had a terrible ten days, —properly a Much Ado about Nothing— It concerned only that projected Letter to the Newspapers about Germany;[6] with a *right* hand valid, & nerves in order, I might have done the Letter in a day; but, with nerves all the contrary & *no* right hand of my own, it was all different. Poor Mary had endless patience, endless assiduity, wrote like a little fairy, sharp as a needle, & all that could be expected of her, when it came to writing; and before that, there was such hauling down of old forgotten books, *Köhlers, Büschings Reichshistories, Biographies*[7] &c &c, in all which my little Helpmate was nimble and unwearied. A terrible hurly-burly, worsened, too, by interruptions very provoking now & then. In fine, we have got the Letter done, & fairly sent away last night to the Times where it will probably appear next week. I do not reckon it a good Letter; but it expresses, in a probably *too* emphatic way, what my convictions are; & is a clearance to my own conscience in that matter, whether it do good or not, whether it *be* good or not. I expect it may be considerably an astonishment to many half & half people, lamenters for the French; but am myself on any terms, right thankful to have done with it, and there an end. Of course I will take care that you see it, if you yourself don't take care. It cannot come before Tuesday

1. Both TC and John A. Carlyle sent money to their relatives in Canada; see TC to JAC, 26 May; this particular gift unidentified further.

2. Thomas Alexander Carlyle (March 1869–Sept. 1870), first son of their nephew Thomas. Jean Aitken wrote, 23 Oct.: "I am sorry to hear of the death of poor Nephew Tom's little child. . . . I can truly feel for them in their trouble having known what it is to be 'in bitterness for a first born.'" Jean's first child had died aged two.

3. Cf. *Aeneid* 1:462

4. See TC to JAC, 28 Oct. John wrote, 8 Nov.: "The enclosed came from [Charles d'] Eichtal late last night, & it gives me some details of the household I used to know when I first went to Munich."

5. Of 15 Oct.

6. Cf. Shakespeare's play, *Much Ado About Nothing*; TC's letter to the *Times*, 11 Nov., pbd. 18 Nov.

7. Johann David Köhler (1684–1755), historian; see 29:73 and 174; Anton Friedrich Büsching (1724–93), geographer and historian; see 29:335; TC used their books while writing *Frederick* (TC's copies; HCC).

or Wednesday next of *Times*; and, withal, it is possible the able Editor there may refuse it,[8] tho' I think that not likely; & in such case, I shall have to select some other able Gentleman. Sterlings Lecture,[9] so soon as I had time to read it, which was only this morning, turns out to be extremely good, clear, flowing & decisive. If you happen to see him anywhere, you can tell him so.

Jeans account of the Harding matter, taken in conjunction with Liverpool Jim's elucidations,[10] which Mary gives me, has acquired a certain sad air of likelihood & reminds me uneasily of Chapmans florid style of promising & undertaking. I have not seen him in these last ten days; but probably shall next week. By a little Note of Forster's which Mary will enclose if she can find it, you will see that the negociation is not yet extinct;[11] nor shall it quite go out till I see it hopeless.

For above a week past we have had fogs,[12] some of them of the blackest ever known to me,—very cold dismal dark & depressing. Happily a light East wind has sprung up, with authentic hoar frost & winter cold, two days ago; & we have now the Sun authentically shining, & one of the brightest winter days.— I always forgot to tell you of the great good I have got of those yellow French shoes.[13] I had heels put on them & walk on those sleek pavements with them morning & evening,—with many silent thanks to Vichy & you.

Adieu, dear Brother, there must not be too much of this babble; and many things lie waiting for me of which this was but the *first*. Thank Jean very

8. John Thadeus Delane (1817–79; *ODNB*), editor of the *Times* 1841–77. The editorial was critical of the letter; see TC to ed. of *Times*, 11 Nov.

9. Sir William Stirling Maxwell delivered a lecture, "The Fall of the Two Empires—1814 and 1870," to the Stirling School of Arts, 8 Nov.; the first part was pbd. in the *Edinburgh Evening Courant*, 10 Nov.; John sent TC, 13 Nov., a clipping from the *Scotsman* that contained the second part of the lecture.

10. Jean Aitken wrote, 30 Oct.: "Mr Harding gives no sign as yet. From yr still looking hopefully at the matter we all try to hope that something may come of it after all; but altogther from the tone of Mr H's letter, I feel almost certain that he wants a 'ready made man' with more experience than Jack can possibly have got by his training in a Bank. . . . Jim tells me many of the young men who come into Mr H's office pay him a premium instead of *receiving* salary. I fear Mr H's letter will turn out to have been meant for a polite but quite final 'no.'"

11. Forster wrote, 8 Nov.: "I forgot . . . to ask you whether anything had been done further in the matter of your nephew and the Mr Harding proposals—and whether it is at all possible that *I* could capably do anything?"

12. The *Times* reported, 10 Nov.: "London and the districts for many miles round were enveloped yesterday in the blackest fog which has been experienced since the winter of 1868. . . . At noon the streets were darker than at night."

13. TC probably refers to the shoes he wore when visiting Edinburgh in early Sept., described by David Masson "a pair of easy shoes of a somewhat glaring buff colour . . . sufficiently remarkable" (David Masson, *Carlyle Personally and in His Writings* [1885] 118) and TC to JAC, 3 Sept. Presumably John gave them to TC when he was in Dumfries.

much for her two Letters; and don't discourage her to write what she likes to me.[14]

With love to all of you

Ever your affectionate
T. Carlyle

TC TO JOHN A. CARLYLE

5 Cheyne Row, Chelsea
16 Nov. 1870

My dear Brother,

You will find that immortal Letter to *The Times* in tomorrow's (Thursday's) Number.[1] We recd yesterday the Proof Slips, — not much misprinted (*points*, capitals &c considerably jumbled, but hardly above one real *error*). The Proofs were sent away by the 5 P.M. post; and this morning Delane's 3 Slips, which I had requested, were punctually delivered; — and so an *end* put to this unexpectedly extensive, and altogether paltry, botheration. No, not quite an end yet!; on view of the Slips, I thought the *Letter* itself had appeared in *The Times* of this morning; & sent out for a Copy on your behalf; — Copy came; but there is nothing of the Letter there! Letter could not appear until tomorrow it would seem? Well, by way of *making* an *end*, I do now enclose to you one of my 3 Copies of the thing (which you need not destroy); — said Copy you can at once read, and the *Newspaper* No in question, if you care for it to send to Alick or the like, can be found, I suppose, in some neighbouring Shop. Enough on that thrice-beggarly concern, — enough and ten times more than enough. — —

Has Harding's Letter actually come to you? I doubt, not yet; but it appears to me, there is good ground for actually expecting it soon. Frederick Chapman, on Monday last, without waiting till I put any question to him, volunteered to assure me that "Harding, who had just left him, meant to write, or perhaps even had written, that very night; appointing John's time of coming; not till after Xmas &c &c." In short, if the matter is not still essentially certain,

14. Jean wrote, 7 Nov.: "I here inclose a note wch I had written to you last Sunday [30 Oct.] the Dr offered to enclose a note to you wch is a modest hint that he wants to see what I am saying. I read over the note & he immediately said 'I must not send it.'" She continued: "as I hate misteries I will send it on today. I see no harm there can be in telling you what we consider to be the cause of Mr Harding's delay in giving John an answer."

TC-JAC, 16 Nov. MS: NLS 527.31. Hitherto unpbd.

1. The letter appeared in the *Times* on Fri., 18 Nov. John A. Carlyle replied, 18 Nov.: "Your letter, I think, will do a great deal of good, both in this country & in Germany. . . . John [Aitken] first read the letter aloud at breakfast downstairs; & then in the evening I had to read it again to the whole household."

Fred*k* Chapman is not only "flaccid" but altogether *made* of gas; and that I really do not suppose him to be.

Adieu, dear Brother: I am partly out of sleep; agitated in nerves (dreadfully easy to agitate, poor Soul!) with those *Times* botherations &c &c; and ought to go out, and profit by the nice frosty sunshine there is

With kind Love to all.

Ever your Affectionate,
T. Carlyle

TC TO UNIDENTIFIED CORRESPONDENT

5 Cheyne Row, Chelsea,
17 Nov. 1870

Dear Sir,

I received by your kindness Mr Greeley['s][1] Book;[2] and have read most part of it, —all the *biographical part*, in its widest sense;—and leave it with a great deal of regard for Mr Greeley.

Much obliged by this polite procedure on your part, I return the Book; and remain,

Dear Sir,

Yours sincerely / T. Carlyle.

MARY AITKEN TO LADY ASHBURTON

5 Cheyne Row / Saturday
[19 Nov. 1870].

My dear Lady,

I am to write a little line today to thank you for the very welcome present of Game which we received yesterday. My Uncle sends you very many thanks for it and for your kind thought of him. He was very sorry not to see you again before you left London. He was busy writing the Letter to *The Times* or he would have gone to you at Stanhope St[1] on Friday (I wrote it to dictation— his hand being so troublesome to him). He is very well just now and says he is so glad to have relieved his conscience by writing this Letter. Nearly all his

TC-UC, 17 Nov. MS: NLS Acc. 9775. Hitherto unpbd.

1. Omitted in MS.

2. Horace Greeley (1811–72), American journalist and politician, founder of the *New York Tribune*; the book was probably Greeley's *Recollections of a Busy Life* (New York, 1868).

MA-Lady A, [19 Nov.]. MS: NLS Acc. 11388. Hitherto unpbd.

1. Lady Ashburton's London house.

Admirers & non admirers seem at once on reading his Letter yesterday to have made a rush to their writing tables & the consequence has been quite a shower of Notes—one side blaming & the other thanking him—which we have been much amused to read.

He sends his Love to you and I am

Yours gratefully & affectly / Mary Carlyle Aitken

TC TO CHARLES KINGSLEY

5 Cheyne Row, Chelsea
22 Nov. 1870.

Dear Kingsley,

Thanks for your kind Note of this morning. It is very serious and true; and does for the poor old lonesome heart what one man can do for another. My comfort as to Germany, in this waste pother of the English Newspapers, is that their talk and their scribble can do nothing in the matter; that the matter depends on Bismarck and the strength of the German heart and arm,—which I always trust will not be wanting in this great Crisis for Europe and for all the world. Considering our Newspapers merely, I rather doubt the *Letter* may have done ill, not good; but it has relieved my own poor conscience somewhat; and that is enough.

The raging whirlwind of delirium that is rising about Russia[1] in these "Best Instructors" fills me with amazement. Determined to fight Russia when we have no Army; but one commanded by Cardwell[2] and Lord Elcho;[3] and for the stupid old brute of a Turk,[4] who, if he had a wise friend in the world, would be advised by him to put himself under the protection and discipline of Russia, as the one chance he had left. The Russians would improve him, poor old

---

TC-CK, 22 Nov. MS: NLS 1796.117. Quot: Patrick Waddington, *Turgenev and England* (1980) 164. Charles Kingsley (1819–77; *ODNB*), clergyman and author.

1. The Russian minister of foreign affairs, Prince Alexander Gorchakov (1798–1883), issued a diplomatic note, 9 Nov., declaring Russia's intention to renounce the stipulation of the Treaty of Paris, 30 March 1856, which prevented all countries from maintaining naval forces and arsenals on the Black Sea. The *Times* warned, 19 Nov., that if Russia "proceeds to fortify the shores of the Black Sea . . . our duty . . . will be painful, but it seems also clear and unavoidable."

2. Edward Cardwell (1813–86; *ODNB*), sec. of state for war in Gladstone's cabinet 1868–74, responsible for re-organization and drastic cutting of military expenditure.

3. Francis Richard Charteris (1818–1914; see 43:201), Lord Elcho, M.P. for East Lothian, was highly critical of Cardwell's military reforms.

4. Abdülaziz (1830–76), 32d sultan of the Ottoman Empire 1861–76; during the 1860s Turkey had very good relations with both Britain and France, but after the Prussian defeat of France, 1871, Turkey turned towards Russia for friendship.

Wretch,—and if they "improved him off the face of the Earth,"[5] it would perhaps be best of all.

Come and see me when you are in town; let me not have seen you for the last time.[6]

Yours always, with many regards,
T. Carlyle

TC TO JOHN A. CARLYLE

5 Cheyne Row Chelsea
26 Nov 1870

My dear Brother,

Before our last post go I must send you a little word though our stock of news is intrinsically small. *Dushty's* Letter[1] came on Thursday afternoon when I was out. I did not get it read till after dinner: rather an indistinct kind of *Dushty* to me, though an affectionate & honest,—dwelling a good deal on the Newspaper rumours & clamours. Stirlings Letter to *The Times* I did not see or hear of;[2] send me a copy, if you have one and I will return it after reading. His Pamphlet-Lecture on *The Two Napoleons*[3] came to us in that shape (a yellow little Pamphlet price 6*d*) above a week ago; and indeed I had already laid by a copy of the thing in slips.

We have had quite a daily jumble of Letters all week on that German-French Affair,—making truly a much ado about nothing; for none of these

5. TC's prediction for the future of African-Americans in "Shooting Niagara: and After?"; see "Critical and Miscellaneous Essays," Carlyle, *Works* 30:7.

6. Kingsley currently lived in Chester as a canon in the cathedral. The last recorded contact between TC and Kingsley was in Sept. 1866; see 44:52 and 59.

TC-JAC, 26 Nov. Addr: The Hill / Dumfries / N.B. PM: London, 26 Nov. 1870. MS: NLS 527.32. Quot: A. Carlyle, *NL* 2:272–73; Wilson, *Carlyle* 6:222; Patrick Waddington, *Turgenev and England* (1980) 164.

1. Charles d'Eichthal (Dushty); see TC to JAC, 28 Oct. John A. Carlyle wrote, 13 Nov.: "I have also written again to Eichthal, postage being only threepence per half ounce to Munich, & he being I know fond of letters"; he sent TC d'Eichthal's next letter, which largely concerned newspaper articles about the war.

2. TC has misunderstood John A. Carlyle's letter of 23 Nov., in which he quoted a letter to himself from Stirling: "I have a letter today . . . from Sir W*m* Stirling Maxwell, in which he speaks of sending copies in pamphlet form to you & me—'much elated by your Brother's approbation. I have read his *Times* letter with more than my usual pleasure. I am daily startled & vexed by the kind of arguments by w*h* people try to extenuate the follies & crimes w*h* have brought France to the pass she is now in & in which—grave as it is—I scarcely hope to see her learn any wisdom.'"

3. Stirling Maxwell's lecture (see TC to JAC, 12 Nov.) was pbd. as *The Fall of Two Empires—1814 and 1870. An Address to the Stirling School of Art* (Stirling, 1870).

missives throws any new light whatever on the matter—and I, for one, am heartily wearied of the process; every day I hope it has ceased; but on the morrow it begins again. "Noisy inanity"[4] that is not a pleasant element to live in; but, by the nature of the case, it must, and will, sink to zero very soon. This morning, for example, I had no Letters but one,—evidently from a raving madman; indeed one of the strangest Letters (adoring or otherwise) that I ever received.[5] For your medical, philological & philosophical study, you get a copy of it by the Book Post this day. Yesterday Mary, I believe, dispatched you a considerable lot of these noisy-inane Epistles. Today you get a selection from the remainder; and that I hope will be finis to this small affair. I have not answered, even by a word, above some 3 of them; those written in the German character I cd not even read, nor need you, to whom the character is familiar, make any report of them, unless (what I don't expect) there be some small particle of practicality involved in so much vapour.[6]

A more important bit of intelligence is, that John's Affair will now be settled, as Yes or No, in a very few days; thanks to Forster chiefly, who has returned yesterday, & will, in the course of next week, have a few minute's articulate speech with Mr Harding,[7] and bring a clear answer from him I have no doubt; which surely will be welcome to us all, whatever it may be! Privately, I have little or no doubt, nor have had, the business is intrinsically safe; but it is very tantalizing to have nothing human or intelligible to report upon it for so long.

Turguénief[8] was here yesterday & walked with me in Hyde Park,— unaltered, or altered for the better, plumper, taller, more stalwart than ever; only his head a little greyer. He was excellent company while we walked to-

4. See Carlyle, *On Heroes* 192.

5. Probably Peter Baines; Jean Aitken wrote, [11 Dec.]: "That 'Madmans' letter w*ch* you sent this day fortnight signed Peter Baines I thought might possibly be by a gealic Clergymans son of that name who lived next door to us in Comely Bank. There were 8 Miss Bains & one brother named Peter. This 'Peter' like his 'honourable synonume' is a Clergyman. . . . I am inclined to think they are one & the same 'Peter' '*but A ken nought about it*.'" Jean stayed with TC and JWC, 21 Comely Bank, Edinburgh, from 5 Dec. 1827 (see 4:294) until they moved to Craigenputtoch, late May 1828. Neither the Baineses nor the Carlyles were listed in the Edinburgh PO Directories of the time. They were possibly the children of Andrew Baines, minister of the United Presbyterian Church in Dunbar, E. Lothian, who fell ill, June 1827, and might have retired with family to a rented house next door to the Carlyles. Otherwise unidentified. "[G]ealic," i.e., Gaelic, presumably indicated the father was from a Gaelic-speaking area of Scotland (mainly the W coast and the Western Isles).

6. John replied, 27 Nov.: "I have read your German letters, & find none of them worth reporting. No doubt the Times letter would stir up the whole of Germany with feelings of real gratitude, but only the shallowest of Germans would find outlet for long letter on the subject."

7. For John Aitken's hope of getting work with Robert Harding, see TC to JAC, 13 Oct.; for Forster's note, see TC to JAC, 12 Nov.

8. Ivan Turgenev.

gether; talking about English Literature (his disappointment with our *recentiores* [moderns], our Brownings, Tennysons Thackerays Dickenses, —nay our Byrons & Shelleys),[9] and giving experiences about the starting of the War in Baden.[10] The sight of him is interesting to me; though it awakens the saddest memories.[11] He talks of being here for 5 or 6 weeks;—intent chiefly on making some acquaintance with real English Literature. Froude is to have an Article on "Progress" next *Fraser*;[12] which you will find worth reading, though it is rather straggly and incondite, not at the bottom of the matter at all.[13] He expected, when I saw him, that the Russian matter[14] was blowing by, which, unless Bedlam has broken loose among us, one would fain hope. My last bit of news was very sad: the death of good Thomas Spedding,[15]—a great shock & surprise to me the last time I met Froude. James Spedding's stoically mournful little Note on the subject (which please return when you have read it)[16] was lying for me when I had parted from Froude and come in from my walk. Another true and valued Friend of mine, whom you, I think hardly knew, I have also lost, poor Foxton, near Rhyader in Wales;[17] sudden and sad, which has equally affected me. Out of my own kindred, I had not two Friends in the world who were so valuable to me. Alas, Alas.

Here is enough, dear Brother. Thank Jean for what she wrote to me, which

9. Robert Browning, Alfred Tennyson, William Makepeace Thackeray (1811–63; *ODNB*), Charles Dickens, George Gordon (1788–1824; *ODNB*), Lord Byron, and Percy Bysshe Shelley (1792–1822; *ODNB*).

10. Turgenev had been living in Baden-Baden, a spa town in SW Germany on the border with France, in the household of his friend Pauline Viardot (1821–1910), French opera singer; when the war began they moved to England for a while.

11. TC and JWC both read and enjoyed Turgenev's *Scènes de la vie russe* (Paris, 1858) in July 1858; see 34:5, 9, 10, and 47.

12. J. A. Froude, "On Progress," *Fraser's Magazine* (Dec. 1870): 671–90.

13. John A. Carlyle replied, 7 Dec.: "Froude's article is well-meant & true, & one wishes 'more power to his elbow.'"

14. See TC to CK, 22 Nov.

15. Thomas Story Spedding d. 21 Nov.

16. See TC to JS, 27 Nov. John replied, 27 Nov.: "Thomas Spedding was well-known to me during the winter of 1859–60 wh he & his family spent in Edinr."

17. Frederick Joseph Foxton (ca. 1807–2 Nov. 70), lapsed Church of Wales clergyman, and writer. Foxton accompanied TC and Joseph Neuberg to Germany, Aug.–Sept. 1858, when TC was researching Frederick the Great's battlefields; see vol. 34. TC had not appreciated him much at the time; see 34:185; for JWC's opinion of him, see 34:127. He latterly did some proof-reading of *Frederick* for TC; see 45:68. Foxton's nephew, G. F. M. Foxton, wrote, 8 Nov., to give TC the news, and TC apparently wrote a letter of condolence to Foxton's widow, Catherine Foxton, as she replied, 21 Nov., thanking TC for his "true Sympathy, which has brought me great comfort. It was most kind your thinking of me, & writing to me in my great affliction. For a moment I felt overpowered, in receiving a note of consolation from you whom my dear husband held as The Foremost of all living men & whom he loved, with a reverential love such as he bore to no other human being."

I read with real pleasure. She writes always with sincerity, with a certain veracity which was peculiar to "Craw Jean"[18] when she was hardly 18 inches high and which is always worthy of much esteem.— Are you not thinking of some outrush in some direction (to London, Edinburgh &c) to break a little the gloomy season of the year? The dark short days fall heavy on one's spirits especially in solitude. The front room here, you know, is always empty.

Ever yr affectionate[19]

TC TO COUNT ALBRECHT VON BERNSTORFF

CHELSEA, *November 26th, 1870.*

Sir,

The telegram from my unknown friends at Hamburg[1] is naturally gratifying to me; and it acquires a double value from the cordial, polite, and emphatic manner in which your Excellency is pleased to concur in that matter. For me, the poor Service in question was, in a sense, compelled by the voice of my own Conscience, and if it can anywhere do any good at all, I am more than rewarded. My persuasion is, withal, that whatever our newspapers may say, the great body of solid English Opinion on the subject is in agreement with my own.

Be pleased to signify my thanks to those unknown friends at Hamburg, and to accept the still more hearty acknowledgments which I owe to Yourself, who have deigned to be their messenger on this occasion.

With many sincere respects, / I have the honour to be / Your Excellency's most obedient, / TH. CARLYLE.

18. Family nickname for Jean Aitken; see 3:414–15 and 44:110.
19. The letter is unsigned.

TC-A von B, 26 Nov. Pbd: *The Bernstorff Papers, the Life of Count Albrecht von Bernstorff*, ed. Dr. Karl Ringhoffer, 2 vols. (1908) 2:293–94. Count Albrecht von Bernstorff (1809–73), Prussian statesman, ambassador to Britain 1854–61 and 1862–73; for TC's earlier acquaintance with him, see 31:86.

1. Bernstorff sent TC a telegram from "unknown friends in Hamburg," 25 Nov., expressing gratitude to Carlyle for his defense of the German cause in his letter to the *Times*, 11 Nov. Karl Ringhoffer explained: "English public opinion had changed after the battle of Sedan [1–2 Sept. 1870]. The greater the successes of Germany, the stronger became the sympathy for France, so that it was sometimes almost impossible for Bernstorff to get the real facts into the Press. All the French newspaper inventions about 'German barbarism' were believed. The only real pleasure which Bernstorff experienced amid all the demonstrations for France was the genuine enthusiasm for German genius and the defence of the German cause, by the celebrated author, Carlyle. In the struggle against a world of prejudice, the old Germanic hero of the pen put forth his whole strength, and his words fell like a sharp sword stroke upon all the Frenchified English!" (*The Bernstorff Papers* 2:293).

TC TO JAMES SPEDDING

5 Cheyne Row—Chelsea
27 Nov: 1870

Dear Spedding

It was with a painful shock & a very sad surprise that I heard from Froude, that morning, what had befallen at Mirehouse, not many hours before, Froude & I walked out together discoursing naturally of Him that has left us; & at my return home your clear & stoically mournful note[1] lay waiting me, bringing home to one's very sight as it were, as well as to one's heart the Fact that had befallen—

We shall all soon follow Him, especially I soon must into that undiscovered country from which there is no return.[2] I feel to have lost one of the truest hearted Friends I ever had, the like of whom I had not now left, or shall ever see again; a man of sterling probity in its gentlest shape— Seldom have I known a human soul gravitating more steadily towards the true & good in all things Telos, Telos [the end]! Our thoughts on it ought rather to be silent; but may well be sad solemn & even devout. His end was peaceful & gentle even as his Life had been blameless quietly manful and noble.

I venture no word to the Bereaved ones[3] he has left, at Mirehouse.

Every one there may know that nothing that belonged to Him can have other than a Friend in me for the remainder of my time in this world

God bless you all—/ Dear Spedding yrs ever / T. Carlyle

TC-JS, 27 Nov. MS: John Spedding. Pbd: K. J. Fielding, "Carlyle and the Speddings: New Letters II," *Carlyle Newsletter* 8 (Spring 1987) 64–65 inc. Quot: *The Carlyle Encyclopedia*, ed. Mark Cumming (Madison, NJ, 2004) 437.

1. James Spedding wrote, ca. 23 Nov.: "You will be sorry to hear what I have to tell you. We have just heard that my Brother died last Monday night [21 Nov.], after a very short illness—with only intervals of pain in the chest—easily and suddenly at last. . . . I have seldom, if ever, seen seventy years worn apparently with less damage and distress. . . . It sometimes seems a pity that a man should die while his faculties are good, but that his faculties should fail *before* he dies is in my apprehension more to be deprecated."
2. Cf. *Hamlet* 3.1.
3. Spedding's wife and family.

TC TO WILLIAM BATHGATE

5 Cheyne Row, Chelsea
1 Decr 1870.

Dear Sir,

I have received your beautiful Volume,[1] and, along with it a Letter full of the friendliest feelings towards me, which, though immensely exaggerated, are evidently altogether loyal and sincere.[2] The sight of so much generous affection, of which I myself know well enough the beauty to the *Giver* as well as to the Receiver cannot be other than welcome to me; and I sincerely thank you for it, and beg from you a continuance of the same.

I have not yet had time to examine the Book as it deserves; but in glancing over it, I find the evident traces of a cultivated, meditative, intelligent and pious man, well worthy of further study; and I think I can assure you that this Copy will have its farther uses, and not be thrown away. I return you many thanks, and wish you heartily all manner of good.[3]

Yours sincerely, / T. Carlyle[4]

TC-WB, 1 Dec. MS: NLS 8992.147. Pbd: "The Rev. William Bathgate, D. D.," *The Worthies of the Evangelical Union* (1883) 434. William Bathgate (1820–79), liberal theologian, minister of Evangelical Union Church, Kilmarnock, 1847–60, and Winton Place Church, Kilmarnock, 1860–79.

1. William Bathgate, *Christ and Man* (1865); Bathgate wrote, 24 Nov.: "I muster courage to send the accompanying volume, — *Christ and Man*, — which indeed I may say has been lying beside me these five years waiting to be sent to you."

2. Bathgate wrote: "I cannot tell you how often during the past quarter of a century I have been on the eve of expressing to you my profound gratitude for good & mighty influence derived from your writings. Whenever I see anything new from your pen the old desire revives within me, & I dare say it is your recent letter on the Franco-German war which induces me to delay no longer the gratification of my own heart at least. No other writer, ancient or modern, outside the 'Sacred Scriptures,' has influenced my spiritual life & being as you have done."

3. TC apparently sent Bathgate a photograph with this letter, as Bathgate replied, 7 Dec.: "My heart will not rest till I have cordially thanked you both for your letter and photograph. The letter is everything I could have desired. It gladdens me very much to be thoroughly understood by you, and to have my sincere tribute sincerely accepted. / Many thanks for the likeness with the name written by the hand that has done so much honest work. I had other likenesses of you taken at earlier dates; but I will look all the oftener at this one, because the expression indicates at once the lateness of the evening and the heaviness of the long day's toil." For a photograph of TC taken around this time by John and Charles Watkins, see opp.

4. Apparently discussions had begun with Chapman about a new popular edn. of TC's *Works*; Forster wrote to Chapman, 29 Nov.: "I must call on you for an additional word about the popular Edn of the Carlyle." He then wrote to Chapman, [5 Dec.]: "I wish you particularly to *bring up here to me yourself tomorrow* (*Friday mrg*), the Specimen &c of Carlyle Popular Edn" (both typescripts, source unknown). It became the "People's Edition," 37 vols., 1871–74. Two more vols. were added, 1874 and 1878; see Tarr 450–51.

Thomas Carlyle, photograph by John and Charles Watkins
© National Portrait Gallery, London

MARY AITKEN TO META WELLMER

5 Cheyne Row, Chelsea,
3 Decr 1870.

Dear Miss Wellmer,

On Thursday night my Uncle (Mr Carlyle) received a long pleasant and kind Letter from you for which he bids me write to thank you. I daresay you will have forgotten about me; but I remember writing a Letter to you about 2 years ago[1] while you were in Paris & receiving a very interesting answer from you. I am to tell you also that after much delay your little Book on Nürnberg[2] came to him & he read it with much pleasure & interest and he says if you are again writing anything of the same kind, he would be very glad to see it.[3] He sends you many kind wishes; & best thanks for your kind remembrance of him.

Your picture of the people weeping and sobbing in the little Village Church is very touching. It is a barbarous cruel War indeed & one longs that it were all ended! Poor foolish France I am very sorry to think of her—not because, as my Uncle says, pity is cheap; but because she is so childish & foolish that she seems incapable of ever learning her Lesson & she has only fools & dishonest untruthful men for her Leaders—and her "Honor" which they are for ever prating about is lying sunk in the mud & has been indeed long before this last folly of theirs was begun. I think every Prussian must be proud to belong to such a country. We in England have little to be proud of in our Government at present! The principal men in it are vulgar wealthy money-loving people.

It is rather strange that you should have been living in Baron Usedom's family— My Uncle used to know him and I think has been in his House.[4]—

My Uncle is I think as well this year as he was last. He has had, like most people who have lived long in the world, to lose many Friends—especially within the last two years— I think he sometimes feels the world rather empty for him now, though he has still many kind and dear Friends left with him. I came from Scotland with him more than two years ago to pay a little visit to

MA-MW, 3 Dec. MS: NLS. Acc. 9207. Hitherto unpbd.

1. Mary Aitken wrote to Meta Wellmer at TC's request, Dec. 1868; see 45:207.

2. Unidentified further.

3. Wellmer sent them her article "Erinnerungen an Pater Hyacinthe [Memories of Father Hyacinthe]" (*Nürnberger Tagblatt*, 1869); Mary Aitken wrote thanking her, 5 Jan. 1871: "We read your article on Père Hyacinthe and thought it very good" (MS: NLS Acc. 9207). Charles Jean Marie Loyson (1827–1912), known as Père Hyacinthe, French preacher and theologian; his preaching against abuses in the Roman Catholic Church had led to his excommunication 1869.

4. Count Karl Georg Guido Ludwig von Usedom (1805–84), Prussian diplomat; see 34: 282; TC had visited him at his home in Carzitz, Isle of Rügen, 26 Aug.–3 Sept. 1858; see 34:159.

him and I have stayed with him ever since & am able to be useful to him in many little ways. I write nearly everything for him now at his dictation, as his hand shakes a good deal & makes writing very unpleasant for him. I am his sister's daughter and am 22 years old (but I may here tell you not only am I not a "Girl of the Period" but I have a great horror of that phenomenon!);[5] and I consider it a great privilege and honour to be with my Uncle. When you have time, he would like if you sent a photograph of yourself—I was going to send you one of his but he thinks you already have one—for he would like to see it.

I was able to read all your Letter; but though I like German better than any other study I ever had I am not able to read or write it fluently.

With my Uncle's best wishes and my own, Believe me Dear Madam

Yours very truly
Mary Carlyle Aitken[6]

TC TO JOHN A. CARLYLE

5 Cheyne Row, Chelsea
3 December 1870

My dear Brother

The clippings from the *Scotsman* which came yesterday morning are of very superior quality; and give a clear synopsis of the French-German History of Alsace and Lorraine,—Elsass & Lothrigen,[1] as I perceive the Germans have all begun to write them again. I cannot fancy what Edinburgh person can have written those two papers, or have known half so much of exact and clear on the subject.[2] Could it be Stirling of Kier,[3] do you imagine? I can guess

5. The phrase comes from "The Girl of the Period," *Saturday Review*, 14 March 1868, written by Eliza Lynn Linton (1822–98; *ODNB*), writer; initially a promoter of women's rights, she became an antifeminist campaigner. She wrote: "The girl of the period is a creature who dyes her hair and paints her face . . . whose sole idea of life is fun; whose sole aim is unbounded luxury; and whose dress is the chief object of such thought and intellect as she possesses" (2).

6. TC wrote in his journal, 4 Dec.: "My 75*th* Birthday, what a tho*t* to me!— Poor little Mary has with some fraction of her poor little income, found me a pretty bit of Birthday gift; an anonymous 'Scotch Lassie of my neighb*d*' contributes a bit of ornate stationary and things, and a German Fraül*n* [Wellmer] w*r* [writes] from Nürnberg, are what the living say to me—while the Silent Dead say so much!" (TC's journal; privately owned).

TC-JAC, 3 Dec. Addr: The Hill / Dumfries / N.B. PM: 3 Dec. 1870. MS: NLS 527.33. Hitherto unpbd.

1. Elsass, German for Alsace, and Lothringen, German for Lorraine; see TC to the editor of the *Times*, 11 Nov.

2. The *Scotsman* editorial, 24 Nov., began: "The question 'How did Alsace and Lorraine become French?' was touched upon, along with many other questions in Mr Carlyle's recent characteristic letter. But it admits of and merits a fuller and more categorical answer,

no other person of the least likelihood. I have stuck the papers together (drying on the Fender at this moment), and will lay them by in a compendious and labelled condition.

Wednesday last the Harding document did actually come to Dumfries; but does not seem to have been at once understood there: Jean seems rather to think it a polite flying-off into space than an actual performance of what Chapman has so long been promising in Mr Harding's name. There is no doubt John actually stands at the top of Mr Harding's List, and will be the first new Clerk he appoints, if John is ready.[4] He keeps, as I understand, 52 Clerks, promotes them according to merit & seniority and rises as high as £400 & £500. The question now is what John has to do in regard to "lying Jamie"[5] and his engagement first of all. I should be inclined to give *it* up with the least possible delay, and to prepare myself with *do* & with all industry in "Bookkeeping by Double Entry"[6] &c against the summons that is likely to come early in the year; but in regard to all that matter I must profess myself entirely incompetent to advise; and should think his best adviser, after those of you immediately about him might be his Brother James in Liverpool;[7] and I hope we shall see it all come right after all and before very long.

The rain of balderdash, foreign and domestic, in regard to that *Times* Letter has not ceased upon me yet; but I hope is now near ceasing. This morning there came nothing upon it; but last night, by the final post, I had no fewer than 16 pieces upon it (Mary counted them), mostly clippings from the Berlin

---

to attain which it is necessary to go a good way back and see how, first of all, Alsace and Lorraine became German." The article gave a history of the provinces from the fifth century, the conquest of Gaul by Germanic tribes up to the 16th century, and the wars between France and the Holy Roman Empire. The history was continued, *Scotsman* 1 Dec., up to the present conflict, concluding: "Whether the Germans would be doing a wise thing in taking back this once German land . . . it is not within our scope to discuss. But in the question of their right, as between them and the French nation, to claim the restitution, it seems to us that nothing more is required than to read the history of the case, to feel that the verdict must be in favour of the Germans."

3. Sir William Stirling Maxwell of Keir; see TC to JAC, 12 Nov. Mary Aitken misspelled "Keir."

4. John A. Carlyle replied, 7 Dec.: "Mr Harding's having placed his name at the head of his list may I suppose be relied on, though in this part of the country his last note would be considered as nothing more than a civil refusal. . . . Neither Jean nor James can know how to decide in such a case, for London ways differ much from those of Dumfries."

5. Presumably James Gordon; see TC to JAC, 13 Oct.

6. John replied, 7 Dec.: "It is my opinion too that he ought to resign his place in the bank without delay; but he tells me he . . . could get free at any time by a single week's warning." Jean Aitken wrote, [11 Dec.]: "Jack is shy and backward to a fault, but if we *cd* only get him farely started, he has both perseverance & ingenuity & I *shd* have no fear of his doing well."

7. John replied, 7 Dec.: "John says he generally gets no satisfactory help or advice from Jem . . . & therefore has asked none in regard to giving up his present work."

Newspapers by some distracted gomeral there. The fire is evidently the true place for such; and I design to keep you in a state of immunity from them henceforth. *The Republican* sent today in *Fraser* seems to have something in it by Maccall,[8]—of very lean rat-trap character. In the *Fraser* I found nothing much worth reading, but that Article on "Progress" & perhaps another slight piece *on Liverpool* by "Patricius Walker" *alias* little Irish Allingham,[9] which however I only stepped through as with seven-leagued boots.

All last week I have had a kind of cold working on me; and for the last two days have been running at the nose like a town-cistern. Not yet quite well, though perhaps growing better; today, for the first time, I omitted my cold bath, and intend to watch well how that answers. Here has John's Letter come to Mary; which she says is all right; and so there-with I end. Sending my Love and blessing to all.

Ever your affectionate Brother
T. Carlyle

TC TO THE DUCHESS OF ARGYLL

5 Cheyne Row, Chelsea
5 Decr 1870

Dear Lady Duchess,

You are very kind to me, His Grace and you. For above four years, I have not, properly speaking, gone out to any dinner; being indeed, bodily and spiritually, unfit for such enterprizes. But perhaps it is right that I again make one exception in respect of distinguished persons so peculiarly good to me. On Friday night, therefore, if nothing bad befal, I will hope to be with you,—at the *hour to be* appointed.[1]

8. *The Republican*, monthly journal ed. by William Maccall, 1870–72. Maccall included a poem called "Penitent France," under which he wrote: "Like many others, I sympathised with Prussia till the Battle of Sedan was fought. From the moment of that momentous and desperate conflict, I have passionately yearned for French victories and Prussian defeats" (*The Republican*, 1 Dec.). For William Maccall, see TC to WM, 17 Oct.

9. For Froude's article, see TC to JAC, 26 Nov. William Allingham's article, "Rambles. By Patricius Walker, Esq. At Liverpool," *Fraser's Magazine* (Dec. 1870) 735–53, was primarily about the British Association Congress in Liverpool, Sept. 1870 (see TC to JT, 28 Sept.) but also contained descriptions of the town, the terrible conditions of the working population, and an indictment of the current economic system that produced such conditions.

TC-duchess of A, 5 Dec. MS: NLS 7197. Hitherto unpbd. Lady Elizabeth Georgiana, b. Leveson-Gower (1824–78), m., 1844, George Douglas Campbell (1823–1900; *ODNB*), 8th duke of Argyll, politician; see 38:79.

1. The duchess of Argyll invited TC, 4 Dec., to dinner on Fri., 9, or Sat., 10 Dec.: "Let us send the carriage for you, as our people know the way better perhaps than your's." They

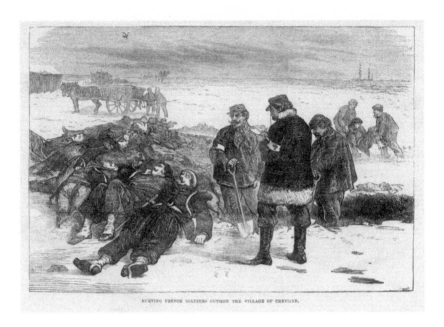

BURYING FRENCH SOLDIERS OUTSIDE THE VILLAGE OF CHEVILLY.

The burial of French soldiers
Illustrated London News, 21 January 1871

That you will beneficently send me a conveyance withal, is a new and welcome piece of favour, —for which I shall endeavour to be punctually waiting. I remain always, with many regards and homages,
Your Grace's / Most obedient, / T. Carlyle.[2]

---

lived at Argyll Lodge, Kensington. She replied, 5 Dec.: "The carriage will call for you in time to bring you here on Friday at ¼ before 8."

2. Mary Aitken wrote to her unidentified married friend, 5 Dec., about the Franco-Prussian War: "My Uncle is pretty well just now since he has relieved his conscience by writing the Letter to The Times. It is very wonderful to see how many really good & clever men here are strong on the side of France; wanting Prussia to believe that France will keep her word now when she has continually broken it for 400 years. It is sad to think so many brave men have been killed fighting against such a crowd of Apes as the French are." For the burial of French soldiers, see above. Mary reported that Hetty (Hedwig) Reichenbach was teaching her German and that "Miss Jewsbury is not home yet she is gone into space—somewhere in Wales I think—& I cant even send her a Note" (MS: Harry Ransom Center, Univ. of Texas). For an earlier letter to her friend, see 46:32.

TC TO JOHN STUART BLACKIE

5 Cheyne Row, Chelsea
6 Decr 1870.

Dear Blackie,

Yesterday your pretty Book[1] came to hand; and I have already read the whole of it, with interest and thanks. The Songs go thundering along with a furious tramp of battle in them; and I suppose if one could *sing*, would be very musical and heart-inspiring. One is glad to see the originals, too, so perfectly printed by your Edinburgh man. On the whole, I say "*Euge, euge* [Well done, well done]";—and especially applaud the clear and vigourous Historical Summary, which will be instructive to so many dark people here at home.

As for the Dedication and Ms. Inscription, what can I say but drop a veil over my blushing face and answer by expressive silence![2]

Good be with you always, dear Blackie. With many thanks, I am ever

Yours truly, / T. Carlyle

TC TO THOMAS DIXON

5 Cheyne Row Chelsea
7 Decr 1870.

Dear Sir,

The *two Hindoo Pamphlets*[1] seem curious as signs of the times;—and I intend to look further into them this evening.

TC-JSB, 6 Dec. MS: NLS 2629.291. Pbd. Anna Stoddart, *John Stuart Blackie* (Edinburgh and London, 1896) 264 inc. Quot: Wilson, *Carlyle* 6:228–29. For John Stuart Blackie, see TC to JAC, 14 May.

1. J. S. Blackie, *War Songs of the Germans with Historical Illustrations of the Liberation War and the Rhine Boundary Question* (Edinburgh, 1870).

2. Blackie wrote in the dedication to TC, dated 23 Nov. 1870: "[I]n two points I have always felt that we are at one—in a stern love of justice, and a hearty detestation of all sickly sentiment. From these two fundamental instincts it has no doubt arisen, that on the subject of the political relations between France and Germany for the last four hundred years, we have arrived . . . at precisely the same conclusion. It was therefore with peculiar pleasure that I received your kind permission to grace with your name the three chapters in prose and verse which I here put forth on this important theme. . . . May you long continue to hold forth in your life and writings, to all English-speaking men, a noble example of that manly independence, lofty fervour, and unbribed truthfulness, without which the greatest literary successes are mere painted flowers" (*War Songs* v–vi).

TC-TD, 7 Dec. MS: Harry Ransom Center, Univ. of Texas. Hitherto unpbd. Thomas Dixon (1831–80), cork-cutter from Sunderland, self-educated working man; see 43:270.

1. Dixon wrote, 6 Dec.: "I . . . send you by Book Post two Pamphlets giving you an idea of the thoughts of modern Hindoos, one of them I felt deeply while I read it when I recollect to my mind your talk with me in 1862 on the effect of your writings and teachings upon

As to the Philanthropy *versus* Justice, I have myself no difficulty; being deeply aware that *Justice is the Soul of this Universe*,[2] *and that against Justice nothing whatever will have weight*. Woe to the People, woe to the Man that imagines he can caudle [mix] right and wrong together, and make up for want of Justice by abundance of miserable Pity for the Criminal who requires it of us! The like of that in our England, I have looked at for the last 40 years, with more and more aversion, growing gradually into ominous foreboding and, of late, I may say into silent anger and even abhorrence. Needing to be kept strictly silent in the present humour of the world! But it seems to me the evident preliminary of universal downbreak into slush and mud. *Justice is eternally the Soul of the Universe*; and it is not always a soft or pleasant thing, it is oftenest a stern and severe. But there has never been any Succedaneum found for it; nor will, or can ever be. That I for myself consider certain though it should have grown doubtful to all the Able-Editors & Stump Orators in this world.[3]

Mr Park tells a dismal story about Ballot-boxing[4] as the substitute for Valour Truth and Wisdom in social affairs; but I have often heard it before, and do not doubt but the whole world will get to know it as well as Park and I one day,—probably centuries hence, and hugely to its cost!

In great haste, but always well-affected towards one so quiet, hopeful, and modestly diligent in his vocation, I remain

Yours sincerely, / T. Carlyle

---

various persons. . . . These will at least prove that your influence is wider by far than you seemed then to think was the case." Pamphlets unidentified further. There is no record of a meeting between TC and Dixon; Dixon had been writing to TC since 1862; see 38:168 and 46:12–13.

2. Cf. *The Sufistic Quatrains of Omar Khayyam*, quatrain 328.

3. Dixon commented on TC's letter to the *Times* on the Franco-Prussian War: "The truthful exposition of matters Historical none can deny. Yet ones Christian feeling somehow is put to the test, at its awful rigid justice upon France. . . . how to reconcile Christian Mercy, with such stern Jewish Law, is to me the task of our Age. . . . Jewish Law or Christian Mercy and forgiveness for sin or Crime."

4. Dixon wrote: "Herewith I enclose you a letter cut from the 'Victorian' bearing out your utterances upon the matter of universal suffrage, or the Benifits to Peoples by Ballot Boxes." Mr. Park and letter untraced, presumably pbd. in *The Victoria Magazine*, monthly periodical, 1863–80, ed. Emily Faithfull; see TC to EF, [16 Feb. 1871].

TC TO SAMUEL CARTER HALL

5 Cheyne Row, Chelsea
8 Decr 1870.

Dear Sir,

Two nights ago there came to this door a weighty Volume;[1] which on opening it proved to be a splendidly beautiful one as well; and a most kind and welcome Gift due to your friendly regard. I have spent all my leisure ever since
on the Book; and find it altogether excellent reading, full of matter strangely
interesting to me. Several of the Pieces I had read before; these also I have
read again in their revised form; in fact I read all,—and only regret to think
I shall probably end it this night. How strange, how grand and tragical, those
silent photograph-shadows of the past, which were once living Figures along
with us, in the loud-roaring present, and whom we are so soon to join! You
have done your work with insight, equity and charity. The Book will be a
cheering guest at many Christmas firesides this year; and may promise itself
a lasting use to this, and the coming generations. Many thanks, many thanks.

Please offer my respects to Mrs Hall;[2] and say her little Pieces seem to me
peculiarly excellent, and have a kind of gem-like brightness where all about
them is polished and bright.

With gratitude and good-wishes,

Yours sincerely / T. Carlyle

S.C. Hall Esq
&c &c

TC-SCH, 8 Dec. MS: Hist. Soc. of Pennsylvania. Pbd: Samuel Carter Hall, *Retrospect
of a Long Life: from 1815 to 1883* (1883) 2:2; Wilson, *Carlyle* 6:223–24 inc. Samuel Carter
Hall (1800–99; *ODNB*), journal editor and writer. He and TC met on the Eyre Committee,
Aug. 1866; see 44:49–50.

1. Samuel Carter Hall, *A Book of Memories of Great Men and Women of the Age from
Personal Acquaintance* (1871); it included biographical portraits of many of TC's friends
and acquaintances. Its title page included the first few phrases of Carlyle's *On Heroes*.

2. Anna Maria, b. Fielding (1800–81; *ODNB*), writer and editor; she m. Hall, 1824. Hall
wrote in his preface: "These 'Memories' will derive much of their value from the aid I receive from my wife. We have worked together for more than forty years: with very few
exceptions my acquaintances were hers. I . . . have freely quoted her view of the characters I depict; and occasionally called upon her for her 'Memories' to add to mine" (*Book of
Memories* viii).

5 Cheyne Row, Chelsea,
10 Decr 1870

Dear Brother,

Thanks for your two Letters. I am sorry you have still your cold hanging about you; though I hope you are nursing it well and that it will soon go altogether. As for mine, it considerably abated after those two days of copious *sniftering*, wh. I suppose were remedial to it; and now I have nothing left of the affair, except perhaps some trifling feeling in the bones, and a dirty aching in one side of the upper jaw, the like of wh. I used to have in the dark *Frederick* seasons; but which is new again this winter. Our weather seems to be as bad as yours or worse, except perhaps in point of black frost. We had two days of that this week, & ever since, a puddle of darkness rainy snow and mud, —yesterday gradually about two inches of snow covering all things; & in spite of all the sloppy thawing, still near an inch of it left:[1] I get through it better can could be expected; omit bathing when the mornings are very cold; one morning omitted going out altogether; button on soft warm coat (not yet quite my warmest), soft cape above that surmounted by a horse collar of comforter wool, with soft hat drawn down as far as it will go; & step out deliberately, defiant of the weather. I really much wish I could persuade you to a Cape exactly like my own: Jean could at once get it you, and have it lined with some soft satiny like thing,[2] and to have it reach to the knee, —of that *same* flexible brownish-grey cloth. You have no idea how much comfort is in it in windy snowing dirty weather. With a comforter and broad hat you are completely warm & independent. Do take my advice in this matter, —*experto crede* [trust my experience].

Last night I was even out to a great or greatish Dinner:[3] strictly speaking, the first time for these 4 or 6 years! But the Duke of Argyle called one morning lately, with a Print for me; was by *Mrs* Warren mistaken for a School-Board Canvasser, and alarmingly dealt with (over which there were peals of

TC-JAC, 10 Dec. Addr: The Hill / Dumfries / N.B. PM: London, 10 Dec. 1870. MS: NLS 527.34. Quot: A. Carlyle, *NL* 2:273–74; Wilson, *Carlyle* 6:224.

1. The *Times* reported the heavy fall of snow, 10 Dec.: "Although the glass stood at freezing point during the day the streets were wretchedly sloppy, but in the suburbs and the parks the snow lay firm and hard."

2. Jean Aitken sent TC a cape, Dec. 1865, made by William Boyd (1811–90), Cummertrees tailor; see 43:84; for a picture of TC wearing the cape, see 43:181. John A. Carlyle replied, 11 Dec.: "I mean to get one of those capes you speak of. It will be good for going out in the night-time or on very cold days." He wrote again, 21 Dec.: "I expect my new Cape tonight. It was finished yesterday . . . made of soft, light, thick, warm cloth, which Jean & I as well as the tailor thought better without lining of any kind."

3. The duke and duchess of Argyll; see TC to duchess of A, 5 Dec.

laughter, when I got the real name and arrived upstairs), invitation from My Lady Duchess was the consequence; and I shudderingly felt I had to go! But it passed all harmlessly, indeed beautifully; they sent their carriage for me, and I went & came as in a big ball of wool. There was an elegant little party (Howards,[4] a L*d* Lowndes,[5] their own Lorne & pretty daughters);[6] Flunkies were grave & solemn creatures in Kilt & Sporn [Sporran]. The Duke himself is a most kindly frank & intelligent man: I dined on a fraction of Venison, d*o* of Grouse, came home with*t* damage & was astonished to find I had been so cheerful.[7]

None of us here has the least doubt about John's case with M*r* Harding.[8] I think it perfectly evident that John ought, according to his promise, straightway to qualify himself in Book-keeping by Double Entry; & if his Tellership is of the least hindrance to that, to quit the same without delay. Thanks for your news of the *S.man* Articles.[9] Pray send me the other when it comes to you. I had a Book from Blackie with blusterous translations of German War-songs interspersed with a kind of similar history of those French-German passages.[10] I sent it to Jean, who no doubt will lend it you, unless you expressly forbid!

Enough of this, dear Brother. I have still various things to do.

Ever your affecte Brother, / T. Carlyle

4. Presumably George James Howard and Rosalind Frances Howard.

5. Possibly William Selby Lowndes (1807–86), known as Lord Winslow.

6. John George Edward Henry Douglas Sutherland Campbell (1845–1914; *ODNB*), marquess of Lorne, eldest son of the duke and duchess of Argyll; probably their two oldest unmarried das., Lady Elisabeth Campbell (ca. 1852–96) and Lady Victoria Campbell (1854–1910). There were four younger das.; the eldest, Lady Edith (1849–1913), m. 1868.

7. TC wrote in his journal, 15 Dec.: "Last Sat*y*, went to dine at the Duke of Argyll's (who had called here, one morning with a Print, & been mistaken for a candidate aiming at Elect*n* to the School Board!) the *first* dinner of the kind since 1866, and, as I felt, probably the *last*. Dinner went well; the Duke a pleas*t* frank and rational man, a pleas*t* Duchess and Family round, & nobody there but pleas*t* honest people (*Howards* mainly): coming home, I was astonished I had been so *cheerful*!" (TC's journal; privately owned).

8. See TC to JAC, 3 Dec.

9. John A. Carlyle wrote, 9 Dec.: "The author of the two articles in the Scotsman is D*r* Findlater, editor of Chambers' Conversations-Lexicon, or whatever it is called. . . . You saw him once, I think, at Masson's . . . a tall gaunt man of sixty or more, very modest, solid & truthful in all respects. . . . There is, it seems, to be a third article." Andrew Findlater (1810–85; *ODNB*), lexicographical editor; he worked on various dictionaries and encyclopædias for the Edinburgh publishing house W. and R. Chambers, 1853–77. For the articles in the *Scotsman*, 24 Nov. and 1 Dec., see TC to JAC, 3 Dec.

10. John Stuart Blackie; for the book, see TC to JSB, 6 Dec.

TC TO KARL VON FOLLER

5 Cheyne Row, Chelsea
10 Decr 1870.

Dear Sir,

Your solidly intelligent and obliging Letter can not be other than gratifying to me; and I return you many thanks for the satisfaction it gave.

According to all the evidence I have or can gather from the rational people I speak with, I believe I can assure you that the real opinion of silent England is much the reverse of that given out in Newspapers by the more frothy and vocal class, and that, in fact, it essentially agrees with my own, and will in the end, as you anticipate openly coincide with it. Certain it is, the conduct of our Government in allowing France to supply itself with Arms from England has excited the surprise regret and disapproval of all or nearly all the considerate and just-minded men whom I have met with; and almost nobody *but* the Newspaper Editors appears to think our Foreign Secretary's arguments[1] altogether satisfactory. My own guess is, our Government, which, at any rate, delights in *governing* as little as possible, is in this instance mindful of its Alabama quarrel with America;[2] and hopes to establish some entirely nugatory principle of contraband, and law of neutrality between Nations, which may, at whatever cost otherwise, help it over that and similar difficulties. Actual Members of the Government known to me are in private very friendly to Germany;—and as to the Newspaper Editors, I fear they are in general of

---

TC-K von F, 10 Dec. Addr: zu Wiesbaden. PM: London, 10 Dec. 1870. MS: NLS Acc. 9775. Hitherto unpbd. Karl von Foller (1821–1912), Regierungsrat [German government administrator], mayor of Bydgoszcz 1857–69, moved to Wiesbaden 1870.

1. George Leveson-Gower, 2d Earl Granville, foreign sec. from July 1870 until Feb. 1874. TC may refer to Lord Granville's letter to the British Ambassador in Berlin, 20 Oct., about Bismarck's manifesto issued to foreign powers, 10 Oct., protesting against Prussia being held responsible for any calamities that might happen if the provisional govt. of France refused to capitulate. Lord Granville explained the British govt.'s efforts to secure an armistice, arguing; "[T]he probability of a new and irreconcilable war must be greatly increased if a generation of Frenchmen behold the spectacle of the destruction of a capital—a spectacle connected with the death of great masses of helpless and unarmed persons, with the destruction of treasures of art, science, and historical reminiscences which are of inestimable value and cannot be replaced. Such a catastrophe would be terrible for France, and dangerous, as I believe, for the future peace of Europe"; Bismarck replied that "English mediation was being misunderstood in Paris and encouraging further resistance" (Joseph Irving, *Annals of our Time . . . 1837 . . . 1871* [1890] 954–55).

2. The *Alabama* was a ship built in Britain for the Confederate States, 1862; this was seen by some as a breach of neutrality, and at the end of the Civil War the U.S. government demanded compensation; the consequent row continued until referred to international arbitration, 1871, both Granville and Gladstone believing that a code of international law, and friendly relations with the U.S., were of paramount importance. The decision, 1872, that Britain should pay £300,000 was unpopular.

another than serious type, and address, not the worthiest or weightiest classes in England, but the most numerous, who can buy their papers to the greatest extent. One has at all times to appeal steadily from that kind of "Philip" to a Philip that is "sober," or at least soberer![3]

I fully participate in all your wishes and anticipations, both for the victorious end of this great controversy with infatuated France, and for the clearer and clearer understanding of one another by our two Nations, which are indeed Brothers both in blood and in spirit if they understood one another.

Believe me / Yours with many thanks,

T. Carlyle

Pray do not think it discourteous in me, if I say that of course I do not wish this Letter to be printed.

TC TO JOHN A. CARLYLE

5 Cheyne Row, Chelsea,
17 Decr 1870.

My dear Brother,

The Letter I got from you yesterday was not for me at all; on opening the cover, it at once addressed Douglas the Bookseller![1] After an hour's consideration, we dispatched it to the Owner, asking in return If *he* hadn't got a Letter for me? Nothing of that kind has come this morning, nor can now till Monday.[2] I suppose there was nothing pressing or of importance in it; and that the fact of your putting the two Letters each into the *other's* cover was evidence of that.[3] This morning Mary has a Letter from one of her Cousins in Canada;[4]

---

3. TC refers to the story told of Philip II of Macedon (see TC to ed. of *Times*, 11 Nov.), when a woman wrongly convicted declared she would appeal to Philip sober against the decision made by Philip drunk; see 8:40.

TC-JAC, 17 Dec. MS: NLS 527.35. Hitherto unpbd.

1. John A. Carlyle wrote, 18 Dec.: "I did intend to write to you on Thursday last, & had a cover addressed for that purpose,—as well as one for Mr Douglas which I find still here in my portfolio! . . . I must have put the letter to D. into the wrong cover! I am sorry for the mistake as it w*d* annoy you not a little." David Douglas (1823–1916), Scottish publisher, of Edmonston & Douglas, Edinburgh; see 45:32 where wrongly identified as George Douglas.

2. TC was writing on Sat., and there were no postal deliveries from Scotland on Sundays.

3. John wrote: "Jean had received a rather vehement letter from Jem about John's business, & we had talked a good deal about it & got somewhat agitated & confused, so that I thought it better not to write to you till I had fully considered the subject, as I have now done since Thursday night. Jean still thinks Mr Harding's second letter, about having 'placed John's name at the head of his list of candidates for employment,' meant nothing in reality. . . . [W]hen Jem first went to Liverpool he had good introductions to some of the most respectable houses, & had his '*name put at the head of some* TEN *lists*' & got nothing thereby except the sorest disappointments & vexations. . . . He therefore strongly advises

which I enclose: it is the only thing worth sending you,—unless perhaps the (emptyish) *Daily News* of this morning, for behoof of Craigenputtock Jamie, whose *Public Opinion* has not come to hand?

We are in an utter drench of tepid rain and mud; swallowed in fact in the Gulf-Stream vapours;—which has at last grown one of the intolerablest elements to live in. Fitter for a duck or a fish, at lowest, for a frog, than for a man. The fall of actual rain is great, and though fitful, hardly ever altogether ceasing; add the darkness, the liquid *glar* of the roadways, & the roaring torrent of wheels:—coming up to Hyde-Park Corner yesterday along with Tait, I was tempted to ejaculate, looking into Piccadilly "*Per me si va nélla città dolente, Per me* [Through me you enter the city of woe, through me]"5—&c! It does not well agree with my poor skin & stomach; but, except that pitiful continual toothache, I have no *cold*, nor other unusual suffering. I do begin, however, to feel that plunging out into the rain, & walking *ad libitum* [at will] in Mackintosh & Wide-awake, is a thing I must avoid. Yesternight, learning by the experience of the night before, I didn't go out at all,—nor suffer specially from it.

Of news we have nothing; the black plunge has even kept visitors for most part away from us; and the Newspaper *Placards* (top of Oakley St.) every morning have indicated sufficiently, for a month past that the paper itself is not *worth* a penny. I am able for no work. I read with relief any Book that has a modicum of sense in it, which a good many that I try have not: last week I read an authentic, but very dim straggly foreign kind of Book, *Life of Bēthoven* by one Schindler;6 sincere Book, but mostly floating invisible to me in the regions of counter-point, artistic rapture &c; & representing to me a dreadfully violent inarticulate gnarl of a man; full of dumb fire, very dark and heavy-laden, though melodious to a degree. "Poor fellow after all!"7 What is better, I have been reading Goethe's *West-Oestlicher Divan*8 again, with increased,9 tho' by no means complete, intelligence, and with abundant gratitude and admiration. I intend to begin Vol. VI this night. Tourguéneff has not

---

John not to give up his present situation. . . . Harding . . . is known to some of his acquaintances in Liverpool & probably has the same method of putting candidates 'at the head of his list' when he wants to be rid of them."

4. From either one of Alexander Carlyle's or Janet Hanning's children.

5. Cf. Dante, *Inferno*, canto 3, "The Gate of Hell."

6. Anton Schindler, *Biographie von Ludwig van Beethoven* (Münster, 1840). TC possibly read this edn., rather than the most recent of 1871 that was printed in German cursive script which TC disliked.

7. John A. Carlyle's phrase; see TC to JAC, 10 June.

8. Goethe, *West-östlicher Divan* (1814–19), a collection of lyrical poems in 12 books.

9. The first two letters of "increased" were repeated with a line over them at turn of page.

been here again;[10] but proposes to come on Tuesday night à *la bonne heure* [well and good]. Here surely you have enough of this.

I know not whether Mary will write to her Mother: she is off, this evening, on a harmless little visit with the Reichenbachs to an amiable Widow in the Regent's Park;[11] till Sunday evening I am to be left alone. Give my Love to Jean, James and all the household. Sister Mary has sent a beautiful basket of eggs. Fair befal you all.

Ever your affectionate, / T. Carlyle

TC TO JEAN CARLYLE AITKEN

5 Cheyne Row Chelsea
24 Decr 1870.

My dear Sister,

This is merely a word to tell you that we are going on here in the common way not a worse than usual, though the weather is for the present settled into steady frost. At a very low temperature, I nevertheless decided this morning, for valid reasons, on a bath; of course I lost not a moment; but on getting downstairs could not put in a button even in my waistcoat; and poor Mary, busy heating everything, had to do the buttoning first! Happily the Streets are all clear of snow again; and I ran out in my comfortable French shoes & muffled to the eyes; getting a great deal of good of the 20 minutes sharp locomotion. Since which I have been quite idle; reading, sorting rubbish, — ready now for a long walk, sun having come out & all being hard & calm.

Yesterday I sent the Dr a bit of German & of Scotsman Newspaper along with a Book about Paris which you may tell him more expressly to keep for me. This day there is a *Macmillan* which contains a capital Article on Versailles & the Seat of War; ask him for me who the sensible and rational "Dr Russell" is:[1]

10. For Turgenev's earlier visit, see TC to JAC, 26 Nov.

11. Oskar and Friedericke von Reichenbach and family. Mary had written to her married friend, 10 Feb., about a party she attended at the Reichenbach household the previous Jan. (MS: Harry Ransom Center, Univ. of Texas); since then she had become friendly with their 2d da., Hetty; see TC to duchess of A, 5 Dec. The widow in Regent's Park unidentified further.

TC-JCA, 24 Dec. MS: NLS 527.36; TC signed the letter on a separate piece of paper that was attached to it. Quot. K. J. Fielding, "Carlyle and Dickens or Dickens and Carlyle?" *The Dickensian* 69 (1973): 118.

1. John A. Carlyle wrote, 25 Dec.: "'John Scott Russell' . . . is probably the Engineer who built the Gt Eastern. He has written also about the Navy &c." John Scott Russell (1808–82; *ODNB*), Scottish engineer and naval architect; for TC's earlier opinion of Russell, see 33: 133, and for pictures of him and the *Great Eastern* steamship, see 33:134 and 129. Russell's article "Into Versailles and Out, Part I," *Macmillan's Magazine* 23 (Jan. 1871): 255–72,

he may send the thing on to Madame Otthenin if he still knows her address.[2] I also inclose him the D'Eichtal Letter, which has several notable points, along with the photog*h* as he ordered.

Poor Forster who is very ill with his Cough & overwhelmed with business, insists on our having Xmas dinner with him tomorrow altogether in private[3] & "without dressing of any kind"—except for purposes of warmth. I am not yet nearly at the end of my clothing resources; indeed I put on tomorrow (*if* this frost hold) one of my new flannel shirts for the first time. Lady Ashburton of whom we otherwise hear nothing sends us this morning, as mute symbol, a Turkey pronounced to be superlative,[4] of which, however, one of us will never be able to judge except by testimony.

I send my best blessing to you all; and am always

Dear Jean / Your affec*te* Brother / T. Carlyle

MARY AITKEN TO LADY ASHBURTON

5 Cheyne Row / Saturday 24*th*
[Dec. 1870]

My dear Lady,

Your munificent and welcome present of a Turkey—which Mrs Warren says is such a beauty—came only an hour ago and I write in my Uncle's name to thank you very cordially[1] not for it only but for your kind remembrance & affection of which tho' it be silent he is always well assured.

I received your kind Letter some little time ago & we were very grateful for it but I had no news to tell so spared you the trouble of reading one from me in return. My Uncle has got rid of his cold now and sleeps at night mostly like his fellow creatures—which is a great mercy. Tomorrow night we are going to

---

warned of the consequences to England of neglecting its defenses and championing free-trade: "To those citizens of Manchester and Leeds who believe in this *Mill-ennium* [play on John Stuart Mill's name] we earnestly recommend that they at once request permission from M. de Bismarck to pass through the lines of the Prussians and to witness in the poor subjugated towns of mill-spinning France the consequences which the unpreparedness for war of the Manchester spinning schools has brought on one country—*our* nearest ally [i.e., France]—and may speedily bring on another, *her* nearest ally [presumably Britain]" (256).

2. Jean Otthenin; see 46:63–64. John wrote: "The Magazine cannot be forwarded to Mad*e* Otthenin as there has been no post to Vassy since August." Mme Otthenin d. in Nov.; because of the war, they did not find out until March 1871; see TC to JAC, 3 March 1871.

3. See MA to Lady A, 24 [Dec.].

4. See MA to Lady A, 24 [Dec.].

MA-Lady A, 24 [Dec.]. MS: NLS Acc. 11388. Dated 1870, as it was the Christmas after Dickens died.

1. TC would not eat the turkey; see TC to JCA, 24 [Dec.].

dine at Forster's;—on account of Dickens's death there is to be nobody at all there except ourselves. What a Xmas this will be in so many desolate homes! "Happy England" (as Gladstone says) to have interfered only with its advice—which I don't think anybody at all cares about.

With every good and kind Christmas wish from my Uncle and myself to the little Lady[2] and you

I have the honour to be / Yours very affectionately / Mary Carlyle Aitken

TC TO ROBERT WALDMÜLLER [CHARLES EDOUARD DUBOC]

5, Cheyne Row, Chelsea,
Dec. 27, 1870.

Dear Sir,—Three nights ago there came to me from Dresden a beautiful little blue book, "*Die tausendjährige Eiche im Elsass*,"[1] which—especially as coupled with your kind inscription on the cover of it, bearing date "vor [in front of] Paris"—I read with very great interest. It is in itself truly a beautiful little book, put together with a great deal of art, and betokening in the writer a delicate, affectionate, poetic, and gifted human brother, well skilled in literary composition—not to speak of still higher things. Nowhere have I seen a more ingenious arrangement of whatever was bright and human in an antiquarian study into a really living and artistic form than this of Elsass and its "Thousand Years' Oak!"[2] That soul capable of such work should now date to

2. Mary Florence, Lady Ashburton's da.

TC-RW, 27 Dec. Pbd: *Daily News*, 11 Jan. 1871; Shepherd, *Carlyle* 2:295–96; Wilson, *Carlyle* 6:221–22 inc. Robert Waldmüller, pseudonym of Charles Edouard Duboc (1822–1910), German writer and painter, living in Dresden. TC attached a clipping of the *Daily News* in his journal, making several corrections to the printed text; these have been incorporated into our text.
    1. Robert Waldmüller, *Die tausendjährige Eiche im Elsass* [The Millennium Oak in Alsace] (Berlin, 1870).
    2. TC wrote, 13 Jan. 1871: "'*Thousand-Years Oak in Elsass*' (Berlin 1870), title of a pretty enough little Book, *wh* came to me, inscribed *der Freunde Deutschld &c*, from the Lines 'before Paris,' *Note*; *wh* has now (yesty 12 jany 1871) come back in the *printed* form; Hooh, hooh, miserable penny-a-liners!" (TC's journal, 13 Jan. 1871; privately owned). The *Daily News* introduced TC's letter: "Our Special Correspondent with the Headquarters of the Crown Prince of Saxony, writing from Ville Evrart on the 7th, says: 'Thomas Carlyle on the foreposts! The "sage of Chelsea," as the penny-a-liners delight to call him, among the besiegers of Paris! Yes, verily, not indeed in the actual flesh; and Scotch plaid, but represented by certain written words, the authorship of which no one could doubt, even if he were not familiar with the handwriting. In the German armies are many who know how to wield the pen as well as the sword. One of these ambidextrous men now in the Saxon Army before Paris here had sent a little book of his to Chelsea, sure that the matter of it would find sympathy there, and as I rode yesterday through the village in which Herr Waldmüller is quar-

Scenes of the siege at Versailles
Illustrated London News, 3 December 1870

me from "Le Vert Galant,"[3] and the heart of a great and terrible World-Event, supremely beneficent and yet supremely terrible, upon which all Europe is waiting with bated breath, is another circumstance which adds immensely to the interest of the kind Gift for me; and I may well keep the little Book in careful preservation as a memorial to me of what will be memorable to all the world for another "thousand years." I wished much to convey some hint of my feeling to you, as at once the writer of such a piece, and the worker and fighter in such a world; and I try to contrive some way of doing so. Alas! my wishes can do little for you or for your valiant comrades, nobly fronting the storms of war and of winter;[4] but if this ever reach you, let it be an assurance that I do in my heart praise you (and might even in a sort, if I were a German and still young, envy you), and that no man, in Germany or out of it, more deeply applauds the heroic, invincible bearing of your comrades and you, or more entirely wishes and augurs a glorious result to it at the appointed hour. My faith is that a *good* genius does guide you, that Heaven itself approves what you are doing, that in the end Victory is sure to you. Accept an old man's blessing; continue to quit yourselves like men, and in that case expect that a

---

tered he brought me the letter which Mr. Carlyle had sent him in acknowledgment. With the permission of the recipient I transcribed it, and here is the copy.'" Frederick Augustus Albert (1828–1902), crown prince of Saxony.

3. Le Vert Galant, district in the Ile-de-France, about 15½ mi. (25 km.) from Paris, the headquarters of the Prussian army.

4. For two scenes of the siege at Versailles, see above.

good issue is beyond the reach of Fortune and her inconstancies. God be with you, dear sir; with you and your brave brethren in arms.—Yours sincerely, / T. CARLYLE.

TC TO [FREDRIC CHAPMAN]

5 Cheyne Row, Chelsea
30 Decr 1870.

My dear Sir,

Many thanks; the three Partridges are very welcome, ditto the three Volumes![1] Two of the latter I had promised yesterday to Mr Lecky[2] with my autograph upon them: these two I request of you to send over to Lecky's Lodging[3] (for that *autograph* reason) and to replace here by another pair. As soon as you like. This is all the needful at present.

With many thanks, / Yours always truly / T. Carlyle

TC TO JOHN A. CARLYLE

5 Cheyne Row, Chelsea,
31 Decr 1870.

My dear Brother,

Yesterday at two o'clock came your Letter; which, and the various details in it, I was thankful to read. Very likely your proposed journey to Edinr may be of real use to you;[1] the breaking up of one's old habits for a time is generally helpful; one may suffer new ways, but they are sure to be *different* ways and, as I sometimes say to rub on new places of the skin. The cold & the solitude you justly complain of will at least be remedied; as to the former sore point, I know well how miserable it is; and I must again give you an advice upon it, supplementary to the Cape[2] which you at length did me the real pleasure to

TC-[FC], 30 Dec. MS: Harvard. Hitherto unpbd. Recipient conjecturally identified as Frederic Chapman by tone and content.

1. Presumably three vols. of the library edn. of *Frederick*; John A. Carlyle wrote, 21 Dec., thanking TC for his copy of vol. 4.
2. William Edward Hartpole Lecky (1838–1903; *ODNB*), historian; see 44:97.
3. Lecky lived at 6 Albemarle St.

TC-JAC, 31 Dec. Addr: The Hill / Dumfries / N. B. PM: London, 31 Dec. 1870. MS: NLS 527.37. Hitherto unpbd.

1. John A. Carlyle wrote, 29 Dec., that he might go to Edinburgh "for a week or two. My old lodgings (Orrocks, 73 George Street) happen to be vacant, & perhaps the change may be beneficial. The distance is short, & my room upstairs here is very cold in the frosty weather." Agnes Orrock (b. 1817) and her sister Elizabeth (b. 1819), lodging house keepers, 73 George St., Edinburgh; John had lodged with them for many years; see 42:147.
2. See TC to JAC, 10 Dec.

follow. You absolutely must provide yourself with a pair of new flannel Shirts. You have no idea of the increase of heat that will surprise you in them; at yr time of life, I reckon it quite unwise to be without them. Do think of this I beg of you! Jean can get you in a couple of days a completely excellent pair; & I am altogether mistaken if, in the course of the first week, or even of the first day, you do not recognise them as real new friends. I that testify have worn them for about 50 years; again therefore I say *Experto crede* [trust the expert]. You could also have *sleeved* waistcoats buttoning to the throat; in fact there are many increments of heat still at hand for you in improvements of costume. Don't, I pray you don't, neglect them any more.

Today there comes a *Blackwood* with a Letter from Lord Neaves enclosed;[3] an innocent enough poor batch, which will wholly explain itself to you. I have not yet answered Lord Neaves; but intend to have a word ready for him on Monday morning. He is a man of sense; and seems to have more of seriousness and affection in him that I had judged by what I saw. If you meet him in Edinburgh, you can also verbally assure him of my esteem. There is farther waiting for you an astonishing Paper by Ruskin;[4] but that shall reserve itself for saluting you in Edinburgh. Quietly I think you never read a madder looking thing; I still hope (though with little confidence) that he will bethink him and drop the matter in time: therefore keep it to yourself in the meanwhile, — though, alas, I fear he will plunge into it all the same. Last night he was here, he and two extremely insipid young women;[5] but the result to me was mostly zero or at least considerable *minus* quantities, — among others loss of a portion of my sleep in the vile cold night it was! For the last fortnight there have been considerable interruptions in that important particular; due mostly to well-intentioned visits and to small mistakes of my own; but I generally make out what the error has been and decide upon more caution and ever more. On the whole there can be nothing but a struggle till this fierce weather pass;

3. Charles Neaves (1800–76; *ODNB*), Scottish judge, lord of justiciary, 1858–76, and rector of the Univ. of St. Andrews, 1872–74. Neaves wrote, 26 Dec., thanking TC for information for his article on "The Late George Moir" pbd. in *Blackwood's* magazine, Jan. 1871. George Moir (1800–70, *ODNB*), literary critic and lawyer, friend of TC's since 1828 (see 4:406–7), d. suddenly 19 Oct.
4. Probably Ruskin's "Looking Down from Ingleborough," *Fors Clavigera: Letters to the Workmen and Labourers of Great Britain* (1871–84), Letter 1. John A. Carlyle replied, 6 Jan. 1871: "Ruskin's mad pamphlet came yesterday. He is a man of very weak intellect, & anything he says will produce small effect on people who have any knowledge." However, TC expressed admiration to Ruskin for his Letter 5 of *Fors Clavigera*; see TC to JR, 30 April 1871.
5. Ruskin wrote to Mary Aitken, 27 Dec.: "I am so glad of your kind note. . . . I shall gratefully bring Joanna with me on Friday evening" (MS: NLS 555.47). Ruskin's cousin Joan Agnew; the other young woman was possibly Constance Hilliard (see TC to JAC, 13 Oct.), otherwise unidentified.

but it, too, will pass. For the last three days I have had no washing except of face & hands in tepid water & I never try to go out except all muffled up, and during the two lucid hours of the day. These changes are real losses to me; but one must put up with them for fear of far worse. Essentially I have nothing to complain of except what belongs to the years I have come to.

Here has come your Letter of yesterday; I keep the Canada Letter[6] till we get it deliberately read. Mary and I send our regards to Jim, who will be a new light in the household at this dim season;[7] you can tell him my thanks that the tobacco has arrived all right. My kindest regards to every member of the family.

Ever your affecte Brother,
T. Carlyle.

TC TO T. H. HUXLEY

5 Cheyne Row, Chelsea
5 January 1871

Dear Huxley,

Pardon the trouble I give you. Mr Burgess,[1] an estimable candidate, a great favourite of Tyndall's,[2] to whom I had given last night a sincere Testimonial for the Under-Secretaryship of the School Board, has this morning, by a fault of his Printer's not of his own, been precisely 10 minutes too late in present-

---

6. John A. Carlyle forwarded, 30 Dec., the letter from Canada sent to their nephew John. In his letter of 29 Dec., John gave TC some of the news: "John had a longish letter last night from his cousin Alick. . . . It gives details about the whole family by name, Father & Mother are 'both very well considering their age.['] Uncle John [their half-brother] had just spent a day at Bield, looked older, but was very cheerful, never stays a night from home 'canna sleep at a' except in his ain bed'; still works diligently & is well off tho' entirely alone in his house. Tom has been getting a new house on his farm. Jane has had hers thoroughly repaired, has two sons who assist her well in the farming, & she looks more cheerful in spite of her husband's continued fits of epilepsy. The money you sent her would do her great good [see TC to JAC, 1 June.]. John has bought himself a house in Brantford & intends working as a carpenter. It was he who was a cavalry sergeant & had a dollar per day. He & young Alick planned Tom's new house & seem to have done all the carpentry of it."

7. Their nephew James Aitken was spending the New Year with his family. TC noted in his checkbook: "21 Jany 1871 / J. C. Aitken Liverpool (for tobacco) / £1 .. 10 .. 6" (TC's checkbook; MS: NLS 20753).

TC-THH, 5 Jan. MS: Huxley Papers, Imperial College of Science and Technology. Hitherto unpbd.

1. Andrew Hutton Burgess (b. 1835), b. Dumfriesshire; journalist, lodging at 36 Park Walk, Chelsea. TC previously helped him find work cataloguing Lady Ashburton's library; see 46:148.

2. See 45:185.

ing his Documents and self; and is in consequence refused admittance altogether; and sees his whole Enterprize sorrowfully go to wreck!

Unless indeed, as he still struggles to hope, *you* could assist him;[3] to which end, he has pressingly requested a word to you from me. The "word" I cannot refuse him; knowing the man's worth & pitying this strange accident that has come on him. Pray listen to his Story for my sake and our absent Tyndall's; & if, on survey, you *can* help, charitably try.

No more except Pardon, Pardon! In very great haste,

Yours sincerely, / T. Carlyle

TC TO JOHN A. CARLYLE

Chelsea 5*th* January 1871

We are glad to think of your safe arrival in Edinburgh,[1] and the new & more stirring world you have got into It can scarcely fail to do good, besides being for the present a sensible enjoyment and variation for the better. Continue to report your Experiences to me, whenever you have leisure. The Old Edinburgh of the Past is—though mournful, for ever interesting to me,—all the more combined with your living presence there! Offer my regards to the few living souls I am still interested in there. To Gordon, Laing, Masson in the first place; I recollect hardly any more—except perhaps *Blackie, David Aitken,*[2] poor *Mrs Stirling*[3] when you have an opportunity.

I have plenty of visitors,—too many rather. Yesterday *Tourgueneff*[4] for an hour, very pleasant and genial, the entered a Gottingen Professor (formerly a

---

3. Huxley was elected to represent Marylebone on the newly constituted London School Board, 29 Nov. 1870. At the Board's second meeting, 16 Dec., it was agreed that "a clerk should be appointed who should devote their whole time to . . . discharge the duties of secretary and to act under the orders of the Board" (*Morning Post*, 22 Dec.). The appointment was delayed by a week because of the large number of candidates applying for the position. On 18 Jan., the Board announced George Hector Croad (1829–1902), formerly secretary of the Bishop of London's fund, as elected to the post.

TC-JAC, 5 Jan. MS copy: Sir Allan Walker's notebook, Ewart Lib., Dumfries, inc. Hitherto unpbd.

1. John A. Carlyle was in Edinburgh for a six week visit; see TC to JAC, 31 Dec. 1870.

2. Friends of both TC and John, whom John always saw on his visits to Edinburgh. For his recent visits to John Gordon (1797–1882; see 43:44), inspector of schools, David Laing, and David Masson, see 46:43. For visits to John Stuart Blackie and Rev. David Aitken (1796–1875), as well as to Masson, see 46:166.

3. Susan Stirling, b. Hunter (1799–1877), old friend of JWC's; see 43:179. John wrote, 10 Jan.: "Mrs Stirling is better, but I have not seen her yet."

4. Ivan Turgenev; see TC to JAC, 26 Nov. 1870.

5. Reinhold Pauli (1823–82; see 26:299), historian and author, prof. of history at the

Bookseller's Writer of Histories here)[5] thick-set, hand-fast, rather common-place and loud; to whom enter *Froude* who happily knew *Pauli* and delivered me from him, till *Tourgueneff* departed, —and the remaining three set out to walk. My little Irish friend *Mr Allingham* calls once a week, or seldomer; really worth something, and easy to banish in a moment, if superfluous. *Forster* I have seen only once at his own house,[6] (busy, partly for my poor bibliopolic concerns)[7] and coughing less than formerly.

I have read some good Books, or passages of Books, —particular Goethe's *Iphigenie*,[8] which was beautiful to me beyond anything for years past, the soul of *Iphigenie* herself especially falling into my poor mournful darkness like a beam of heavenly light, and remote Eternal Summer. I am now upon *Tasso*[9] but don't yet like that so well. *Goethe* is by far my best reading. Indeed is latterly the only good thing I *do*; unhappily the type (Cotta's 12*mo* Ed)[10] at night is difficult to read.[11]

TC TO JOHN A. CARLYLE

5 Cheyne Row, Chelsea
13 Jan*y* 1871

My dear Brother,

Though in great haste today, with proof-sheets &c, I must write you a little word before sallying out into the frost. We have miserable continually fluctuating weather of the same kind as yours and certainly quite as bad: I am very glad to hear that you stand it without damage; & I beg you very much to be careful of yourself and avoid tumbling! I had fancied the Edin*r* people threw ashes on their streets; but seemingly they are as mad as we in that respect.[1]

Univ. of Göttingen 1870–82. TC met him April 1851 (see 26:74–75) and again, 1853, when they met in the London Lib. (see 28:64), but rarely mentioned him since.

6. TC and Mary Aitken went to the Forsters' for Christmas lunch; see TC to JCA, 24 Dec. 1870.

7. The new popular or people's edn. being planned by Frederic Chapman and John Forster; see TC to WB, 1 Dec. 1870.

8. Goethe's verse drama, *Iphigenie auf Tauris* (1786).

9. TC refers to Goethe's verse drama, *Torquato Tasso* (1790), about the life of the Italian poet Torquato Tasso (1544–95) (see TC to JAC, 13 Jan.), rather than to the poet's own works, although he did have a 1764 edn. of Tasso's *La Gerusalemme Liberata* (1581); see *Carlyle's House* 79.

10. Johann Friedrich Cotta (1764–1832), publisher of Goethe's *Werke*, 54 vols. (Stuttgart, 1828–33); see 46:117.

11. MS copy ends here.

TC-JAC, 13 Jan. MS: NLS 527.38. Hitherto unpbd.

1. John A. Carlyle replied, 10 Jan.: "Our frosty weather still continues, with short intervals of thaw now & then in the day time, slippery streets, sprinklings of snow . . . but I . . .

The last oxen in Paris
Illustrated London News, 14 January 1871

I for most part sleep, if not well, yet not intolerably ill & endeavour to fence myself against the unfriendly elements till their time of departure do come.

Dushty's Vienna Newspaper did get both read & burnt;[2] it was dark as the bellow of a mad radical ox; & had been more cheering to Dushty but to me also was significant. I daresay you have read in the Edinburgh paper that little Note to the *Eiche im Elsass*, and how it came back to me from Le Vert-galant. "Plague on all Penny-a-liners!"[3] I begin to say: yesterday Froude told me they were all busy with their leading Articles &c on that small occasion (most likely

---

have not yet had any fall in the streets." It was against London bylaws to throw ashes into the streets to prevent accidents even in times of frost and icy pavements; see 44:151.

2. Charles d'Eichthal; Vienna newspaper unidentified further. John had received a letter from d'Eichthal: "I confine myself to enclosing a newspaper cutting, w*h* he asks me to forward, & which can easily be burnt if found worthless."

3. For Robert Waldmüller's *Die tausendjährige Eiche im Elsass* [The Millennium Oak in Alsace], Le Vert Galant, and "Penny-a-liners," see TC to RW, 27 Dec. 1870; TC's letter was widely reprinted and discussed in newspapers throughout Scotland and England. The *Illustrated London News*, 14 Jan., published a sketch of "The last oxen in Paris," in illustration of the privations within the besieged Paris; see above.

all squirting dirty water on me);—for above a week before it seems they were all busy Leading-Articling upon some Note I had written to a stupidest of intrusive mortals, perhaps 20 years before;[4] of Whom it was now tragic for me to think. To shove up one's umbrella with strict constancy ag*t* all that is the on[5] recipe; and that I do strictly follow. "Can neither d'ye ill n'a gude"[6] pff! By this post I send you certain poor pamphlets & Ms. which I dont wish returned. Playfair[7] seems to me rather a pinchbeck, would-be golden article. If you care to read the Manchester Letter & look into the d*o* Pamphlet,—especially if *you* have any light about the "£50's worth of shares,"[8] or can get any handily, as I cannot, please say a word upon it farther. Mary has got an excellent reading lamp, which, except for the gas, might be well worth y*r* attention; it illuminates like a Sun, Colza oil[9] & no bad gas to be perceived:—I can read *Goethe* even with freedom; have done *Tasso* & the *Naturliche* Tochter[10] with new admiration, especially of the former. This, with reading over *Meister* (which is to be printed in Library Edition shape)[11] is properly the only shadow of work I do. Good be with you, dear Brother, now and always; I hope we shall soon,[12] possibly tomorrow itself have another glimpse of Edin*r* from you.

Ever y*r* Affectionate

T. Carlyle

4. The *Glasgow Herald*, 6 Jan., pbd. an extract from TC's letter to W. C. Bennett of 14 July 1847 (see 22:15–16), in "Mr Thomas Carlyle on Verse Writing." This letter was also widely discussed in other Scottish and English newspapers. William Cox Bennett (1820–95; *ODNB*), journalist and author.

5. Mary wrote "on," presumably for "only."

6. Coterie speech; see 4:369.

7. Presumably Lyon Playfair (1818–98; *ODNB*), politician and chemist, M.P. for Edinburgh and St. Andrews Universities, 1868–85; possibly either *On Primary and Technical Education. Two lectures delivered to the Philosophical Institute of Edinburgh* (Edinburgh, 1870), or *The Inosculation of the Arts and Sciences, Address delivered to the Midland Institute, 29 Sept. 1870* (Birmingham, 1870).

8. TC had been sent a prospectus from the Artizans, Labourers & General Dwellings Co., a philanthropic property company; the first group of houses were built in Battersea, S London; they were now planning to build at Salford, nr. Manchester. The pamphlet was sent by J. Royle Martin, unidentified further. John replied, 17 Jan.: "Martin's [pamphlet] seems . . . interesting . . . & I should think you might do good by lending your name to his project by taking the Five Shares of £10 each as he requests."

9. Colza oil is produced from rapeseed, a heavy viscous oil popular in lamps at the time.

10. Goethe's verse drama, *Die natüralich Tochter* (1803).

11. TC's trans. of Goethe's *Wilhelm Meister* became vols. 31–32 (1872) in the library edn. of Carlyle's *Works*.

12. Word repeated with a line over it at turn of page.

MARY AITKEN TO MARTIN TUPPER

[mid-January 1871]

Dear Sir,

Mr Carlyle, my uncle, bids me send you this; and say he has read your Letter and Verses with much pleasure. He does not know what the Newspapers have been saying lately about him and his hatred of *Verse*; he has read none of their Leading articles and has heard it is all about some forgotten Note he sent long ago to a foolish intrusive fellow, Bennet,[1] who used to plague him dreadfully with his stupid Poems.

Yours very truly, / MARY CARLYLE AITKEN[2]

TC TO JOHN A. CARLYLE

5 Cheyne Row, Chelsea
21 Jany 1871.

Dear Brother,

Here, before the week quite end, is a little word of answer to your Letter of Monday.[1] Nothing of the least importance has befallen us in the way of good or evil: I am reading & slightly revising (with hardly any change at all) the three volumes of German Translations;[2] & am more than half through the 2d Vol., —that is to say *nearly* half through Meister's Travels; which with the Apprenticeship is full of strange impressiveness to me while I read it again after

MA-MT, [mid-Jan. 1871]. Pbd: Derek Hudson, *Martin Tupper: His Rise and Fall* (1949) 238. Martin Tupper (1810–89; *ODNB*), poet and writer, "read in some newspaper that Carlyle objected to poetry, and promptly sent him some attempts of his own" (Hudson 238). This letter is presumably dated soon after the republication of TC to W. C. Bennett, 14 July 1847 (see TC to JAC, 13 Jan.). Tupper also wrote to TC, 11 March, that he had "written more than one paper on the German side of this now late War" and asked for information about "any AngloGerman Review or Newspaper, or of any Editor Germanically disposed"; no reply has been traced.

1. William Cox Bennett.

2. Tupper wrote on the reverse of Mary Aitken's note: "On the 5th of July [1871] I had an interview with Carlyle at his house . . . and found him genial and kindly and very glad to welcome me. We talked of many things literary and political: he denouncing the meannesses and dishonesties of the age, and now and then using his favourite words 'shams' and 'unwisdoms'" (Hudson 239).

TC-JAC, 21 Jan. MS: NLS 527.39. Pbd: A. Carlyle, *NL* 2:274–75 inc. Quot: Susanne Howe, *Geraldine Jewsbury: Her Life and Errors* (1935) 187.

1. John A. Carlyle wrote from Edinburgh, Tues. 17 Jan.; he presumably also wrote on Mon. 16 Jan. as there are gaps in the correspondence of TC and John at this time.

2. The three vols. of the *Translations from the German* in the library edn. (1872) consisted of TC's trans. of *Wilhelm Meister* (vols. 31–32) and of *Tales of Musaeus, Tieck, and Richter* (vol. 33).

so many years! F̄red Frederick[3] Chapman with a clever-looking Engraver has been here; bent upon a new print of Watts's new & final Edition of my poor maltreated face,[4] to usher in that People's Edition he is so busy with.[5] Has printed he tells me 150,000 advertisements to be stitched into the Magazines of the coming month; one of the strongest blasts it is hoped that Fame thro' her biggest tin trumpet *cd* produce upon the lazy ear of a too-enlightened Public.[6] I am not to be plagued, it appears, with reading proofs of that People's Edition[7] at 2/ a volume; and it will bring in, covenants Chapman, a good sum of money,—I altogether forget how much. Mary in the meanwhile is strenuously busy about Signatures for a Pension for poor Geraldine,[8] which, in the sickness of Forster & the laziness of Froude, Mary has had to undertake and is managing with great vigour and success.

Nothing has arrived worth sending forward to you,—except perhaps this Yankee synopsis[9] of the Letter on the German War; which, especially the

3. "Fred" repeated at turn of page.

4. Probably Joseph Brown; see TC to FC, 9 Sept. 1870. Watts's portrait was originally engraved for the library edn. by William Holl the younger (1807–71; *ODNB*); see 46:121.

5. *The People's Edition of the Works of Thomas Carlyle*, 37 vols. (1871–74); see TC to WB, 1 Dec. 1870.

6. The advert. read: "Mr. Thomas Carlyle's Works. People's Edition. In compliance with urgent applications from large classes of readers interested in Mr. Carlyle's Writings, to whom the existing Editions are not accessible because of their price, the Publishers have obtained Mr. Carlyle's consent to the issue of a CHEAP EDITION, printed from the Library Volumes which have received his latest revision, and which will appear in MONTHLY TWO SHILLING VOLUMES, small crown 8vo. The Volumes will be handsomely printed in clear type, with good paper and binding, and issued in the following order: / SARTOR RESARTUS. 1 vol., with Portrait of Mr. Carlyle. (*In March*, / The FRENCH REVOLUTION. 3 vols. / LIFE OF JOHN STERLING. 1 vol. / OLIVER CROMWELL'S LETTERS AND SPEECHES. 5 vols. / HERO-WORSHIP. 1 vol. / PAST and PRESENT. 1 vol. / CRITICAL and MISCELLANEOUS ESSAYS. 7 vols." (*Athenaeum*, 11 Feb.; *Daily News*, 13 Feb.; and others).

7. In his edn. of *Sartor*, Tarr noted: "The People's Edition was clearly based on the Library Edition, preserving most of its punctuation and spelling, but it is a complete resetting, not using the 'stereotyped' plates of the Library Edition." Tarr added that there "are no variants in the 1871 *Sartor Resartus* that suggest authorial revision" (Carlyle, *Sartor* cxxv).

8. Geraldine Jewsbury. Forster had been attempting to get a Civil List pension for her since May 1869; see 46:49. Jewsbury suffered from various health problems, particularly with her eyes, which hindered her from working. Mary Aitken wrote to Jewsbury, [26 Jan.], about the progress of the campaign, informing her that the Memorial was being sent around the country from supporter to supporter for their signatures, and "it is all like clockwork which one cannot hasten at all. . . . Forster thinks it has been signed very well." She continued: "I think if you are at all able . . . to come to town either on *Saturday* or *Monday* first—so that when Mr Forster begins his campaign you may be here for consultation" (Howe, *Geraldine Jewsbury* 210). As well as TC, the supporters were to include Tennyson, Forster, Tyndall, Huxley, Woolner, Kingsley, Ruskin, and Blunt (Howe 211).

9. Unidentified further.

winding up of it with a reference to Moltke[10] and Bismarck to the Sermon on the Mount,[11] might cause even the Iron Duke to try if he could execute a smile;[12] burn the thing as soon as you have looked into it. You have, like myself, a good opinion of that Manchester Enterprize;[13] but what I wanted, if it came in your way or you chanced to meet some Broker or Public-Person suitable is what the practical character of the thing and of the persons doing it is:—but no; you have little better chance for information than myself; and we can let the little project sink to nothing for the present as so many others do.

If Kirkpatrick[14] happen to take a Photograph of your Portrait, don't neglect to send me a Copy. I send my best regards to Mrs Stirling, my warmest hopes that she is getting well again:[15] Ah me Ah me!— For the last three nights I am reading a Book of Moltke's, The Prussian-Turk war of 1827,[16] which is written with great talent veracity and vigour; and betokens to me a truly superior kind of man. That is the one attraction to me, and holds me fast hitherto, in the total absence even of Maps which my Copy (lent by Reichenbach) altogether has *not*. Our weather here is one whirlpool of mud rain and darkness; the very air seems to be a kind of solution of GLAR. But for the last three days it sometimes seems to be mending. Courage, Courage. Adieu, dear Brother.

Ever yours affectionately[17]

10. Helmuth Carl Bernhard von Moltke (1800–91), German field marshal, leader of the Prussian armies in the Franco-Prussian War.

11. See Matt. 5–7.

12. Arthur Wellesley (1769–1852; *ODNB*), 1st duke of Wellington, army officer and politician; nicknamed "Iron Duke" for his strong will and resolution, also known for his dislike of showing emotion. TC possibly meant the "iron chancellor," i.e., Bismarck.

13. See TC to JAC, 13 Jan.

14. Edward Kirkpatrick, living at 5 Picardy Pl., Edinburgh; he exhibited at Royal Scottish Academy Exhibitions 1867–78; unidentified further. John A. Carlyle sat for the portrait spring 1870; see 46:173. John wrote, 17 Jan.: "Mr Kirk*k* is to have one more sitting for the Portrait tomorrow morning, & then it is to be framed & sent to this year's Exhibition w*h* opens first week of February. It is not a bad picture." The portrait was not sold from the Exhibition and is untraced.

15. John replied, 23 Jan.: "Mrs Stirling is quite better now & has been out today for a drive though the weather is still cold. Her husband had a threatening of apoplexy lately & looks thinner than usual." Her husband was James Stirling (1802–76).

16. Mary wrote "Prussian" in error for "Russian." Moltke's *Der russisch-türkische Feldzug in der europäischen Türkei 1828 und 1829 [The Russo-Turkish Campaign in Europe, 1828–29]* (Berlin, 1845).

17. The letter is unsigned.

TC TO ROBERT CARRUTHERS

Cheyne Row, Chelsea,
25th Jan. 1871

Dear Sir,

I thank you much for the kind little note you sent me, which was deeply interesting after the sad news we had had.[1] Sad always is death, sad and solemn the departure of our loved ones into the silent unknown land; but in this case it could truly be regarded as a solemn blessing and release from sufferings grown intolerable.[2]

Beautiful and gentle, softly heroic, had the life all along been; and now at last the end has been peace. It was a wild surprise to me, some three months ago, to find on my return one evening that poor Munro had actually been at this door! I hastened out next day in search, but there was no address on the card, and I could find nothing: it was near night of the second day before I came on any clear trace; and he had sailed for Antwerp some hours before. We were not to meet again in this world. He was much loved here, and has left a pathetically beautiful remembrance with many friends. It is perhaps a still better consolation that he left his widow and children provided for, and his house well set in order.[3] To such a life we can piously say well done, well done!

MARY AITKEN TO AN UNIDENTIFIED CORRESPONDENT

5 Cheyne Row, Chelsea,
27 Jan. 1871

Dear Sir,

Mr Carlyle, my Uncle, desires me to say he has received the Book[1] you have been so kind as send him; and he intends to read it the first leisure he has. Meanwhile he sends you his cordial thanks.

Yours very truly
Mary Carlyle Aitken

TC-RC, 25 Jan. Pbd: David Garnett, "Eight Unpublished Letters of Thomas Carlyle," *Archiv für das Studium der neueren Sprachen und Literaturen* n.s. 2 (1899) 329-330 inc. Quot: Wilson, *Carlyle* 6:222. Robert Carruthers (1799-1878), writer and editor; owner and editor of the *Inverness Courier*; see 26:225.
1. The death of Alexander Munro (1825-71; *ODNB*), sculptor; he d., 1 Jan., in Cannes where he wintered; see also 46:42. For the sketch of him, *Illustrated London News*, 28 Jan., see 144.
2. Munro had been suffering from cancer since 1865.
3. Munro m., 1861, Mary, b. Carruthers (1834-72), 4th da. of Robert Carruthers; they had two sons, John Arthur Ruskin (1864-1944) and Henry Acland; they lived at 6 Upper Belgrave Pl., London.

MA-UC, 27 Jan. MS: Hornel. Hitherto unpbd.
1. Unidentified further.

"The late Alexander Munro, Sculptor"
Illustrated London News, 28 January 1871

TC TO JEAN CARLYLE AITKEN

5 Cheyne Row, Chelsea,
28 January 1871.

My dear Sister,

Out of this cold element let me send you a word of assurance that nothing special has gone wrong here and that we are lovingly remembering you all. I have this moment had a Letter from the Doctor; who as you observe seems to be enjoying himself not ill at Edin*r*, & going out a good deal to dinner or lunch.[1] I am very glad he should have some benefit from the considerable bit of variation, which after his long solitary rustication must be welcome to him.

Paris City you no doubt perceive with thankfulness *has* now got to the end of its tether;[2] and is evidently within a very few days of making complete surrender.[3] One hopes, though that is not so certain, that the War itself will soon go the same road:[4]—it is the only bit of glad news I have had from these Placards for a very long time. Poor France one *cd* observe all the while had, in spite of its boastings and the rumours of the Editors, no success in any enterprize whatever; & every "Victory," each in its turn, turned out within two days to have been a *defeat* cloaked by lies and fallacious hope. Poor France, what a bitter cup she is getting to drink! But it is of her own brewing;—let us hope only that all these frightful sufferings may prove instructive to her, and spare her any more of the like!

That Glasgow Sermon I doubt will do little for you, in spite of the great

TC-JCA, 28 Jan. MS: NLS 531.6. Hitherto unpbd.

1. John A. Carlyle wrote regularly to TC detailing the people he was seeing in Edinburgh.

2. The *Illustrated London News*, 28 Jan., published examples of the privations of Paris inhabitants: the killing of an elephant for food, see 146; the bringing of their cats and dogs to the fleshmarket, *ILN*, 28 Jan.; tree stumps in the Bois de Boulogne, see 147. On 25 Feb., they published two illustrations of the internal effects of bombardment on a house, see 148.

3. The *Times* reported, 28 Jan., the "capitulation of Paris" and the onset of "armistice negotiations" between France and Prussia, represented respectively by Jules Favre (1809–80), French statesman, vice president and minister for foreign affairs in the Government of National Defense, and Bismarck: "The negotiations . . . are so far advanced that the terms are expected to be concluded to-day. . . . Count Bismarck is desirous of treating for Peace on the basis of the cession of Alsace and a part of Lorraine. If M. Jules Favre accepts these proposals made to him by Count Bismarck, Germany will recognize the French Republic. It is certain that these proposals would be accepted by the Imperialists."

4. John A. Carlyle wrote to Janet Hanning, 2 Feb.: "The terrible war which is not yet ended or likely soon to be distresses everybody in this country. I have some German friends engaged in it, & heard a few days ago that they were all safe though exposed to great cold & hardship near Paris. One of them is a grand nephew of the German Baron with whom I spent a year at Munich long ago when studying medicine" (MS: Hilles); the d'Eichthal "grand nephew" was possibly Julius Brunn; John wrote to TC, 31 March, that he had heard from Julius's mother ("widow of my old friend D*r* Brunn at Coethen") that he was safely home, having survived both the siege of Strasburg and of Paris.

Killing an elephant, Jardin des Plantes, Paris
Illustrated London News, 28 January 1871

Caird's name;[5] nor can the Essay on Hamlet[6] pretend to be anything but what has been far better said before. Glance into both of them however; & if you find nothing give them to James[7] to light his pipe with.

5. Rev. John Caird (1820–98; *ODNB*), Church of Scotland minister, prof. of Divinity at the Univ. of Glasgow, chaplain-in-ordinary in Scotland to Queen Victoria 1857–86; his sermon *What is Religion?* (Glasgow, 1871) was delivered, 8 Jan., at the opening of the Univ. of Glasgow's new chapel.
6. Probably Arthur Meadows, *An Essay on Hamlet* (1871).
7. Her husband, James Aitken.

Bois de Boulogne, Paris
Illustrated London News, 28 January 1871

Last night Mary & I, on the absolute pressure of importunity long continued, had to go and dine at the Blunts'.[8] The Blunts were excessively kind; but there was a load of dull Parsons[9] there relieved only by the wit of Brookfield[10] and by two unattractive Ladies[11] in the tea-room: the evening itself was not difficult, or altogether miserable while it lasted, but unfortunately I found on coming home that I had eaten (or found possible to eat) nothing but one small mutton cutlet, weight about an ounce;—and that a baddish night was inevitable; as indeed it partly proved; sorrow on all dinner givers of a quality at once importunate & dull; I wish they w*d* at least let me alone Adieu,[12] d*r* Sister: Tait[13] &c have come in!

Ever y*rs* / T. Carlyle

8. Rev. Gerald Blunt, rector of St. Luke's, Chelsea, and his wife, Frances.
9. Unidentified further.
10. William Henry Brookfield (1809–74; *ODNB*), clergyman and school inspector; known to TC since 1841.
11. Unidentified further.
12. From "Adieu" to the end, the letter is in TC's hand.
13. Robert Scott Tait.

BOMBARDMENT OF PARIS: EFFECTS OF A SHELL BURSTING IN THE THIRD AND FOURTH STORIES OF A HOUSE.

Internal effects of bombardment on a single house
Illustrated London News, 28 February 1871

TC TO JOHN A. CARLYLE

5 Cheyne Row, Chelsea,

30 January 1871.

My dear Brother,

I wished to write you on Saturday; but was prevented by various paltry interruptions, such as are continually occurring here. Today also most part of my time is gone by a similar or worse process of waste! Your Letter had many interesting Edin*r* details, — especially that about poor Mary Welsh, whose considerable degree of recovery,[1] by stricter and better regulated treatment, was truly gratifying to me. Maggie herself is expected here (date not fixed at all, *duration* only fixed to be not too long); she is a good cheerful patient creature, especially for one so sensitive by nature, and bears her burden well,[2] as indeed few could do. — You never yet called again at Morningside[3] I suppose: please do some day soon; and send me authentic report. Tell Ann she knows my poor old right hand now refuses to write but that there is nothing else in me that refuses; and that my interest in these two last branches of a kindred ever dear and venerable to me[4] will continue so long as I do. Pray make my compliments to D*r* Hunter;[5] and thank him from me for his great and constant kindness to these Two.

TC-JAC, 30 Jan. MS: NLS 527.40. Quot: Patrick Waddington, *Turgenev and England* (1980) 166.

1. Mary Welsh had become addicted to opium; see 46:46–47. John A. Carlyle wrote, 27 Jan.: "Yesterday I had a private interview with Maggie Welsh, & she told me about her sister Mary. After spending more than a year at Bridge of Allan, boarded with a lady who undertook to keep her as much as possible from opium, her brother Alick came to see her in September last, & found no improvement in her case; so by advice of D*r* Skay physician to the large Morningside Asylum here, he had her placed as I advised two years ago in the Perth Asylum where there are other ladies in a similar condition—separate from the general patients & with walking ground as well as apartments of their own. Jeanie (M*rs* Chrystal) [Mary and Maggie's sister] saw her in November & found her greatly improved & not at all dissatisfied, & last month (Dec*r*) Maggie saw her, was cheerfully welcomed & spent some hours in her company. She had lost all her stoutness, become as active as she ever was, & looked much the same as she was before she began to take any opium, & she gets none at present, but the D*r* at Perth thinks it w*d* not be safe to trust her alone just yet." Dr. David Skae (ca. 1815–73), F.R.C.S. (Fellow of the Royal College of Surgeons), 1836; d. 18 April 1873 at Tipperlinn House, part of the Morningside Asylum. Perth doctor not further identified.

2. Maggie Welsh's brother Walter, with whom she lived, was deep in debt; see 45:170.

3. JWC's aunts, Elizabeth and Ann Welsh, lived in Craigen Villa, Morningside. John replied, 31 Jan.: "I have been thrice at Craigen Villa, but will go again one of these days."

4. Because of their relationship to JWC; Ann wrote regularly to TC.

5. Presumably the same Dr. Hunter (Jacob Dickson Hunter) who attended the Welsh aunts; see TC to JAC, 26 May 1870. John wrote, 6 Jan.: "D*r* Hunter has just come in & sends his kind respects. He entirely agreed with you in everything you said in your Times Letter."

Mary and I had a dismal dinner with the Blunts on Friday night; the results of which have not been beneficial to any temporal or spiritual interest of
mine. Oh dear, Oh dear! Miss Bromley was here last night;—treating herself
to a week's Hotel-Life in London, in relief from the murky imprisonment at
Shirley.[6] Turguéneff whom I have not seen since I last mentioned is coming
on Tuesday night to take leave on return to Russia for a three or four months.
With him come Allingham and *again* Miss Bromley, who is an admirer of his.[7]
Him I myself consider to be a truly interesting and gifted man; but, alas, these
evening visits are a real misery and peril for me. Sleep, Oh gentle Sleep,[8] these
do considerably affright thee. Tuesday, however, *is* believed to be the last of
them within sight. Yesterday there had come a kind of incipiency of thaw,
roads still good; but this morning there lies a powdering of sloppy snow, with
darkness as of Egypt over-head, and I found the roads all as if soaped and fitter for being skated on (with my woolen shoes) than travelled on. Patience,
Patience, the end must come. Enough, enough, dear Brother.

Ever your affectionate
T. Carlyle

TC TO UNIDENTIFIED CORRESPONDENT

Consider the issue!
T. Carlyle
Chelsea, 2 Feby 1871

---

6. Caroline Davenport Bromley; there are several places in England called Shirley, unidentified further.

7. According to Waddington: "Miss Bromley arrived at Cheyne Row first, then Allingham
and then, at 10 o'clock, Turgenev" (Waddington 166). Allingham recorded in his diary: "*February* 2.—At Carlyle's meet Tourgueneff, and the talk turns upon Russia. T. says that every
one speaks good Russian in his country, not French, except the lower people. He speaks
well, softly, naturally, tellingly, politely; his gentle speech flowed round Carlyle's rocks—
a big strong man, over fifty, about 6½ feet, good linguist, and curious about English Literature of the time" (*Allingham Diary* 203–4); TC wrote "Tuesday" (31 Jan.) twice; 2 Feb. was
a Thurs.; it is not known which date the visit took place.

8. Cf. *Henry IV, Part II*, 3.1.

TC-UC, 2 Feb. MS: EUL, in TC's hand in blue pencil. Hitherto unpbd. TC wrote on a
small piece of paper, folded to fit in an envelope; presumably an autograph.

TC TO ROBERT LAWSON

5 Cheyne Row, Chelsea,
9 Feb. 1871.

Dear Sir,

It is with reluctance that I write anything to you on this subject of Female Emancipation which is now rising to such a height; and I do it only on the strict condition that whatever I say shall be private, and nothing of it get into the Newspapers. The truth is, the topic for five & twenty years past, especially for the last three or four, has been a mere sorrow to me; one of the most afflicting proofs of the miserable Anarchy that prevails in human society; and I have avoided thinking of it, except when fairly compelled; what little has become clear to me on it I will now endeavour to tell you.

In the first place, then, I have never doubted that the true and noble function of a woman in this world was, is, and forever will be, that of being Wife and Helpmate to a worthy Man; & discharging well the duties that devolve on her in consequence as mother of children, and mistress of a Household, duties high, noble, silently important as any that can fall to a human creature: duties which, if well discharged, constitute woman, in a soft beautiful and almost sacred way, the Queen of the World, and, by her natural faculties, graces, strengths and weaknesses, are every way indicated as specifically hers. The true destiny of a Woman, therefore, is to wed a Man she can love and esteem; and to lead noiselessly, under his protection, with all the wisdom grace and heroism that is in her, the life presented in consequence.

It seems, furthermore indubitable that if a Woman miss this destiny, or have renounced it, she has every right, before God and man, to take up whatever honest employment she can find open to her in the world; probably there are several or many employments, now exclusively in the hands of men, for which women might be more or less fit;—printing, tailoring, weaving, clerking &c &c. That Medicine is intrinsically not unfit for them is proved from the fact that in much more sound and earnest ages than ours, before the Medical Profession rose into being, they were virtually the Physicians and Surgeons as well as Sick-nurses, all that the world had. Their form of intellect, their sympathy, their wonderful acuteness of observation &c seem to indicate in

TC-RL, 9 Feb. MS: NLS 98.99. Pbd: Conway, *Carlyle* 87–88; Shepherd, *Carlyle* 2:297–99 inc; *Scotsman*, 20 Feb. 1907; Wilson, *Carlyle* 6:234–35. Robert Lawson (1846–96), studied medicine at Edinburgh Univ., where he had supported TC for rector; he qualified as a surgeon 1871; he was to work in the West Riding Asylum, Yorkshire; Wonford House, a hospital in Devon; and became, 1878, a commissioner of the Lunacy Board. The issue of admission of women to medical classes at Edinburgh Univ. was current, see below. Lawson had apparently asked TC for his opinion.

them peculiar qualities for dealing with disease; and evidently in certain departments (that of female diseases) they have quite peculiar opportunities of being useful.— My answer to your question, then, may be that two things are not doubtful to me in this matter.

1°. That Women, any Woman who deliberately so determines, have a right to study Medicine; and that it might be profitable and serviceable to have facilities, or at least possibilities offered them for so doing.[1] But

2°. That, for obvious reasons, Female Students of Medicine ought to have, if possible Female Teachers, or else an extremely select kind of Men; and in particular that to have young Women present among young Men in Anatomical Classes, Clinical Lectures, or generally studying Medicine in concert, is an incongruity of the first magnitude; and shocking to think of to every pure and modest mind.

This is all I have to say; and I send it to you, under the condition above mentioned, as a Friend for the use of Friends.

Yours sincerely, / T. Carlyle

To / Robert Lawson Esq

TC TO JOHN A. CARLYLE

5 Cheyne Row, Chelsea,
10 Feb. 1871.

My dear Brother,

Nothing has happened during this week that could much deserve record: in fact I may define myself as one that has no history at all except a passive one, or dumb struggle against the winter elements and their aggravation of

---

1. John A. Carlyle wrote from Edinburgh, 12 Feb.: "The question about admissions of ladies to the medical classes is much talked of, & several meetings on the subject have been held. Of all my acquaintances amongst the professors Masson is the only one who votes for mixed classes of women & men. . . . I . . . distinctly & emphatically told him I could by no means agree with him, & believed that the introduction of any such classes might do great injury to the university. . . . One of the 7 or 8 female students is a Miss Sophia Jex Blake— a stout, rather tall & clever-talking lady of forty or more with large under jaw. . . . I met her one day at luncheon, sat next her, found her smart & clever, but talked little about her fixed ideas." Sophia Louisa Jex-Blake (1840–1912; *ODNB*), physician and campaigner for women's rights; already a qualified mathematics teacher, she applied to Edinburgh Univ. to study medicine in 1869, but was refused on the grounds that she could not attend the men's classes, and it would not be practicable to hold classes for just one woman; when five women applied, they were admitted, but as lecturers were paid directly by their students, and they were so few, they were charged very high fees. By 1870 there were seven women altogether; although they all passed their examinations, the Univ. decided, Jan. 1872, that they could not be granted degrees.

TC-JAC, 10 Feb. MS: NLS 527.41. Hitherto unpbd.

[152]

the burdens inexorably due to old age and its sorrows. For the last four weeks I have at last fallen much bankrupt in regard to sleep; and am not yet in a state of safe liquidation,—tho' again at this date I have a *second* night of tolerable sleep; and, as usual, am trying to hope for a *third*, which would make things surer. Except this, which means merely weaker and weaker faculty of digestion, I have no complaint whatever; and ought to know, and partly do, that there is no room for discontent with my situation, but for much the reverse. The worst is, I have lost my right hand, and faculty of penmanship; otherwise I might have daily an interesting hour or two, which is now forbidden me. Two hours of reading in *Goethe*, after tea, is fairly the best employment my day yields me,—the rest of it a series of bothers & futilities; without either action or discourse which can be called either genial or satisfactory. Well, Well. Let us hope the Winter is now going or gone; let us, at least, be patient, thoughtful and, so far as may be, silent.

The Geraldine Petition, splendidly signed (thanks to Mary's eminent industry),[1] is now out of our hands into those of Gladstone; and with it at least we have *done*. Poor Forster is still coughing sadly; and much oppressed with ill-health and continual labour;—to him also the *finale* of the Geraldine affair will be a real deliverance; we went together, he and I, and solemnly delivered it to Dilke[2] last Saturday; right glad both of us to wash our hands of it.

Sunday last I had an unexpected visit from the Political Forster (of Bradford),[3] accompanied by Lord Houghton (*ci-devant* Milnes); they sat about an hour; and got a great deal of contemptuous denunciation, and *Latter-Day Pamphletism* from me; which they took, especially Forster did,[4] with some appearance of real seriousness, and *quasi*-penitent admission that perhaps it was too true. Forster in particular rather pleased me; had more of solidity, and less of "soft-soap" than I had expected, after his sudden rise to what is called

---

1. For the campaign for Geraldine Jewsbury's pension, see TC to JAC, 21 Jan.

2. Sir Charles Wentworth Dilke (1843–1911; *ODNB*), writer and politician; as the Liberal M.P. for Chelsea, 1868–86, he was the appropriate person to whom to deliver a petition for a constituent.

3. William Edward Forster (1818–86; *ODNB*), reforming politician, Liberal M.P. for Bradford 1861–80; known to the Carlyles since 1843 (15:229), see also TC's note to JWC's "Much Ado About Nothing," 24:171.

4. Richard Monckton Milnes, 1st Baron Houghton, wrote to his wife, Annabella, 5 Feb.: "I have seen a number of people to-day, beginning with the Prophet of Chelsea. . . . I went . . . with Forster (W. E.), and it was touching to hear him tell the old man that if he ever did or became anything useful or notable, he owed it to the influence of his writings. I am sorry to say the Prophet cursed and swore a great deal, saying the Government might drag the nation down to hell, but he was not going with them, or with any Ministry that left the country with six guns, one torpedo, and a Cardwell" (T. Wemyss Reid, *The Life, Letters and Friendships of Richard Monckton Milnes, First Lord Houghton*, 2 vols. (1890) 2:250). For Edward Cardwell and his military reforms, see below.

eminence in the Parliamentary line.[5] There is great emotion, he told me, on the matter of Army Reform, and some other points of practicality.[6] Surely not a moment too soon! Gladstone, I hear in other quarters, has decided to take the Army Reform "enthusiastically" into his own hand, —the admirable man intent to ride on whatever puff of vapour rises, and be at the top so long as possible. Perhaps this movement may really carry him thro' another session (his horoscope was thought to be bad otherwise); what it will do for the Army nobody yet can know, except in general that, till the British Constitution please to change itself, no right Army is possible to the British Nation or its Gladstones. n.l.[7] Three days ago I went to Mazzini's Lodgings, to take leave of him on his departure from England for good.[8] I had not seen him for two years; the look of his now aged face bro't many thoughts to me which were sad and strange, and, in some sort, even great. We talked for about an hour, he mostly the Speaker, with eloquence, with affectionate vivacity: he looks very old and hoary, but the eyes are still beautiful and genially bright. He is to settle in Rome; and set forth some *"truly* patriotic" Newspaper there.[9] He discribed himself as one dead all but the brain part, which belonged to his Country till the very end; he himself having rather the feeling of a *Revenant* than of a Man still living. Poor Fellow, it was impossible not to wish him well, and commend him silently to the Good Powers of this Universe. A really pious, heroic little man. We parted with real emotion on both sides; and shall probably not meet again in this scene of things. I have felt a peculiar shade of sadness ever since.[10]— Tonight there is a Col*l* Davidson from Edinburgh coming: he also is a mournful phenomenon, though on far other grounds.[11]

5. Forster was appointed vice-president of the council (with responsibility for education), Dec. 1868, in Gladstone's government; the 1870 Elementary Education Act became known as Forster's Act; see also 45:90.

6. Gladstone's secretary of state for war, Edward Cardwell, was instituting army reforms, re-organizing the War Office, replacing a large standing army with a smaller permanent force and a large number of trained reservists, and, most controversially, abolishing the purchase of commissions; see also TC to CK, 22 Nov. 1870.

7. TC wrote "n.l." (new line) to indicate new paragraph.

8. Giuseppe Mazzini's last recorded contact with TC was Aug. 1867; see 45:16. TC wrote in his journal, 8 Feb.: "Yesterday . . . took leave of Mazzini, who is just about returning permanently to Rome, to publish a Newspaper there. I had not seen him for a long time: we talked for about an hour, in a cordial & sincere way, with real emotion (I do believe) on both sides; —and parted, hardly expecting, either of us, to meet again in this world. . . . Mazzini is the most *pious* living man I now know" (TC's journal; privately owned). Mazzini was lodging with Mrs. France at 18 Fulham Rd. He did not mention TC's visit in his letters at the time, but he wrote to Emilie Venturi from Pisa, 13 March: "Remember me to Carlyle, whose sympathy and good opinion is very much valued by me" (*Scritti* 90:312).

9. Mazzini founded and edited *La Roma del Popolo*, Feb. 1871–March 1872.

10. JWC had been a close friend of Mazzini's, while TC was more detached.

11. David Davidson and JWC had been childhood friends.

I enclose two Letters which touch on specifically Edinburgh topics; the Medical one I answered yesterday after some delay; voting *for* the Young Man and his party who writes;[12]—they are *not* to print my bit of Letter. To the Sheriff, and indeed to the Scott Centenary question from the first, I have continued dumb;—do you hear of it in Edinburgh much, and in what sense?[13] To myself Scott was never of heroic quality; and seems to be far too young yet for *Centenary* operations;—which, at any rate, are apt to be blaring nonentities of a rather disgusting nature. Everybody here now expects a speedy Peace for France; since Gambetta's evanescence[14] that seems now the likely issue. The German management throughout seems to have been well nigh perfect; and with such consummation the Victory may be considered of benifit to all the earth.

This is enough of tedious babble, dear Brother; and I will release you, for the time. Tomorrow perhaps we may hear from you.

Ever your affectionate[15]

TC TO JANET CARLYLE HANNING

5 Cheyne Row Chelsea
13 Feb. 1871.

My dear Sister Jenny,

Here is a little bit of a present[1] which you must accept from me; it was intended for the New-Year's time, but has been belated; which will do it no

12. Presumably those in favor of training women as doctors; see TC to RL, 9 Feb.

13. Archibald Davidson, Edinburgh sheriff, unidentified further; presumably he had written to TC to ask for some kind of contribution to one of the celebrations which were to be held in many Scottish towns for the centenary of Sir Walter Scott's birth, 15 Aug. 1871; TC had already been approached for contributions to the centenary; see 46:17. John wrote, 12 Feb.: "The Centenary of Sir W. Scott I have not heard once mentioned in any company since I came to Edinr. . . . Now & then advertisements & short statements about it appear in the papers."

14. Léon Gambetta (1838–82), French republican politician; minister of the interior in the Government of National Defence 1870–71; he tried to organize the army from Tours to relieve Paris, but lost power in the general elections, 8 Feb., to Adolphe Thiers (1797–1877), French conservative politician and historian, new leader of the National Assembly. TC had apparently written to John about him, as John replied, 5 Feb.: "I was . . . especially struck by what you say concerning Gambetta. The situation of things in France seems very critical still though Paris has surrendered; & Gambetta's projects not only may meet with approbation amongst mad Frenchmen, but also with many ignorant people in this country. . . . And another letter to the Times might do great good, as the first did, both in Germany & England, & indirectly also in France."

15. The signature has been cut off.

TC-JCH, 13 Feb. MS: Yale. Pbd: Copeland, "Unpublished Letters" 82:788–90; Copeland 238–42.

1. Mary Aitken noted in TC's checkbook: "Chelsea 11 Feb. 1871 / John C. Aitken (for Canada) ('Jenie') / £10 .. o .. o" (TC's checkbook; MS: NLS 20753); "('Jenie')": in TC's hand.

great ill with you. Buy yourself something nice with it; and consider at all times that my affectionate best wishes are with you; and that if I could in any way do you a useful kindness, I gladly would.

We get a good few Canada Newspapers from you; welcome tokens of your remembrance: in one of the last, there was a very melancholy item of news marked by your hand,—the death of your dear little grandchild, poor Mary's Bairn;[2] we conceived painfully how sad it must have made you all; & were ourselves sad & sorry. Poor Mary, she was herself a Child when I saw her last,[3] & she is now a bereaved Mother;—Death snatches us from one another at all ages! I often think with silent gratitude to Providence how gently we older ones have been dealt with in this respect; saved, a whole family of us, for so many years; none lost but poor Margaret[4] (very dear, and very sacred to me at this hour) and a wee wee *Jenny*[5] whom you never saw, but whose death, and my Mother's unappeasable grief for it, are still strangely present to me, after near seventy years. All we can say is, both the Living and the Dead are with God; & we have to obey, and be of hope.

You regret sometimes that I do not write to you; but it is not my blame, it is my misfortune rather. For rather above five years past my right hand has been getting useless for writing (the left, strangely enough, is still steady, and holds good); the weight of years, too, 75 of them gone December last, presses heavy on me; and all work, but most especially all kinds of writing are a thing I avoid as sorrowfully disagreeable. Mary Aitken, who drives an admirable pen, is indeed ever willing to be "dictated" to; and I do, in cases of necessity try that method; but find, on the whole, that it never will succeed with me. From the Dr and from Jean I believe you get all the news that are worth writing; and that is the main interest in the matter.

The Dr is in Edinr, of late weeks; & seems to be enjoying himself among old friends;—and finds it, no doubt, a pleasant & useful interruption of his Dumfries solitude, to which he will return with fresh appetite. He is much stronger and cheerier than I; five years *younger*, and at least twice five lighter of heart.

2. Jenny Hanning wrote to John A. Carlyle, 5 Jan.: "When I wrote to you five weeks ago I mentioned . . . that my little Granddaughter Jeny C. Holden was sick . . . she grew weaker and weaker, and poor Mary was nearly worn off her feet . . . she died so very suddenly. . . . I thought [Mary] would lose her reason at the time but she is trying to say that Gods will be done. / Maggie had a letter from her cousin Maggie Carlyle two days ago: they were all well at Bield then. Tom's Wife [Margaret] had a Daughter [Hellen] about a week ago. / Please give my kind love to sister Jean: she too knows what it is to part with her children: a few lines from her might help to comfort Mary in her affliction" (MS: NLS 1775E.7). Jean Aitken had now lost three sons; see also TC to JAC, 12 Nov.

3. TC last saw Mary Sept. 1850 (see 25:211); Jenny and her das. left for Canada, June 1851 (see 26:86).

4. Their sister Margaret (1803–30); for her death, see 5:116–20.

5. Their sister Janet Carlyle (1799–1801); for her death, see Carlyle, *Reminiscences* 115.

He has an excellent Lodging at Dumfries, yonder; and is of much service to all the kindred; every one of whom he is continually ready to help. Mary Aitken has been here with me above two years;—a bright little soul writing for me, trying to be useful and cheerful to me. I have plenty of Friends here; but none of them do me much good, except by their evident good-will; company in general is at once wearisome & hurtful to me; silence, and the company of my own sombre thoughts, sad probably but also loving and beautiful, are wholesomer than talking; these and a little serious reading are my chief resource. I have no bodily ailment, except what belongs to the gradual decay of a digestive faculty which was always weak; except when sleepless nights afflict me too much, I have no reason to complain but the contrary. This winter, now nearly done, has been a blusterous cold inclement one as any I can latterly remember; it grew at last to tell upon me as the unfriendliest of all its brethren;—but I think, after all, it may have done me little or no intrinsic damage. With the new Spring and its bright days I hope to awaken again and shake away this torpor of nerves and mind.

I have long owed Alick a Letter,—that is to say, intended to write him one, though by count it is his turn. I often think of you all on that side the Sea as well as this; if that could do you any good, Alas! I will end here, dear little Sister; wishing all that is good to you and yours, as at all times. I am and remain,

Ever your affectionate Brother,
T. Carlyle.[6]

Send a *Newspaper* with 3 strokes when this comes: don't trouble yrself with any other announcement.[7]

TC TO JOSEPH LAWTON

5, Cheyne-row, Chelsea
Feb. 14, 1871.

Mr. Jos. Lawton.

Dear Sir,—Your letter has pleased and interested me; and certainly I wish you progress in your ingenuous pursuit, which may be defined as the highest

6. The signature and postscript are in TC's hand.

7. TC wrote in his journal, 14 Feb.: "Spring prophesying of itself,—once ag*n*! To me how useless hitherto; mournful, barren of earthly hope. Truth is I have suffered from the bad Winter, for 4 or 5 weeks back suffering considerably from *want of sleep*; wh*h*, at all times, acts frightfully on the *nerves*, and thereby on the *sensations* and even the *thots*,—such are our condit*ns* in this world. I strive to believe I shall get above this ag*n* in some measure, and be good for something: but every ill fit that takes me now can persuade one, more or less that *it* is the invincible and final one" (TC's journal; privately owned).

TC-JL, 14 Feb. Pbd: *The Best Hundred Books* (*Pall Mall Gazette Extra* 24 [Feb. 1886] 3); *Pall Mall Gazette*, 17 Feb. 1886. Joseph Lawton (d. 1916), journalist; after working on vari-

and truest for all men in all ranks of life. Evermore is *Wisdom* the highest of conquests to every son of Adam, nay, in a large sense, the one conquest; and the precept to every one of us is ever, "Above all thy gettings, get understanding."[1] Books are certainly a great help in this pursuit; but I know not if they are the greatest; the greatest I rather judge are one's own earnest reflections and meditations, and, to begin with, a candid, just, and sincere mind in oneself. Books, however, especially the Books of sincere and true-seeing men, are indisputably a great resource of guidance and assistance; and indeed are at present almost the only one we have left.

I have more than once thought of such a list as you speak of (for we all, in universities as well as workshops, labour under that difficulty, and in the end each of us has to pick his own way); but a good list of the kind would be extremely difficult to do; and would be both an envious and precarious one. Impossible to be right in all your judgments of Books; and still more impossible to please everybody with it if you even were! Perhaps I may try something of it some good day nevertheless.[2]

For the rest, I can assure you that your choice of a Homer is perfectly successful: I reckon Pope's still fairly the best English translation,[3] though there are several newer, and one older, not without merit; in regard to style, or outward garniture, neither Pope nor one of them has the least resemblance to rough old Homer; but you will get the *shape* and essential meaning out of Pope as well as another. In regard to Plato (Socrates didn't *write* anything; and he is known chiefly by what Plato and Xenophon say of him) your best re-

---

ous newspapers in Darlington, County Durham, Lawton worked on the *Northern Echo* (also Darlington) and then, 1880, succeeded W. T. Stead (1849–1912; *ODNB*) as its ed., Stead having moved to the *Pall Mall Gazette*. The letter was first pbd. in the *Pall Mall Gazette Extra*, then in the *Pall Mall Gazette* itself; text: *Pall Mall Gazette Extra*. The 1886 *Pall Mall Gazette* pbd. several letters on the subject of the best hundred books; these were so popular that they were reprinted in a pamphlet, with others added, including this letter from TC, which was introduced: "Exactly fifteen years ago a North-country lad who was seeking after knowledge in the midst of his work in a printer's office wrote to Carlyle for his advice on the best books." The *Pall Mall Gazette* added: "His correspondent had justified the sage's good wishes and is now director of an important journal in the north of England."

1. See Prov. 4:7.

2. TC had several times compiled reading lists for friends; see, for instance, 38:209–10 and (for Lord and Lady Ashburton) 38:257–58. He wrote in his journal, 14 Feb.: "I wanted to write down sevl things . . . some List (perhaps) of '*Books* best worth reading by *workmen* & the eager unguided;' &c &c: but except by 'dictatn' I cannot, and that never will go rightly with me" (TC's journal; privately owned).

3. Alexander Pope (1688–1744; *ODNB*), poet; there are many edns. of his trans. of Homer's *Iliad* (1715–20) and *Odyssey* (1726); TC owned the 1761 edn. of the *Odyssey* (see *Carlyle's House* 88), and he gave Mary Aitken, 16 June 1875, a 1784 edn. of the *Iliad*, which he probably already owned (see *Sotheby's* [1932] item 75).

source will probably by Bohn's Classical Library[4] (Bohn, York-street, Covent-garden), a readable translation at four or five shillings, which any country bookseller can get for you on order: and, indeed, I may say, in regard to all manner of books, Bohn's Publication Series is the usefullest thing I know; and you might as well send to him for a catalogue, which, doubtless, he would willingly send you for the postage stamp. As to English History, Hume's[5] is universally regarded as the best; but perhaps none of them can rigorously be called good; and you will be sure to take the first book you can come at, and to read that with all your attention, keeping a map before you, and looking round you on all sides; especially looking before and after for chronology's sake,[6]—upon which latter at least, if not upon various other things, you may find it useful to take notes. Pinkerton's Geography, even the 8vo abridgment (still more the 2 vol. 4to original),[7] is a useful book in such studies. In Political Economy I consider Smith's "Wealth of Nations,"[8] which is the beginning of all the books since, to be still, by many degrees, the best, as well as the pleasantest to read; and in regard to that of "Political Economy," nay even to that of Plato, &c, &c, you must not be surprised if the results arrived at considerably disappoint you; and sometimes, though also sometimes not, completely deserve to do so.

Wishing you heartily well, and recommending silence, sincerity, diligence, and patience as the grand conditions of every useful success in your pursuit, I remain, yours sincerely,

T. CARLYLE.

4. Henry George Bohn (1796–1884; *ODNB*), translator and publisher; see 23:108. Bohn retired in 1864, and his business, at 4 York St., Covent Garden, was continued by George Bell (1814–90; *ODNB*) and Frederick Daldy (1825–1905).

5. David Hume (1711–76; *ODNB*), Scottish philosopher and historian, *The History of England, from the Invasion of Julius Caesar to the Revolution in 1688*, 6 vols. (1762).

6. For a very similar instruction to Jean Aitken, see 26:225.

7. Sir John Pinkerton (1758–1826; *ODNB*), Scottish historian and poet, *Modern Geography*, 2 vols. (1802); TC owned the updated 2 vol. 1817 edn.; see *Carlyle's House* 97.

8. Adam Smith (bap. 1723–90; *ODNB*), Scottish moral philosopher and political economist; his major work is *Wealth of Nations* (1776); TC owned the 1835–39 edn. (4 vols.); see *Carlyle's House* 85.

TC TO EMILY FAITHFULL

[16 February 1871]

5, Cheyne-row, Chelsea,—Dear Madam,—I regret that I cannot get to hear your lecture,[1] which would have been interesting and pleasant to me; but I send a little ear of corn to join with the charitable harvest you are reaping,[2] which I trust will be abundant for the sake of those poor Frenchwomen whom with all my heart I pity, as you do.—With many kind wishes, I remain, always yours sincerely, T. Carlyle.

TC TO LADY STANLEY

5 Cheyne Row, Chelsea
22 Feb. 1871.

Dear Lady Stanley,

For a long time I have been anxious to see you, after so unexampled a period of absence! I am very much obliged by your kind offer of 5 o'clock to my little Niece and me:[1] but tea in the afternoon is a thing I am forbidden to take; and at that hour I am regularly hastening home, or already got home, with an eye to try for a little sleep before dinner. That, therefore, I grieve to say is not possible at present.

On the contrary I could, and will, any day you appoint, call on you at *four* o'clock; and from twelve till *three* I am, all days, here at home; and should rejoice to be honoured with a call from you.

Yours always, with affectionate regards,

T. Carlyle

TC-EF, [16 Feb.]. Pbd: *Pall Mall Gazette*, 21 Feb.; *Daily Telegraph*, 21 Feb. Dated by TC's check, see below. Emily Faithfull (1835–95; *ODNB*), women's activist and publisher of the Victoria Press, 1860–69.

1. Emily Faithfull's lecture, 20 Feb., was on "Women's Work and Women's Sphere"; it was given on behalf of French female refugees in the Franco-Prussian War and hosted by the Refugees Benevolent Fund. Before beginning her lecture, Faithfull read TC's letter, which proved "that the strong enthusiasm for Germany which beat in that great heart of his by no means excluded a tender sympathy for the suffering entailed by the unprecedented success of German arms" (*Pall Mall Gazette*, 21 Feb.).

2. Mary Aitken noted in TC's checkbook: "16 Feb 1871 / Miss Emily Faithful / £1 .. 1 .. 0" (TC's checkbook; MS: NLS 20753).

TC-Lady S, 22 Feb. MS: Strouse. Hitherto unpbd.

1. Lady Stanley wrote, 21 Feb.: "I have been hoping to see you this long time & now write to ask if it would be possible for you to come to tea here at 5 oclock next Monday the *27th* & do me the favor to bring your niece. I have a particular reason for asking you to come to me & if Monday is not convenient for you tell me what other day will be for have you here I must with Miss Aitkin." TC and Mary Aitken called on Lady Stanley 27 Feb.; see TC to JCA, 25 Feb., and TC to MO, 11 April.

TC TO JEAN CARLYLE AITKEN

5 Cheyne Row, Chelsea,
25 Feb. 1871.

Dear Sister,

There was talk last week of a letter from you on Sunday, which however did not come; today I send to you a word upon the principle of Mahomet's miracle, "Since the Mountain cannot come to Mahomet, Mahomet can and will come to the Mountain."[1]

It will relieve you to hear that I seem to be slowly recovering out of my dreary contention with want of sleep, which has made my life unusually miserable for the last 7 or 8 weeks. I have not yet had one night of what can be called good sleep; but it is several nights, perhaps 5 or 6, since I absolutely failed to sleep and got into nocturnal chaos, with the certainty of an utterly smashed feeling for the following day. The getting out of sleep, as I have heard you often say, is an altogether easy matter, but the getting into a steady tract of it again is a most ticklish process. I do not yet call myself successful; but I have a better hope than hitherto. It seems purely the fruit of damages, a "sundries at different dates" inflicted on me by the bad winter, and coming in at last for settlement when the Winter itself is gone.

That I have been entirely idle, incapable of anything deserving, never so little, the name of Work I need not tell you; and certainly that degrading element is a great aggravation of all one's other miseries. I feel sometimes as if there were things in me which I still wished to say; and poor Mary is often encouraging me to try if I cannot, though without a hand of my own, begin: she is a most swift and willing scribe, poor creature; but I never can go on at all as if there were nothing between the paper and me, —no third party guessing what I was about! This is a haggle which I feel I shall never altogether overcome;—nor indeed till I get considerably relieved from this stomachie "Slough of Despond"[2] can I fairly try; nothing else, I find, but Indigestion is the matter with me, the gradual decay of that indispensable operation, which has been my misery for fifty years; and which cannot be expected now to do other than *de*crease till it stop altogether. Let it be as God wills; that is a duty eminently incumbent, which I hope is at no time doubtful to me.

We had a Letter from the D*r* yesterday; but it was vague and of little interest, evidently written in a great hurry; the one bit of important news, that he still purposed returning home in the beginning of the week. I confidently expect he will find himself sensibly improved by this Town-adventure, and winnowed clear of much country dust by the new and stirring scene he has

TC-JCA, 25 Feb. MS: NLS 531.7. Hitherto unpbd.
1. Proverbial; cf. Francis Bacon, *Essays* (1625).
2. See John Bunyan, *Pilgrim's Progress* (1678).

been in. Sometime in Summer, not too far on, I privately expect him here, though he has said nothing about it. I often, indeed generally more or less, have an outlook towards the Sea in Summer; other hopeful shift of lodgings I have now none left,—if in this itself there be any hope left. One ought to try it at least.

I have plenty of company, perhaps too much, and of the kind called good; but, though there is a certain stimulus in conversation, and in uttering, in the least faithfully, what one thinks and feels, I seldom feel much real pleasure in these colloquies; and visits of people, in the evening especially, are apt to do me evident hurt;—these latter accordingly I strive more and more to forbid. Yesterday I made no fewer than three calls; found a clever old Gentleman, whom I had not seen for two years (Lord Stratford de Redcliffe, long our Ambassador in Turkey,[3] a really shrewd, experienced and honest minded old Man): with him I sat in vigorous talk for above an hour; then *walked* home (three new miles, making six in all); but, except perhaps some transitory pleasure to the old Diplomatist I could myself trace little or no benifit; and might about as well have been plodding along with no companion but my own solitary thoughts. On Monday Mary and I are solemnly invited to some (doubtless quite insignificant) interview[4] with a big Lady Stanley, whom I know not if you ever saw, though she is now my oldest Friend among the Aristocracy here (once very beautiful, now a Widow and obliged to apply to Banting for fat);[5] of course we shall go; but know already that nothing will come of it but *fee-fah-fum* in a good humoured dialect.

Yesterday I sent you Sinclair's Pamphlet on the War;[6] if you are not busy, it is really worth reading. The *Daily News*, sent along with this, contains our latest rumours out of France;[7] perhaps some of you may like to look into it.

3. Stratford Canning Redcliffe (1786–1880; *ODNB*), 1st Viscount Stratford de Redcliffe, diplomat; much of his career was spent as the British ambassador in Constantinople, where he became known as the "Great Elchi." TC met him early Nov. 1867; see 45:65.

4. It was for the presentation of a clock for TC's 75th birthday, 4 Dec. 1870; see TC to MO, 11 April.

5. William Banting (1796/97–1878, *ODNB*), writer on diet; having been extremely overweight, he cut out starch and fat from his diet, lost weight and felt much healthier; he then wrote *A Letter on Corpulence, Addressed to the Public* (1863), which became an overnight success; his name became a synonym for a slimming diet.

6. Sir John George Tollemache Sinclair (1825–1912), *The Franco-German War* (1871). He lived in Norwood, and was the son of TC's old friend Sir George Sinclair (1790–1868; *ODNB*); see 36:286. TC had met him when Sir George was staying with him April 1864; see 40:66.

7. The Paris correspondent of the London *Daily News* reported, 24 Feb.: "Of news there is an absolute dearth; of rumours there is no end. . . . Upon one point all the newspapers seem to be unanimous; and the same opinion is entertained by every class of politician. . . . [T]hat Prussia will make a cession of territory a *sine quá non*, and that Count Bismarck,

Peace does appear in spite of all that babbling and guessing, to be now really at hand; Thiers's Speech itself indicates that he is prepared to accept almost any terms,—which indeed is wise on his part.[8] Poor old Thiers, last time I saw him, 16 years ago,[9] he little expected such an adventure as this! But all his Politics and all his Writings (especially his huge lying Life of Nap$n$ I)[10] have led his Nation straight in this direction; and now poor Souls they have arrived.

Jim has sent us a Tin of Brazil Coffee, which on tasting it this morning, I find to be excellent; if there were any good way of roasting it I would have a good lot more. My new Stockings are capital. You farther sent me a pair of new Snow Shoes, for which I never yet thanked you in words; tho' otherwise I did not fail; they were handsome shoes & of excellent quality, but were from 2 to 3 inches too short: Mrs Warren says she can alter them; and if we live to see another Winter, they shall do duty.[11] The proposed indoor pair of woolen Shoes, we need not meddle with till there is a surer opportunity of fitting them.

Adieu, dear Sister; here is an abundance of Babble for you & even a superabundance; my heart's blessing to you and all yours. Ever Yr affectionate
T. Carlyle

TC TO JOHN A. CARLYLE

5 Cheyne Row, Chelsea,
27 Feb. 1871

My dear Brother,

You got nothing from us on Saturday but Newspapers; nor has anything come from you today; but we understand that yr rooms are *engaged* for Thursday coming, and we conclude that probably you will go home on Wednesday. All right; & may your Town-adventure make the Spring beauties of the Coun-

---

though he is said to be inclined towards leniency, urged by the military party, will submit hard terms. . . . Whatever man can do M. Thiers and his colleagues will strive to accomplish to save the honour and the dignity of France; but that they are resolved to make peace is evident from the tone of M. Thiers' remarks to the Assembly on the 19th, on his formal acceptance of office." For Adolphe Thiers, see TC to JAC, 10 Feb.

8. The *Daily News* reported, 21 Feb., Thiers's speech to the National Assembly, 19 Feb.: "[A]t the present time there was only one line of policy to follow, and it was urgent to put an end to the evils afflicting the country, and to put an end to the occupation of the enemy. The country had need of peace which must be courageously discussed, and only accepted if honourable."

9. TC met Thiers several times while he was visiting England in 1852; see 27:89.

10. Adolphe Thiers, *Histoire du consulat et de l'empire*, 21 vols. (Paris, 1845–69). For TC's opinion of his *Histoire de la Révolution Française* (Paris, 1823–27), see 6:302–3.

11. "[D]uty" repeated with a line over it at turn of page.

TC-JAC, 27 Feb. MS: NLS 527.42. Hitherto unpbd.

try all the more tasteful and profitable to you![1] I recollect no farther messages to Edin*r*; nor have I have anything specially to report of myself,[2] nothing indeed, except that I find the Winter has done me considerable injury, which I w*d* fain judge to be slowly but gradually in *fact* repairing itself. Hope springs eternal![3] —

What I write about today is a sad discovery I came upon yesterday in reference to poor Anthony Sterling. I had heard, in a vague accidental manner, that he was unwell; and I yesterday, thinking it was nothing particular, strolled up in that direction to enquire and see. The Servant could not admit me; and had a grave look; but he went at my request to announce me,[4] and produced the Nephew, Capt*n* John Sterling;[5] from whom I at once learned that the business was of an altogeth*r* grave & gravest character; & that in fact poor Anthony was rapidly advancing towards the inexorable bourne![6] I was much struck; and the longer I have thought of the matter since, it grows the sadder and more tragic to me, —tumbling up into confused and mournful memory so much that has come & gone during the 35 years past.[7] Anthony has been evidently in a suffering grim unwieldy state for years past, especially since we last returned from Scotland; during which period he got into the way of occasionally calling on me again. About the end of October last, it must have been, he called here one day;[8] bringing down his Nephew's Wife,[9] a showy kind of Lady of whom he seemed to be rather proud, & indeed he looked a degree cheerfuller and fresher than I had seen him of late. Alas, it was the last time I was ever to see him in this world. It appears, "about 3 months ago," I suppose just when Winter had set in, he became much worse; and indeed, in the course of a few weeks, broke down altogether: kidneys, heart, stomach, all manner of functions, ceasing work; the whole system in rapid collapse;[10] so that, several weeks ago, "Dr Gull,"[11] the Celebrated of the present day, de-

1. John A. Carlyle replied, Wed. 1 March, that he had returned home that day: "& find all well here—fully better than when I left . . . at the beginning of January."
2. Mary wrote "of myself to report"; TC corrected by reversing the phrases.
3. Cf. Alexander Pope, *Essay on Man* (1733–34) 1.95.
4. TC inserted the phrase "at my request to announce me."
5. Capt. John Barton Sterling, soldier in the Coldstream Guards.
6. Anthony Sterling d. 1 March.
7. TC and Anthony Sterling first met late Dec. 1836 or early Jan. 1837; see 9:119.
8. This visit is unrecorded; TC's last mention of Sterling was in Sept. 1870, just after his return from Scotland; see TC to JAC, 17 Sept. 1870.
9. Apparently Caroline and John Barton Sterling lived with Anthony Sterling; from 1872, the PO directory listed John Barton at "South Lodge, South Place," i.e., Anthony Sterling's address of 3 South Pl.
10. John wrote, 1 March, that Stirling Maxwell had told him that he had seen Sterling about a month ago, and "found him hopelessly ill."
11. William Withey Gull (1816–90; *ODNB*), physician.

clared his visits to be useless henceforth, and ceased to come. The brain itself is now gone; poor Anthony has now no consciousness of where or what he is; dimly and with difficulty recognises his Nephew John, hardly any other; & is evidently hastening towards the last goal. The way of all the earth, —of *all* the earth and its million generations, past and coming, till Time itself shall die!—

This is all I will write today, dear Brother: somebody is waiting for Mary; & we have both together to go on some quasi-mysterious visit to Lady Stanley at 4.

Ever yr affecte Brother
T. Carlyle

TC TO ALEXANDER CARLYLE

5 Cheyne Row, Chelsea,
28 Feb. 1871.

My dear Brother,

I heard of some intention you had to "write me a long Letter" a good while ago; but nothing has yet come: indeed I guess well enough, by sad experience of my own, how unwilling you are to write at all, if it can be helped; I myself, with a shaking right hand, have almost lost the power of writing. But having got a willing Clerk here (gleg little Mary Aitken who is very good to me), I overcome my languours, and will this day at last accomplish my small purpose of sending *you* an articulate word. Alas, if the thoughts I send you could go without writing, you would hardly any day want a Letter: that I firmly believe too is my own case on your side; so we will endeavour to be patient; to be justly thankful, both of us, that we are still spared to send one another *silent* Letters, and to be Brothers to one another in this world yet a while!—

The Winter here, singularly wild tempestuous and inclement one, has been perceptibly unkind to me; though now, in the Spring, I flatter myself with thoughts of coming back to the old poor level again;—whether ever of getting to do any Work more, I dare not promise, or even confidently hope. I have no bodily ailment, except what I have always had for above half a century now, namely, the inability to digest; which of course is increasing as years increase, and is not in the possibility of doing other. I can still walk a great deal in my better days; and it is a thing I try daily as the one medicine I have, or ever really had. Outward things go what might be called altogether prosperously with me; much printing and new printing of my poor bits of Books; which never had such a degree of circulation as now; honour enough, all sorts of honour from my poor fellow creatures &c &c; all which sure enough is good

TC-AC, 28 Feb. MS: MUL. Pbd: Marrs 770–74. Quot: A. Carlyle, *NL* 2:275–77.

in its kind, is at least better than the contrary would have been; but has all become of small moment, and indeed to a degree that astonishes myself utterly *indifferent*, in sight of the Immensities & Eternities which I now see close ahead. Plenty of personal friends there are too, who are abundantly kind, and several of them clever and ingenious to talk with; I do not shun these altogether, but neither do I seek them; conversation generally wearies rather than delights me, and I find the company of my own thoughts and recollections; what may be called conversing with the Dead, a more salutary, though far mournfuller employment. In fact, dear Brother, I am now in my 76*th* year, and for the last five years especially am left altogether solitary in these waste whirlwinds of existence: that is as you perceive, the summary of my history at present. I think I was always a serious creature too, and always had in the heart of me a feeling that was unspeakable for those I loved. No wonder one's thoughts, in such case, are solemn, and one's heart indisposed for worldly trivialities, however big these think themselves. — But I must get out of this; which is leading us nowhither, and fast wasting the space left me for more definite objects at present.

The last Letter I saw of yours was the one to John several months ago, directly on the death of Tom's poor little Boy.[1] That was a sternly sad event. I can never since forget the speech of the poor little creature to his Father as the clouds of Death were sweeping him away! — We hear lately from Sister Jenny that she has lost a little Grand-child:[2] no doubt there, too, there is sorrow and mourning. Death at all times lies under the flowers & the thorns of existence, whatever or wherever these may be. —

In late times, looking at you all in Canada, where you are as it were a little Colony of yourselves; I cannot help feeling thankful that you are there and not here. This Country seems to me to grow more & more uninhabitable for the natural minded man of any rank, and especially for the poor man, who has to work for his Bread, and determines to be honest withal. More and more does that become impracticable to him as matters now go; the proportion of false work and of false ware, —*shoddy* in all departments, practical and spiritual, — increases steadily from year to year. Wealth in enormous masses becomes ever more frequent; &, in a still higher proportion, poverty, grim famine and the impossibility to live among larger and larger masses of the Working People, in the lower kinds of them. Among the higher kinds of them, intemperance, mutiny, bad behaviour increases daily: in fact, I apprehend before many years the huge abominable Boil will *burst*, and the British Empire fall into convulsions; perhaps into horrors and confusions which nobody is yet counting on. All Europe, indeed the whole civilized World, is in weltering confused

1. Thomas Alexander Carlyle; see TC to JAC, 12 Nov.
2. Jenny Holden; see TC to JCH, 13 Feb.

struggle and mutiny: I can find nobody so safe as he that is piously and faithfully tilling the earth and leading a manful life in silence far away from all that, divided by the Sea from all that.—

Of our kindred in Scotland, I think you hear pretty regularly; and probably I have nothing new to tell you: I will say only that nothing has gone wrong there since you heard last; and that the Dr (which also perhaps you know) has been spending a six weeks in Edinburgh; seemingly with both satisfaction and profit, and expects to return tomorrow (Wednesday) afternoon and resume his solitary habits, his Books and his old rural walks at Dumfries, now when the bright Spring has come. He is usually very solitary there and cultivates hardly any Company, but what the walls of the house contain for him. At Scotsbrig, at The Gill, or elsewhere among us, there is nothing changed, still less anything changed for the worse. Let us be thankful, thankful!

I often think of your Boys and Girls, especially of Tom and Jane, and am always glad to have any details about them. It is very long since I had a Letter from your Jane: do not bother her about determining to write to me; say I remember some pretty Letters from her long ago, and if she ever did come upon the thought of writing to me again, it would be very welcome. As to Tom, he knows I always read his Letters with pleasure, especially when he expands freely into the historical and biographical. Some of you tell me at least about this new Edition of my Book, *Whether any of you get an actual Copy of it?* There are to be 30 or even 33 volumes; and about 25 are already printed. In a smaller form, there is an older handy Edition, in 23 volumes, I surely think I sent that to Tom or to some of you! There is also to be straightway a *People's Edition*; very neat, tho' very cheap. Any or all of these, I could readily send, and would to such of you as really needed them. To Boston our Bookseller[3] here has a regular transit of Books; from Boston to you I think the road also is open. Tell me something about this soon as you like.

We have had, as you doubtless know, an agitated six months with the German-French War. Not since we were Boys, and the *First* Napoleon was getting handcuffed and flung out of doors,[4] have I seen so much emotion or so universal about any Continental thing. Yesterday, and not till then, we learn that the *Preliminaries* of Peace are actually signed,[5]—not yet Peace itself; though that latter too is to be looked for as certain in a few days; and so an end to the most furious controversy Europe has ever seen; at least to the completest brashing into ruinous defeat that vain and quarrelsome France has ever had. "Such a thrashing as probably one creature of the human kind

3. Field, Osgood, & Co; see TC to RWE, 28 Sept.

4. For TC on Napoleon I's abdication and first imprisonment, see 1:6–7.

5. Thiers was negotiating a peace treaty with the Prussians; it was signed 26 Feb. and ratified 1 March.

never gave another" to use poor Will Brown's[6] expression; —and sure enough *this* "Scoury Devil from the Priestside"[7] did richly deserve it; and we all hope will be the better for it; no event has taken place in Europe in my time that pleased me better; and, for my own part, I expect that the results, which are certain to be many-fold, and are much dreaded by the ignorant English, will be salutary & of benifit to all the world. —Adieu, my dear Brother, I will weary you no more today: I am in fact utterly stupid, and have not, except symbolically, been able to express anything of my feelings towards you or what I most wanted to say. But you understand it all well enough without my saying. Give my Love and Blessing to all the Canadian kindred, big and little, young and old. Be diligent and faithful, patient and hopeful one and all of you; and may we all know, at all times, that verily the Eternal rules above us, and that nothing finally *wrong* has happened or can happen.

Send some news, the more copious the better, some willing hand of you; it will be welcome whenever it comes.

> Ever your affectionate Brother,
> T. Carlyle

TC TO JOHN BARTON STERLING

> 5 Cheyne Row, Chelsea,
> 1 March 1871

Dear Sterling,

On Sunday last it was but a small part of my feelings that I expressed to you, on hearing your sad news. The weight of the event first became sensible to me when I got out of doors and was left alone;[1] and indeed I may say it has grown weightier and sadder to me ever since. Your Uncle's many fine qualities were from of old well known to me; and never could be hidde[n] in the latter times by his outward asperities and unreasonable impetuosities: I counted him always a right honest, true minded, and even superiorly gifted man, who loved me well (me and mine); and whose own life had been obstructed by many sore and heavy contradictions. And now, in addition to all that, his departure is to me, more than to almost any other, a source of tragic thoughts; it is as it were the last living root, now also disappearing, of what was once a beautiful and fruitful grove or friendly umbrageous wood in the common-

6. William ("Wull") Brown (d. 1838; see 10:248), their paternal cousin.

7. TC presumably used the term *Priestside* to mean that the French were Catholics, rather than as a reference to the place in Ruthwell parish, Dumfriesshire.

TC-JBS, 1 March. MS: NLS 3823.197. Hitherto unpbd.

1. TC called at the Sterling household, 3 South Pl., Sun. 26 Feb., when he was told by John Barton Sterling that Anthony Coningham Sterling was dying; see TC to JAC, 27 Feb.

place wilderness of things: you well know by tradition how we were related to your Grandfather's house, to your Father, your Grandmother, your Uncle;[2] and you can understand how the sudden *finis* of all that tumbles up on me a world of recollections of the most mournful and also of the most tender and even sacred kind!

In brief the practical point I have to impress upon you, my dear young Friend, is, the very great desire I feel to have speedy and frequent news from that Sick-room; to hear from you at once when the least change occurs for the better or the worse; at lowest to hear from you, never so briefly, or, what were still better, to see you once every week till the Inexorable and Inevitable itself arrive.[3] Do not deny me this request; probably one of the last I shall ever have to make of you.

Yours affectionately
T. Carlyle.

TC TO JOHN A. CARLYLE

5 Cheyne Row, Chelsea
3 March 1871.

My dear Brother,

I am very glad you have got safe home to Dumfries ag*n*; I have no doubt you will find yourself improved, refreshed & strengthened more or less in resuming your old ways after this interval of pause. We got your Letter yesterday; many thanks for writing so soon. I learned with a kind of shock the fate of poor Madame Otthenin;[1] and how, without effort of *hers*, poor bewildered heavy-laden old Lady, she had found an inespugnable refuge, and covert from the storm of War and of Life, "*Ja ja*"; all does find its end, all has its measure and bounds. Poor Irma seemed greatly agitated, as is natural. I could not make out from her handwriting what the disease which proved fatal had been; it read like 'ederme of the arm'; but the words refused to have any sense to me. You might now forward to her the *Macmillan* which I send today; espe-

---

2. John Barton Sterling's grandfather was Edward Sterling (1773–1847), journalist, known as the "Thunderer of the *Times*," his grandmother was Hester, b. Coningham (1783–1843), and his father was John Sterling, TC's great friend. The Carlyles had been friendly with the whole family; see Carlyle, *Reminiscences* 94, 95–96, and earlier vols.

3. Anthony C. Sterling d. 1 March.

TC-JAC, 3 March. MS: NLS 527.43. Hitherto unpbd.

1. Jean Otthenin had been living in France with her das., Irma Durival and Margaret Otthenin; because of the Franco-Prussian War there had been no communication possible since Aug.; see TC to JCA, 24 Dec. John A. Carlyle wrote, 1 March, with the news of her death in Nov., and enclosed a letter from Irma to Dr. Hunter (see TC to JAC, 30 Jan.) with the details; he himself received a similar letter, 3 March.

cially I hope you will at once write to her,—and do not fail to express my real sympathy,[2] withal; for it is real enough, and mournful enough; if it cd do her any good at all.

Poor Anthony Sterling has likewise rapidly reached the goal. I had written to Captain John earnestly enforcing the request left with him to send me frequent news; before there was time for an answer, the enclosed line came from him; and yesterday, by way of answer he had called here while I was out. All is ended there too.

I am still not a little bothered with my sleep; but I continue to hope it is mending, and will not just now trouble you further on the subject.— Miss Jewsbury's Memorial for a Pension seems, after all our trouble upon it, to have failed again;—evidently hopeless under Gladstone's Ministry. Forster is very angry; nor can any of us well account for the failure of so natural a request, backed as it was by what everybody calls 32 of the best names in England. Some little pique of Gladstone's,[3] perhaps spite against some name of the 32, and willingness to give that one a slap as he passes? Roebuck, who, with all his eagerness to help in the matter, charitably refused for such a reason,[4] said to Mary "His (Gladstone's) *smallness* of mind is quite appalling, and only over*topped* by his vanity which reaches towards the Infinite!" It is reckoned probable *he* will not long continue helmsman; so there may be room for a new trial.[5] Poor Geraldine seems gradually losing her eyes; becoming old too, and in "merit" if such a word be applicable at all fairly rises above the average of the Applicants favoured by Gladstone and Co.

Here is Frederick Chapman[6] come about *People's Edition* &c &c: no

2. John wrote, 3 March: "I mean to write to Irma on Sunday . . . so if you have any message for her & her sister [Margaret] please send it by tomorrow's post."

3. Gladstone wrote to Tennyson, 9 Feb. 1872, explaining his criteria for granting civil list pensions: "With respect to literary pensions I think it was the intention of parliament that they should be given to really distinguished literary men. . . . I have found that it was necessary, in practice, to recognise loss of health, old age or calamity, as elements in the case for pensions of this class; but I have endeavoured to limit this admission to those cases only where some real service had been rendered, by works of intrinsic value, to the cause of letters" (Hallam Tennyson, *Alfred Lord Tennyson: A Memoir By His Son* [London and New York, 1897] 2:112). Jewsbury was a distinguished literary reviewer, one of the *Athenæum's* main reviewers, and had pbd. five novels and two children's books.

4. John Arthur Roebuck (1802–79; *ODNB*), politician, M.P. for Sheffield 1849–68 and 1874 to his death; radical in his youth, he was unaligned to either of the main parties, but more often anti-Liberal (Gladstone's party) in his positions; presumably Roebuck did not sign knowing that Gladstone was hostile to him.

5. Jewsbury was finally granted a civil list pension of £40 a year by Disraeli, 19 June 1874.

6. TC signed a receipt, 6 March: "Received from Messrs. Chapman & Hall, by Bill payable in four months, Three Hundred and Fifty Pounds, in payment of my account with them till 31 December last / T. Carlyle / (£350) / 5 Cheyne Row, Chelsea / 6 March 1871" (MS: William Andrews Clark Memorial Lib., UCLA).

more of that or of any thing else today as it is already three oclock all but 10 minutes.

My love and blessings to you all. Ever your affectionate Brother, / T. Carlyle[7]

MARY AITKEN TO META WELLMER

5 Cheyne Row, Chelsea,
London, 12 March 1871

My dear Miss Wellmer,

My Uncle and I are very sorry to know that you are in such sorrow at present[1]— We sympathize very much with you; but speaking is of little use in such case—the heart knoweth its own bitterness and a Stranger intermeddleth not therewith.[2] I am very glad you cared to write to me at such a time and that you wished me to write in return, though I have little news to tell you that you would care to hear. My Uncle and I are sitting here together, he reading and I writing, by the same Lamp; he bids me tell you he "is profoundly sorry to hear of your great grief, which only time and reflection can in the least smooth down and make more easy to bear; he has only one advice to offer you, that is: not to remain alone and not to be idle, for he says work is the only thing which can for a moment make one forget or cease to remember one's own cares."— Our drawingroom is a small room[3] prettily furnished by my late Aunt who was a very graceful clever woman and made everything pretty round my Uncle wherever they might be; she died very suddenly five years ago and my Uncle never seems to forget that he has lost her even for a day. The Street we live in is old fashioned and rather dingy, but it is less disagreeable to look at than the ugly new Streets they are making now in London,—the houses all covered with plaster carved into all sorts of ugly shapes to cover the bad bricks of which they are made—this house as my Uncle often says is at least "solid & honest" and doesnot pretend to be anything but what it really is.—

7. TC wrote in his journal, 6 March: "Went to Forster's yesterday to dinner, as appointed,—tho the night before, I had not slept, and the day had been passed in strict solitude, solitary walk &c, and a sadness and depression *complete* so far as Earth and its affairs went, tho' not quite otherwise. Home ag*n* with Mary before 11; improved, not wretched;—& have had the one tolerably human *sleep* that has fallen to me since jan*y* last!— A dismal, mean and as it were, degrading time to me these last 10 weeks! Utter incapacity of work or effort; slavish sorrow & misery. . . . Reading of Goethe has been my best employ*t*" (TC's journal; privately owned).

MA-MW, 12 March. MS: NLS Acc. 9207. Hitherto unpbd.
1. Meta Wellmer's mother, Eva Margaretha Wellmer, b. Wirth, had d. recently.
2. See Prov. 14:10.
3. The drawing room was at the front of the first (second in U.S.) floor; see 172.

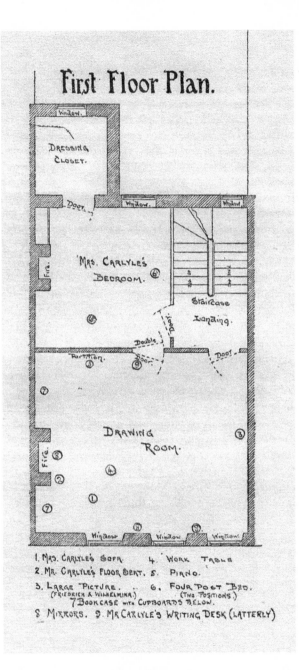

"First Floor Plan"
Reginald Blunt, *The Carlyles' Chelsea Home* (1895)

Some little time ago I got the little Book of your own[4] you were so kind as send me; and also the newspaper cuttings which latter were very interesting and lively to read. I have not yet read Theophille;[5] because I wished first to finish *Wallenstein*[6] which I was reading with a young Lady here who was so kind as help me with my German;[7] but I *will* gladly read it—and I meanwhile send you many thanks for them all. Thanks also for the two interesting enclosures in yr last Letter.— I am rather an idle reader. I read a great deal but in rather a wandering style which often reminds me of the attempts at improving their minds which Philine and Friedrich in *Wilhelm Meister* made.[8] I don't exactly spread the Books out on the table all together but I have often half a dozen very interesting Books which I read alternately according to my mood—so that when I finish one Book I generally finish five or so at the same time.—

You will not be able to care very much for the Peace which has come at last to your Country—I often think when I hear of the glorious Victory of the Germans how many sad homes there will be both in Germany & poor degraded France—to which the news of peace will now give no joy. It is a horrible pitch of civilization we are arriving at now—when people go out & have each other killed by machinery by way of settling disputes. We had a very orthodox religious man[9] here who talked to me very much before my Uncle came into the room about the advisibility of giving up one's life to Christ, visiting the sick &c; later in the evening he became lively on the War, and having been himself a Soldier in India, he told us he had just invented out of his own pious head a gun which cd be made to go on taking aim and firing *both night and day!*[10]

---

4. Possibly Wellmer, *Gedichte* [*Poems*] (Leipzig, 1871).

5. Wellmer was to publish *Theophile, A Story* but not until 1876; perhaps she sent them a manuscript.

6. Presumably Friedrich Schiller (1759–1805), German poet, philosopher, playwright and historian, *Wallenstein*, a drama in three parts (Weimar, 1780). For JBW's difficulties with the German, but also huge enjoyment, of *Wallenstein*, see 2:197, 207, and 248.

7. Hedwig von Reichenbach; see TC to duchess of A, 5 Dec. 1870.

8. Friedrich, a wild young man, ran away with Philine, whom Wilhelm had loved; when Friedrich reappeared, he told Wilhelm that his "stock of erudition" derived from "a pleasant plan" of Philine's; they lived together in a house with "a small but choice library" from which they laid books out on the large table; they then read to each other "first from this book, then from that!" (*Wilhelm Meister's Apprenticeship*, bk. 8, chap. 6; Carlyle, *Works* 24:137).

9. Col. David Davidson; see TC to JAC, 10 Feb.

10. Davidson invented telescopic sights for rifles that were adopted both by the British army and by the Confederate army in the American Civil War; see K. J. Fielding and Mary Sebag-Montefiore, "Jane Carlyle and Sir David Davidson: Belief and Unbelief—The Story of a Friendship," *Studies in Scottish Literature* 35 (2007): 26–43. See also David Davidson, *Memories of a Long Life* (1890) 210–12, 251–54, and 332–33.

I dont quite know how he reconciled his ideas but I suppose he managed it somehow or other.— — I am at the end of my sheet—I feel ashamed to send you this Letter—by way of greeting to you in your sadness. I would so willingly say something to comfort you if I c*d* but that I think is seldom possible and never in the case of a stranger like myself—so I wll leave all unsaid and only With our kindest wishes & sincere sympathy sign myself

Yours very truly
Mary Carlyle Aitken

Perhaps you will have leisure & I sh*d* be most happy to hear again from you.

TC TO [JOHN BARTON STERLING]

5 Cheyne Row, Chelsea
13 March 1871.

Dear Sir,

Accept many thanks from me, cordial and mournful, for the Volume[1] I received on Saturday night. Your good Sister[2] did not over estimate the interest it would have for me. It is the express image, more than writing can well be, of the pure clear-seeing high and pious soul that threw it out on paper; I have read it with many thoughts indeed; it is very mournful and very beautiful to me; and will remain a precious memorial of days that are no more.

With many grateful regards to your Sister[3] and self. I remain

Sincerely yours, / T. Carlyle

TC-[JBS], 13 March. MS: Bloomsbury Auctions. Hitherto unpbd. Recipient identified as John Barton Sterling; see TC to JBS, 1 March. The letter was pasted into the 1871 people's edn. of *Sartor Resartus*, probably one of the books TC sent to the Sterling sisters; see below.

1. Presumably a work of either John Sterling, John Barton's father, or Anthony C. Sterling; unidentified further.

2. Either Julia Maria or Hester Isabella Sterling.

3. TC apparently sent some books to Julia and Hester, probably vols. 1–5 of the people's edn. of TC's works, *Sartor Resartus* (vol. 1), *The French Revolution* (vols. 2–4), and the *Life of John Sterling* (vol. 5), all pbd. 1871; Julia Sterling wrote, 24 March: "Many thanks for sending us the books & for so kindly writing our names yourself. We are very glad to have them from you. Sometimes when I open that book I think there is nothing *except* friendship that does not grow old . . . & I need hardly say what a tender feeling we must always have for one who loves my Father as you do"; "that book" was probably TC's *Life of John Sterling*. Julia wrote from 6 Bolton Row (where she lived with her sister, Hester), and hoped to see TC "before we return to Cornwall."

TC TO JOHN A. CARLYLE

5 Cheyne Row, Chelsea
18 March 1871

My dear Brother,

We rec*d* yr Photographs; which seem good and tolerably like; Mary has put them into a Book she has been instituting here for such objects and has already furnished to some extent.[1] I hoped at first it might have been some Photograph of the Kirkpatrick Picture; but I suppose there has none hitherto been taken of that.[2] If there ever be, dont forget us here.

Maggie Welsh is to come to us on Thursday next: it is a long time ago that I had promised her a little visit up hither; & alas, it is only in fulfilment of such promise that I can be said to have invited her, — so broken feeble & dispirited as I now feel; certainly in no want of *visitors* for one thing, but we expect the visit will not last long; I had said "some three weeks"; Mary said "two or three." We may expect one calendar month will handsomely complete the affair. Poor Maggie is one of the pliablest and softest of guests; creates no noise or mischief anywhere, and is altogether glad and ready to be useful wherever she sees the least chance. I am often sorry to think of the life she has had and that it is not improving as the weight of years advances.[3]

Forster is better; is gone upon his journeyings;[4] and reports the business to agree with him. He was really miserably ill all winter; coughing like a volcano, missing sleep, full of suppressed gout &c &c &c; and all the time overwhelmed with business, not for himself only but for others; I have more than once recommended a warm climate for his Winters; but he really cannot well go; he has still one winter to front here at his post (and so become 60 of age) before he can apply for *any* retiring pension, directly on attaining 60, he can retire with £700 a year from his "Lunacy" affairs. I hope and pray the good obliging Forster may accordingly get through his next winter well, and retire comfortably into *otium cum dignitate* [leisure with dignity], as befits. — Froude is at St. Andrews; went on Wednesday night to deliver his Fare-

---

TC-JAC, 18 March. MS: NLS 527.44. Hitherto unpbd.

1. John A. Carlyle wrote, 15 March: "Here are two photographs that have just arrived from the artist"; possibly the two photographs of John A. Carlyle in vol. 6 of the Thomas Carlyle Photograph Albums, Columbia: "Dr Carlyle / my Brr," see 176, and one of John in a hat; see 177.

2. For Edward Kirkpatrick's portrait of John, see TC to JAC, 21 Jan. John replied, 19 March: "There was no time for having a photograph of Kirkpatricks picture taken before it was sent to the Exhibition; & it will have to remain till the end of May at least in the Exhibition."

3. Maggie's sister Mary was addicted to opium and their brother Walter was in debt; see TC to JAC, 30 Jan.

4. Forster wrote, 7 March, that he was leaving that day.

"Dr Carlyle my Brr," [1871]
Thomas Carlyle Papers, Rare Book & Manuscript Library,
Columbia University in the City of New York

John A. Carlyle, [1871]
Thomas Carlyle Papers, Rare Book & Manuscript Library,
Columbia University in the City of New York

well Address and end the Rectorship there;[5] that feat he would do yesterday; and is probably getting under way just now with intention to be here before tomorrow morning. His Address was to be on the Meaning (eternal worth and meaning) of Scottish Calvinism; upon which subject, I have little doubt he will be new and well worth hearing to the St. Andrews people. He had the Address in print before leaving London; but could not give me a Copy, though anxious to do it; there will be copies enough straightway and you shall have one properly printed by about Tuesday or Wednesday next.[6] Froude is a very honest clear and stedfast kind of man, with a fine ringing tone of eloquence and talent belonging him; in a quiet way, very quiet and almost unnoticeable, I can perceive he honours me with a degree of affection considerably more than I deserve.

Last Sunday Froude & I made a call on Lady Derby:[7] we there found a large fat bald-headed man, with large melancholy, lazy grey eyes; whom neither of us knew, nor could learn the name of; though I now find, by putting guesses together, that is must have been Morier (a kind of Diplomatist and Novelist, Brother of a *former* Do Do—who is now dead);[8] this one is evidently a clever kind of man; and to my surprise lazily said several wise things, and, most surprising of all, plainly hinted an opinion of "Constitutional Government" which I imagined had been fully shared by no mortal except my own poor self, for many years back! Froude reported to me of a former call where I was not, that the Lady had informed him, "Both Lord Derby and Mr Lowe[9] were completely discouraged from political enterprise, and foresaw nothing for England but rapid subsidence into what we Scotch call the *Lowe Pot*."[10]

5. Froude had been elected rector of St. Andrews Univ., March 1868.

6. John wrote, 19 March: "I send yesterday's Scotsman which contains Froude's Lecture at St Andrews, though not perhaps in a perfect form. . . . I shall be glad to have the perfect copy . . . which you promise me. It is a most interesting lecture"; J. A. Froude, *Calvinism: An Address Delivered at St. Andrew's, March 17, 1871* (1871). The *Athenæum* reported, 25 March: "It may be mentioned as an illustration of Scottish character that the daily newspapers in Edinburgh and Glasgow containing the report of Mr. Froude's lecture on Calvinism at St. Andrews were run out of print in the course of last Saturday."

7. Mary Stanley, countess of Derby; for TC's visits to her, June 1870, see TC to AC, 3 June 1870. He also visited her 12 Feb.: "Visit to Lady Derby's last sunday: Froude, E*l* Stanhope, She (amiablest intellig*t*;—with*t* real benefit to me, or even temporary satisfact*n*, so far am I down" (TC's journal; privately owned). Philip Henry Stanhope (1805–75; *ODNB*), 5th earl; known to TC through their work on founding the National Portrait Gallery.

8. David Richard Morier (1784–1877; *ODNB*); diplomat and author; for JWC's meeting with his son, Robert Burnet David Morier (1826–93; *ODNB*), also very fat, see 36:170. Two of his three deceased brothers were also diplomats, James Justinian Morier (1782–1849; *ODNB*) and John Philip Morier (1778–1853; *ODNB*); the third, William (1790–1864; *ODNB*), was a naval officer.

9. For Lord Derby and Robert Lowe, see TC to AC, 3 June 1870.

10. Fire pot. Lady Derby had no apparent connections with Scotland.

Which a little surprised me: pray do not mention it again, lest it may have been more a transient mood than a settled conviction on the part of these two great Men,—whom one w*d* not wish to hurt in any way!

I get various Letters from German *Vereins* [associations], one in Leith, one in Bradford &c &c, intending solemn Dinner and Palaver about German unity and the victory over France and the Devil.[11] I make no answer though I do right heartily recognize, as everybody does or will at last do, that the Germans have done their French job in a right workmanlike manner. I continue to get many Letters, but not one in twenty is worth the ink it is written in; and deserves nothing but the fire. Here is one, which came this morning from a reverend Yankee[12] of whom I cannot recall the faintest shadow; this I enclose (*if* the l*d* will carry it!); it will at least light your pipe; for I dont the least want it again.

I have been considerably bothered this week with the Sleep question (weak old Being that I am); but there is again hope that I *may* have got over the hill this time. Hope springs eternal! One hope I do always know, that *cannot* be doubted or be distant God's good will be at all times done; other deliberate pray we can now have none. n.l.[13]

I send my constant and best Love to Jean[14] and everybody;[15]

TC TO JOHN A. CARLYLE

> 5 Cheyne Row, Chelsea,
> 25 March 1871.

My dear Brother,

Yr two Letters, the second of them this morning, punctually arrived; many thanks for them. At this moment, 3 P.M., I have just returned from a long

11. The *Glasgow Herald* reported, 24 March: "On Wednesday evening, the Germans resident in Edinburgh and Leith, held a festival in the Free Mason's Hall, Edinburgh, to celebrate the unification of German restoration of peace, and the seventy-fifth anniversary of the Emperor-King's birth. . . . Letters sympathising with the object of the meeting were read from . . . Dr. John Carlyle of the Hill, Dumfries." The *Illustrated Times*, 6 May, reported on a similar "German Peace Festival" in London, held "in the Gymnasium of the Turn-verein, St. Pancras-road. . . . Among the Englishmen invited were . . . Mr. Thomas Carlyle."

12. Not further identified.

13. TC wrote "n.l." to indicate new line.

14. Jean Aitken wrote, 12 March: "I have to thank you very heartily for the nice 'Sartor' w*ch* came along with your kind and welcome letter. . . . I am delighted to hear of the 10,000 copies bespoke already it is wonderful to think of the good this will bring to ten thousand readers at least. It of all your B*ks* used to be thought the most difficult to understand (tho' I never thought so)."

15. The end of the letter, with signature, has been cut away.

TC-JAC, 25 March. MS: NLS 527.45. Quot: A. Carlyle, *NL* 2:278; Wilson, *Carlyle* 6:236.

drive with Lady Ashburton, round by Hampstead &c, in beautiful sunshine and Spring air;—a drive by appointment;—am now due for a walk; and have hardly a moment left, were there even no other impediment upon me. But there is unfortunately; and, to myself, a very grievous one. My Sleep-history—for the last two weeks, especially for the last week, has been quite deplorable; and last night the worst of all: so that literally I am good for nothing today, and can write only to say that I am so. This miserable affair of Sleep does not yet quite discourage me; but it does seems to indicate, such are the new phases of it, some crisis coming on or taking place; crisis towards good or towards what might be called bad I cannot say; and indeed, speaking with all calmness, cannot be said to care. All I have to pray for—is, that it would be speedy, and that I may have patience for it, pious silent patience, given me, whether it be long or short. So we will say no more of that at present.

Maggie Welsh came duly, and adjusts herself, with the utmost quietness and kindly good humour, as her knack is, into the fluctuating element. I never hear her more than if she were a shadow; Mary & she breakfast together independent of my irregularities; sit down stairs & lovingly do their respective functions; so that Maggie at least does us no manner of ill; and if my sleep were back, or even whether or not, might almost be reckoned a small increment rather. Mary is very good and kind, poor little Soul; has been up three times in the hollow of the night ministering to me like a benificent little Fairy: yesterday she had from Lady Ashburton a shining testimony of that Lady's about her,[1] which I doubt not is rather agreeable to the little wretch;—but I leave her to report the thing to her own Mother (as of course she will do in a day or two) having no authority of my own to speak of such matters. She has already done out of her own little head four Letters for me to correspondents requiring nothing but second hand; and had just got done five minutes before I was set down at this door.

Your accounts of Lorimer[2] and Shairpe[3] are interesting to me; I wonder only who Mrs Shairpe, a "Douglas of Kellhead," can be: there was, long years ago, a young Lady at Kinmont who wd now be Aunt of the present Marquis;

1. "A gift of a gold watch"; note by A. Carlyle on MS; otherwise unidentified.

2. James Lorimer (1818–90; *ODNB*; see 33:40), advocate, jurist, and political philosopher. John A. Carlyle wrote, 24 March: "Thanks for the parcel of books which came by the post of this day. . . . Your 'Sage' who sends the open paper about France & Germany & their 'Fraternity' & 'Paternity' is Mr Lorimer, Professor of International law in Edinr whom I . . . have known many years. He is a very honourable painstaking man, was entirely in favour of the Germans, & often sent me German newspapers which were interesting at the time. . . . He is a sincere & old admirer of yours."

3. John Campbell Shairp (1819–85; *ODNB*; see 46:188), literary scholar, principal of the United College at St. Andrews; John wrote, 24 March: "I already had got a copy of Principal Shairp's Culture & Religion, but found it heavy reading."

can this be she I wonder?[4] I have also asked myself sometimes whether the speculating Law-Professor is a descendant or connection of a certain Rev*d* Dr Lorimer, once of Haddington;[5] whom, not for his own sake at all, but for other good reasons, I vividly remember![6]— It was Froude who brought me these Books home from St. Andrews. His Speech, it appears, was thoughtfully rather welcomed at St. Andrews. I think it capital both in matter & manner.

Mr Erskine (*ci-devant* [formerly] Patterson) with his Wife were duly welcomed here; with a glad surprise even, for I did not know he had changed his name:[7] they sat half an hour in very pleasant colloquy with me; and I engaged to consider if there w*d* be any possibility of my putting down on paper some reminiscences of good old Erskine;[8] which so far as yet appears I hardly think there will.[9]

Write to me soon, dear Brother, when you have a deliberate hour. Jean I suppose will hear from Mary about Tuesday. To her and every member of the household my always loving regards.

Your affectionate Brother,

T. Carlyle

4. John replied, 31 March: "Mrs Shairp, 'née Douglas of Kilhead,' may be the daughter of Douglas of Lockerbie House who lived many years at the Glen, Kinmount." He had written, 24 March: "[Shairp's] wife, who sends you the book, I have not seen. Both were very intimate friends of Erskine." Eliza, b. Douglas (d. 1903), m. Shairp, 1853; she was the da. of Henry Alexander Douglas (1781–1837), younger brother of Charles (1777–1837), 6th marquess, and John (1779–1856), 7th marquess of Queensberry; she was the cousin of Archibald (1818–58), 8th marquess (for his death see 34:109–10 and 126), and first cousin once removed of John Sholto Douglas (1844–1900; *ODNB*), 9th marquess of Queensberry.

5. Rev. Robert Lorimer (1765–1848), minister of Haddington, 1796–1843, who had left in the Disruption. John wrote, 31 March: "Professor Lorimer's father was a Perthshire laird, not any relation of the Haddington D*r* Lorimer, I think, as I never heard the professor say anything on the subject." The professor's father was James Lorimer (1779–1868), factor of the earl of Kinnoul in Perthshire.

6. Rev. Lorimer and his wife, Elizabeth, b. Gordon (d. 1843), m. 1801, were both very kind and supportive to JBW after her father's death, Sept. 1819; see 1:203–4.

7. James Erskine Paterson, m., 1852, Mary Jane, b. Macnabb (b. 1826); see 46:188. John wrote, 24 March: "A letter from Mr Paterson (Erskine's nephew & heir who has now taken the name of Erskine) was forwarded to me . . . & in it he asked permission to call with his wife to see you before leaving London. . . . Both he & his wife were most attentive & kind to Erskine at all times . . . & they are both warm-hearted people."

8. Thomas Erskine d. March 1870; see TC to JAC, 1 June 1870.

9. TC did not write anything; see TC to JCA, 13 Oct.

TC TO AN UNIDENTIFIED CORRESPONDENT

29 March 1871

Sir,

I am obliged for the honour you do me. It is certain I at all times wish cordially well to all real interests of Germany, material and still more spiritual; certain therefore that I wish to your new projected *Verein* for "*Volksbildung* [Association for Popular Education]" all manner of prosperity, so far as it can tend to forward that high object.[1]

n.l.[2] At the same time, I am in such complete ignorance of all the circumstances, personages and conditions of your Enterprize;[3] and at any rate, feel in these advanced years, so imperatively bound to cultivate retirement and quietude in every sense, that I must decline the honour offered me; and trust you will find me excused in doing so.

I remain / Yours, with many thanks / and true good-wishes,

T. Carlyle[4]

TC-UC, 29 March. MS: Strouse. Hitherto unpbd.

1. John A. Carlyle wrote, 31 March: "The prospectus of that German *Gesellschaft für Verbreitung von Volksbildung*, together with the little note accompanying it, asking you to become a member or at least give countenance of favour, is remarkable as coming from Berlin." The German Society for the Propagation of National Education was founded 14 June 1871. There were three main organizers of the "Verein für Volksbildung": Fritz Kalle (1837–1915), merchant from Wiesbaden, Franz Leibing (1836–75), teacher from Elberfeld, and Herman Scutze-Delitzsch (1808–83), politician from Potsdam.

2. TC inserted "n.l. [new line]."

3. John wrote: "The names of 'German subscribers' are mostly names of republicans. Thus 'Dr v. Virchow Professor in the University Berlin' is the most eminent physiologist in Europe." Rudolf Ludwig Carl Virchow, prof. of Pathological Anatomy and Physiology at Berlin Univ. from 1856. Although John gives him the honorary "von" title, he did not have such a title, and indeed refused one in 1873.

4. The Paris Commune, radical socialist govt. now in control of Paris, began 18 March; two generals, Claude Lemonte (1817–71) and Jacques Léonard Clément-Thomas (1809–71), commander in chief of the National Guard, were both murdered on the first day. TC knew Clément-Thomas and wrote in his journal, 26 March, of his shock at the death: "Some four days I heard from Froude of the miserable death of Commandant Clement Thomas in the horrid insurrectionary puddle now going on in Paris. From all likelihoods I had & have the sorrowful idea that it is the same M. Thomas I knew—some 26 years ago as one of the companions of Cavaignac here,—who had broken out from political imprisonment in Ham, & fled to Cavaignac resourceless, as so many others did. Cavaignac repeatedly brought him here; and, apart from his fixed but quiet republicanism, was well esteemed by both of *us*. I can vividly remember smoking with him in company of Cavaignac &c one evening, & even what we said to one another. He was a most good-humoured, strong-built, well-conditioned man; had a fine bright smile, & shewed, on occasion, a lively sense of humour. He had returned to Paris on amnesty, which was granted by Louis-Philippe shortly before the Finis of Louis. For ten years afterwards I heard no more of Thomas (except from the Newspapers once in 1848 that he had been appointed commandant of the National Guard); but in 1857

6 April, 1871. The Ms. (of which there are two copies) entitled *"Letters and Memorials of Jane Welsh Carlyle"* is to me, naturally in my now bereaved state, of endless value, tho' of what value to others I cannot in the least clearly judge; and indeed for the last two years am imperatively *forbidden* to work farther on it, or even to look farther into it.[1] Of that *Ms.*, my kind, considerate and ever-faithful friend, James Anthony Froude (as he has lovingly promised me) takes precious charge in my stead;[2] to him therefore I appoint that the better of the Two Copies be given up, with whatever other furtherances and elucidations may be possible;—and I solemnly request of him to do his best and wisest in the matter, as I feel assured he will. There is incidentally a quantity of *auto*biographic record in my Notes there; but *except* as subsidiary and elucidative of the Text, I put no value on such: express Biography of *me* I had really rather that there should be none. Mr. Froude, Mr. Forster and my Brother, will make earnest survey of the *Ms.*, and its subsidiaries, there or elsewhere in respect to this as well as to its other bearings; their united ut-

---

(or 8? [Aug.–Sept. 1858]), in returning from my *second* Tour in Germany, somewhere in the country of Spa, in a railway carriage, he & I recognised one another and rode a stage together. He was there an exile of Napoleon's making; still fresh & strong of hope, tho' his dark red hair was getting grizzled; & our tone together was much less merry than formerly.— The next account I get of him is *this* which I have recovered with difficulty from the ever-flowing stream of Newspaper rubbish. [TC included a clipping from the *Times*, 21 March, about Clément-Thomas's death, with TC's hand at top: 'Poor *Clément-Thomas*, on the Place Pigalle Montmartre, Sat*y* 18 March 1871!']. Since then I have often had the face & attitude of Thomas in that horrible scene before my mind, almost to a visual degree; and, mid my waste miseries in the sleepless nights, his undaunted bearing has been a rebuke to me. *Good* be with him, the valiant Thomas now at rest" (TC's journal; privately owned). Eléonore Louis Godefroy Cavaignac (1801–45), revolutionary republican, in exile in London, 1835–41; friend of both Carlyles; see 7:53. Neither Clément-Thomas's visit to Cheyne Row nor the meeting on the train, Sept. 1858, were noted at the time. Louis Philippe (1773–1850; see 5:139), king of France 1838–48.

TC's 1871 Will, 6 April. Typescript: privately owned. Pbd: Froude, *My Relations* 74–75; K. J. Fielding, "Carlyle Makes His Will (1865–1871): New Documents Discovered," *CA* 10: 61–62. For TC's earlier drafts of his intentions in regard to Craigenputtoch, see 44:197–200 and 220–22, and K. J. Fielding, "Carlyle Makes His Will," *CA* 10:57–59. Text: Fielding, except for one paragraph (in square brackets) taken from Froude, *My Relations*.

1. Although TC was looking at JWC's letters to the Forsters of early Nov. 1869 (see 46: 93), most of his work on JWC's letters was complete by Sept. 1869: "The '*Task*,' in a sort, *done*;—Mary *finish* my Notes (of 1866) this very day;—I shrinking, for weeks past, from any revisal of interference there, as a thing evidently *hurtful*, (evid*tly* anti-somnial *even*!) in my pre*st* state of nerves.— Essentially, how*r* Her Letters & Memorials are saved" (TC's journal; privately owned); see 46:80.

2. TC gave one of the copies to Froude for his consideration, mid-June; see TC to JAF, 7 July; for Froude's response, see TC to JAF, 26 Sept.

most candour and impartiality (taking always Mr. Froude's PRACTICALITY along with it) will evidently furnish a better judgement than mine can be.[3] The *Ms.* is by no means ready for publication; nay the questions, How, When (after what delay 7 years, 10 years?)[4] it, or any portion of it, should be publishable are still dark to me; but on all such points Mr. Froude's practical summing-up is to be taken as mine. — The other Copy (with the *Original Letters*) can be given to my Niece Mary; to whom also, dear little soul, I bequeath Five Hundred Pounds for the loving care, and unwearied patience and helpfulness she has shown to me in these my last solitary and infirm years. To her also are to be given, at her choice, whatever memorials of my Dear Departed One she has seen me silently preserving here, — especially this *Writing-table*,[5] and the little *Child's-Chair*[6] (in the China-Closet), which latter to my eyes has always a brightness as of Time's morning and a sadness as of Death and Eternity, when I look on it; and which, with the other dear articles, I have the weak wish to preserve in loving hands yet a while when I am gone.——

[My other Manuscripts I leave to my brother John. They are with one exception of no moment to me. I have never seen any of them since they were written. One of them is a set of fragments about James First which were loyally fished out for me from much other Cromwellian rubbish, and doubtless carefully copied more than twenty years ago by the late John Chorley[7] who was always so good to me. But neither this latter nor perhaps any of the others is worth printing. On this point however my Brother can take Counsel with John Forster and James Anthony Froude and do what is then judged fittest. Many or most of these papers I often feel that I myself should burn; but probably I never shall after all. The "one exception" spoken of above is a sketch of my Father and his life hastily thrown off in the nights between his death and

3. From "There is incidentally" to "mine can be" was written on a separate sheet of paper; see below, n. 14.

4. Froude pbd. *Letters and Memorials of Jane Welsh Carlyle* in 1883, two years after TC's death. TC's *Reminiscences* (including that of JWC) came out a few weeks after TC's death, Feb. 1881.

5. TC's writing table (see 32:frontis. and 41:23) had belonged to John Welsh, JWC's father; see 41:24.

6. TC wrote, 1 July 1866: "Her little bit of a first chair, its wee wee arms etc., visible to me in the closet at this moment, is still here, and always was; I have looked at it hundreds of times; from of *old*, with many thoughts. No daughter or son of *hers* was to sit there; so it had been appointed to us, my Darling. I have no Book thousandth-part so beautiful as Thou; but these were *our* only 'Children,' — and, in a true sense, these *were* verily *ours*" (Carlyle, *Reminiscences* 153). The chair is in Carlyle's House; see opp.

7. For Chorley's copying of material on James VI and I (1565–1625; *ODNB*), king of Scotland, England, and Ireland, described by TC in Feb. 1865 as "About James I. and Charles I. The Chorley Transcript, with the *Original*, probably about 1849"; see 26:1–2. The Chorley transcript is untraced. John Rutter Chorley (1806–67); see 44:242.

Jane Welsh Carlyle's childhood chair
Courtesy of Carlyle's House, National Trust

burial,[8] full of earnest affection and veracity, most likely unfit for printing; but I wish it to be taken charge of by my Brother John and preserved in the Family. Since, I think, the very night of my Father's Funeral (far away from London and me) I have never seen a word of that poor bit of writing. In regard to all business matters about my Books (of which not only the Copyrights but all the Stereotype plates from which the three several collected Editions have been respectively printed and which are at present deposited with my Printers Messrs. Robson and Son belong exclusively to me[9]) Copyrights, Editions, and dealings with Booksellers and others in relation thereto[,] John Forster's advice is to be taken as supreme and complete, better than my own ever could have been. His faithful, wise, and ever punctual care about all that has been a miracle of generous helpfulness, literally invaluable to me in that field of things. Thanks, poor thanks, are all that I can return, alas!]][10]

If my brother Alick survive me, I bequeath him, over and above his joint share as brother,[11] One thousand Pounds. To Maggie Welsh, my dear good Cousin and HERS, One hundred Pounds. To my House-servant, Mrs. Warren, if she continue here at my decease, Fifty Pounds. Till "Captain" Baillie and his Wife both decease (ask my Nephew James Aitken), I wish the bit of annuity (£20, payable 21 April £10, and 21 October £10) to be continued on them, on the same veiled terms.[12] — To my dear Friends Forster, Froude (Masson[13] too I should remember in this moment, and perhaps some other?) I have

8. For James Carlyle the elder's death, 16 Jan. 1832, see 6:105–8; for TC's "sketch," see Carlyle, *Reminiscences* 4–39.

9. For TC's ownership of the stereotype plates, see 46:45 and TC to FC, 31 July 1870.

10. The passage in square brackets (from "My other Manuscripts" to "alas!") was left out of K. J. Fielding's text, because the original was "more-or-less the same as Froude's text" (Fielding 61). From "In regard to all" to "alas" was written on a separate sheet of paper; see below, n. 14. The text included here is taken from Froude's publication of TC's Will of 6 Feb. 1873 (Froude, *My Relations* 74–75).

11. In his provisional Will of 12 May 1865, TC had left equal portions of his property (except Craigenputtoch) to "my two Brothers, Alexander and James, and my three sisters, Mary, Jean, Janet." John A. Carlyle was exempted because he had "no need of my money or help" (K. J. Fielding 58). This joint division of property remaining after specific bequests was confirmed in TC's Will of 6 Feb. 1873 (Froude, *My Relations* 74–75).

12. TC gave money regularly to James Baillie and his wife, Anna-Maria, via James Aitken; see 46:28 and 45. After James Aitken's death, 20 Sept., the money was channeled via the Rev. Wodehouse Raven (1806–90), vicar of Christchurch, Streatham. By the time of the 1871 census, the Baillies had moved to 12 Caroline St., London; the Caroline St. that they lived in is untraced; possibly TC was introduced to Raven by Lady Ashburton who owned Addiscombe, not far from Streatham.

13. James Baillie (d. 1873), Alexander Carlyle (d. 1876), John A. Carlyle (d. 1879), and John Forster (d. 1876) pre-deceased TC. Only David Masson outlived him. Maggie Welsh d. 4 May 1875. TC's last check for £20 via Wodehouse Raven was in April 1876, so Anna-Maria Baillie possibly d. later in 1876 or 1877. Sarah Warren left TC's employment some-

nothing to leave that could be in the least worthy of them: but if *they*, any one of them, could find among my reliques a memorial they would like who of men deserve it better! — No man at this time.

T. Carlyle.

Chelsea, 11 April, 1871 (not till now got signed, and finished with its two carets, &c, — owing to intolerable interruptions).[14]

TC TO ARTHUR HELPS

5 Cheyne Row, Chelsea
10 April 1871.

Dear Helps,

I am very much gratified by that kind dedication of your *Cortes*[1] to me. It has in the very tone of it a beautiful simplicity and sincerity; it puts on record, before I leave this world, a relation which was always gracious cheerful profitable and pleasant to me; — in short it gives me more satisfaction than all the "dedications" that were ever made to me, or are like to be.[2]

Cortes himself I believe will profit not a little by being disengaged from the

---

time between the 1871 census (when she is listed as at 5 Cheyne Row) and the 1881 census (when she is not).

14. K. J. Fielding included the note by A. Carlyle: "The 'Two carets' refer to two passages which are written on separate slips of paper gummed to the large sheet of foolscap on which the rest of the Will is inscribed. The first of these carets begins 'There is incidentally' &c; and ends 'better judgement than mine can be.' The second begins with the words: 'In regard to all business matters,' &c; and ends: 'thanks, poor *thanks*, are all I can return alas!' / Typed from the originals / by A. Carlyle." Fielding noted that these final words (presumably from "Typed") were written and signed.

TC-AH, 10 April. MS: NLS 3823.222. Pbd: *Correspondence of Sir Arthur Helps*, ed. E. A. Helps (London and New York, 1917) 308–9.
1. Arthur Helps, *The Life of Hernando Cortes*, 2 vols. (1871).
2. The dedication was written in the form of a letter to TC: "I dedicate this work to you, because I desire an occasion to record my gratitude for all your kindness to me in times past. When you first honoured me by making me your friend, I was a mere youth, while you were in the full maturity of manhood; but you were always kind and tolerant to me; and we were from the first, as we have been ever since, the best of friends. . . . / I do remember that we were not always of the same mind in our discussions on things in general; but there were some points on which we did agree, and do agree, thoroughly. We both believe that there is such a thing possible as good government, and that it would decidedly be desirable that men should live under good government. / We also think that whatever a man does, he should take great pains in doing it, — that in short, good work is an admirable thing. . . . / I have now only to say . . . that I should not have presumed to dedicate to so indefatigable student as yourself, this book of mine, if it had cost me no new researches, and if it did not contain my last and most carefully weighed observations upon the matters to which it relates" (Helps, *Life of Hernando Cortes* 1:v, vi, x).

[187]

big Book[3] where so many cannot well afford to follow him; and to the select few who, like myself, desire also to know his connections there, he still remains attainable in that form. I return you many thanks for Dedication and Copy both, the latter of which is again in process of being read here. Long may you live, dear Helps, to write new Books and purify and pacify your distracted fellow creatures with sprinklings of mild wisdom, in a form all your own!

It has not been want of will that has kept me so long from answering your message,[4] but simply an imbroglio of interruptions and botheration, excelling any strength I now have to deal with them.

With grateful and affectionate feelings, / Yours always truly,

T. Carlyle

TC TO MARGARET OLIPHANT

5 Cheyne Row, Chelsea,
11 April 1871.

Dear Mrs Oliphant,

Thank you very much for what you are doing in behalf of the poor Pension for Miss Jewsbury.[1] If Colonel Ponsonby[2] could, in some good moment, bring the matter, in all its evidence, before Her Majesty's clear and gracious mind, I think it could not fail to have a good effect there,—and indeed might *end* the tedious hagglings and dubieties of Mr Gladstone;[3]—with whom it has hung uncertain for above two years; a request signed first by only three of us, who thought ourselves sufficient as witnesses to the facts;[4] but now signed by

3. Arthur Helps, *The Spanish Conquest in America, and its Relation to the History of Slavery and to the Government of Colonies*, 4 vols. (1855–61); see 37:117. Helps wrote in the *Life*: "This Life is not a mere extract from my History of the Spanish Conquest. . . . I went carefully . . . over every sentence quoted from that History, to see whether, by the aid of additional knowledge, I could correct or improve it; and I have added greatly to those parts which especially concern the private life of Cortes" (*The Life of Hernando Cortes* 1:v).

4. Helps wrote to TC, 9 March 1870, forewarning him: "An infliction will come upon you in the course of the next three months. It is now your turn to have a 'tremmock.' I meditate dedicating to you my 'Life of Cortes,' in a long epistle, which will give me an opportunity of saying some things which I want to say—especially to declare that this book is not a mere warmed-up portion of the Spanish Conquest" (MS: NLS 1769.185); see 46:170. For "tremmock," a kind of trepidation, see 46:169.

TC-MO, 11 April. MS: NLS 23194.156. Hitherto unpbd.

1. See TC to JAC, 21 Jan.

2. Sir Henry Frederick Ponsonby (1825–95; *ODNB*), soldier and courtier, appointed private sec. to Queen Victoria, April 1870.

3. For Gladstone's restrictive views of literary pensions, see TC to JAC, 3 March.

4. Mary Aitken wrote to Margaret Oliphant, 25 April, explaining the history of the cam-

Presentation clock for Thomas Carlyle's 75th birthday
Privately owned, on loan to Carlyle's House, National Trust

---

paign to get a pension for Jewsbury: "The only Gift Miss Jewsbury has ever had from the Royal Bounty is £50 which Mr Gladstone sent two years ago by way of answer to the first Petition, which was signed only by Mr John Forster, Mr Froude & my Uncle: Froude having verbally expressed his firm conviction that poor Miss Jewsbury well deserved such a pension & having received from Mr Gladstone an answer which he considered decidedly encouraging. They accepted this £50 as a 'subvention' such as is often given when the List for the year is already full, thinking that next year her claim to a *Pension* would be accepted; but unfortunately no such thing happened; and then came this more formal Petition" (MS: NLS 23194.158).

Presentation clock in its traveling case
Privately owned, on loan to Carlyle's House, National Trust

some three and thirty of what one may fairly call the best names in England, who still do not seem to prevail in that quarter, somewhat to their surprise perhaps!

Tomorrow I will endeavour to put on paper my own poor word of testimony on Miss Jewsbury and her claims; and will send it off to *you* for transmittal, as the briefest and easiest way of getting it to Colonel Ponsonby's kind hands; and saving him the trouble of superfluous responses on the subject. Today I have not a moment left.

It will give me great pleasure to see you here again. The five minutes at Lady Stanley's was far from a "bother" to me;[5] and indeed the whole trans-

5. The presentation of a clock to TC for his 75th birthday; for Lady Stanley's insistence on TC calling on her, without telling him why, see TC to Lady S, 22 Feb. Anne Thackeray (1837–1919; *ODNB*), writer (da. of William Makepeace Thackeray, longtime friend of the Carlyles [see 39:278]), wrote to Emily Tennyson, [Oct. 1870]: "I . . . ask if you would join in a little conspiracy to give Mr. Carlyle a small token, like the seal he sent to Goethe [see 5:304–8]? I have written to Lady Ashburton and to Lady Stanley, his faithful friends. Lady Airlie suggests a clock. I have asked her and Mrs. Froude, about twelve ladies in all, and we

Presentation clock (detail)
Privately owned, on loan to Carlyle's House, National Trust

action there grows prettier and more gratifying, the longer that melodious little clock (it has a bell comparable almost to Big Ben's) measures out to me the remainder of my time.[6] Thanks, many and cordial, to you all, ye fourteen

---

think the clock should cost £12.0.0" (*Letters of Anne Thackeray Ritchie*, ed. Hester Ritchie [1924] 141). For the clock, see 189; it came in a traveling case; see opp.

6. Anne Thackeray later wrote: "It was . . . a dismal winter's day, the streets were shrouded in greenish vapours, and the houses looked no less dreary within, than the streets through which we had come. Somewhat chilled and depressed, we all assembled in Lady Stanley's great drawing-room in Dover Street, where the fog had also penetrated, and presently from the further end of the room, advancing through shifting darkness, came

honourable women,[7]—whose names I now have, safe, in a venerable brass tobacco-box,[8] once the property of a Soldier of the Great Friedrich's.

Believe me always, / Dear Mrs Oliphant, / Sincerely Yours,

T. Carlyle

TC TO JEAN CARLYLE AITKEN

5 Cheyne Row, Chelsea
17 April 1871.

Dear Sister,

It is very interesting to me, that account you give of the poor body Carruthers and his shipwrecks, and adventures, bad and good,[1]—especially of his

---

Carlyle. There was a moment's pause. No one moved; he stood in the middle of the room without speaking. . . . Lady Stanley went to meet him. 'Here is a little birthday present we want you to accept from us all, Mr. Carlyle,' said she, quickly pushing up before him a small table, upon which stood the clock ticking all ready for his acceptance. Then came another silence, broken by a knell sadly sounding in our ears. 'Eh, what have I got to do with Time any more?' he said. It was a melancholy moment" (Anne Thackeray Ritchie, *Chapters from Some Memoirs* [1894] 143). Intended to mark TC's 75th birthday (4 Dec. 1870), the clock was inscribed with the date of presentation "Thomas Carlyle 27th Feby 1871" (see 191); see also TC to JAC, 27 Feb.

7. The clock was accompanied by a "paper of signatures" inscribed "to Mr. Carlyle from his affectionate friends," 27 February 1871 (Carlyle House); it was signed by Lady Stanley, Juliet Pollock, b. Creed (1818–99), Lady Airlie, Anne Farrer (1818–1910; see 38:279), Margaret Oliphant, Frances Blunt, Maude Stanley, Anne Thackeray, Emily Tennyson, Mary Richenda Stephen, Henrietta Froude, Harriet Marian (Minny) Stephen, b. Thackeray (1840–75; *ODNB*), "A nameless Friend" ("my mother" [Ritchie, *Chapters* 142]), Isabella Thackeray, b. Shawe (1816–93), mother of Anne Thackeray and Harriet Stephen, and Lady Ashburton. Alexander Carlyle was to loan Carlyle House the "paper of signatures" (*Carlyle's House* 92).

8. Presumably the box sent to TC by an unidentified admirer (April 1865), with a picture of Frederick on the lid; see 42:172.

TC-JCA, 17 April. MS: NLS 531.8. Hitherto unpbd.

1. Jean Aitken wrote, 14 April, detailing the adventures of "Geordie Carruthers nephew to Carruthers of Haregills & Carruthers who married old Mrs Garthwait. He was brought up at the Kirksyke with old John & Jenny Jardine . . . & went out to Canada 39 years ago. He had to work as 'fireman' in the Packets [steam ships] till he got a knowledge of the machinery when he got to be engineer. . . . He is too old to work in the steamers now (67 years) & lives at Toronto with his son, his wife being dead. . . . This luckless little ingineer . . . was wrecked on his passage 5 weeks ago one other passenger & six of the crew only being picked up in a boat reshipped & sent on to Glasgow & Ecclefechan without a penny or a rag but what was on their backs." George Carruthers (b. 1805). Jean described him at length: "A stout active shrewd looking little old man with a broad short face, very much tanned, grey eyes set wide apart & bushy steel grey hair. He wore a brown fur cap & short blue sailor looking coat. . . . But very rusty looking, & *no vestige of linen visible*."

experiences, as eye-witness, in our dear old Alick's establishment.[2] I perfectly recollect both Carrutherses (all the Carrutherses) of Haregills[3] and Sooty Rob, his elder Brother, at the upper end of the Haggs (Tailor Garthwaite's Stepfather),[4] a *blethering* noisy, ever-unwashed man. With an effort, too, I think I can at last summon out a third, considerably younger Brother, called Jamie Carruthers, probably a kind of Journeyman Clogger;[5] who had come out from Dumfries, and was working at Ecclefechan for a livelihood in the later years of his life. He also was, in the physical sense, an overwhelmingly dirty man; seems in my recollection to have had a running scrofula (with cabbage blades &c) about the abominable neck of him; had a snoring, indistinct, pockmarked face, with the eyes swiming in it, as if half-boiled and nearly blind,—a most ugly physiognomy, though rather to be pitied and avoided than in any way *hated*. This surely must have been the Father of your present *Gangrel* Carruthers[6] in the brown cap? who the Gangrell himself can have been I cannot in the least make out. Probably he is of a more recent date than my personal remembrances of the Kirksyke[7] reach to? I very well remember old Crury Jardine, the Mason (how well!) and his big sack of a Wife,—a Sister of these Carrutherses:[8] but the Jardine pair had nothing of young about them in my time, except one big harl of a daughter, hardy and coarse as hemp, not a bad lass otherwise, whom I know not what became of. There was, at that time, no Boy in the establishment.[9] Can this Gangrel Carruthers, now at Dumfries, be by chance the upshot of a certain "Billy-Bobby,"[10] of whom

2. Jean wrote that Geordie "recognised Alick & his wife when they came on board his ship when they were in search of a 'location' [Alick and family sailed for the U.S., June 1843, finally settling in Canada, June 1844; see 18:71–72] and has known them ever since. . . . He saw Alick 16*th* Feb, shortly before he started for this Country." Geordie had spent a week at New Year, 1871, with Alick and his family and told Jean: "They have a nice comfortable house & farm, & no man stands higher in the public estimation in Brantford than yr brother Sandy."

3. The Carruthers brothers lived at Haregills, farm about 4 mi. (6.5 km.) N of Ecclefechan; one of them was m. to Jean, b. Bell, cousin of TC's mother; see 1:172. Alick had considered taking Haregills Farm before he emigrated in 1843; see 16:97.

4. Sooty Rob Carruthers lived at The Haggs, on the road out of Ecclefechan to the NW, and m. the widow Garthwaite, mother of Tom Garthwaite (ca. 1810–94), tailor, who made clothes for TC for many years; see Wilson, *Carlyle* 2:142–43. His father was possibly John Garthwaite (b. ca. 1791).

5. Maker of clogs; James Carruthers, shoemaker, Ecclefechan.

6. According to parish records, George's parents were John and Agnes Carruthers, Gretna.

7. Kirksyke, farm in Hoddom parish.

8. John Curry Jardine (b. ca. 1784), mason, m. Agnes, b. Carruthers (b. ca. 1791).

9. Their da. was Jane (b. ca. 1814); they later had two boys, George (b. ca. 1821) and Thomas (b. ca. 1825).

10. John A. Carlyle wrote, 27 April: "[George] Carruthers is himself the 'Billie Bobbie' of

there rises on me a pale shadow or faint echo, of certainly belonging to the Kirksyke, though at a time when that locality was not in my neighbourhood any more? The Kirksyke, the Helgills (Halygills) well, the vanished old Kirk, Eccles of St Fechan,[11]—alas the poor old Kirkyard tree itself is now a vanished quantity! all vanishes and fades away like a dream; as TIME itself, with all its edifices and achievements, shall do; swallowed in ETERNITY's Silent Sea, whose record is with God only.

I was really interested in these ancient Ecclefechan trifles; to me they are impressive naturally as to few others. If you can get any trace of this Billy-Bobby shadow, and fix it down as belonging to your now Gangrel in the brown cap, it would be really worth my while to know it. For the rest, he seems to be a really worthy kind of body;—and if he *need* any farther help I shall be very willing to add my sovereign for him to the Drs.[12] The Wull Carruthers, Andrew's Brother Gabriel's Son,[13] I recollect in every lineament; a peaceable, but dreadfully fighting man when you provoked him,—who, by certain signal fist-victories at Dumfries, in volunteer time,[14] had gained the hearts of us patriotic boys:—I am really gratified that Wull and his children have prospered in America. There was something good in all that kin of Carrutherses.[15]

Excuse all this clatter; it comes from a warm place in the heart.

Ever your affectionate Brother

T. Carlyle

old times, Jamie says . . . & was thought to be given to lying at that time & other vices—w*h* it is to be hoped he has quitted."

11. The medieval church of St. Fechan was demolished in the 17th century after the parishes of Ecclefechan and Hoddom were united in 1609; the churchyard was still used for burials.

12. Jean wrote: "Mr Shankland the Banker at Ecclef*n* has written to his (George's) son at Toronto to tell him of his Father's misfortunes & I fear the poor old soul must be ill off in the meantime. I gave him a few shillings . . . & the Dr sent him a £1." John wrote, 27 April, to say that he had given TC's sovereign to Carruthers.

13. Jean wrote: "He told me also about 'Road Wull' i.e. W*m* Carruthers who lived at the solitary house on the north side of the road at the top of the Hags." William Carruthers, known as "Road Wull," was the son of Gabriel Carruthers (b. 1764), who was the brother of Andrew Carruthers (1775–1837), mason; see 29:307.

14. Volunteer Corps of part-time soldiers were set up in the late 1790s and early 1800s during the Napoleonic wars, due to fear of invasion.

15. Jean replied, 23 April, that she had not been able to find out anything more; Carruthers was staying in Ecclefechan and rarely came to Dumfries.

TC TO JOHN A. CARLYLE

5 Cheyne Row, Chelsea
22 April 1871

My dear Brother,

Thanks for the Letter you have written about Irma; you will at least get to the bottom of that wild looking project of hers, and see whether there is any possibility in it or none.[1] That was all I undertook for her in the answer I sent the other day;[2] and that will be accomplished. — If poor Maggie is actually left resourceless; dependent altogether on the pity of others, might it not be feasible to combine the help of all the friends she has to make up some little fund for her against a still worse day? Irma would have to take charge of the affair: I recollect only the Cressfields (if any of them survive in New S. Wales);[3] but doubtless there are various others more or less able who might be willing? I will readily to your £50 add another; — but you did well not to *send* any money during the present War troubles; and indeed I almost think it would be worth while and better to aim at the above general enterprise first; and ascertain what feasibility is in it; judge *you* altogether;[4] *I* have next to no data for judging.

TC-JAC, 22 April. MS: NLS 527.46. Hitherto unpbd.

1. Apparently Jean Otthenin had received a pension of £50 a year from the heirs of Lord Balgray. David Robertson Williamson (1761–1837), Lord Balgray, of Balgray House, Dumfriesshire, Scottish judge. Jean Otthenin d. in France, Nov. 1870; see TC to JAC, 3 March. She and her elder da., Margaret, who suffered from ill-health (see 45:146), had been living in France with her other da., Irma Durival; see 45:130.

2. TC evidently sent on to John A. Carlyle his letter from Irma, as John wrote, 15 April: "Poor Irma is evidently in a sea of troubles, & one would be glad to help her if possible; but she has very little common sense or true veracity of character, & her statements often depend on mere imagination & are not to be relied on without due investigation." But the pension was real as John then wrote, 20 April: "I had a letter yesterday from Mr Steuart of India Street about Madame Otthenin's Pension. He & his father . . . 'have long acted for her in little business matters gratuitously'; & had not heard of her death till he got Irma's letter & mine. . . . He is to forward both 'to the representatives of Lord Balgray,' by my permission, & see if there be any chance of continuing the pension."

3. Dr. William Little (1760–1847), of Cressfield House, 1 mi. (1.5 km.) S of Ecclefechan, who was often known as Cressfield; see 4:419–20. His sons, Francis and Archibald (1803–88), emigrated to New South Wales in Australia, Francis in 1822 (see 2:163) and Archibald in 1825: "In May 1829, the estate of Cressfield was established by Archibald Little, just north of his brother Francis's earlier grant [of land] named Invermein" (Sharon Veale, *Remembering Country: History & Memories of Towarri National Park*, [NSW, 2001] 11). There were also two das., Mary (1796–1857) and Maxwell (b. 1799, still alive in 1862; see 38:128); TC played with Mary as a child (see 33:19) when he was also friendly with Jean Otthenin, so presumably the families were all close.

4. John wrote, 15 April, that he had thought of sending a gift of £50 to Maggie, once it was safe to send money through France. John replied, 25 April, that he knew almost no-

Thanks also for what you have done in the "Artizan's Dwellings" matter.[5] I had a private notion you *would* probably go along with me in the adventure; and now it seems you have actually done it: thanks again for good company on such a questionable adventure! —

In regard to the Adamson account,[6] which you always take such punctual trouble with, I have practically no doubt whatever but it is all right, but somehow or other my Balance there seems to be less than I had vaguely guessed. Could you undertake the farther bother of writing down to me in two columns what my *payings in* have been and what my *drawings out*; adding only what the Balance this time twelve months was: I should then see clearly *where* my guess is faulty.[7] One of the points I suppose is that a *second* Bill on Chapman (I think, for some £350)[8] has not yet become payable, and does not appear in the Account at all. — If it be less trouble to you; — as indeed it surely will! — pray send me the Account itself instead, and let the fash lie on my own oblivious head.

This has been the worst of all my weeks in regard to sleep and its adjuncts;[9]

---

one else who knew Jean Otthenin: "Miss Maxwell Little was poor herself when she left & sold Cressfield, & none of the children of her brothers Frank & Archy are known to me even by name. . . . Perhaps it might be best to send the order for £50, which I still have, as a joint gift from you & me . . . & then send another for the same sum later. Both Maggie & Irma have a good deal of family pride or vanity; & I dont feel sure how a gift from me alone w*d* be received."

5. See TC to JAC, 13 Jan. John wrote to TC, 12 April: "That pamphlet about the Artizans', Labourers' &c Dwellings is the same as one you sent me in Jan*y* last, & the newspaper accompanying it gives report of last year up to 8*th* inst. It is a society which one would like to see successful; but its task is difficult to accomplish. You might, as I said in January, do a good deed by taking, say five, £10 Shares or £50 worth in all." John wrote again, 20 April: "[Adamson] knows nothing about the 'Housebuilding Society,' but said the utmost one can lose is the price of Shares as the concern is Limited, I have therefore written to Martin, your Birmingham correspondent, & ordered five Shares of £10 each for you, & also five for myself."

6. John wrote, 20 April: "At Adamsons I also got your Bank Acc*t* up to 15*th* April of this year. It shews a Balance in your favour at that date of £844 .. 7 .. o, & seems quite correct. I need scarcely forward it to you."

7. He replied, 23 April: "I at once send your Bank Acc*t* about which you seem uneasy. It is all quite correct, I think, & has been well examined. I have your Cheques here, & List of all your Railway Stock — w*h* for this year's Acc*t* bring in £45 more than for last year, some of the Dividends being better. I mark with + the sum sent to your London Bank, & with – the sums given away (more than £860) during last year. Money on Deposit Receipts is never entered in Current Acc*ts*. Last year's Balance £2575, this year's £844 with Deposit of £2000 = £2844 — or £269 more in Bank than last year, w*h* with the £860 of gifts w*d* have made £1129 more than last year. Rents of Craig*k* paid in full tho' marked only £120, as usual, public burdens being deducted."

8. For TC's signed receipt, 6 March, for Chapman's check for £350, see TC to JAC, 3 March.

9. TC wrote in his journal, 3 June: "'*April 21* [date of JWC's death; see 43:211]' has

after four or five sensible improvements, each rashly accepted as a recovery, this is a little disheartening; but I do not yet in the least give in. I have a thought of trying Melchet[10] for a little while, if things don't soon mend; still more confidently an *actual* attempt at trying the Sea were Summer here; — in short courage, courage!

Adieu, dear Brother. With constant ever-kind Love to all of you

Yours ever,

T. Carlyle[11]

"Kitty's"[12] Letter (the *first* for a year or years back, it seems to me!) is intrinsically worth nothing; but you may return it if there is a chance.

TC TO CATHERINE PHILLIPPS

5 Cheyne Row, Chelsea
23 April 1871.

Dear Mrs Phillipps,

It is long since we heard with any distinctness of you; and this word that now arrives is very welcome. On my side, too, I have sent many a thought and enquiry after you; not able to do more than guess vaguely as to your whereabout, still less as to what you might be doing or how it was faring with you and yours. Happily there seems to have nothing essential gone wrong; and I am much obliged by the assurance to that effect.[1]

To me also Dover, where I once was, and properly only once for a few hours some years ago, was a most mournful place; scattered irrecognisably hither & thither,[2] full of noise and confusion, and populous only with pale shadows

---

passed since I last wrote here; solemn, sad, unspeakable; —the *fifth* year of my *solitude* in this Earth is now completed, therefore; solitude *increasing* rather than diminishg. *God* is about us Both; no other solace, —but that in some strong moments is one.— Ever since jan*y*, a miserable state of health; incapacitating for any real work at all, —and tho*ts*, sometimes tender enough, oftener merely heavy-laden, dim, and drearily weary, all the 'work' done" (TC's journal; privately owned).

10. Lady Ashburton's house, Melchet Court, in Hampshire; TC's last visit there had been 5-21 Feb. 1870; see 46:159.

11. Signature and postscript in TC's hand.

12. Catherine Phillipps; see TC to CP, 23 April.

TC-CP, 23 April. MS: Yale. Hitherto unpbd.

1. Catherine Phillipps wrote, 18 April, from Dover, where she now lived: "I so often think of you in this Dover that I cannot help writing you a few lines. I want to know how you are in *bodily* health and what you are really about—and if I write I cannot get an answer except from your kind little niece if she is still with you— I hope you are well; for you are one of the very few of my real old friends left me on this earth." TC and Phillipps had become reacquainted in Oct. 1868, but had had little contact since then; see 45:191-95.

2. TC visited Caroline Davenport Bromley at her home, Ripple Court, Ringwould, nr.

and recollections more or less ghastly of the things and persons that had made it human to me in the years long fled for ever. I, with great difficulty, found a Liverpool St, which I tried to believe might be the old Liverpool Terrace, though no feature of it was recognisable to me as such. Edward Irving's Lodging I could not even trace or guess at to the extent you have done:[3] in short all was jumbled into chaotic wreck for me; and I left the place not wishing ever to behold it again.

Our poor little French Tour,[4] so pleasant and full of interest in those old days,—alas, what it has grown to! Surely no Country I have read or heard of ever by its own delirium and ill luck, fell into such an ignominious welter of anarc[h]y and misery as poor France is now in. With you I altogether heartily and sorrowfully pity it; with the ardent *wish*, which struggles to be the sure *hope*, that it may recover its pristine beauty and brilliancy and be once more the ornament of Europe.[5] But too evidently it has infinite delirium, vainglorious unveracity and open disregard of the Laws of God and Man to cast out of it, with sore travail enough, before any real prosperity or well-doing can return to it. Few persons, I believe, perhaps *au fond* [deep down] not you yourself, have a deeper sense of the beautiful graceful and shining qualities Nature has lodged in the French; but except in *conforming*, in perpetually striving to conform to the Laws which Nature has eternally appointed, no Nation can prosper, or at length can exist at all in this world. Alas, my coṁon idea, withal, is, that England's turn must come next, and that, in exact proportion to England's folly, wickedness and worldly baseness, must England's disasters and disgraces like-wise be. And often it strikes me moreover that the hour cannot now be distant, and is fast hastening on. But let us quit these sad considerations; too dismal to be dwelt on here,—or elsewhere, if one could help it.

Dover, 13–27 Aug. 1866; traveling through Dover on arrival, he remarked: "a country whh I cd not recognise one yard of"; see 44:36.

3. Phillipps wrote: "[T]he old Dover no longer exists, either for me or for others—A large uncomfortable straggling Town is built upon the Sands & elsewhere—Liverpool Terrace, is now Liverpool street & no longer looks upon the Sea, having several rows of ugly houses between it & the Sea, & I cannot find out the house where poor Mrs Irving used to give me lectures upon my forward behaviour & used to drill me upon *les convenances* & then end by expressing some desperately unmoral sentiment.... [T]he house in Townwall street where the Irvings & you lived, when the Stracheys came down here—I see no trace of the house—tho' I know it exists behind some mildewed wall." TC visited Dover, Oct. 1824, in company with Edward Irving, his wife, Isabella, b. Martin (1797–1854), and their son, Edward (1824–25); Phillipps had been there with her cousin Julia Strachey, b. Kirkpatrick, and Edward Strachey; see 3:165–72.

4. TC, Edward Strachey, and Phillipps went to Paris together, 23 Oct.–6 Nov. 1824; see 3:178–188 and Carlyle, *Reminiscences* 305–7.

5. Phillipps wrote: "I think you have been hard upon the French if those ... leaves collected again by the Newspapers are your real opinion. I grieve ... the desolation of dear beautiful Paris & hope her children may yet return to order."

I can really hope you will soon see the "Purchase System"[6] put an end to,—though that England will thereupon get a real Army, as every Nation ought to have, I can by no means believe. England, I sorrowfully calculate, will have to change its ways, parliamentary and other, a good deal, and that to an extent she little thinks of, before that can arrive!— But at all events in September or October next we can hope your interest in it will substantially be set at rest. This is a little bit of blessing which we can thankfully appropriate. You are then to be free of Army matters and free to choose a residence where you please.[7] Let us hope it may not be too far from London and the old scenes connected with your young history,—and not too inaccessible to the old friends, especially to one old Friend who still lingers in that region, and cannot now calculate on lingering long!— I have been decidedly below par in point of health,—got sensibly hurt by the puddles and rages of last winter (the first winter that ever did sensibly hurt me); have twice or thrice fancied I was recovering since Spring came; but have never yet been able quite to do it. However I still keep hoping, keep endeavouring.

My little Niece is still here, as you perceive; still helps me faithfully all she can. I am to send her kind regards to you; my own you are at all times assured of. Do you never come to London? If so why do you neglect to call or warn us?

Believe me ever, / Dear Mrs Phillipps, / faithfully and

affectionately yours,

T. Carlyle

TC TO JOHN RUSKIN

5 Cheyne Row, Chelsea,
30 April 1871

Dear Ruskin,

This *Fors Clavigera*, Letter 5*th*,[1] which I have just finished reading, is incomparable; a quasi-sacred consolation to me, which almost brings tears into

6. See TC to JAC, 10 Feb.

7. Phillipps wrote: "I have been here with my youngest daughter since Sept*r* last. Her husband's regiment is here & here we shall remain till this new state of army regulations gives him his next step without purchase & then I shall be free, free to live where & how as I please— Dover will not be the place, if my life is preserved till then (w*h* I think will be about September or October). Dover is so cold that I have spent all the winter coughing— my old weakness of lungs is returned upon me."

TC-JR, 30 April. MS: previously Helen Viljoen, inherited by Van Akin Burd (d. 2015), present location unknown. Pbd: W. G. Collingwood, *The Life and Work of John Ruskin*, 2 vols. (1893) 2:411; *Ruskin's Works* 27:lxxxvi; Wilson, *Carlyle* 6:247; Cate 159.

1. John Ruskin, "The White Thorn Blossom," *Fors Clavigera. Letters to the workmen and labourers of Great Britain*, Letter 5, dated 1 May.

my eyes! Every word of it is as if spoken, not out of my poor heart only, but out of the eternal Skies; words winged with Empyrean wisdom, piercing as lightning, — and which I really do not remember to have heard the like of.[2] *Continue*, while you have such utterances in you, to give them voice.[3] They will find and force entrance into human hearts, *whatever* the "angle of incidence" may be; that is to say, whether, — for the degraded and *in*human Blockhead-isms we, so-called "Men," have mostly now become, — you come in upon them at the broadside, at the top, or even at the bottom *Euge, euge* [bravo]! —

[yrs ever / T. Carlyle[4]]

TC TO JOHN A. CARLYLE

[ca. 6 May 1871]

Burn this; — we have utterly *denied* him, as you may suppose.[1]

Mary writes instead of me,[2] — for cause. I do feel sensibly freshened & *piously* delighted (at intervals) by the beautiful fresh air divine *silence* and blessed skyey influences, — tho' I slept but little. My love to one and all of you, — T.C.

2. Ruskin argues that the current debasement of the human spirit is a byproduct of the values and enterprises of the industrial revolution, and he offers an alternative vision of how society ought to be organized, based on an appreciation of nature.

3. Ruskin replied, 1 May: "I am deeply thankful to have your letter . . . I think the great help it gives me is . . . the pleasure of giving you pleasure — and knowing that you accept what I am doing as the fulfilment so far as in me is, of what you have taught me." The first letter of *Fors Clavigera* was pbd. 1 Jan. 1871, the last, no. 96, in 1884.

4. According to a note on MS, the signature in TC's hand, "yrs ever / T. Carlyle," was cut away and "given to young Harvey Goodwin of Orton Hall"; Harvey Goodwin (b. 1850), son of Harvey Goodwin (1819–91; *ODNB*), bishop of Carlisle 1869–91).

TC-JAC, [ca. 6 May]. MS: NLS 527.47. Hitherto unpbd. Written in TC's hand from Melchet; dated soon after TC's arrival on 5 May.

1. TC wrote on the reverse of a letter from Thomas Hedderwick (1850–1918), 3 May. Hedderwick was sec. of the Committee of the Glasgow Univ. Liberal Association, and asked TC's permission to nominate him as their candidate for the office of Lord Rector of the univ. Hedderwick wrote: "The Committee are anxious to secure your assent to this application; — not only because they feel that there is none other living whose name would more worthily sustain the illustrious character of the Rectorship of this University but also on account of the unfortunate miscarriage of 1854." The Glasgow Univ. Liberal Association nominated TC for Rector, 1854, but his name was withdrawn because of widespread objections to his religious views; see 29:217–18.

2. Mary's letter is untraced; Hedderwick replied, 24 May: "From the kindly tone of your letter . . . the Committee could not avoid entertaining a hope that you might ultimately reconsider your decision if their petition were more ably and fully stated than can be done by letter"; two of their number therefore proposed calling on him: "if you will be so good as to grant them an interview." TC's reply is untraced.

TC TO JOHN A. CARLYLE

Melchet Court, Romsey,
13 May 1871.

My dear Brother,

Your little Note came duly to me here; almost the only one I have yet had, — for except the farewell note from Maggie Welsh, wh. enclosed 2 splendid looking American Letters, Mrs Warren forwarded nothing, and all manner of trash, no doubt daily accumulating, lies comfortably out of my sight for the time being. Nay the splendid Yankee Letters themselves contained nothing but more or less impudent requests for Autographs and had the destiny of merely lighting pipes. There is something really comfortable in living day after day without any letters at all from such impertinent correspondents as mine usually consist of.

It is not for want of thinking of you all that I have written nothing in answer to your Note; but the truth is I am so overwhelmed with mournful languour total indisposition to write or even to speak if I cd get it well helped, that I have absolutely written[1] nothing at all till this moment; & shall probably write nothing till forced by something on getting back to Chelsea. I read almost nothing either, & in fact do nothing; but am content to look upon *being in the open air*, sitting walking, being driven through the New Forest[2] sceneries (and one day) riding a too a firey horse in hope of benifit from that variety of inaction wh. however I have not repeated hitherto. Tourguéneff came duly on Monday; but unhappily had to go again on Wednesday morning[3] I say unhappily not only because he is really a friendly intelligent man, a general favourite with high & low, but because he entirely relieved me from any labour of talking; being himself a most copious & entertaining talker, — by far the best I have ever heard who talks so much. We have had various other people here but none that did me the least good; nothing in fact is so tolerable to me at present as being well let alone.[4] The pure clean air, the sometimes shining skies, the great *sough* of the woods, the otherwise entire silence: all that comes to me with an unspeakable welcome; and though steeped in sadness all of it is a real blessing for me (*Enter*[5] Lady A. we can't proceed!) — In brief, we are doing altogr *well*; —for the rest, we don't think of

TC-JAC, 13 May. MS: NLS 527.48. Quot: A. Carlyle, *NL* 2:278–79.

1. TC inserted "2" and "1" above the words to indicate that "absolutely written" should be reversed.

2. The New Forest, large area of unenclosed land, mainly in SW Hampshire, S of Melchet.

3. Ivan Turgenev visited Melchet 8–10 May.

4. Coterie speech; see 18:231.

5. From "*Enter*," the letter is in TC's hand.

homewards till ab*t* a week hence. I sleep visibly *more*; oftenest I rather feel as if slightly *better*,—but don't *know*!— Post-time is within 3 minutes too. I can add no more except that our treatment here is *Supreme*; and that Mary is a first favourite with everybody. Tell Jean that with my love. God bless you all.— Ever y*rs* dear Brother,

T. Carlyle

TC TO JOHN A. CARLYLE

Melchet, Romsey, 15 May, 1871

My dear Bro*r*,—Here is one of the Yankee Letters[1] (one, indeed *both*) still left; and before trying anything else, I make it the excuse of a word in my own *slow* hand to you, by way of thankfulness and blessing for the bright May morning and beautiful solitude prepared for me this day!—Lady A*n* is gone to London Sat*y* night last, and does not return till tomorrow; great was her joy, profuse her *gratitude*, to find that we w*d* stay here alone, and not fly off when she herself had to take wing! A small fav*r* surely; wh*h* only increases as one's freedom, power of unlimited roaming on the woody hills,—with hour of dinner *certain*,—and of being *monarch* of all one surveys. But certainly this noble Hostess excels in genial effusive kindness of heart all that one c*d* find elsewhere; and fairly "beats the world":[2]—all that one c*d* object to is laxity of purpose as to time and space; whereby much gets *jumbled* daily, in a way *not* welcome to Dyspepsia and Insomnia, to whomever else!—

I have been utterly idle, as I told you, all week; yesterday, I struck into the "Lady-Nelson" woods;[3] roved ab*t* on footpaths and horse-paths, for 2 hours and more, in a silence as of Hades: saw nobody, only once far off a human hab- itat*n*; kindled my pipe in a fav*ble* place, and sat smoking, with tho*ts* enough, tho*ts* very sad for most part, but not unblessed some of them.— I don't think we are likely to *return* till the last of this week; it may be not till this day week (Monday), if Froude & Wife be invited in the "Sat*y* to Monday" way: wh*h* alone suits Froude for Melchet. *Meinetwegen* [for my part], either way. I continue to believe (especially this morning) that I grow a little better: it is cert*n* I have not had any *utter* downbreak in sleep hitherto, tho' no night

TC-JAC, 15 May. MS: NLS 527.49. Quot: Surtees, *Ludovisi* 154. Written in TC's hand, on the reverse of George Reed's letter.

1. George Reed (unidentified further) wrote from New York, 25 April: "Pardon this intru- sion but owing to the very high respect I hold towards you as the leader of modern thought I venture to ask for your autograph."

2. Coterie speech; see 8:223.

3. Landford Wood, on the W side of the Melchet estate, named after its proprietor Lady Frances Elizabeth Nelson, b. Eyre (1797–1878).

"sleeping well" (how far from that, alas!); perhaps tongue & mouth are a little cleaner (*venia verbo* [pardon the word]!),—and the wilderness of *muscae volitantes* [floaters] in my left eye, inumerable in quantity, and strange in shape & quality some late few, has certainly abated in savagery since I came. Let us hope, let us hope,—if it be worth while at all!

We shall be 2 only when Chelsea ag*n*: poor Maggie, as I told you, will not be there:—good cheerful Maggie; she was really very good, quiet, well-bred; a quietly much-enduring woman if one think of all that has come and gone![4]— The House being empty, we are now ready for you when you like to come. I want to know what y*r* plans are if you have formed any? Tell me, so far as you can. I am myself bent ag*n* on the sea; and hope I shall not ag*n* be disappointed as in the last 2 summers. But perhaps I shall still! *Voyons* [let us see].

You have no idea what a *time* this scribble has cost me;—almost as if I had been *engraving* it, say on *lead!* This loss of my hand is the worst of all I have had for the 5 years that have now fled since 1866.[5] It completely disfurnishes my life; makes real "employ*t*" impossible in it: I perceive too well I shall never learn to write by "dictat*n*"; it is as if one were learning to "laugh thro *wool.*" Well, well.——— All my press-correct*g* is done. "Pop*r* Edit*n Sartor*," by Chap*n*'s reckoning (and even *Bill* of £371) *has* come to 21,000,[6] if never farther. Ah me; too late, too late!

I cannot fully read that *1000*-jahrig *Eiche* [one-thousand-year-old oak tree] Letter;[7] but gather that it is of no import*ce*. Being so very *thin*, how*r*, you may send it (interpreted a little),—unless you forget. Adieu d*r* Brr. My loving regards to Jean & to all of you.

Yr affect*e* T. Carlyle

4. Maggie Welsh stayed at Cheyne Row from 23 March until early May; for her troubles, see TC to JAC, 30 Jan. TC gave her a copy of the people's edn. of *Sartor*, inscribed: "To my dear Cousin Maggie, with many regards, T. Carlyle (Chelsea, 27 April 1871)."

5. TC meant the years since JWC's death, 21 April 1866.

6. *Sartor Resartus* in the people's edn. was pbd. 25 March; see TC to JAC, 21 Jan. The *Dundee Courier* reported, 29 March: "Of the first volume of Messrs Chapman and Hall's People's Edition . . . which was only published on Saturday, more than 11,000 copies have been sold. It appears that the publishers of the work greatly under-estimated the popularity of their author, and the publication of the work, which was announced for the 15th inst., had to be delayed. Even now the booksellers in this and other towns have only received a moiety of their orders, and it is estimated the present issue will have to be more than doubled." The *Morning Post* announced, 31 March, that "The third issue (making 20,000 copies) is now ready."

7. Robert Waldmüller had sent TC his book *Die tausendjährige Eiche im Elsass* [The Millennium Oak in Alsace]; see TC to RW, 27 Dec.; he wrote to TC in German, 7 May; TC enclosed it to John, who replied, 18 May: "The German letter is not easily read, but I have succeeded in making a copy which you will find legible enough. . . . [It] is modest & interesting, & hardly requires an answer."

MARY AITKEN TO W. D. CHRISTIE

Melchet Court, Romsey,
18 May 1871.

Dear Sir,

Mr Carlyle, my Uncle, desires me to thank you cordially for you kind note and say when he returns to Chelsea he will be most happy to go some afternoon between 3 and 4 (which is his best time) and see Mrs Christie and you.[1] He is sorry you and your Daughter had the trouble of coming to Chelsea without seeing him.[2]

We came down here a fortnight ago—to try if the change would do my Uncle any good; and he is much better and intends to return home in another week.

With his kind regards to you all

Yours truly
Mary Carlyle Aitken

TC TO JOHN A. CARLYLE

5 Cheyne Row, Chelsea,
23 May 1871

My dear Brother,

We got home yesternight between 8 & 9 without accident of any kind:— we did indeed aim at starting 2 hours earlier, but by disrespect for the rigorous nature of Time (which it is the custom at Melchet too much to treat as an elastic entity), arrived at Romsey[1] some minutes after our train had passed; and were obliged, Mary & I, to saunter about in the lanes & shady places for a 2 hours & more, waiting next train; but found the time slip easily enough, & the actual journey in all its details a quite successful affair.

People say, as their wont is, I have an air of great improvement; I myself feel that perhaps I am a little improved; certainly I don't feel worse; and

MA-WDC, 18 May. MS: EUL. Hitherto unpbd.

1. Christie wrote, 14 May: "I have long wished to say to you that my wife [Mary Christie] often expresses her strong desire to see you once again. . . . I wish you might be induced to extend one daily walk in this direction . . . to visit here any afternoon . . . (5 o'clock tea has become a natural hour). . . . If you would do so, it would make her very glad."

2. Christie wrote: "I endeavoured to find you this day week, but unsuccessfully, and a daughter of mine accompanied me." Christie had several das., including Mary Elizabeth Christie.

TC-JAC, 23 May. MS: NLS 527.50. Quot: Surtees, *Ludovisi* 155.

1. Romsey Station, the junction on the London and South-Western railway line nearest to Melchet.

the 17 days of pure air on the hill tops & quiet lanes were beyond dispute a healthier element than noisy dusty Chelsea; and at all events were a new one. I have yet seen nobody; indeed am very busy getting into the poor old harness again; dealing with the litter that has accumulated in this absence. To you is the first Note I write, which will enclose at least the 2 Letters, Butler's[2] and Alick's;[3] the latter of which was left lying by a small mistake of mine or Mary's. The house is very quiet; all things clear & clean; and will be the eligiblest of lodgings I sh*d* think till the weather grow too hot. Your room upstairs is in perfect readiness, and, I think, will be found to have gained by the Peabody frontage.[4] Pray let one hear of y*r* plans immediately, so far as they have yet come into shape.[5] Mine hitherto are hanging very much in the vague. Lady Ashburton indeed has been talking about Yachts & sea Voyages, for weeks past; the very day before we left she had a fine little programme about going to the Island of Lewis (beautiful silent Isle placed far amid the melancholy main);[6] I to go with her to lodge in some aristocrat summer cottage which she knew of close by the solitary shore and there bathe & swim about completely at discretion till the 10*th* of Aug*t* next—when the above said Cottage w*d* be required again by the aristocratic owner.[7] To this fine scheme I had only to assent; and did so with great readiness, as one of the suitablest things imaginable. She overjoyed will at once go into the preliminary inquiries &c; and at an early date ("June 4*th*" she said; but let us call it June 10*th* or 20*th*) begin executing! What the degree of "execution" will amount to I can by no means certainly say; nor what, on failure of this I ought to decide on. My object is very simple; I have nearly altogether lost the power of digestion, consequently of sleeping or almost of living; and ought, if I could, to seek for some improvement; likeliest by help of the *sea*, while the Summer lasts. It seems

2. Charles Butler (1802–97); see 45:223. Butler had looked after TC's American investments until 1868; see 45:125–26. John A. Carlyle and Butler continued to correspond. John wrote to Butler, 6 June: "The stay of three weeks . . . at Melchet proved very beneficial, & my brother looks fully as well as usual. . . . He bids me send his very kindest regards to you, & say that he intends to send you a book of which the last volume is not yet quite ready. He has always a very lively sense of your kindness & the pleasure he had in seeing you while you were in this country."

3. Their brother Alexander.

4. Peabody Mansions, Lawrence St., Chelsea, completed April 1870; see 46:94. Lawrence St. is parallel to Cheyne Row. John A. Carlyle's bedroom was on the 2nd (3rd in U.S.) floor at the front (see 45:173), presumably overlooking the rear of Peabody Mansions. Peabody Estates were founded by George Peabody (1795–1869; *ODNB*), to provide housing for the deserving poor.

5. John replied, 24 May: "My plans like yours are still undecided, except that I purpose going to see you at Chelsea again early next week if all goes well."

6. Isle of Lewis in the Outer Hebrides, about 43 mi. (70 km.) W of mainland Scotland.

7. Unidentified.

my one chance;—and I do intend making some attempt that way; but in what particular shape is no more fixed than you see.

Two cards were left here, "Mr Alex. Forrest,[8] Beswick Manchester" & "Mr Alexr. Gibson," without any further address. Mary thinks one of these may have been the Edinr Student, or Advocate,[9] who was to call upon me? If so, take what order on it seems fittest. I am now ready to sign the Railway Papers; for your trouble in regard to which many, many thanks.[10] I should like well to hear what the finale of Irma Otthenin's application has been,[11] if any finale has yet ensued. I am this morning sending off to Adamson a Bill, which in writing to you the other day I described as for £371;[12] whereas when I now look on it the real reading is £271. Is not this the sign of a first rate financeer!— I had some other trifles to talk about or send you but will say no more in the hurry of today. Jean's Letter to Mary was by much my liveliest bit of epistolary reading last night. There is a posthumous little vol. by Erskine from Edmonstone & Douglas,[13] which probably you have got; a really interesting German, originally old Danish, Biography, or Autobiography[14] lies waiting for you here by the next opportunity: but doubtless your 9th vol. of *Frederick*[15] has already gone its road; and come to hand before now.

With my kindest regards to Sister Jean & all the household.

Yours ever affectionately

T. Carlyle

8. Alexander Forrest (d. 1898), Manchester liberal leader, oil refiner, and manufacturer.

9. Alexander Gibson (1843–87), advocate; chairman of the committee for TC's election as rector, 1866; see 43:36. He wrote to John A. Carlyle, 27 April: "You kindly promised . . . to let your brother know that I wished to call on him when I went to London. I am going up tomorrow night for eight or ten days."

10. TC had shares in several British and American railway companies, his investments being handled by John; see TC to JAC, 22 April, and vol. 45. John wrote, 18 May, that he was expecting the transfers for the railway stock he had recently bought for TC, "& mean to send them all together for your signature when you get home again. I was lucky in getting £2000 of it at one per cent lower last week than it now is." He wrote, 24 May: "I at once forward your four Transfers for £500 each. Your usual signature of 'T. Carlyle' will suffice, & your witness (any *man*) must give his profession & address along with his signature. . . . I enclose a cover ready stamped, & addressed to . . . the Edinr Broker, wh will contain them all."

11. Irma Durival was seeking a pension for her sister Margaret; see TC to JAC, 22 April. John replied, 24 May, that he had no further news.

12. See TC to JAC, 15 May.

13. Thomas Erksine, *Spiritual Order and Other Papers Selected from the Manuscripts of the Late Thomas Erskine of Linlathen* (Edinburgh, 1871).

14. Not further identified.

15. Presumably of the library edn. of *Frederick*.

TC TO JOHN A. CARLYLE

5 Cheyne Row, Chelsea,
29 May 1871.

My dear Brother,

Thursday is as good for us as any day; we will expect you then, about what hour you may appoint, — or any other day do.[1]

After one or two very bad nights, I have had three of what may fairly be counted beyond the average; and I begin again to think I may be actually improving in this fine Summer weather. Hope springs eternal in the human breast.[2]

Last night we were at Forster's dining. Poor F. has had a bad turn lately; sudden staggering on the street, and would have fallen had he not caught by the railing, — evidently something in the head; which has considerably alarmed him; and even the ever-hoping Dr Quain,[3] though he persists in calling it "congestion of the liver"; seems clearly to have his own apprehensions on the subject, and enjoins earnestly on Forster less labour for the brain. I never saw poor F. so dull as last night; he is to go ("if possible" which was to be considered today) on his Business Tour, along with a comrade Official,[4] tomorrow morning: his good little Wife too, in speaking to Mary, was in great anxiety. The recent fate of Landseer,[5] and indeed the case itself, naturally gives rise to such feelings. I do trust and pray that nothing of all these sinister forebodings will take effect; but that caution, moderation and the Summer air, for the next three weeks, will work a favourable change for poor Forster. Certainly a more obliging, helpful man to all the help-needing, especially to myself (whether falling under that category or not) I have no where met with. Last night, for the first time, what I noted as a bad symptom, he did *not* say anything of me or my Chapman or other affairs; but dwelt mainly on his own,

TC-JAC, 29 May. MS: NLS 527.51. Quot: Froude, *Carlyle* 4:405–6; Surtees, *Ludovisi* 155.

1. John A. Carlyle wrote, 28 May: "I think of starting for Chelsea on Thursday next [1 June] if all goes well till then. . . . Please let me have two words from you . . . to say whether that day will suit you." TC wrote in his journal, 3 June: "My Brr John expected today. Once ag*n*! — " (TC's journal; privately owned). For his thoughts about himself in "the *fifth* year of my *solitude*," also written in his journal, 3 June, see TC to JAC, 22 April.

2. See Alexander Pope, *An Essay on Man* (1733–34) 1.95.

3. Richard Quain; see TC to JF, 22 July 1870.

4. Not further identified. Forster's work as a Lunacy Commissioner took him traveling around the country.

5. Sir Edwin Landseer (1802–73; *ODNB*), artist, had been suffering from bouts of insanity. The *Times* reported, 1 May, remarks of Sir Francis Grant (1803–78; *ODNB*), president of the Royal Academy, 29 April: "The protracted and distressing illness of Sir Edwin Landseer has been a source of great sorrow and anxiety to the members of the Academy."

especially on a Biography of Dickens.[6] One thing he seemed even to have forgotten his promise about, and did not allude to at all. Near a month ago he had promptly undertaken to see Mr Harding[7] himself, and confidentially ascertain from him whether he did mean anything practical with Nephew John, in regard to that Clerkship or merely a polite dismissal of the thing (as nephew Jim thought,[8] and doubtless still thinks). Of course I took no notice last night; but I do design not to let the matter drop; and either thro' Chapman, Harding himself, or some other channel, shall hope to be at the bottom of the matter now before long.

Of Lady Ashburton, we have heard nothing definite, far less seen, Her Ladyship since Monday last. She is of flighty fitful habit in her appointments, — this we already knew! — She was to have been here on Wednesday on &c (passing thro' Town on some visit to a sick Friend);[9] I called yesterday at her house, found she had not come till Friday, was to return "tomorrow"; i.e, today, and be home at Melchet tonight; in short we *may* see her today or not see; and she is still an unknown quantity, *not* yet eliminated farther, in our equation! That probably will come in good time however.

Today I bought a *Daily News*; struck by these unexampled horrors that have been going on in Paris;[10] but I gained no glimmer of real instruction from my penny worth *there*; and indeed am much in the dark about the real meaning of all these quaisi-infernal Bedlamisms; upon which no Newspaper that I look into has anything to say, except "horrible and shameful!" and "Oh Lord, I thank Thee that we Englishmen are not as other men!" One thing I can see in these murderous ragings by the poorest classes in Paris, that they are a tre-

6. John Forster, *The Life of Charles Dickens* (1872–74).

7. Robert Palmer Harding; see TC to JAC, 13 Oct. 1870. Forster had offered in Nov. 1870 (see TC to JAC, 12 Nov. 1870) to try and help in the matter of John Aitken applying to Harding for work; presumably he had repeated the offer more recently.

8. For James Aitken Jr.'s view, see TC to JAC, 17 Dec. 1870.

9. Unidentified.

10. During the Franco-Prussian War, Paris was under siege, and the new National Assembly, under Adolphe Thiers, moved to Tours; see TC to JCA, 25 Feb. Paris then came under the control of the radical socialist Paris Commune, backed by the national guard, 18 March; TC had been particularly shocked to hear of the murder on that day by the national guards of their commandant, J. L. Clément-Thomas, whom he had known; see TC to UC, 29 March. Thiers assembled an army to re-take the city, which finally triumphed, 28 May. The *Daily News*'s "Special Correspondent," 29 May, under the headline "The Struggle in Paris, Scenes in the Streets," described the scene: "The soldiers were exasperated enough when they entered Paris, but they were all the more when they found that the Commune, forced to surrender their ground, had set fire to the town. I will state more in detail hereafter, what ravages have been committed by the flames — but one can see at once that nothing can exceed the wickedness of the designs of the Commune. Paris shall not exist, if Paris does not belong to the Commune — such is their hellish resolve; and they proceed to carry out their threat of destroying the capital which they could not retain."

mendous Proclamation to the Upper classes in all countries, *"Our* condition, after 82 years of struggling, Oh ye quack Upper Classes, is still unimproved, more intolerable, from year to year and from revolution to revolution; and by the Eternal Powers, if you cannot mend it we will blow the world up, along with ourselves and you!"[11]

Enough for this day, dear Brother;—nay I *ought* to add, By no means forget my Straw hat;[12] your own, you will find in perfect preservation here; hanging for you on its nail, and we will gladly exchange again.

Give my kindest Love to Jean and everybody.

Your affectionate Brother[13]

P.s. *Item.* Don't forget to bring on record for me Alick's instruction about the Chapman new Books,—that is to say, the names of the two Boys to whom *People's Edition* might be fitly sent.[14] I did make memorandum of the thing; and put it in a clip, but it has since got drowned and washed away.[15]

TC TO RALPH WALDO EMERSON

5 Cheyne Row, Chelsea,
4 June 1871

Dear Emerson,

Your Letter gave me great pleasure. A gleam of sunshine after a long tract of of[1] lowering weather. It is not you that are to blame for this sad gap in our correspondence; it is I,[2] or rather it is my misfortune, and miserable inabilities, broken resolutions &c &c. The truth is the winter here was very unfriendly to me; broke ruinously into my sleep; and through that into every other department of my businesses, spiritual and temporal; so that from about New-year's Day last I have been, in a manner, good for nothing,—nor am yet,

---

11. TC refers to the mood of the "poorest classes" in France after finding no improvement from the beginning of the French Revolution, 1789, to the present.

12. John wrote, 2 June: "Your old black Straw Hat has been cleaned & new-lined by Jean & looks as good as new again. I shall take it with me tomorrow."

13. TC's signature has been cut away.

14. Probably copies of the new edn. of *Sartor* to be sent to two of Alick's sons.

15. Mary Aitken wrote to Lady Stanley, 26 May, thanking her for thinking of making TC a new cap: "as the one he at present wears is nearly worn out, I am sure he would be most happy to have it. / I enclose you a little paper pattern of the shape he likes best with the *size* marked on it. I will not tell him of your kind offer so that he might be surprised by the present" (MS: Strouse).

TC-RWE, 4 June. MS: RWEMA. Pbd: Norton *CE* 2:338–42; Slater, *CEC* 579–81.

1. Word repeated.

2. Emerson wrote, 10 April: "I fear there is no pardon from you, none from myself, for this immense new gap in our correspondence."

though I do again feel as if the beautiful Summer weather might perhaps do something for me. This it was that choked every enterprize; and postponed your Letter, week after week, through so many months. Let us not speak of it farther!

Note, meanwhile, I have no disease about me; nothing but the gradual decay of any poor digestive faculty I latterly had,—or indeed ever had since I was three and twenty years of age. Let us be quiet with it; accept it as a mode of exit, of which always there must be *some* mode.

I have got done with all my press-correctings, editionings and paltry bother of that kind: vol 30 will embark for you about the middle of this month; there are then to follow ("uniform," as the printer's call it, though in smaller type) a little vol. called *General Index* and 3 more voll. of *Translations from the German;*—after which we two will reckon and count; and if there is any *lacuna* on the Concord shelf, at once make it good.³ Enough enough on that score.

The Hotten who has got hold of you here is a dirty little pirate, who snatches at everybody grown fat enough to yield him a bite (paltry, unhanged creature);⁴ so that in fact he is a symbol to you of your visible rise in the world here; and, with Conway's vigilance to help, will do you good and not evil.⁵ Glad am I, in any case, to see so much new spiritual produce still ripening around you; and you ought to be glad too. Pray Heaven you may long *keep your right hand* steady: you too, I can perceive, will never, any more than myself, learn to "write by dictation" in a manner that will be supportable to you. I rejoice also to hear of such a magnificent adventure as that you are now upon. Climbing the back bone of America; looking into the Pacific Ocean too, and the gigantic wonders going on there.⁶ I fear you wont see see⁷ Brigham

3. Emerson wrote: "Meantime, you have been monthly loading me with good for evil. I have just counted 23 vols. of Carlyle's Library Edition, in order, on my shelves, besides 2, or perhaps 3, which Ellery Channing has borrowed. Add, that the precious Chapmans' Homer came safely, though not till months after you had told me of its departure, & shall be guarded henceforward with joy"; see TC to RWE, 31 May 1870. William Ellery Channing (1819–1901), poet.

4. John Camden Hotten (1832–73; *ODNB*) had pbd. without permission TC's *On the Choice of Books* (the rectorial address); see 43:188–89, 197, 207.

5. Emerson wrote: "Now I come to the raid of a London bookseller, Hotten . . . on my forgotten papers. . . . Conway wrote me that he could not be resisted,—would certainly steal good & bad,—but might be guided in the selection. I replied, that the act was odious to me, & I promised to denounce the man & his theft to any friends I might have in England: but if, instead of printing then, he would wait a year, I would make my own selection . . . & permit the book." The vol. Emerson intended to publish appeared, 1875, after his death, as *Letters and Social Aims*. Daniel Moncure Conway (1832–1907), American Unitarian minister; see 43:269.

6. Emerson wrote that he was going to visit "California, the Yosemite, the Mammoth [Redwood] trees, & the Pacific."

7. Word repeated.

Young,[8] however? He also to me is one of the products out there;—and indeed I may confess to you that the doings in that region are not only of a big character, but of a great;—and that in my *occasional* explosions against "Anarchy," and my inextinguishable hatred of *it*, I privately whisper to myself, "Could any Friedrich Wilhelm, now, or Friedrich, or most perfect Governor you could hope to realise, guide forward what is America's essential task at present faster or more completely than 'anarchic America' herself is now doing?" *Such* "Anarchy" has a great deal to say for itself,—(w*d* to Heaven ours of England had as much)[9]—and points towards grand *anti*-Anarchies in the future; in fact, I can already discern in it huge quantities of Anti-Anarchy in the "impalpable-powder" condition; and I hope, with the aid of centuries, immense things from it, in my private mind!

Good M*rs* Lowell has never yet made her appearance;[10] but shall be welcome whenever she does— Did you ever hear the name of an aged or elderly, fantastic fellow-citizen of yours, called J. Lee Bliss, who designates himself O.F and A.K, *i.e.* "Old Fogey" and "Amiable Kuss?"[11] He sent me the other night, a wonderful miscellany of symbolical shreds and patches;[12] which considerably amused me; and withal indicated good will on the man's part; who is not without humour, insight and serious intention or disposition. If you ever did hear of him, say a word on the subject next time you write.

8. Brigham Young (1801–77), Mormon religious leader and politician, president of the Mormon church 1847–77, governor of Utah Territory 1851–58; he held various religious beliefs in conflict with accepted Christianity, including polygamy. Emerson replied, 30 June, that he had been to see Brigham Young: "a strong-built, self-possessed, sufficient man with plain manners. . . . Our interview was peaceable enough, & rather mended my impression of the man. . . . He is clearly a sufficient ruler, & perhaps civilizer of his kingdom of blockheads . . . but I found that the San Franciscans believe that this exceptional power cannot survive Brigham."

9. The sentence in brackets inserted in TC's hand, with "had as" repeated with a line over it at turn of page.

10. Emerson wrote, 10 April: "Effie Lowell, widow of one of the noblest of our young martyrs in the War, Col. Lowell . . . sends me word that she wishes me to give her a note of introduction to you, confiding to me that she has once written a letter to you which procured her the happiest reply from you." Josephine Shaw Lowell (1843–1905), author, social reformer, and philanthropist; she m. 1863, Charles Russell Lowell (1835–64). For TC's reply to her earlier letter, see 46:171. Emerson replied, 30 June: "I am glad that Mrs Lowell . . . has seen you & I hope that you have seen her as I do." Emerson wrote again, 4 Sept.: "I have heard from Mrs Lowell twice lately, who exults in your kindness to her."

11. Judah Lee Bliss (1803–73); American author and teacher, who wrote under several pseudonyms; possibly *On Reform in General, and Prison Reform in particular* (New York, 1855), or *Footprints of Travel in France and Italy, with Occasional Divagations* (New York, 1858), both listed as "by an Old Fogy" in William Cushing, *Initials and Pseudonyms, A Dictionary*, 2 vols. (New York, 1885 and 1888) 1:211 and 357. Emerson replied that he had not heard of him.

12. Cf. *Hamlet* 3.4.

And above all things *write*. The instant you get home from California, or see this, let me hear from you what your adventures have been and what the next are to be. Adieu, dear Emerson.

Yours ever affectionately,
T. Carlyle[13]

Mrs Lowell sends a Note from Piccadilly *this* new morning (june 5th); *call* to be made there today by Niece Mary, card left, &c &c. Promises to be an agreeable Lady.

Did you ever hear of such a thing as this suicidal Finis of the French "*Copper Captaincy*";[14] gratutitous attack on Germany, and do Blowing-up of Paris by its own hand! An event with meanings unspeakable;—deep as the *Abyss.— —*

If you ever write to C. Norton in Italy,[15] send him my kind remembrances.

T.C. (with abt the velocity of
Engraving,—on lead!)[16]

TC TO DAVID LAING

5 Cheyne Row, Chelsea
10 June 1871.

Dear Laing,

I am very much obliged by the two Volumes of *Lindsay*, which my Brother has brought me;[1] you are always very kind and attentive to me;—and what is still better, you are always busy at your work. As soon as the Third Volume reaches me I design to have a stroke at the old Gentleman, and try if I can understand what he has to say to me.

---

13. From TC's signature to the end written in TC's hand.

14. TC's epithet for Napoleon III; see TC to JF, 26 Aug. 1870.

15. Charles Eliot Norton, currently living in the Villa d'Elsi, San Gallo, Florence; see 46:163.

16. Emerson's letter of 30 June was delivered to TC by George Partridge Bradford (1807–90), one of Emerson's closest friends, with an accompanying letter of introduction (Slater 584); he hoped to pay his respects to TC while passing through London.

TC-DL, 10 June. MS: EUL. Hitherto unpbd.

1. *The Poetical Works of Sir David Lyndsay of the Mount, Lion King of Arms*, ed. David Laing, 2 vols. (Edinburgh, 1871). Sir David Lyndsay (ca. 1486–1555; *ODNB*), writer and herald, with estates in Fife and East Lothian. John A. Carlyle wrote, 25 April: "Two volumes of Laing's new Edition of Sir David Lyndsays works have come today, with a letter from him, in wh he asks me to forward them to you after satisfying my own curiosity, & wait till the 3d & final vol. comes out 'in a few months' when he will send *me* a complete copy of the whole." The third vol. was pbd. 1879.

There has come an expensive new Book to me, Twistleton's[2] conclusive endeavour to identify *Junius* and Sir Philip Francis by hand-writing—in which, so far as I can judge, he is completely successful;[3] and so *ends* that weary and useless riddle-ma-ree, which has employed many idle people so long. I know not whether such a Book as of the least interest to you; but as it is of none at all to me, I mean to send it you:—the Signet Library[4] will at least require the Book; and if you reject it for yourself, it may save the Library the expense of a Copy; and may silently testify the gratitude I feel to that Institution for help often rendered me, always in so frank and kind a manner. You must not reject the Book under one or other of these categories. Absolutely not!— I mean to send it *franco* by Chapman's Edinburgh Parcel, about the middle of this month.[5]

Believe me

Yours ever faithfully,

T. Carlyle[6]

2. Edward Turner Boyd Twisleton (1809–74; *ODNB*), civil servant, close and respected friend of the Carlyles; he saw JWC shortly before her death (see 43:192), and attended her funeral (see 43:249).

3. *The Handwriting of Junius Professionally Investigated by Mr. Charles Chabot, expert. With Preface and Collateral Evidence by the Hon. Edward Twisleton* (1871). Charles Chabot (1815–82; *ODNB*), graphologist. "Junius" was the pseudonym of a writer (or writers) who contributed political letters to the *Public Advertiser*, 21 Jan. 1769–21 Jan. 1772, opposing the policies of George III and his prime ministers. Sir Philip Francis (1740–1818; *ODNB*), politician and political writer, was a probable author of the letters of Junius; there were more than 50 other possible authors suggested at various times.

4. Laing was librarian of the Signet Lib., 1837–78.

5. Laing replied, 23 June: "I delayed answering your kind letter till the parcel arrived, and I have just seen the handsome book on *Junius* for the first time. I shall have much pleasure in presenting it to the Signet Library in your name. . . . Personally, I feel as grateful to you as if I had retained the volume for my own use. . . . I am so put about for want of room, that I generally find it easier to come here [to the library] to look than to search out for those that I actually possess." Laing had been a bookseller and had accumulated a massive collection of books and manuscripts. The Signet Lib. catalog lists it but does not note TC's name.

6. TC wrote in his journal, 4 June: "Household much in confus*n* (by poor John's advent, &c) nothing or almost that, to be done;—enough to be mournfully tho*t* of, and *suppressed*! Cold gray north-wind days (c*d*n't I actually *write* ag*n*, with pencil, in here? Alas!— John sitting beside me reading Ruskin's *Fors Clavigera* (strange project, and strange book!)—no more today, in such a posture & such a mood" (TC's journal; privately owned).

TC TO JEAN CARLYLE AITKIN

5 Cheyne Row, Chelsea
17 June 1871.

Dear Sister,

If it were not for your formidable Railway Station,[1] I feel as if I would almost rush off to you this very day. For ten days past I have been in such a state of "health" as I never knew in my life before. It is indeed a matter of six months not of 10 days; but on Wed. gone a week it came to a crisis; by various accidents that day, by cold East wind, indigestable dinner, and a carpenter[2] taking to splitting sticks within earshot of me, I found before bedtime that I had got a new dose of cold (coughing and *clochering* ever since and still going on); and all capacity of eating food as nearly as possible in complete abeyance ever since. For a long time all food had been as physic to me; swallowed from duty not desire; but for the last 6 days I have been obliged to renounce eating solid food altogether (cannot prevail upon myself to look where cooked beef or mutton is). I swallow in large draughts my basin of brown soup and fly out of the way of dinner altogether. You can fancy what a vigorous condition of body and of soul this indicates; and how pressing the necessity is to get out of it without delay,—to change one's place in it, if getting out be a vain chimera!— I ought to add that of heart sickness I intrinsically feel nothing; and what will surprise you that I oftener sleep than otherwise; such the entire weariness and prostration, and am surprised for the last 3 mornings to find how little strength or benefit the fair amount of sleep has yielded me.

Lady Ashburton's plans have all gone to windy uncertainty; and nothing is left me but what plans I can form for myself. John proposes we should go next Wed. towards the Orkney Islands no less by Aberdeen Steamer; and tho' the venture seems sharp for one in this skinless condition, I rather feel inclined to try it; my actual condition as you see being plainly unendurable. "To try a sail again," let us at least execute that. If the Orknies prosper we should have more sailing; come round by the west coast &c &c; and I think it likely I should land at Dumfries any way in one form or another of stranded goods.

Besides sailing, there is only one other measure from which I have ever expected benefit, that of riding. I tried it at Melchet, on a high-going, rough-paced, almost intolerable horse, 3 times lately; and it seemed clearly to do me more good than anything else. What I practically want of you today therefore,

TC-JCA, 17 June. MS: NLS 527.52. Hitherto unpbd.

1. TC presumably meant the noise of the railways around Dumfries; see TC to Sir JMN, 4 July 1870, and TC to JAF, 25 July.

2. Probably Frederick Freure (b. 1835), who had worked for the Carlyles since at least 1864; see 41:231.

is that you w*d* make a little serious enquiry as to my possibilities for getting a horse to carry me about while among me.[3] John and Mary both agree with me in thinking that you ought to question young Jamie of Craigenputtock on the subject and report to me what his counsel is. I am perfectly willing to buy a horse and pay the proper price for a good one, about 14 hands or so, with good sure paces: your own James knows very well the kind of thing that w*d* suit; and *he* perhaps is the person you had best consult about it. Do what you find wisest in that small matter;—and excuse this long *clish maclaver*, which is due purely to the vice of dictating; had my own right hand been still mine I sh*d* have written in 5 lines what here occupies as many pages. So soon as any project comes to execution you shall at once hear.— My blessing with you and all the house.

Ever y*r* affect*e* Brother
T. Carlyle[4]

MARY AITKEN TO UNIDENTIFIED CORRESPONDENT

5 Cheyne Row, Chelsea
3 July 1871.

Dear Sir,

Mr Carlyle, my Uncle, desires me to thank you for your little Note & the Paper[1] you have been so kind as send him. He read the latter with approval and thinks you have done it in a very good spirit.

I am / Yours very truly / Mary Carlyle Aitken

TC TO J. A. FROUDE

5 Cheyne Row, Chelsea
7 July 1871

My dear Froude,

Your letter is very kind and cordial; your invitation altogether tempting, hopeful-looking and pleasant,—except that, by ill-luck, it is 24 hours too late![1]

---

3. Mary wrote "me" instead of "you."
4. Jean wrote on the reverse of the last page, presumably forwarding it to her son James in Liverpool: "Please send this back at once. All well no news but what you see here. WRITE."

MA-UC, 3 July. MS: EUL. Hitherto unpbd.
1. Unidentified.

TC-JAF, 7 July. Pbd: Waldo H. Dunn, "Carlyle's Last Letters to Froude II," *Twentieth Century* 159 (March, 1956): 259.
1. Froude presumably invited TC to visit him in Devonshire; see below.

Yesterday morning, after endless haggling & hesitating, John, my Brother, was dispatched to engage a cabin in the Aberdeen Steamer;[2] by that vehicle we are to take the Northern Seas tomorrow! Dr. Quain (for he has been twice or thrice to see me) seemed to prescribe this as the next stage in his treatment; all my acquaintances have been here daily asking, "When are you to go?" "Are you not to go on such a day?" So that, in mere self-defence, I had half desperately to decide as above. After Aberdeen, it would appear, there are Steamers for the Orkneys, for the Shetlands;[3] Steamers that go through the Pentland Firth, and shew you the Western Isles, all down to Glasgow; Steamers enough; but a very dubious reception in them for the like of me in my present mood! However, I have long had, or have long talked about, the notion of benefit from a Sea-voyage, and now, if ever, may really be the time for trying it. I am fairly a little better than when you left me; but only a little; and indeed feel generally weaker, and less fit for taking things in the rough, than almost ever in my life before.

After Aberdeen and the Sea-voyaging there remains to me, much approved by Quain, a second, somewhat hopefuller project, that of getting into some soft quiet friendly place, and taking to a spell of daily riding. Into this latter project beneficent Holne Park, with its quiet woods and waters, and loved and loving Friends,[4] might perhaps still enter as a lively possibility! Let us all hope so. If there were a gentle riding horse procurable (still more if there were *two*), Holne Park would be in reality, of all places now known to me, the likeliest. That hope I will keep for the present, it is already a cheerful possession to me.

No more today; all being in a stir with packing. Mary I think goes to Dumfries next week. My surest address will be there (The Hill, Dumfries) till you hear farther from me:—The deepest thanks of my heart are due to you in regard to that MS.[5]— With kindest regards to Mrs. Froude and all the Household,

Yours ever faithfully
T. Carlyle

2. TC wrote in his journal, 28 July: "On Saty 8 july 1871, embarked with Brr John, at Wapping, on the Aberdeen Steamer, being totally broken down with dyspeptic misery and utmost inanity,—to try whether 'a sail' w*d* not help" (TC's journal; privately owned).

3. The *Times* advertised, 3 June: "TO TOURISTS.—Steam to CAITHNESS and the Isles of ORKNEY and SHETLAND twice a week from EDINBURGH and ABERDEEN by the steamship ST. MAGNUS, ST. CLAIR and QUEEN. . . . Fares very low."

4. Holne Park, nr. Ashburton, Devon, estate of Sir Henry Bourchier Toke Wrey, (1829–1900), 10th bart. The *Western Times*, 16 June, reported: "J. A. Froude, Esq., the historian, has taken Holne Park House, on the banks of the Dart."

5. TC had already recorded his intentions as to his MSS of JWC's letters and memorials and his reminiscences of JWC; see TC's 1871 Will, 6 April. Froude wrote later: "One

TC TO BETTY BRAID

Loch Luichart Lodge, Dingwall
14 july 1871

Dear Betty,

I am far away from home on this to me ever sacred 14 july,[1] which to you always has a dear meaning. My good little Niece will have written to Green End about my special remembrance of *you* on this solemn day,[2]—more grand and memorable to you and to me than to any others now living on the Earth:—but I cannot help, withal, sending you the little Token here inclosed,[3] the many meanings of wh*h* are clear to to y*r*self, dear faithful Betty, with*t* farther words of mine.

Nor need you *write* ab*t this*; merely address an old Newspaper to me here (one word of it in y*r* own hand),—that will itself signify that the thing has come safe, and abundantly suffice.— I do indeed want to hear from you spe-

---

day—the middle or end of June, 1871—he brought, himself, to my house a large parcel of papers. . . . He told me to take it simply and absolutely as my own, without reference to any other person or persons, and to do with it as I pleased after he was gone. He explained, when he saw me surprised, that it was an account of his wife's history, that it was incomplete, that he could himself form no opinion whether it ought to be published or not, that he could do no more to it, and must pass it over to me. He wished never to hear of it again. I must judge. I must publish it, the whole, or part—or else destroy it all. . . . I was to wait only until he was dead, and he was then in constant expectation of his end. . . . I was then going into the country for the summer. I said that I would take the MS. with me, and either write to him or would give him an answer when we met in the autumn. . . . I found that it consisted of a transcript of the 'Reminiscence' of Mrs. Carlyle, which he had written immediately after her death, with a copy of the old direction of 1866, that it was not to be published [28 July 1866; see Carlyle, *Reminiscences* 198-99]. . . . The rest was the collection of her own letters, &c . . . with notes, commentaries, and introductory explanations of his own. The perusal was infinitely affecting" (Froude, *Carlyle* 4:408-9).

TC-BB, 14 July. MS: NLS 3278.158. Hitherto unpbd. Written in TC's hand in pencil.
1. JWC's birthday.
2. Mary Aitken wrote to Betty Braid, 13 July: "On Saturday last my two Uncles went off to Aberdeen in the Steamer. I went down to the Wharf with them and staid on board for an hour; it was a beautiful ship and they seemed very comfortable. . . . As you know, Uncle's hand shakes a good deal and makes writing hard work for him now; but he said he would if he was at all able for it, write you a little Letter today so that you might have it tomorrow morning. However in case he could not manage it I was to write and tell you the reason of your not getting the customary Letter from him on the now sad anniversary of his Wife's Birthday. . . . I know he will be disappointed if he has not got it done; but in any case he will write to you by my hand as soon as he and I meet again. . . . I am going home to Dumfries either tomorrow or Monday & I hope when Uncle is tired of the Highlands he will come there too" (MS: NLS 3278.156).
3. John A. Carlyle recorded in TC's checkbook: "14*th* July 1871 / To Mrs Braid of Green-end, Edin*r* / £5 .. o .. o" (TC's checkbook; MS: NLS 20753).

cially how you are after the sore Winter we had; by no means neglect that, the first convenient day you have; and a few words, remember, will be of real value to me. I have myself been sensibly weaker ever since jan*y* last;—and have come hither, thro' much confusion by sea and land, to this remote still place in hope of recovering myself a little,—a very little is the extent of my hope; nor indeed can I be said to *care* much or almost at all. *God's* will be done, not *mine* if contrary!— The mistress of this place is "Louisa Lady Ashburton," a most bounteous Lady, long a warm-hearted friend both of me and of *Her* that is now not Here.

God ever bless you, dear Betty;—and, at His blessed time, call us both *home*, to rest eternally with Those our hearts dwell with, who are already There! Amen; Amen.

Yrs ever truly / T. Carlyle

TC TO J. A. FROUDE

Loch Luichart Lodge,
Dingwall, N.B.
July 25/71

Dear Froude,

Your second kind little Word from Holne Park reached me safely via Dumfries, three days ago. I would have answered at once had I had Mary as my Amanuensis, but could not: having none; till now as you will see, with a witness.

My brother & I had a prosperous sail to Aberdeen—prosperous though noisy & confused;—& had a pleasant view of the old granite city, & its brisk populations for a few hours till the Railway started with us for Inverness, for Dingwall, & finally for this remote little paradise in the middle of the wild, rocky hills, & torrents; where we lived, as yet no Hostess here, a week of the strangest most benignant solitude I have experienced for long. Hostess with complete equipments, & with the warmest of welcomes, has come about ten days; brother John, has gone to the Wells of Strathpeffer to drink the sulphurous waters (much good may they do him) & I am here;[1] still on *"probation"*

TC-JAF, 25 July. Pbd: Waldo H. Dunn, "Carlyle's Last Letters to Froude II," *Twentieth Century* 159 (March, 1956): 260–61. Written on Loch Luichart headed notepaper, "dictated to an unknown amanuensis" (Dunn 261), probably Lady Ashburton. The postscript was written by TC.

1. TC wrote in his journal, 28 July: "Chaos come ag*n* was, to the usual extent, the hist*y* of our otherwise pleas*t* voyage; and we did duly land on Aberd*n* on Monday [10 July], not the worse for our rude tumblings;—made for thrice habitable Loch Luichart,—where have been for us three of the strangest weeks in this bright solitude (for myself 3, for John 2, who shifted to Strathpeffer on Monday last), no *Hostess* here for the first week, but only ready

as to sleep for a week to come;—much wishing the probation might fall out affirmative, in which case, I continue longer,[2] if it fall negative, my course is uncertain—probably round by Skye, & the Western Isles to Glasgow & Dumfries, with uncertain results (so loud are the railways there) when I do arrive.

In spite of continued irregularities as to sleep I do feel perceptibly better— Now this is all my news— Your surest address in future is The Hill, Dumfries. We heard only yesternight of Gladstone's coup d'état;[3] let us pity the poor white man.[4] I am glad purchase is condemned at any rate; no improvement can even be thought of till that is utterly extinguished, & anathematized; for the rest, you are sufficiently aware, I expect no *army* in England till parliamentary palavering cease to be the form of Government in that country (seemingly a very distant date!) & I do not participate in the horror felt in the House of Lords & elsewhere, at the terrible spasm that has seized poor Gladstone—may the Lord pity him & us!

Yours ever truly

T. Carlyle

With kind regards to Madam,—and request for a word about the *young* Lady's health[5] amid the rains.

TC TO JOHN A. CARLYLE

Loch L*t* 1 Aug*t*, 1871—

Dear Br*r*,—I am passably well (by no means brill*tly* so);—just going for windy[1] to Grudy Bridge[2] and back. — — These 2 are my sole Letters of today & yesterday. I can, as you see, form no prognosis of Mary's actual *coming*;[3]

---

servants & equip*ts*, and a silence and a pure seclusion except from sky and earth,—wh*h* reminded me of Craigenp*h*, and almost made me weep!" (TC's journal; privately owned). Dingwall, about 14 mi. (22.5 km.) NW of Inverness; Loch Luichart, about 18½ mi. (30 km.) W of Dingwall; and Strathpeffer, spa town, about 5½ mi. (9 km.) W of Dingwall.

2. TC wrote: "Today [28 July] I have consented to write for Mary, & try if I can stay another 3 weeks. Very strange it still all is to me; and (in spite of bad sleep) does me evid*t* good" (TC's journal; privately owned).

3. Gladstone announced in the House of Commons, 20 July, that, despite the objections of the House of Lords, the practice of purchasing commissions in the army would be abolished by Royal Warrant. See also TC to JAC, 10 Feb.

4. See *Past and Present*, Carlyle, *Works* 10:211.

5. Henrietta Froude and Rose Mary Froude, who was an invalid.

TC-JAC, 1 Aug. MS: NLS 527.54a. Hitherto unpbd. Written by TC in blue pencil, on the reverse of a letter from Jean Aitken to TC, 30 July.

1. Word omitted, presumably "walk."

2. Grudie Bridge, 1½ mi. (2.5 km.) WSW of Loch Luichart.

3. Jean wrote, 30 July: "[Mary] desired me to write a word to say she got your letter only

Alexander Carlyle, Alexander and Janet Carlyle's son
Thomas Carlyle Papers, Rare Book & Manuscript Library,
Columbia University in the City of New York

James Carlyle, Alexander and Janet Carlyle's son
Thomas Carlyle Papers, Rare Book & Manuscript Library,
Columbia University in the City of New York

and, some report, there *are difficulties* abt telegrams BEYOND *Garve*?[4]— If you had a fair chance of sending one to STOP *Mary altogr*, I sh*d* now incline to vote for that!— — — I hope you are prospering in your.[5]— We really ought to SEE (or be *seen by* at Dingw*ll* Inverness) those Canad*n* Nephews of ours?[6] *somewhere* surely! Adieu d*r* Brr: Write

T.C.

TC TO SARAH WARREN

Loch Luichart
Dingwall, N.B.
9*th* Aug*t*, 1871

Mrs Warren,

These are my two Canadian nephews[1] who are come to spend a few days in London. Having said this, I need hardly add that I wish you to do your very best not to let them feel that I am absent, but to lodge and help and forward them in all ways while they continue in their uncle's house. As I have no doubt you will in all ways faithfully do.

I am fairly a little better; you shall hear from me again soon.

Yrs truly / T. Carlyle[2]

---

this morning . . . and will write tomorrow when she has made due enquiries about the journey."

4. Garve, village 5 mi. (8 km.) E of Loch Luichart.

5. Word omitted, presumably "visit"; John was in Strathpeffer.

6. Alexander (Alick) and James Carlyle, sons of their brother Alick; Jean wrote, 30 July: "Mary has gone out with her Canadian Cousins. . . . The two young men are very kindly well conditioned fellows. Alick the oldest is a Teacher & is spending his summer holiday by trying to see the mother country & what friends are still left to his Father & Mother. They talk of going to the Gill & Scotsbrig . . . & then return to us . . . before going to see Edinburgh &c"; see also TC to AC, 16 Dec. For a photograph of Alick, see 220, and of James, see 221; both are in vol. 6 of Thomas Carlyle Photograph Albums.

TC-SW, 9 Aug. MS: Hornel. Hitherto unpbd. Written on Loch Luichart headed notepaper, by John A. Carlyle. Apparently he and TC met in Inverness, Wed. 9 Aug., as John wrote, 11 Aug., hoping that TC "got rest on Wednesday night after returning from Inverness."

1. Alick Jr. and James Carlyle; see TC to JAC, 1 Aug.

2. From "I am" to the end, the letter is in TC's hand.

TC TO JOHN FORSTER

Loch Luichart / Dingwall. N.B.
Aug*t* 18*th*/71

Dear Forster,

I have often longed to shoot a little word of enquiry towards you, but since the 7*th* July, I have had no Secretary (Mary at Dumfries all this while;) & I am obliged, as you see, to a foreign hand on this occasion.

I want, in brief, and truly want very much, to hear how it is with Madame & you, where, how in regard to health & otherwise you both now are, — in short a little history of your events & vicissitudes since the day I last saw you — don't neglect to send it instantly;[1] regardless of the languid cunctatory & indeed quite torpid silence I have so long observed towards you, & all other friends. You cannot fancy with what a spasm of remorseful endeavour I am now at last animated to write —

My own history since landing at Aberdeen (prosperously enough, considering the tumults & confusions of the Sea) may be comprised in three words. We made directly hitherwards, brother John & I, *to end* at once brother John's dubitations about Orkney, about Shetland, about Iceland &c &c, waited here some days till Mylady in person arrived; after which John took himself to the baths of Strath peffer, where he is still ducking, or drinking, & I lay down in the most perfect envelopment of idleness, of soft kindness, & in fact of unlimited cotton, spiritual & physical which it is well possible to conceive (the fittest of all elements for a broken down old creature) where I still continue;[2] & only regret that such a course of life cannot be destined to continue for

---

TC-JF, 18 Aug. Addr: Palace Gate House / Kensington / London / S.W. PM: Dingwall, 18 Aug. 1871. MS: FC. Hitherto unpbd. Written on Loch Luichart headed notepaper, in Lady Ashburton's hand, signed by TC.

1. Forster replied, 21 Aug.: "This morning brings me your welcome letter, dear Carlyle, and, *only last night*, myself went to Mrs. Warren for your address, it being my intention to write to you today: which in any case I should have done. I returned here on Friday night, after a weary absence of three weeks and upward.... Of myself, & the small one here, there is the usual mingled yarn." He reported that his wife had not been very well, and continued: "My health has not been very brave but I have had no absolute break-down — except in the way of sleep. How I have thought of you in the dreary watches!"

2. Richard Owen (1804–92; *ODNB*), anatomist and palaeontologist, known to TC since 1842 (see 42:19–20), was visiting John Fowler (1817–98; *ODNB*), railway engineer, at Braemore, Ross-shire; he wrote to his wife, Caroline Amelia, b. Clift (1801–73), 13 Aug.: "Lady Ashburton and T. Carlyle drove over and took tea with us on Friday (11th), and strolled along the easier walks. He is much emaciated, can digest but little, and hardly gets any sleep. He was most friendly and, I thought, took his last leave of me at parting. They drive twenty-six miles, and the same in returning. Lady A. intimated it was mainly his wish to see me that brought them so far. He painfully, with a pencil, put his name in the Visitors' Book" (Richard S. Owen, *The Life of Richard Owen*, 2 vols. (1894) 2:209–10).

ever—in effect John quits Strathpeffer (with a *pocket compass* of his own) on Monday next, & I, in about ten days more, possibly with some touch of Steaming through the Sounds of the Western Isles (Skye & Iona[3] at least I shd rather like to see) am to be landed at Glasgow, & in four hours more be carried by little Mary home to Dumfries; whence without further circuiting back home to Chelsea so soon as the Weather &c seem to promise well. There, of all friends, you of Palace Gate House, are I thin[k] almost the Only that I can look forward to—

Write hither at once dear Forster—letters take 2 days, don't put off I entreat you

Your's ever faithfully silent or not,

T. Carlyle

TC TO GEORGE HOWARD

Loch Luichart / Dingwall. N.B.
Aug. 23*rd* [1871]

Dear Howard—

Your kind present of Grouse, I have authentically heard, arrived in perfect preservation at Cheyne Row; & though I myself at a distance of 500 miles could not bear a hand in eating it, it was turned to excellent account there in part, I believe, by friends whom I wished much to be good to— Many thanks to you, & to madam—for this kind mark of your attention.

I have been here ever since the second week of July; & am still to continue about eight days— No life has been quieter & more hospitably dealt with than mine among these solitudes which ought to have benefitted me,—& indeed has if anything earthly could now benefit such an article. Sometime in September my little niece & I will be journeying from Dumfries to Chelsea & will at least gratefully remember the Nawarth[1] invitation if it be not possible (which I fear is too likely) to do more with a scene so interesting & friendly— With many regards to that bright Lady[2] (whom I rejoice always

3. The *Scotsman* advertised, 27 July: "The Royal Mail Steamer 'IONA' passengers only.... / From Inverness Daily ... at 7 A.M. .... From Oban Daily ... at 8 A.M. ... / From OBAN to ... IONA Daily (Sunday and Monday excepted)." Skye, largest island of the Inner Hebrides; Iona, small island, known for its medieval abbey, off SW coast of the much larger Isle of Mull, both in the Inner Hebrides; for TC's route to Oban, then Glasgow, see TC to JAF, 26 Sept.

TC-GH, 23 Aug. MS: NLS 1770.73. Hitherto unpbd. Written on Loch Luichart headed notepaper, in Lady Ashburton's hand, signed by TC.

1. Naworth Castle in Cumberland, country house belonging to the Howards.

2. Presumably Howard's wife, Rosalind, b. Stanley; JWC used to call the Stanley daughters "bright young Beings"; see 36:214. For a photograph of Rosalind Howard before mar-

to picture as *not* following the Medical profession)[3]

I remain / Yours ever truly
T. Carlyle

TC TO J. A. FROUDE

The Hill, Dumfries
26 Sep. 1871

Dear Froude,

Your friendly and affectionate Letter reached me above a week ago; and was read very gladly: I would have answered far sooner; but I was suddenly deprived of my *pen*,—that is to say, my good little Mary was suddenly summoned off to London with her Mother on the saddest of errands, and only returned last night; so that till now I could not write at all. Mary's eldest Brother, my poor Nephew "Jim," an excellent, affectionate, loving, diligent and truthful young man, much loved by us all, who was settled in Liverpool of late years, and prospering honestly as Manager and Partner of a big London House there; had come up on business, Saturday gone a fortnight last, intending to return on Monday; on Saturday night returning to his quarters at a younger Brother's,[1] who has come to London since you went away, and lodges in Brompton Road,—got upon a Chelsea Omnibus at Cheapside, and rode beside the driver to the head of Sloane Street, where, being in haste to get down, and probably not knowing that the Chelsea Omnibuses turn *into* Sloane St. before pausing, he appears to have sprung hastily from his seat, and

---

riage, see 41:68; for a photograph of Rosalind and George Howard around the time of their 1864 marriage, see 41:69.

3. Howard replied, 3 Sept.: "We very much hope that you will be able to find your way here 'between Dumfries & Chelsea'.... [I]t would not be taking you out of your way to come here—and if you are in a hurry you might spend even a night here to break the journey, though I hope you could make your visit longer. Your friend John Stanley is coming here with his bride next Friday. I daresay you know her too as she was a niece of Lady Ashburton's.... [A]fter that perhaps the Amberleys are coming on their way to Scotland; but I can promise that they will not have a medical woman with them." John Stanley m., 15 Aug., Susan Mary Elizabeth Stewart-Mackenzie, da. of Lady Ashburton's brother Keith William Stewart-Mackenzie (1818–81). John Russell Amberley, Viscount Amberley, and Katherine (Kate), Viscountess Amberley, who was a promoter of women's education, including medical education. For a photograph of Kate Stanley, 1860, see 41:32, and of "Kate & her Amberley," see 41:100.

TC-JAF, 26 Sept. Pbd: Waldo H. Dunn, "Carlyle's Last Letters to Froude II," *Twentieth Century* 159 (March, 1956): 261–63.

1. John Aitken, who was now working in London; the work with Robert Harding's firm (see TC to JAC, 13 Oct. 1870, and TC to JAC, 29 May) had apparently not materialized, but he was apparently now working for Chapman & Hall; see vol. 48.

in half jumping down (for he was in the flower of his strength and recklessly nimble of limb) caught a foot in the apron of the carriage, as is supposed, and came headlong down upon a street laid with new-broken stones, probably upon the sharp angle of one, and fractured his knee-pan (fracture both "compound & comminuted"): one of the most tragic incidents I have ever known. For such a wound, I now understand, was probably fatal from the very first; and not even instant amputation could have saved him. He was carried to St. George's Hospital, totally insensible all night; not till next morning could he write a line in pencil to his Brother, — the last he was to write in this world. We were all of course thrown into consternation at this news; but foolishly kept hoping till at length one bad telegram came to the effect that Mary and his Mother ought to come up at once. Which they at once did, deeply to his satisfaction; and thrice deeply now to their own for the rest of their lives. Though labouring for most part under continual clouds of hallucination, his intellect, his affections and his courage were essentially as clear as ever: he appears to have behaved himself with a beautiful simple magnanimity; to have known for the last six days that the end was here, and to have met it in a way that one cannot but lovingly honour. They had removed him into an Apartment all his own; and the nursing and attendance on him has filled his poor Mother's heart with gratitude and surprise. He died on Wednesday 9.20 p.m.;[2] Mother and surviving Brother returned early yesterday morning, Mary who had gone round by Liverpool not till night;—the funeral was yesterday at noon (all wisely and beautifully adjusted, I think by my dear little Mary mainly); and all is now over; all of work that we could do *done*; and only the suffering and sorrow now to deal with. It has of course made a dismal house here,[3]— concerning all which I need say no more. The sad Story itself I thought *you* had a right to hear from me; and now all is said.

I was myself minded to have been in Chelsea before this; but now mean to stay a day or two long[er]; day of departure not yet fixed but some day this week it must be; I rejoice much in the prospect of seeing you in ten days farther; indeed I may say it is the chief attraction London now has for me. I pray Heaven your little "Rose" may not be doomed to go abroad; and that we shall *not* forfeit a season of walks; of which there can now so few remain

2. Wed. was 20 Sept. James Aitken Jr.'s death was announced in the obituary column of the *Liverpool Mercury*, 25 Sept., as on 21 Sept.: "AITKEN,—Sept. 21, at St. George's Hospital, London, from the effects of an accident, James Carlyle Aitken, son of James Aitken, The Hill, Dumfries."

3. TC wrote about Jim's death in his journal, 5 Dec.: "Dismal sudden tragedy there [Dumfries]: accid*t*, at London, to poor 'Jim' (Mary's eldest Bro*r*): sudden summons thither of Mary and her poor Mother; return of them in few days with the Body of their Dead Loved One:—one of the saddest and cruelest-looking calamities I ever was concerned in" (TC's journal; privately owned).

for that painful reason.[4] — I have never been so long from home before; what benefit I have gained is still uncertain, though benefit there surely is more or less. I have had the usual continuity of difficulties and sufferings about sleep; but did lazily taste somewhat the solitary Lotus-eating life of the Highlands; had a week of beautiful beneficial Sea-bathing in the Isle of Skye; was picked up there by a Glasgow Steamer, and conveyed through these strange and mournfully beautiful Hebrides Isles and their many sounding Seas in the space of a day and night to Oban and Greenock;[5] from which in a few hours more, the Ayrshire Railway[6] landed me safe here. I felt considerably better at first; but begin to suspect, that might be in good part the effect of novelty and beautiful environment, outward and inward. We shall see better at Chelsea; — and in effect the better ought not to be too momentous to me just now.

It gives me real pleasure to see you so interested and ardently diligent about your Irish Book;[7] there is not a doubt you will make an interesting two Volumes of it, and set the matter in a new light, new and profitable to the English mind; which infinitely needs instruction in that matter. — I long much with a tremulous deep and almost painful feeling about that other manuscript, which you were kind enough to read at the very first.[8] Be prepared to tell me, with all your candour, the *pros* and *contras* there.[9]

4. Presumably Froude thought he might have to take his da. Rose abroad for her health.

5. Oban, port on the W coast of mainland Scotland, 93 mi. (150 km.) NW of Glasgow; Greenock, port on the Firth of Clyde. TC commented in his journal, 5 Dec.: "continued at L*h* Luichart, with a final short flight to Skye, for above 2 *months*; — The loneliest *almost*, and, altog*r* the *idlest* bit of life I ever had; — life as of 'Lotus-eating' I defined it, & not quite with*t* remorse, perhaps just! Home by Mull, Oban, Greenock directly to Dumfries" (TC's journal; privately owned).

6. Presumably TC took the Ayrshire Railway from Greenock via Glasgow to Paisley, then the Glasgow and South Western Railway from Paisley to Dumfries. In 1858, he had recommended the Ayrshire railway to Lord Ashburton: "from Carlisle there is a fine gentle (ill-paying) railway the *quietest* and handiest I ever travelled in . . . then by Dumfries . . . Ayrshire and places you have never been" (see 34:83).

7. Froude was currently working on *The English in Ireland*; the first vol. was pbd. 1872, the second and third vols. 1874.

8. The MSS of JWC's letters and of TC's reminiscences of her; see TC's 1871 Will, 6 April, and TC to JAF, 7 July.

9. Froude wrote later: "When I saw him again after the summer we talked the subject over with the fullest confidence. He was nervously anxious to know my resolution. I told him that, so far as I could then form an opinion, I thought that the letters *might* be published, provided the prohibition was withdrawn against publishing his own Memoir of Mrs. Carlyle. . . . It would have been hard on both of them if the sharp censures of Mrs. Carlyle's pen [in her letters] had been left unrelieved. To this Carlyle instantly assented. The copy of the Memoir . . . [was] among the other papers, that I might make use of it if I liked . . . but I required, and I received, a direct permission to print it" (Froude, *Carlyle* 4:411–12). For TC's view that Froude should consult John A. Carlyle and Forster, see TC's 1871 Will, 6 April. Froude "presumed that John Carlyle was acquainted with his brother's inten-

I send my kindest grateful regards to you and Madam, to poor Rose and all the kind household. I remain

> Very sincerely, dear Froude,
> Your thankful & affectionate
> T. Carlyle[10]

---

tions, and would communicate with me on the subject if he wished to do so" (Froude, *Carlyle* 4:412); he gave the papers to Forster for his consideration: "He, if any one, could say whether so open a revelation of the life at Cheyne Row was one which ought to be made. Forster read the letters. I suppose that he felt as uncertain as I had done, the reasons against the publication being so obvious and so weighty. . . . To me at any rate he gave no opinion at all. He merely said that he would talk to Carlyle himself, and would tell him that he must make my position perfectly clear in his will, or trouble would certainly arise about it. Nothing more passed between Forster and myself upon the subject. Carlyle, however, in the will which he made two years later bequeathed the MS. to me specifically in terms of the tenderest confidence" (Froude, *Carlyle* 4:413); for TC's Will, 6 Feb. 1873 (this was TC's formal and witnessed will, along with the codicil of 8 Nov. 1878), see Froude, *My Relations* 71–77.

10. From "dear Froude" to the end was written in TC's hand.

BIOGRAPHICAL NOTES

Notes on the Carlyles' contemporaries referred to more than once in the present volume are given below, cross-referenced to earlier information. Some relatives or old friends who died before the starting date of this volume are retained because of frequent references to them. Otherwise, individuals are accounted for in headnotes and footnotes when they appear in the letters.

Adamson, Samuel (1831–80), of British Linen Co. bank, Dumfries, where TC had an account; son of Robert Adamson (1787–1861; see 10:23 and 37:261).

Agnew, Joan (1846–1924), cousin of John Ruskin; she m., 20 April 1871, the artist Arthur Severn (1842–1931).

Airlie; see Stanley.

Aitken, James Jr. (1836–20 Sept. 71), son of Jean and James; he worked in a mercantile house in London 1858–ca. 1864, then moved to work in Liverpool 1864–66, tried to establish himself as a shipbroker on his own in London 1866–67, then went back to work in Liverpool ("salary £400 & work easy & interesting for him" [JAC-TC, 27 Dec. 1868; MS: NLS 1775C.296]), living at 29 Rock Terrace, Claughton, Birkenhead (across the river Mersey from Liverpool), initially with his sister Margaret (1845–1932) as housekeeper.

Aitken, Jean ("Craw") Carlyle (1810–88), TC's sister; m., 1833, James Aitken (1809–87) from Troqueer, housepainter of English St., Dumfries; they moved from Assembly St., Dumfries, to their new house, The Hill, Lochmaben Rd., Dumfries, 1863. They had two sons who d. in infancy (1834–36 and 1855–56), both named Alexander; James Jr. (see above); Thomas (1841–69), who was at an inst. for the deaf in Glasgow from 1854 (see 29:186), then lived at home from ca. 1864; and John (1843–1911), bank clerk at the Commercial Bank, Dumfries, moved to London, Sept. 1871. Their das. were Anne (1839–1919), Margaret, and Mary (see below).

Aitken, Mary (1848–95), worked as a pupil teacher in Peebles, March-Sept. 1867, then returned home. She accompanied TC to London, Sept. 1868, "for about three weeks," but stayed for more than three years. She continued to live in London and to help TC, though not always living in Cheyne Row. She m., 1879, her cousin Alexander Carlyle (see below).

Allingham, William (1824–89; *ODNB*), Irish poet; he worked in the Customs

Service 1846–70; friendly with TC since early 1850s. He m., 1874, Helen Mary Elizabeth, b. Paterson (1848–1926; *ODNB*), watercolorist; she later painted portraits of TC; she also compiled the list of pictures for *Carlyle's House Catalogue.*

Amberley; see Stanley.

Ashburton, Lady Louisa Caroline, b. Stewart-Mackenzie (1827–1903), m., 1858, William Bingham Baring (1799–1864; *ODNB*; see 11:40 and later vols.), 2d baron, politician, and partner in Baring Bros., bankers. They had one da., Mary Florence (1860–1902). Lady Louisa was the da. of Mary Elizabeth Frederica, b. Mackenzie (1783–1862; *ODNB*), chief of Clan Mackenzie, and James Alexander Stewart (1784–1843); on their marriage (1817) the name Mackenzie was added to that of Stewart. Lady Ashburton lived at Melchet Court (see 38:8), a country house 6 mi. (9.5 km.) W of Romsey, Hampshire, on the border between Hampshire and Wiltshire; she also owned a farm at Addiscombe, near Croydon, and Seaforth Lodge, Devon. Lord Ashburton's first wife, m. 1823, was Harriet, b. Montagu (1805–57; *ODNB*; see 11:40 and 26:ix–xv); they met the Carlyles in 1839 and became close friends. Where necessary for clarity, we refer in notes to Lord Ashburton's first and second wives as Lady Harriet Ashburton and Lady Louisa Ashburton respectively, although these are not the correct forms.

Austin, Mary Carlyle (1808–88), TC's sister, m., 1831, James Austin (1805–78), farmer of The Gill, 6 mi. (9.5 km.) SW of Ecclefechan. They had eight das.: Margaret (see Stewart); Grace (1833–1922), who m., 1856, William Yeoward (ca. 1824–1911), of Toronto, Ontario; Jessie (b. 1836), who m., 1859, George Grierson (b. 1835); Jane (b. 1840); Mary Anne (b. 1842); Catherine (see James Carlyle Jr.); Isabella (b. ca. 1846); and Mary Carlyle (b. 1851); and one surviving son, James Jr. (b. 1848).

Baillie, James Augustus (1799–1873), impoverished cousin of JWC's mother, and his wife, Anna-Maria (1812–after 1876); they had lived in Dover (see 39:136–37), but by the 1871 census they were living at 12 Caroline St., London.

Baring; see Ashburton.

Bismarck, Otto von (1815–98), chancellor of the North German Confederation 1867–71, chancellor of the German Empire 1871–90.

Blackie, John Stuart (1809–95; *ODNB*), classical scholar and Scottish Gaelic scholar, prof. of Greek at Edinburgh Univ. from 1852; m., 1842, Eliza, b. Wyld (1819–1908).

Blunt, Abel Gerald Wilson (1827–1902), rector of St. Luke's, Chelsea, from 1860; m., 1851, Frances Mary, b. Forssteen (1820–99); see 40:224.

Braid, Betty, b. Pringle (1795–1875), Grace Welsh's Haddington servant, close to JWC (see 21:82 and 24:221); b. in Prestonkirk, E. Lothian; m. Alexander (1792–1874), stonemason and shopkeeper. Three sons d. in infancy: Alexander (b. 1826), James (b. 1829), and James (b. 1831); George (1827–65) was the only child who survived into adulthood. Previously living at 15 Adam St. (see 17:127), they moved, 1858, to Upper Stenhouse, Greenend, Liberton, S Edinburgh.

Bromley, Caroline Davenport (1820–91), da. of Rev. Walter Davenport Bromley (1787–1862) of Wootton Hall, Staffordshire, and his first wife, m., 1818, Caroline Barbara, b. Gooch (1791–1827). A friend of Lady Louisa Ashburton, she became a close friend of JWC's; she was now friendly with TC. Her London home was at 32 Grosvenor St.

Browning, Robert (1812–89; *ODNB*), poet; friend of the Carlyles since mid-1830s.

Carlyle, Alexander (Alick) (1797–1876), TC's brother; emigrated with his family to Canada, 1843; settled at the Bield, 4½ mi. (7 km.) W of Brantford, Ontario. He m., 1830, Janet, b. Clow (1809–91); they had six surviving sons: Thomas (1833–1921), m., 1867, Margaret, b. MacVicar (1847–1917), who had at least seven children, including Thomas Alexander (1869–70), and Hellen (b. ca. Dec. 1870); John (1839–1924), moved to Brantford and became a carpenter, 1870, m., 1871, Helen, b. McVicar (1851–1927); Alexander (see below); James (1846–1924); William (1849–1935); and Robert (1851–1932); and three surviving das.: Jane Welsh (1831–84), m., 1852, Robert Sims (1825–80), they had three sons, Alexander (1855–1922), Thomas (1856–1934), and John (b. ca. 1862), and a da., Jessie (b. ca. 1859); Janet (Jessie) (1836–1916), m., 1864, William Apps (1834–1911), miller from Ontario, they had at least five children, including Jessie (b. ca. 1867), Alfred (b. ca. 1870), and a da. (b. ca. Jan. 1872 ["Jessie has another daughter two months old I am sorry they are living so far from us," JH to JAC, 7 March 1872; MS: NLS 1775E.125]); and Margaret (1847–1935), m. Edward Marrs (d. 1927), widower from Okmulgee, Oklahoma; see 1:166. An unidentified son (1832–33), Margaret (1835–36), James (b. 1840), and Euphemia (1853–54) all d. in infancy; see 32:4.

Carlyle, Alexander (Alick) (1843–1931; see 16:153), Alexander and Janet's son, school headmaster; m., 1879, his cousin Mary Aitken; lived with TC from 1879 and ed. various collections of the Carlyles' letters and TC's writings. After Mary's death in 1895, he m. Lillias, b. MacVicar (d. 1929), sister of the wives of his brothers Tom and John.

Carlyle, James (Jamie) (1805–90), TC's brother, farmer at Scotsbrig; m., 1834, Isabella, b. Calvert (ca. 1813–59). Their children were James Jr. (see below); John (see below); Thomas (1839–41); and Janet (Jenny) (see Scott).

Carlyle, James Jr. (1835–88 [mistakenly given as 1871 in previous vols.]), m., 1866, his cousin Catherine, b. Austin (1844–1908); see 44:64. Their first child, James, d. at birth 1867; they had nine further children, including Isabella (1868-post-1901), and Mary (b. March 1871). They lived at Craigenputtoch, the tenancy of which had been taken on jointly by James and his father, June 1867; see 44:196.

Carlyle, John (ca. 1792-1872), TC's half-brother; emigrated to the U.S. in 1837, then moved to Canada (see 12:228); he lived on a small farm at Mount Pleasant, nr. Brantford, Ontario. He m., 1817, Margaret (Peggy), b. Benn (1798-1867); they had six children: Janet (1818-89), m., 1844, John Randall Ellis (1810-1911), postmaster and carpenter; Mary (1821-50); John (1825-26); John (1827-97), m., ca. 1852, Mary Catherine, b. Smith (1835-79); James (1830-1900), qualified as a doctor but worked for most of his life as a teacher, m. Wilhelmina Deborah, b. Patten (1847-1926); and William (1833-1911), a teacher and later a school inspector, m., 1860, Emily, b. Youmans (1835-1912); their da. Florence Emily Carlyle (1864-1923) became a prominent Canadian artist. William visited TC in London, Aug. 1864.

Carlyle, John Aitken (Jack, "The Doctor") (1801-79; *ODNB*), TC's brother, physician, and translator. He m., 1852, Phoebe Elizabeth Hough Watt, b. Fowler (1810-54), wealthy widow of Fitzjames Watt (1809-48), from Leek in Staffordshire, with four sons; she d. in childbirth, the child was stillborn. John A. Carlyle assumed responsibility for his stepsons: Thomas Fowler (1838-62), went to Australia, 1861, and d. on his return (see 38:115); Henry (b. 1839), at sea from 1854 (see 29:121), m., 1863, Jane Wilson, b. Hunter (1837-1908), da. of John A. Carlyle's friend John Hunter (1801-69; see 8:161) and Helen, b. Vary (1804-85); Arthur (b. 1840), joined the civil service 1862, and was currently serving in India; and William (b. 1842), an officer in the Dragoons, m., 1866, Mary, b. Smith, da. of E. H. Smith of Grouville, Jersey.

Carlyle, John Calvert (1836-1901), m., 1868, Margaret Little, b. Murray (1848-92), of Blackwood Ridge, Middlebie; they lived at Scotsbrig with his father; they had 13 children, including Isabella Calvert (1869-1915), Elisabeth Carruthers (Oct. 1870-1947), and James (1872-1931).

Carlyle, Margaret, b. Aitken (1771-1853), TC's mother; TC's father was James Carlyle (1758-1832); they m. 1795.

Chapman, Frederic (1823-95; *ODNB*), partner in Chapman & Hall, took over the management of the company 1864; he m., 1861, Clara, b. Woodin (1842-66), they had one surviving son, Frederic, and a baby who d. early 1866. He then m., autumn 1870, Annie Marion, b. Harding (b. 1848).

Christie, William Dougal (1816-74; *ODNB*), diplomat and author; known to TC since 1840; see 12:56; see also 44:67-68. He m., 1841, Mary, b. Grant (1819-1908), they had several children, including Mary Elizabeth Christie (1847-1906), novelist.

Davidson, David (1811–1900), army engineer and inventor, childhood friend of JWC's; see 35:255; see also 46:192.

Derby, Edward Henry Stanley (1826–93; *ODNB*), 15th earl of; politician and diarist; m., 5 July 1870, Mary Catherine, b. Sackville-West (1824–1900; *ODNB*), dowager marchioness of Salisbury, widow of James Gascoyne-Cecil (1791–1868), 2d marquess of Salisbury.

Dickens, Charles (1812–9 June 70; *ODNB*), novelist; friend of the Carlyles since the early 1840s; m., 1836, Catherine Thomson, b. Hogarth (1816–79), separated from her in 1858; see 33:233.

Disraeli, Benjamin (1804–81; *ODNB*), politician and author; prime minister 1868 and 1874–80.

Duffy, Charles Gavan (1816–1903; *ODNB*), Irish nationalist, lawyer, and politician, friend of TC's since 1845. He m., 1847, Susan, b. Hughes (1826–78); they emigrated to Australia 1855.

Durival; see Otthenin.

Eichthal, Charles d' (1813–80), baron, from a wealthy German Jewish banking family in Munich whom John A. Carlyle met in 1827; see 5:277; Charles first visited the Carlyles in Dec. 1835; see 8:277. His son was Karl (1845–1909).

Emerson, Ralph Waldo (1803–82; see 6:425), philosopher, essayist, poet, and transcendentalist. He first met TC in Aug. 1833; in spite of their philosophical and political differences they had close ties; he introduced many Americans to TC and played a leading part in arranging the publication of TC's works in the U.S. Emerson m., 1835, as his second wife, Lydia, b. Jackson (1802–92); their children were Waldo (1836–42); Ellen Tucker (1839–1909); Edith (1841–1929), m., 1865, William Hathaway Forbes (1840–97), businessman; they were to have eight children, including Ralph Emerson (1866–1937), Edith (1867–1926), William Cameron (1870–1959), and John (1871–88); and Edward Waldo (1844–1930).

Erskine, Thomas (1788–20 March 1870; *ODNB*; see 10:18), theologian and retired advocate, living at Linlathen, Dundee; known to the Carlyles since the mid-1830s. He had had two widowed sisters: Christian Stirling (1789–1866), m., 1817, Charles Stirling (d. 1830); she had lived with Erskine; during the winter they had usually lived in Edinburgh; and David Paterson (1791–1867), m., 1821, Capt. James Paterson (1795–1856); she had lived with her son, James Erskine Paterson (b. 1826) and his family at 8 Newbattle Terr., Morningside.

Forster, John ("Fuz") (1812–76; *ODNB*; see 6:118 and 11:7), historian, journalist, and biographer; ed. of the *Examiner* 1847–55; sec. of, 1855–61, and commissioner of, from Feb. 1861, the Lunacy Commission; friend of the Carlyles since the late 1830s and TC's literary adviser; began his *Life of Charles Dickens* after Dickens's death and pbd. it 1872–74. He m., 1856,

Eliza Ann, b. Crosbie (ca. 1819–94), widow of the publisher Henry Colburn (ca. 1784–1855; *ODNB*); from late 1863 they lived at Palace Gate House, Kensington.

Froude, James Anthony (1818–94; *ODNB*), journalist and historian, ed. of *Fraser's Magazine* 1860–74; he m., first, 1849, Charlotte Maria, b. Grenfell (1812–60); they had two das., Georgina Margaret (1850–1935) and Rose Mary (1852–75), and a son, Pascall Grenfell (1854–79). He m., second, 1861, Henrietta Elizabeth, b. Warre (1824–74); they had a son, Ashley Anthony (1863–1949), and a da., May (b. 1867). They lived at 5 Onslow Gdns., Fulham Rd.

Gladstone, William Ewart (1809–98; *ODNB*), politician; leader of the liberal party 1867–94, prime minister 1868–74, 1880–85, 1886, 1892–94. He m., 1839, Catherine, b. Glynne (1812–1900; *ODNB*).

Hanning, Janet Carlyle (1813–97), TC's sister; m., 1836, Robert Hanning (1796–1878), who had emigrated to Canada in mysterious disgrace in 1841; she joined him in Hamilton, Ontario, Aug. 1851, with their two das., Margaret (b. 1838), and Mary (b. 1840), who m., 1864, Charles Coates Holden (b. 1836); they had at least two das., Jenny (d. Dec. 1870 [JH-JAC, 5 Jan. 1871; MS: NLS 1775E.7]) and Jane. Janet and Robert had two more das., b. in Canada, Catherine (b. ca. 1852), a school teacher, and Jane.

Harding, Robert Palmer (1821–93; *ODNB*), head of a London accounting firm. See also Chapman.

Helps, Arthur (1813–75; *ODNB*), historian, civil servant, clerk to the privy council 1860–75; friend of the Carlyles since the 1840s. He suffered financial ruin and was given a "grace and favour" residence in Kew Gardens by Queen Victoria in 1869.

Houghton, Richard Monckton Milnes (1809–85; *ODNB*), 1st Baron, author and politician; friend of the Carlyles since the late 1830s; m., 1851, Annabella, b. Hungerford Crewe (1814–74), they had two das. and a son; see 37:270.

Howard, George James (1843–1911; *ODNB*), artist and politician, m., 1864, Rosalind Frances, b. Stanley (1845–1921; *ODNB*), women's rights and temperance activist.

Huxley, Thomas Henry (1825–95; *ODNB*), biologist and educationist.

Irving, Edward (1792–1834; *ODNB*; see 1:92, later vols., and Carlyle, *Reminiscences*), the Carlyles' great friend; religious leader and preacher.

Jewsbury, Geraldine Endsor (1812–80; *ODNB*; see 12:103–4), novelist, reviewer, and misc. writer; friend of the Carlyles, particularly of JWC's, since 1841. She lived at 41 Markham Sq., Chelsea.

Laing, David (1793–1878; *ODNB*), antiquary; librarian of the Signet Lib., Edinburgh, 1837–78. When TC became rector of Edinburgh Univ. he chose Laing as his assessor on the Senatus Academicus. Laing's youngest sister, Euphemia (1808–96), lived with him as his housekeeper after the death of their mother, Helen, b. Kirk (1767–1837); since 1845 they had lived in East Villa, 12 James St., Portobello (see 43:122).

Lowe, Georgiana, b. Orred (d. 1884), m., 1836, Robert Lowe (1811–92; *ODNB*), politician, chancellor of the exchequer 1868–73; both members of the Ashburton circle, and liked by both Carlyles; for JWC on them, see 30:213. The *ODNB* describes her as his "plain-spoken, garrulous, eccentric wife, Georgiana, from whom he had unsuccessfully tried to separate in the late 1860s."

Maccall, William (1812–88; *ODNB*), impoverished writer, Unitarian preacher, lecturer, and author; m., 1842, Alice, b. Haselden (1813–78); they had one da., Elizabeth (b. 1843). They lived at Fountain Villa, Woolwich Rd., Bexley Heath, Kent. See K. J. Fielding, "Carlyle, Charles Dickens, and William Maccall," *Notes and Queries* n.s. 1 (1954): 488–90.

Masson, David (1822–1907; *ODNB*; see 16:312), writer and editor, prof. of rhetoric and English lit., Edinburgh Univ., 1865–95. He m., 1853, Emily Rosaline, b. Orme (1835–1915); they had a son, David Orme Masson (1858–1937; *ODNB*), and three das, Flora (1856–1937), Helen (b. 1864), and Rosaline (1867–1947); they lived at 10 Regent Terr., Edinburgh. He was also ed. of *Macmillan's Magazine* 1859–68.

Maxwell, Sir William Stirling (1818–78; *ODNB*), art historian, book collector, and politician; known to TC since 1848; for his family, see 43:278.

Mazzini, Guiseppe (1805–72; see 11:225), Italian revolutionary, friend of the Carlyles since the late 1830s.

Mill, John Stuart (1806–73; *ODNB*), utilitarian philosopher and economist; m., 1851, Harriet Taylor, b. Hardy (1807–58; *ODNB*), who strongly influenced his thinking. Mill met TC in Sept. 1831 (see 5:398); they remained on friendly terms even after the MS of vol. 1 of *The French Revolution* was burned while in Mill's keeping (see 8:66–68), but later became estranged because of many differences in temperament and attitudes to social questions; Mill also believed that TC and other friends disapproved of his marriage. Elected Liberal M.P. for Westminster 1865.

Milnes; see Houghton.

Napoleon, Louis (1808–73), president of France, 1848–52, emperor (as Napoleon III), 1852–70.

Neuberg, Joseph (1806–67; see 11:231), a German Jewish businessman, naturalized British 1845, and retired 1849; m., 1841, Marian (d. 1848; see 23:77). He was introduced to TC, whom he had long admired, by Emerson, 1848; helped TC as an unpaid sec., translated his work into German, and twice accompanied him on visits to Germany (1852 and 1858). He lived at Roslyn Park, Hampstead, with his widowed sister, Rosetta (or Rosette) Frankau (ca. 1816–98) and her children; see 45:227–28.

Norton, Charles Eliot (1827–1908), author, journalist, and Harvard Coll. prof. of Art 1875–98. He m., 1862, Susan Ridley, b. Sedgwick (1838–72); they had six children. He and his family spent 1868–72 in Europe, mostly in London, where he became friendly with TC.

Oliphant, Margaret Oliphant, b. Wilson (1828–97; *ODNB*), prolific novelist, biographer, reviewer, and misc. writer; friend of JWC's since 1860; see 37:62; she lived at 6 Clarence Cres., Windsor.

Otthenin, Jean, b. Johnston (ca. 1800–Nov. 70; see 42:236), old school friend of TC, who had lived for several years with her das., Margaret and Irma (1838–97), at 33 Northumberland St., Edinburgh. Irma had m., 1867, Jean Charles Louis Eugène Durival (1811–92), and now lived in Vassy, Haute Marne, France, where her mother and sister joined her.

Paterson; see Erskine.

Phillipps, Catherine Aurora "Kitty," b. Kirkpatrick (1802–89; see 3:166–67), da. of James Achilles Kirkpatrick (1764–1805), Resident at the court of Hyderabad, and col. in the British East India Company army, and his wife, m. 1801, Khair-un-Nissa (ca. 1786–1813), a Hyderabadi noblewoman. Catherine m., 1829, Maj. James Winsloe Phillipps (ca. 1801–64), 7th hussars; they had four surviving children: Mary Augusta (b. ca. 1830), John James Winsloe (ca. 1833–99), Emily Georgiana (b. 1834), and Bertha Elizabeth (1840–75). She was currently living with her da. Bertha and her husband, Lucius Falkland Brancaleone Cary (1839–78), in Dover. TC had known Kitty since 1824, and she was said to be one of the sources of inspiration for "Blumine" in *Sartor Resartus*; see 3:81.

Quain, Richard (1816–98; *ODNB*), physician; see 45:101. He had attended both Lord Ashburton and JWC.

Reichenbach, Oskar von (1815–93), Silesian landowner, liberal deputy to the Frankfurt parliament 1848–49, exiled to London in 1850. His wife was Friederike, b. Plattnauer (b. 1817), sister of Richard Eduard Plattnauer (b. 1814; see 41:234), political refugee from Prussia (see 22:10), who suffered periods of insanity; old friend of the Carlyles. Their children were Elizabeth (b. 1843), Hedwig (Hetty) (1844–92), and Oskar (b. 1845). They had emigrated to the U.S. in 1853 and had moved back to London sometime after 1865; they lived at 5 Carlisle Ter., Kensington.

Robson, Charles (1805–76), TC's typesetter and printer since 1837; initially of Robson, Levey, & Franklyn, printers, 23 Gt. New St., Fetter Lane, which went bankrupt early 1864. He then went into partnership with one or both of his sons, John (b. ca. 1837) and Christopher (b. 1843), forming Robson & Son, Great Northern Printing Works, St. Pancras Rd.

Ruskin, John (1819–1900; *ODNB*), author, artist, and social reformer; m., 1848, Euphemia Chalmers, b. Gray (1828–97); marriage annulled 1854 (she then m., 1855, John Everett Millais [1829–96; *ODNB*], artist). Ruskin lived in the family home at 163 Denmark Hill, S London, with his mother, Margaret, b. Cock (1781–5 Dec. 1871). His father, John James Ruskin (1785–1864), was a wine merchant.

Russell, Mary, b. Dobbie (1802–75; see 6:145), close friend of JWC and her mother. She m., 1829, Dr. James Russell (ca. 1796–1878); they had moved to Holmhill, nr. Thornhill, Dumfriesshire, by Oct. 1859.

Scott, Janet (Jenny), b. Carlyle (1843–74), youngest child of James and Isabella Carlyle of Scotsbrig; m., 1864, William Scott (b. ca. 1829), draper; they lived at 27 Bradford St., Birmingham, and had a son, John James Carlyle (b. 1865), and two das., Isabella (b. late 1860s) and Jessie Beattie (b. May/June 1870).

Spedding, Thomas Story (1800–21 Nov. 1870; see 10:32), m., 1839, Frances Elizabeth (previously called Emily in error), b. Headlam (1811–96); their children were Margaret Emily (1842–73), Frances Ellen (1843–1900), Maria Isabella (d. in infancy 1845), Henry Anthony (1846–87), and Mildred Eyre (1848–1918). They lived at Mirehouse, nr. Keswick, Cumberland. A lawyer, he devoted his life to local interests in Cumberland. He and his brother James Spedding (1808–81; *ODNB*; see 8:196 and 19:205), literary editor and biographer, known as "Lord Bacon" had been friends of TC's since the late 1830s. James lived in Westbourne Grove, London.

Stanley, Henrietta Maria, b. Dillon (1807–95; *ODNB*), m., 1826, Edward John (1802–1869; *ODNB*; see 12:59), 2d Baron Stanley of Alderley, Whig politician; living at Alderley Park, Cheshire; their London home was at 40 Dover St. Both were friends of the Carlyles. They had nine surviving children including Henrietta Blanche (1829–1921), 5th countess of Airlie; Maude (1833–1915; *ODNB*), women's welfare activist; John Constantine (1837–78), soldier, m., 15 Aug. 1871, Susan Mary Elizabeth Stewart-Mackenzie (d. 1931); Edward Lyulph (1839–1925; *ODNB*), educationist; Katharine Louisa Russell (1842–74; *ODNB*), Viscountess Amberley, radical and suffragist, m., 1864, John Russell Amberley (1842–76; *ODNB*), Viscount Amberley; and Rosalind Howard (see above); see also 45:222 and 229–30.

Stephen, James Fitzjames (1829–94; *ODNB*; see 41:24), judge and writer, m., 1855, Mary Richenda, b. Cunningham (1829–1912); they had eight children: Katharine (1856–1924), Herbert (1857–1932), James Kenneth (1859–92), Harry Lushington (1860–1945), Rosamond (b. 1869), Dorothea (b. 1871), and 2 other das. Their London home was at 4 Cornwall Gds., Queen's Gate.

Sterling, Sir Anthony Coningham (1805–1 March 71; *ODNB*; see 9:103 and later vols.), soldier; m., 1829, Charlotte, b. Baird (d. 1863), who suffered attacks of insanity and was jealous of JWC (see 18:266–67 and 19:9); he lived at 3 South Pl., Knightsbridge. His brother John (1806–44; *ODNB*), writer, had been a particular friend of TC's; see *CL* vols. 8–18 and Carlyle's *Life of John Sterling* (1851); his surviving children were Edward Coningham (1831–77); Julia Maria (1836–1910); John Barton (1840–1926), m., 1863, Caroline Matilda, b. Salusbury-Trelawny (1842–1917); and Hester Isabella (1843–1908).

Stewart, Margaret, b. Austin (1831–74), da. of Mary and James Austin, m., 1859, Thomas Stewart (1832–69), farmer from Hollybush, now living at Ernhirst (Ironhirst), about 5½ mi. (9 km.) SW of Dumfries; see 38:19; they had a da., Mary (b. ca. 1861), and four sons, William (b. 1863), James (b. 1864), Hugh (b. 1866, dead by April 1868) and Thomas (b. 1869). Thomas Stewart's brothers were Hugh (b. ca. 1826), James (b. ca. 1831), and John (b. ca. 1839).

Stirling, Christian; see Erskine.

Strachey, Sir Edward (1812–1901; *ODNB*), 3d bart., religious and philosophical writer, son of Edward Strachey (1774–1832; *ODNB*), East India Company diplomat and judge, and his wife, m. 1808, Julia Woodburn, b. Kirkpatrick (1790–1846); the family had been friends of TC's since the 1820s; see Carlyle, *Reminiscences* 283–84.

Tait, Robert Scott (1816–97), portrait painter and pioneer photographer; friend of the Carlyles since 1853, he painted TC (see 31:84), and *A Chelsea Interior* (see 33:197), as well as photographing both Carlyles.

Tennyson, Alfred (1809–92; *ODNB*), poet; poet laureate 1850–92; m., 1850, Emily Sarah, b. Sellwood (1813–96); friends of the Carlyles since the early 1840s.

Turgenev, Ivan (1818–83), Russian novelist and dramatist, whom TC first met in 1857; see 32:157.

Tyndall, John (1820–93; *ODNB*), physicist, prof. of natural philosophy at the Royal Institution, Albemarle St., London, from 1853; TC's admirer and friend from the mid-1850s; see 31:1–2.

Venturi, Emilie (ca. 1819–93; *ODNB*), da. of William Henry Ashurst (ca. 1791–1855; *ODNB*; portrait painter), supporter of Italian independence and campaigner for women's rights; unhappily m. to Sydney Hawkes, whom she divorced 1861; see 30:215 and 235. She m., 1861, Carlo Venturi (ca. 1830–66). A strong supporter of Giuseppe Mazzini and the Young Italy movement, she published various English editions of his writings and *Joseph Mazzini: A Memoir* (1875).

Victoria (1819–1901; *ODNB*), queen of Great Britain and Ireland 1837–1901; m., 1840, Albert (1819–61; *ODNB*), prince consort.

Ward, Charles Augustus (1828–1914), vintner, author, antiquarian, and bookseller; see 45:230–31.

Warren, Sarah (b. ca. 1812 in Norfolk), a widow with adult children (see 41:96), cook and housekeeper at Cheyne Row from Nov. 1864 until at least 1871 (listed in the 1871 census as still at 5 Cheyne Row). Mrs. Warren was previously wrongly identified as Eliza Warren (ca. 1816–1905) in vols. 41 and 42.

Watt; see John. A. Carlyle.

Watts, George Frederic (1817–1904; *ODNB*), artist. He lived at Little Holland House, Kensington. He m., first, 1865, Ellen Alice, b. Terry (1847–1928; *ODNB*), actress, but they separated after less than a year; he m., second, 1886, Mary Seton, b. Fraser-Tytler (1849–1938).

Wellmer, Meta (1826–89; see 43:21 and 45:207), German writer, teacher, feminist, vegetarian, and spiritualist. Her publications later included *German Educators and their Sphere of Influence* (Leipzig 1877), and *The Vegetarian Way of Life and the Vegetarians* (Berlin, 1889).

Welsh, Alexander (Alick) (b. 1816), son of JWC's maternal uncle John; m., ca. 1849, Sophy, b. Martin (b. ca. 1824). Their children were John (Jackie) (ca. 1853–64), Isabella Helen (b. 1856; see 31:201), Margaret (b. 1858), and Jean (b. 1860); they lived at Sandown Park, Wavertree, Liverpool.

Welsh, Ann (1799–1877), Elizabeth (1792–1877), and Grace (1801–67), JWC's paternal aunts (see 14:67 and 16:219), living at Craigen Villa, Morningside, Edinburgh.

Welsh, Grace, b. Welsh (1782–1842), JWC's mother; m., 1800, John Welsh (1776–1819; see 1:202–3), JWC's father, doctor in Haddington.

Welsh, John (1785–1853; see 28:286–87), JWC's maternal uncle, brass and copper founder, who had lived at 20 Maryland St., Liverpool; m., 1808, Mary, b. Colliver (d. 1838; see 10:200); their children were Helen (ca. 1813–53); Walter; Alexander; Jeannie (Babbie) (1818–95), m., 1853, Andrew Chrystal (ca. 1811–83), wine merchant from Glasgow, they had a da., Mary (1857–1937), see 40:226–27; John (1820–60); Margaret; and Mary.

Welsh, Margaret (Maggie) (b. 1821), da. of JWC's maternal uncle John; lived in Auchtertool with her brother Walter; was JWC's nurse, Dec. 1863–May 1864; she came to Chelsea to look after TC after JWC's death, late April–mid-Aug. 1866, and June-Oct. 1867.

Welsh, Mary (1823–79), da. of JWC's maternal uncle John; usually lived in Auchtertool with her brother Walter, but had been living in Bridge of Allan for over a year to try and combat her opium addiction.

Welsh, Rev. Walter (1815–1879; see 16:12), son of JWC's maternal uncle John; minister at Auchtertool, Fife, since 1842. His sisters Margaret (Maggie) and Mary usually lived with him.

Woolner, Thomas (1825–92; *ODNB*; see 26:37 and 29:176–77), sculptor and poet; he lived at 29 Welbeck St., London. He m., 1864, Alice Gertrude, b. Waugh (b. 1845), da. of George and Mary Waugh; they had six children, including Amy (b. 1865), Hugh (1866–1925), and Geoffrey (1867–82).

VOLUMES OF
THE COLLECTED LETTERS OF
THOMAS AND JANE WELSH CARLYLE
PUBLISHED TO DATE

This list of previously published volumes gives the period each volume covers. Through volume 24, the *Collected Letters* were published in sets, with an index in the last volume of each set; these volumes are indicated. From volume 25 onward, an index is included in each. Also included in each, from volume 25 onward, is a separate list of biographical notes for frequently mentioned contemporaries. The list also specifies any appendix or appendices included in a volume.

1: 1812–21
2: 1822–23
3: 1824–25
4: 1826–28; index
5: Jan. 1829–Sept. 1831
6: Oct. 1831–Sept. 1833
7: Oct. 1833–Dec. 1834; JBW's "The Rival Brothers" and letters found too late to be placed chronologically; index
8: Jan. 1835–June 1836
9: July 1836–Dec. 1837; letters found too late to be placed chronologically; index
10: 1838
11: 1839
12: 1840; letters found too late to be placed chronologically; index
13: 1841
14: Jan.–July 1842
15: Aug.–Dec. 1842; index
16: Jan.–July 1843
17: Aug. 1843–March 1844
18: Apr.–Dec. 1844; index
19: Jan.–Sept. 1845
20: Oct. 1845–July 1846
21: Aug. 1846–June 1847; index
22: July 1847–March 1848
23: Apr. 1848–March 1849

24: Apr.–Dec. 1849; index

25: 1850

26: 1851

27: 1852

28: 1853

29: 1854–June 1855

30: July–Dec. 1855; JWC's Notebook (1845–52), *Simple Story*, and Journals (Oct. 1855–July 1856); Jewsbury and Twisleton appendices

31: Jan.–Sept. 1856

32: Oct. 1856–July 1857; appendices: *Athenaeum* advertisements for TC's *Collected Works* and TC's comments on *Aurora Leigh*

33: Aug. 1857–June 1858

34: July–Dec. 1858; TC's letters to Charles Butler found too late to be placed chronologically

35: Jan.–Oct. 1859

36: Nov. 1859–Sept. 1860; TC's letters to his family, May–July 1859, found too late to be placed chronologically

37: Oct. 1860–Oct. 1861; volume divisions of the first edition of *Frederick the Great*

38: Nov. 1861–Nov. 1862

39: Dec. 1862–Dec. 1863

40: Jan.–Aug. 1864

41: Sept. 1864–April 1865

42: May–Sept. 1865

43: Oct. 1865–June 1866; with material relating to JWC's death and its aftermath

44: July 1866–June 1867; TC's letters, 1850–66, found too late to be placed chronologically

45: July 1867–Dec. 1868; TC's notes to Henry Larkin, found too late to be placed chronologically

46: 1869–April 1870; JWC's letters to Isabella McTurk / Dinwoodie, found too late to be placed chronologically; JWC's letters, 1850–66, found too late to be placed chronologically

INDEXES TO VOLUME 47

The index uses italic type for an identifying or substantial note or important passage. For complete reference to any correspondent, use needs to be made of both indexes. The Index of Correspondents gives only the first page of any letter, and the correspondents' names are capitalized in the General Index.

Women are indexed normally by their married names; couples often only under one of the two concerned. Selected subjects, as well as names, are indexed alphabetically, and some selected topics, which are personal rather than general, are also indexed under the Carlyles' main entries. Works and characters in works are usually indexed only under the name of the author; writings of unknown authorship are indexed by title. TC's works are indexed alphabetically. Scottish words are italicized, listed and glossed.

Identified quotations from published works are footnoted and indexed under their authors' main entries; unidentified quotations, and all but the most common sayings, are given under the first or most important word. The index usually gives the correct spelling of a name, and notes TC's misspellings only when this seems necessary. Problems have sometimes arisen with the Carlyles' "coterie speech": such expressions are now indexed but not always noted after their first appearance.

INDEX OF CORRESPONDENTS

Aitken Jean Carlyle 22 32 129 145 161 192 214
Anderson Frederick 1
Argyll Duchess of 119
Ashburton Lady 6 46
Ashburton Lady [from Mary Aitken] 107 130

Bathgate William 114
Bernstorff Count Albrecht von 112
Blackie John Stuart 121
Braid Betty 43 217
Bromley Caroline Davenport 42

Carlyle Alexander (TC's brother) 17 74 165
Carlyle Dr. John A. 4 6 11 15 25 30 32 34 49 54 63 81 86 103 106 109 117 124 127 133 136 137 140 149 152 163 169 175 179 195 200 201 202 204 207 219
Carlyle Thomas (Alick and Janet's son) 1
Carruthers Robert 143
Chapman Frederic 38 43 47 62 133
Christie William Dougal 39 204

Dixon Thomas 121
Duncan George Alexander 23
Duncan Margaret 64

Editor of the *Times* 91
Emerson Ralph Waldo 13 70 209

Faithfull Emily 160
Foller Karl von 126
Forster John 28 38 44 52 89 223
Froude James A. 50 56 215 218 225

Hall Samuel Carter 123
Hanning Janet Carlyle 155
Helps Arthur 187
Hogarth Georgina 39
Howard George 224
Huxley Thomas Henry 135

Kerr Ralph Drury Lord 41
Kingsley Charles 108

Laing David 212
Lawson Robert 151
Lawton Joseph 157
Lüders Dr. Ferdinand 35

Maccall William 82
MacFarlane James 9
Masson David 55

Naesmyth Sir John Murray 40

Oliphant Margaret 188

Parkes Henry 65
Phillipps Catherine 197

Rogers Charles 35
Ruskin John 77 199

Spedding James 113
Spedding Thomas Story 60
Stanley Lady 160
Stephen James Fitzjames 20
Sterling Capt. John Barton 168 174

Thompson John R. 67
Tupper Martin [from Mary Aitken] 140
Tyndall John 72

Unidentified Correspondents 8 107 143 150
    182 215

Waldmüller Robert 131
Wallace Rev. Jardine 49
Ward Charles A. 83
Warren Sarah 222
Wellmer Meta [from Mary Aitken] 116 171
Wilson Thomas 73

GENERAL INDEX

Abbey Church / Kirk *See* St. Mary's Abbey
    Church / Kirk (Haddington)
Aberdeen 32 216 218 223
—Steamer 50 214 216 217
Abdülaziz sultan 108
Abingdon (Lanarkshire) 55
Abyssinia 20
Academy The 64
Adam St. (Edinburgh) 231
Adamson Robert 229
Adamson Samuel 15 196 206 229
Addiscombe (Croydon) 186 230
Aeneid 104
African-American xviii 67–8 109
Agnew Joan 80 81 134 229
Airlie Henrietta Blanche countess of 190 192
    237
Aitken Alexander 229
Aitken Anne (Jean and James's da.) 31 229
Aitken Rev. David and Eliza 136
Aitken James (Jean's husband) 4 12 16 63 146
    215 226 229
Aitken James (Jean and James's son) xx 31 63
    105 118 127 135 163 186 208 215 225–6 229
AITKEN Jean Carlyle (TC's sister) xiv 4 6
    8 12 16 22 31 32 33 34 47 55 63 65 75 82
    89 104 105 106 110 111 112 116 118 124 125

127 129 134 156 159 179 180 181 186 192
    193 194 202 203 206 209 215 219 222 225
    226 229
Aitken John (Jean and James's son) 8 63 81–2
    105 106 110 118 119 125 127 128 135 208 225
    226 229
Aitken Margaret (Maggie) (Jean and James's
    da.) 31 229
Aitken Mary (Jean and James's da. "Child of
    Nature") xiii xiv xv xvi xx 3 8 10 13 23 31 34
    38 40 42 43 46 47 48 55 63 68 70 75 80 81
    82 89 90 104 105 110 116 117 118 119 120 127
    129 134 135 137 139 140 141 147 150 153
    155 156 157 158 160 161 162 164 165 170 175
    180 181 184 188 199 200 202 204 205 206
    207 209 212 215 216 217 218 219 222 223
    224 225 226 229 231
Aitken Thomas (Jean and James's son) 229
Alabama (ship) 126
Albemarle St. (London) 133
Albert Prince 238
Alderley Park (Cheshire) 237
Alexander the Great 103
Allingham William and Mary Elizabeth 7 8
    60 82 119 137 150 229–30
Alsace Elsass xv 60 73 91 96 97 101 102 117
    118 131 145

Alsace-Lorraine (France) 60
Amberley family 225 230
Amberley John Russell and Katherine Viscount and Viscountess 225 237
America American xviii 68 71 95 107 126 141
  179 193 194 201 202 210 211 232 233
—Civil War xviii 211
—Confederate States 126
—Confederates 67 173
—Republicans 67
—TC's investments 205
American Express Co. 63
American Unitarians 210
ANDERSON Frederick xv 1
Annan Annandale 18 45 51 75 76 87
Anne (queen of Great Britain and Ireland) 95
Anne Boleyn (queen) 7 51 52
Antwerp (Belgium) 143
Arabic 27
Arbuckle Anna Maria and family 31 32
Arbuckle Dr. Robert 31
Arched House (Ecclefechan) 33
ARGYLL Lady Elizabeth Georgiana duchess
  of and George Douglas Campbell 8th duke
  of 119 124-5
Argyll Lodge (Kensington London) 120
Arouet François-Marie See Voltaire
Artizans Labourers & General Dwellings Co.
  139 142 196
Ashburton (Devon) 216
Ashburton Lady Harriet 18 230
ASHBURTON Lady Louisa 12 23 26 27 38
  40 46 47 50 81 82 90 107 130 135 158 180
  186 190 192 201 202 205 208 214 218 223
  225 230 231 235
Ashburton William Bingham Baring Lord 158
  227 230 236
Assembly St. (Dumfries) 229
Athenaeum 141 170 178
Athens Athenian 10
Atlantic (ocean) 22
Auchenhay (Kirkcudbrightshire) 31
Auchtertool (Fife) 239
Audiffret Henri d' 27
Augsburg (Germany) 93
Augsburg Peace of 98
Augsburg War of the League of 95 See also
  Louis XIV
Austin James (Mary's husband) 4 230 238
Austin Mary (Carlyle) (TC's sister) and family
  4 8 22 62 76 186 230 238
Australia xvii 65 195 233
Austria Austrians 7 101

Austrian Succession War of 101 102
Austro-Prussian War 61
Auvergne (France) 5
Ayrshire 227

Bacon Francis 161
—Essays 161
Baden-Baden (Germany) 111
"Bahadur" 27
Baillie James Augustus and Anna-Maria 186
  230
Bain Alexander 7
Baines Rev. Andrew 110
Baines Peter and family 110
Balgray David Robertson Williamson Lord
  195
Balgray House (Dumfriesshire) 195
Ballyare (Gweedore Ireland) 50
Bannockburn battle of 35
Banting William 162
Barbarossa See Frederick I
Baring Bros. & Co. (bankers) 230
Baring Mary Florence (Lord and Lady
  Louisa Ashburton's da.) 47 131 230
Barton Mills (Suffolk) 21
BATHGATE William 114
—Christ and Man 114
Battersea (London) 139
Bavaria/n 87
Bayard Pierre Terrail seigneur de 101
"Beats the world" (coterie speech) 202
Beattie James and Jennie 33
Beck Leonhard 93
Bedlam 111 208
Belgium 94
Bell Davy and Lizzie 33
Bell George 159
Bell William 33
Belle-Isle Charles Louis Auguste Fouquet
  duc de 95
Belvoir Castle (Leicestershire) 47
Bengal (India) 13 20
Bennett William Cox 139 140
Bequest of TC's books to Harvard See
  Harvard
Bergenroth Gustav Adolph 52
Berlin (Germany) 64 96 118 126
—University 182
BERNSTORFF Count Albrecht von 112
Beswick (Manchester) 206
Bible
—Cor. 100
—Exod. 20

—Isa. 99
—Job 61
—Matt. 142
—Prov. 158 171
—Ps. 75
—2 Thess. 100
Bield (Brantford Ontario Canada) 77 135 231
"Big Ben" (bell London) 191
Biographie Universelle 27
Birkenhead (Cheshire) 229
Birmingham 31 32 76 196 237
Bishop of London fund 136
Bismarck Otto Eduard Leopold von xvi xvii
　53 73 78 91 93 101 102 103 108 126 130 142
　145 162 *230*
Bitzius Albrecht 80
Black Sea 108
BLACKIE John Stuart and Eliza 7 121 125
　136 *230*
—*War Songs* 121 125
Blackwood's Edinburgh Magazine 134
Bliss Judah Lee 211
Blue pill 26
Blunt Rev. Gerald and Frances 31 141 147 150
　192 *230*
Bohn Henry George 159
Bolton Row (London) 174
Bonheur Rosa 77
Boston (Massachusetts) 3 63 70 71 72 167
Bouillon duc de *See* Turenne
Bourbon monarchy 96
Boyd William (tailor) 124
Bradford (Yorkshire) 153 178
Bradford George Partridge 212
Braemore (Rossshire) 223
Braid Alexander 230
BRAID Betty 43 *56* 65 217 *230-1*
—and family 230
Brantford (Ontario Canada) 135 193 232
Brazil coffee 163
Bridge of Allan (Stirlingshire) 149 239
Brissac (France) 97
Britain British xvii xviii 9 20 31 57 67 73 95
　101 108 112 126 130 154 166 235
British army 173 199
British Association / Congress 73 119
"British Cable" 72
British Colonies xviii 57
British East India Co. 236 *See also* East
　India Co.
British Empire 166
British Linen Co. (bank Dumfries) 15 229

British Museum (London) 6
British North America Act *See* Canada
BROMLEY Caroline Davenport xviii 150
　197 *231*
Bromley Walter Arthur Davenport 231
Brompton Rd. (London) 225
Brookfield William Henry 147
Brown Joseph (engraver) 62 141
Brown William "Wull" 168
Browning Robert and "Pen" 90 111 *231*
Bruce Henry Austin 21
Brunn Dr. 145
Brunn Julius 145 *See also* Baron Charles
　d'Eichthal
Buccleuch dukes of 46
Büsching Anton Friedrich xvi 104
Bugenhagen Johannes 35
Bunyan John
—*Pilgrim's Progress* 161
Burford (South Brant Ontario) 2
Burgess Andrew Hutton 135-6
Burgher Church of Scotland 9
Burghley William Cecil 1st Baron 18-19
Burgkmair Hans 93
Burgundy 93
Burgundy dukes of 91
Burns Robert 47
Burnswark (Dumfriesshire) 38
Butler Charles xv 205
Byron George Gordon Lord 111

Cable 72
Caird Rev. John 146
Calcutta (India) 20
Caledonian Canal (Scottish Highlands) 27
California 210 212
Calton Tunnel (Edinburgh) 54
Cambridge University 6 27
Campbell Lady Edith Lady Elisabeth and
　Lady Victoria 125
Campbell John George Edward Henry
　Douglas Sutherland 125
"Can naither d'ye ill n'a gude" (coterie
　speech) 139
Canada Canadian xv 1 3 8 11 15 17 63 67 75
　95 104 127 135 156 166 168 192 193 222 231
　232 234
Candlemas 8
Cannes (France) 143
Cardwell Edward 108 153 154
Carlisle (Cumberland) 227
Carlton Terr. (London) 41 236

CARLYLE Alexander (TC's brother Alick Sandy) Janet and family 1 2 3 4 5 11 15 17 18 19 26 74 103 104 106 128 135 157 186 193 205 209 222 *231*

Carlyle Alexander (Alick) (Alick and Janet's son) 135 222 229 *231*

—Photograph 220

Carlyle Isabella Calvert (James Carlyle's wife) 76 231

Carlyle James (TC's father) 9 38 56 184 185 232

Carlyle James (TC's brother Jamie) and family 31 32 34 76 186 194 *231* 237

Carlyle James (Jamie's son) and Catherine 4 5 45 46 76 128 215 230 *231*

Carlyle James (Alick and Janet's son) 222 231

—Photograph 221

Carlyle Jane Welsh *See also* chronology Cheyne Row No. 5 and Thomas Carlyle— On JWC

—Birthday 43 192 217

—Chair 184

—Comments on 12 13 17 33 86 111 154 171 173 217 224 236

—Death 203 239

—Funeral 55

—Grave 54 56 57 65 76 *See also* St. Mary's Abbey Church / Kirk (Haddington)

—Letters xiii 167 183 227

—"Much Ado about Nothing" 153

Carlyle Janet 156

Carlyle John (1754–1801) and Janet 33

Carlyle John (TC's half-brother) and family 11 76 135 232

Carlyle John (Alick and Janet's son) and Helen 3 4 135 231

Carlyle John (Jamie's son) and Margaret 8 34 76 156 *232*

CARLYLE Dr. John Aitken (TC's brother Jack) xv 4 5 8 11 12 13 16 19 22 26 28 34 46 49 50 53 55 63 65 74 75 76 81 86 89 104 105 106 109 110 111 118 124 125 128 129 130 133 134 135 136 137 138 139 142 145 149 152 155 156 161 164 166 167 169 170 175 178 179 180 181 182 183 184 186 193 194 195 196 205 206 207 209 213 215 216 217 218 223 224 227 232 233

—Photographs 175–7

—Portrait 142

Carlyle Margaret (TC's sister) 56 156

Carlyle Margaret Aitken (TC's mother) 9 56 75

CARLYLE Thomas *See also* chronology and individual entries for works topics and opinions

—Advice and encouragement to friends and family 5 16 64 81–2 124 133–4 158

—Amanuensis *See* Mary Aitken

—Anarchy 211

—Autographs 47 150 201 202

—Bathing 119 124 129 135

—Bequests 184 186

—Biography 183

—Birthday 117 162 190

—Charity 160 194

—Checkbook 15 43 135 155 160 217

—Clock presentation 162 190 191 *192*

—Clothes hats buttons shoes slippers 105 124 129 130 133–4 163 209

—Coffee 77 163

—Comments on 13 17 27 38 40 54 55 66 71 82 90 *103* 107 112 114 *116* 117–18 120 130 140 153 171 179 189 *191–2* 204 205 215 217 223 227 228–9

—Dedications 121 188

—Dictating letters xiii xiv xv 11 26 75 90 117 156 202 210 215

—Dining 125 130 147 150 207

—Driving 180 201

—Fog 105

—Food and drink 67 77 147 214

—Gifts to and from 2 3 9 14 19 26 43 68 83 104 107 114 121 123 130 131 133 143 163 212 *See also* TC—Clock presentation

—Grouse and pheasants and venison 107 125 133 224

—Health ill-health xiii xiv 3 7 11 25 32 75 82 119 124 130 157 161 165 199 202 203 204–5 210 214 218

—Holidays / House for summer 12 15–16 22–3 26–7 31 205 214

—Horse for TC 12 215

—Investments *196* 206

—Invitations to and from 6 32 40 60 71 73 80 86 109 119 160 162

—Journal xiv xv 1 2 10 18 31 32 54 56 61 62–3 65 80 117 125 131 154 157 158 171 178 182 183 196–7 207 213 216 218–19 227

—Letter-writing 1–2 165

—Letters of condolence xiv 41 111 113 143 168–9 171

—Mackintosh 55 128

—Noise 214 *See also* —Railway noises

—On books 158

—On colonization xviii
—On emigration xvii 66 67
—On female emancipation xix *151–2* 224–5
—On himself xiv 11 21 25–6 49 53 56 57 62–3
   65 68 75 107 128 153 157 161 165–6 171 175
   199 201 202 204 210 214 223
—On JWC 3 19 184–5 217 218
—On newspaper editors 126–7
—On old age 26 75 76 77 153
—On parliament 30–1 42
—On prayer *24*
—On society 166
—On women and medicine *151–2* 224–5
—Photographs 3 27 114 117 123 130
—Portraits *See* George Frederic Watts
—"Prophet of Chelsea" 154
—Railway noises / whistles xiii 22 40 44 45
   46 51 54 56 57 62–3 75 214 219
—Reading 49 53 128 129 137 139
—Riding xiv 5 16 201 214 216
—"Sage of Chelsea" 27 *131*
—"Scotch Calvinist" 66
—Sea-bathing 12 16 22 31 49 65
—Sea-voyaging xiv 26 65 205 214 216 223
—Shaky right hand xiii 2 3 4 11 20 22 26 53
   57 65 68 75 82 90 117 149 153 156 165 203
   210 215 217
—Silence and solitude 2 4 24 45 53 62 112
   171 197 201 202 207
—Sleep xiii 19 22 25 49 54 62 63 65 75 76 82
   130 137 150 157 161 170 171 179 180 183 196
   200 202 203 205 207 209 219
—Thomas Carlyle's Photograph Album xviii
   68 175 222
—Travel 40 54 57 63 71–2 76 218
—Turkey (bird) 130
—Visits visiting 13 27 54 55 70 80 128 136 175
—Walking 23 49 54 83 113 128 129 180 201
   202 226
—Weather xiii 11 22 26 31 34 48 49 53 57 89
   105 124 128 129 134 137 150 157 165 180
   207 210 213 214
—Wide-awake (hat) 128
—Will 1871 xiii 183–87
—Work xiii xiv 64 128
—Writing table 184
—Writing with a pencil xiii 2 20 26 28 81 213
—Writing with left hand 75
CARLYLE Thomas (Alick and Janet's son)
   and Margaret 1 5 11 15 17 18 19 26 63 74 75
   77 104 135 156 166 167 231
Carlyle Thomas Alexander (son of Thomas
   and Margaret) 104 166

Carlyle's Works (various edns.) 6–7
—General index 210
—Illustrations 6–7
—Library edn. xiii xv 6 139 140 210
—People's edn. xiii xv 114 137 *141* 167 170
   209
—Proofs 106
—Translation of 82
—Uniform (Cheap) edn. 210
Caroline St. (London) 186 230
Carruthers Andrew (mason) 194
Carruthers Gabriel 194
Carruthers George (Geordie) ("Billy Bobby")
   192–3 194
Carruthers John and Agnes 193
Carruthers Rob ("Sooty") 193
CARRUTHERS Robert 143
Carruthers William ("Road Wull") 194
Carsitz (Isle of Rügen Germany) 116
Carteret John 2nd Baron *See* Granville
Cartes de visite 28 30
"Cartouche" *See* Louis Dominique
   Garthausen
Cartwright William Cornwallis 52
Cary Lucius Falkland Brancaleone and
   Bertha 236 *See also* Catherine PHILLIPPS
Castle Ashby (Northamptonshire) 46
Catholic Church 30 66 95 97 168
Caucasian 27
Caudle mix 122
Cavaignac Eléonore Louis Godfroy 182
Chabot Charles 213
Chambers William & Robert 125
"Chambers' Conversations-Lexicon" 125
Chambord Treaty of 98
"Chambres de Réunion" 97
Channing William Ellery 210
Chapman & Hall xiii 13 14 38 62 70 71 203
   213 225 232
—Receipt 170 196
Chapman Annie Marion 81 232
CHAPMAN Frederic 38 48 62 70 71 81 82
   105 106 107 114 118 133 137 141 207 208
   209 232
Chapman George 14 70 210
—*The Iliads of Homer* 14 70 210
Chapuys Eustace 7 51 52
Charlemagne 91
Charles I (king of England Scotland and Ire-
   land) 94 102 184
Charles V duke of Burgundy 7 93 94 97
Charteris Francis Richard 108
Chartism 42

Chatham William Pitt 1st Earl 101
Cheapside (London) 225
Chelsea xiv 17 40 48 49 57 63 73 86 131 153
    201 203 204 205 207 224 225 226
—Omnibus 225
Chester (Cheshire) 109
Cheyne Row 7 87 171
Cheyne Row No.5 63 150 *171* 183 203 205
    224 228 229 239
Chorley John Rutter 184
Christ Christianity 9 45 80 94 122 211
"Christ of Nations" 100 101
Christchurch (Streatham Croydon) 186
Christie Manson &Wood 45
CHRISTIE William Dougal and Mary and
    Mary Elizabeth 39 204 232
—*The Poetical Works of Dryden* 39
Christmas 106 123 130 131 137
Chrystal Jeannie (JWC's cousin) 149 239
Church of England 32
Church of Scotland 146
Church of Wales 111
Cincinnati (Ohio) 70 71
Clarence Cres. (Windsor) 236
Clarence Rd. (Clapham Park London) 41
Classen Johannes 34
Clément-Thomas Jacques Léonard 182 183
    208
Clish maclaver idle talk gossip wordy dis-
    course xv 215
Clochering phlegmy coughing 214
Clyde Firth of 27 30 227
Clydesdale 46 47
Cobbe Francis Power xix
Coethen (Germany) 145
Coldstream Guards 164
Collins Charles Allston and Kate Macready
    39 40 *See also* Dickens
Colvend (Kirkcudbrightshire) 12 15 16
Colza oil 139
Comely Bank (Edinburgh) 33 110
Commercial Bank (Dumfries) 82 229
Concord (Massachusetts) 72 210
Constantinople 162
Conway Moncure Daniel 210
Cook Ann (servant) 87
"Copper Captain Emperor" *See* Napoleon III
Corbie raven or carrion crow 5
Cornwall 31 174
Corrie Hash and Jean (Lockhart) 33
Corrie Jenny 33 *See also* James Beattie
Corry Andrew 33
Corson Samuel and Mary 4

Corson Rev. William 4
Cortes Hernando 187 8
Cotta Johann Friedrich 137
Craigen Villa (Morningside Edinburgh) 149
    239
Craigenputtoch Craigenputtock 4 8 18 33 44
    46 65 75–6 110 128 186 196 215 219
—Rabbits 5
—Stumpy 4
Crank snare difficulty 11
"Craw Jean" *See* Jean Carlyle Aitken
Cressfield (farm New South Wales) 195
Cressfield House (Dumfriesshire) 195 196
Critical and Miscellaneous Essays 109
—People's edn. 141
Croad George Hector 136
Cromwell Elizabeth 44
Cromwell Oliver 184 *See also Oliver Crom-
    well's Letters and Speeches*
Croydon (London) 230
Cumberland / Cumbria 60 224
Cummertrees (Dumfriesshire) 124
Cundall & Fleming 43
Cundall Joseph 43 62
Currie Andrew 35
Customs Service 7 229

Daily Evening Transcript (Boston) 72
Daily News 128 131 162 163 208
Daily Telegraph xvi 21 77
Daldy Frederick 159
Dante Alighieri
—*Inferno* 30 128
Darlington (Co. Durham) 158
Dart (river) 216
Darwin Charles xix
Davidson Archibald 155
Davidson Col. David 154 *173–4 233*
—Gun invention *173–4*
Dawyck and Posso (Peebleshire) 40
Delacour Benjamin 62
Delane John Thadeus 105 106
Delhi (India) 27
Denmark Danish 18 103 206
Denmark Hill (London) 81 237
Derby Edward Henry Stanley 15th earl of
    and Mary Catherine Stanley countess of
    18 178 233
Devolution War of 95 *See also* Louis XVI
Devon 215
Dickens Charles xx 18 *28* 31 39 53 71 89 111
    131 208 233
—Auction 45 53

—Funeral 28 31 32
—*The Mystery of Edwin Drood* 53
—Will 39
Dickens Charles Culliford Box 53
Dickens Mary ("Mamie") 39 40
Diderot Denis 34
Dilke Sir Charles Wentworth 153
Dingwall (Ross & Cromarty) 218 219 222
Disraeli Benjamin 21 179 *233*
—*Lothair* 21
DIXON Thomas 121 122
Dodds James 65
Dodds Rev. James and Barbara Ann 25 65
—*Lays of the Covenanters* 65
Dods Jane and William 54
Donegal (Ireland) 50
Douglas family *See* Queensberry
Douglas David 127
Douglas George 127
Douglas Henry Alexander 181 *See also* Queensberry
Douglas of Kilhead *See also* Douglas family and Queensberry
Dover (Kent) 197 198 199 230
Dover St. (London) 191 237
Dresden (Germany) 131
Drumlanrig Castle (Dumfriesshire) 46 47
Dublin (Ireland) 90
—Dublin Castle 21
Duboc Charles Edouard *See* Robert Waldmüller
Duffy Charles Gavan xvii 66 *233*
Dumfries/shire xiv 3 4 5 12 16 31 33 34 38 40 45 47 54 55 64 65 75 82 105 118 135 156 157 167 168 169 194 214 216 217 218 219 223 224 225 227 229
—Bank *See* British Linen Company Bank
Dumfries and Galloway Courier 12 16
Dunbar (East Lothian) 65 110
Duncan Barbara Ann *See* Rev. James Dodds
DUNCAN George Alexander 23 27 *64*
Duncan George John 25
Duncan Henry and Agnes 24 25
DUNCAN Margaret Ann Borthwick 64
Duncan Mary 24
Duncan William Wallace and Rachel 25
Dundas (New South Wales) 66
Dundee Courier 203
Dundrennan (Kirkcudbrightshire) 26
Durival Irma and Jean Charles and family 169 170 195 206 *233* 236 *See also* Jean Otthenin

"Dushty" *See* Baron Charles d'Eichthal
Dutch 80 95

East India Co. (British) 236 238
East India Co. (French) 95
East Lothian 108 212
Ecclefechan (Dumfriesshire) 9 23 33 56 76 192 193 194 230
Edinburgh xix xx 1 7 13 17 27 35 43 49 51 52 54 55 56 57 76 105 110 111 112 121 125 133 134 136 138 139 140 145 152 155 156 161 163 167 178 206 213 216 222 *233* 236
Edinburgh Evening Courant 105
Edinburgh Review 10 90
"Edinburgh Seven" xix xx
Edinburgh University xix 64 139 151 152 230
—International Law 180
—Rectorship xix 17 206 234
—Rhetoric and English Literature 235
Edmonstone & Douglas (publishers Edinburgh) 127 206
Egypt Egyptian 27 150
Eichthal Baron Charles d' 86 87 104 109 130 138 145 *233*
Eichthal Gustav d' 87 *233*
Elberfeld (Germany) 182
Elcho Lord *See* Francis Richard Charteris
Eliot Charles William 72
"Elsass" *See* Alsace
Elwin Whitwell 32
EMERSON Ralph Waldo and Lidian and Edward and Ellen xv 13 14 17 70 72 104 209 210 211 212 *233* 235
—*English Traits* 14
—*Letters and social aims* 210
—*Prose Works* 17
—*Society and Solitude* 13 14
England English xvi xviii 7 8 9 18 27 35 57 61 67 74 87 91 93 101 102 108 112 116 122 126 127 130 138 154 155 158 163 168 170 178 190 198 199 208 211 219 227
—History 159
—Literature 111 150
—Long Parliament 102
—Newspapers 102 108
English Illustrated Magazine 1
English St. (Dumfries) 229
Engraver *See* Joseph Brown
Ernhirst *See* Ironhirst (Dumfriesshire)
Erskine Thomas 16 17 43 181 206 *233*
Europe European xv xvi xvii 27 74 86 91 94 95 101 108 132 166 167 168 198 236

Euston Sq. Station 34
Evangelical Union Church 114
Examiner 233

Fait feat graceful smart 33
FAITHFULL Emily 122 160
Farrer Anne 92
Fash bother 6
Favre Jules Claude Gabriel 145
Fayetteville (N. Carolina) 67
Field Osgood & Co. (Boston publishers) 70
    71 167
Fife 212
Findlater Andrew 125
Florence (Italy) 212
"Fluellen" *See* Shakespeare —*Henry* V
FOLLER Karl von 126
Forbes William Hathaway and Edith 233 *See*
    also Emerson
Forrest Alexander 206
Forster Eliza 45 54 89 90 207 223 234
FORSTER John xiii xx 28 31 32 34 38 39
    44–5 48 50 53 62 89 90 105 110 114 130 131
    137 141 153 170 171 *175* 183 184 186 189
    207–8 223 227 228 233
—Accident 44 50 52
—*Life of Charles Dickens* 89 208 233
—Lunacy Board / Commission 44 175 207 233
—Retirement 175
FORSTER William Edward 153 154
—Forster's Act *See* Parliament—Elementary
    Education Act
Fort William (Invernessshire) 27
Fortnightly Review 28 62
Fowler John 223
Foxton Frederick J. and Catherine 111
Foxton G.F.M. 111
France French xv xvi xvii 5 8 53 54 60 61 73 74
    80 86 89 91 93 94 95 96 97 98 99 100 101
    102 103 104 108 109 111 116 117 118 119 120
    122 125 126 127 130 145 150 155 160 162 163
    167 168 169 173 179 195 209 212 236
—First Empire 96
—Government of National Defense 145 155
—Literature 100
—National Assembly 155 163 208
—Republican government 86 145
—Second Empire 60
France Mrs. 154
Francis I (king of France) 93 94 96
Francis Sir Philip 213
Franco-Dutch War 95

Franco-Prussian War xiii xv xviii xix 53–4 57
    60 61 73 74 77 83 89 90 114 116 120 122 130
    142 145 160 167 169 195 198 208
Frankau Rosetta 235
Frankfurt Parliament 236
Fraser's Magazine xviii 7 51 57 60 111 119 234
Frederick I Holy Roman Emperor 74
Frederick II the Great 78 111 192 211
Frederick the Great 78 104 124
—German translation 235
—Library edn. 32 33 44 48 62 70 133 206
—Maps 47 48
—Photographs for Library edn. 44
—Pictures for 62
—Portrait for Library edn. 6 7
—Proof-reading 32 33 48 49 87
—Stereotype plates 48 53
—Uniform (cheap) edn. 47 48
Free Church of Scotland 25
Freemason's Hall (Edinburgh) 178
Freeman Edward Augustus 51
French Revolution 96 100 209
—Directory and Consulate and First French
    Empire 96
—War of Fourth Coalition 96
French Revolution 28 174 235
—Library edn. 70
—People's edn. 141
French and Indian War 95
Frère Édouard 77
Freure Frederick 214
Friedrich Wilhelm elector of Brandenburg
    62 211
Froude Georgina Margaret and Rose Mary
    219 226 228 234
Froude Henrietta Elizabeth and children 52
    60 90 190 192 202 216 219 234
FROUDE James Anthony xiii xviii 5 7 8 21 22
    26 41 51 56 60 61 82 90 111 113 119 138 141
    175 178 181 182 183 184 186 189 202 215
    216 227 234
—*History of England* 7 51
—*The English in Ireland in the Eighteenth
    Century* 227
Fulham Rd. (London) 154 234

Gad's Hill (Kent) 28–9 31 45 54
Gaelic 100 110 230
Gaius Sallustius Crispus 9
Galloway 16 26 47
Galloway Alexander Stewart 6th earl of 47
Gambetta Léon 98 155

Gangrel tramp vagrant 193
Garlieston (Wigtownshire) 15 16 47
Garrick David 28
Garthausen Louis Dominique 89 101
Garthwaite Mrs. 192
Garthwaite James (shoemaker) 193
Garthwaite John 193
Garthwaite Tom (tailor) 193
Garve (Ross and Cromarty) 222
Gatehouse-of-Fleet (Kirkcudbrightshire) 26
Gaul 118
Geikie Sir Archibald 54
Geneva (Switzerland) 7
George III (king of Great Britain and Ireland) 213
George St. (Edinburgh) 133
"German Empire" *See* Holy Roman Empire
German Jewish 233 235
German Peace Festival 179
German Society for the Propagation of National Education 182
German states 53
German War-songs *See* John Stuart Blackie
Germany Germans German xv xvi xvii 18 34
   35 54 60 74 78 80 83 86 90 91 93 94 95 96
   97 99 101 102 103 104 106 108 109 110 111
   112 117 118 120 125 126 131 132 142 145
   155 160 173 179 182 183 203 206 210 212
   235 239
—Cursive script 110 128
—Literature 87
—Newspapers 129 180
Gesellschaft für Verbreitung von Volksbildung *See* German Society
Gibson Alexander 206
Gill (farm Dumfriesshire) 22 76 167 222 230
Girvan (Ayrshire) 4
Gladstone William Ewart xiv 21 30 42 57 90
   108 126 131 153 154 170 188 189 219 234
Glar glaur sticky mud 128 142
Glasgow 46 47 146 178 192 216 219 224 227
   229 239
—Steamer 227
Glasgow Herald 139 179
Glasgow University 146
—Liberal Assoc. 200
—Lord Rector nomination 200
Gleg glegness alert alertness 165
Glen (Kinmount Dumfriesshire) 181
Goethe Johann Wolfgang von 26 27 74 137
   153 171 190
—*Die natürliche Tochter* 139
—*Faust* 24

—*Iphigenie auf Taurus* 137
—*Torquato Tasso* 137
—*Werke* 137
—*West-östlicher Divan* 128
—"Wilhelm Meister's Apprenticeship" 64 139
   140 173
—"Wilhelm Meister's Travels" 140
Göttingen University of 136 137
Gomeral fool 119
Goodwin Harvey bishop of Carlisle 200
Goodwin Harvey 200
Gorchakov Prince Alexander 108
Gordon George *See* Byron
Gordon James 82 118
Gordon John 136
Goschen George Joachim 57
Graham George Farquhar 27
Grant Sir Francis 207
Granville George Leveson-Gower 2nd Earl
   101 102 126
Granville John Carteret 2nd Earl 101
Gravelotte battle of 54
Great Eastern (steamship) 129
"Great Elchi" *See* Stratford de Redcliffe
Great Northern Printing Works 236
Greece Greek 10 21 35
Greek mythology 103
Greeley Horace 107
Green Park (London) 90
Greenend (Stenhouse Edinburgh) 43 231
Greenock (Renfrewshire) 27 30 227
Greenside *See* Greenend
Gregory Dr. James 35
Gretna (parish Dumfriesshire) 193
Grey Sir George xvii 67
Grierson Jessie and George 230 *See also*
   Austin
Grosvenor St. (London) 231
Grudie / Grudy Bridge (Invernessshire) 219
Gulf Stream 128
Gull William Withey 164
Gweedore (Donegal Ireland) 50
Gymnasium of the Turnverein 179

Habsburg dynasty 94
Haddington (East Lothian) 33 54 55 56 65
   76 181
—Churchyard *See* St. Mary's Abbey Church /
   Kirk
—Prison 33
Haggs The (Ecclefechan) 193
HALL Samuel Carter and Anna Maria 123
—*Book of Memories* 123

Hamburg (Germany) 34 35 112
Hamilton (Ontario) 234
Hampshire 201 230
Hampstead (London) 180
HANNING Janet Carlyle (TC's sister Jenny)
    and Robert and family 11 63 128 135 145
    156 166 186 234
Hanning Maggie 156 234
Hanning Thomas and Margaret and Helen
    156
Harding Pullein Whinney & Gibbons
    (accountants) 81
Harding Robert Palmer 81 105 106 110 118
    125 127 128 208 225 234
Haregills (farm Dumfriesshire) 192 193
Harl slattern 193
Harrison Frederic 28
Harvard University 14 71 72 236
—Bequest of TC's books 72
Harwood Philip 51
Haute-Marne (France) 236
Hebrides Inner and Outer 205 224
Hedderwick Thomas 200
Hegel Georg Wilhelm Friedrich 71
Heidelberg (Germany) 97
Helgills / Hallygills well (Ecclefechan) 194
HELPS Arthur xvii 187 234
—*Casimir Maremma* xvii
—*The Life of Hernando Cortes* 187 188
—*The Spanish Conquest in America* 188
Henry II (king of France) 97 98
Henry V (king of England) 103
Henry VIII (king of England and Ireland)
    51 93
Heroes and Hero-Worship 27 110 123
—People's edn. 141
Hight James 21
Hill The (Dumfries) 16 75 179 216 219 226
    229
Hill George A. Lord 50
Hilliard Constance 81 134
Hindi Hindu 27
Hindoos 121
—Pamphlets 121–2
Hoddam (Dumfriesshire) 193 194
HOGARTH Georgina 39 45 *See also* Dickens
Holden Jenny C. and Mary 156 166 *See also*
    Hanning
Holl William the younger 141
Holland Lady Emma 10
Holmhill (Thornhill Dumfriesshire) 12 31 237
Holne Park (Devon) 216 218
Holy Roman Emperor *See* Charles V

Holy Roman Empire 91 93 94 95 97 118 230
Homer 158
—*Iliad and Odyssey* 158 *See also* Alexander
    Pope and George Chapman
Hooper Rev. Richard 14
Hotten John Camden 210
—*On the Choice of Books* 210
Houghton Richard Monckton Milnes Lord
    and Annabella 153 234
HOWARD George James and Rosalind
    Frances 125 224 224 235 237 *See also*
    Stanley
Hübner Johann 35
—*Genealogische Tabellen* 35
Huguenots 94 97
Hume David 159
—*History of England* 159
Hungary 94
Hunsrück (mountains) 98
Hunter Dr. Jacob Dickson 13 149 169
HUXLEY Thomas Henry 135 136 141 234
Hyde Park (London) 61 110 128
Hyderabad (India) 236

Iceland 223
Ile-de-France 132
Illustrated London News 78 86 87 91 99 138
    143 145 179
Illustrated Times 179
India Indians 20 23 44 95 173
India St. (Edinburgh) 195
Invermein (farm New South Wales) 195
Inverness/shire 12 27 46 218 219 222 224
Inverness Courier 143
Iona (island) 224
Iona (steamship) 224
Ireland Irish 7 8 21 22 30 46 49 50 57 60 81
    82 119 137 229 233
—Catholics 166
—Emigrants 57
—Priests 66
Irish Channel 90
Irish St. (Dumfries) 33
"Iron duke" *See* Wellington duke of
Ironhirst (Dumfriesshire) 5 8 11 12 238
Irving Edward and Isabella and Edward 198
    234 *See also Reminiscences*
Italy Italians 212 235 238

James VI and I (king of Scotland England
    and Ireland) 184
James St. (Portobello) 234
Jardine John and Agnes and family 192 193

Jeffrey Francis 10
Jenkins John Edward xviii 42
—*Ginx's Baby* xvii 42
"Jeremias Gotthelf" *See* Albrecht Bitzius
Jerusalem 45
Jews Jewish 122
Jewsbury Geraldine Endsor xiv 120 141 *170*
188 189 190 234
—Civil List Pension xiv 141 153 170 188 190
Jex-Blake Sophia Louisa xix 152
Johanneum (Hamburg) 34 35
Johnson Samuel 8 28
Johnstone Rev. John 9
"Junius" *See* Sir Philip Francis

Kalle Fritz 182
Kant Immanuel 73
Keir (Stirlingshire) 117
Keith James Francis Edward Marshal 44
Kensington (London) 120
Kentish Town (London) 1
KERR Ralph Drury Lord 41 42
Kerry (Ireland) 21 22 90
Keswick (Cumbria) 237
Kew Gardens (London) 234
Khan Syed Ahmed 23 27
—*Essays on the Life of Mohammed* 27
Khan Syed Mahmood 27
Kilhead *See* Kinmount
Kilrush *See* Portrush
KINGSLEY Charles 108 109 141
Kinlochluichart (Ross and Cromarty) 12 46
Kinmount (Perthshire) 181
Kinnoul (Perthshire) 181
Kirkandrews (Kirkcudbrightshire) 16 31
Kirkcudbright/shire 12 22 31 34
Kirkpatrick Catherine Aurora ("Kitty") *See*
Catherine PHILLIPPS
Kirkpatrick Edward 142 175
Kirkpatrick James Achilles and Khair-un-
Nissa 236
Kirksyke (farm Dumfriesshire) 192 193
Knockbreck (Kirkcudbrightshire) 31
Köhler Johann David xvi 104

La Marck Charlotte de 97
La Marck Erard de 94
La Marck Robert II de 94
La Rochelle 94
La Roma del Popolo 154
LAING David 136 212 213 234
Landford Wood (Melchet estate) 202

Landseer Sir Edwin 207
Latin 9 35
Latter-Day Pamphlets 153
Lawrence St. (Chelsea) 205 *See also* Peabody
Mansions
Lawson George *9–10*
LAWSON Robert xix xx 151
LAWTON Joseph 157
Le Vert Galant (France) 132 138
Lecky William Hartpole 133
Leeds (Yorkshire) 130
Leek (Staffordshire) 232
Leibing Franz 182
Leith (Edinburgh) 179
Lemonte Jacques 182
"Letter to the *Times*" 86 89 *91–103* 104 108
109 112 118 120 122 149 *See also* Franco-
Prussian War
Letters and Memorials of JWC 183
Lewis Isle of (Outer Hebrides) 205
Lewis Stewart 23
Liberton (Edinburgh) 231
Liège (Belgium) 94
Life of Sterling 174 238
—People's edn. 141 174
Linlathen (Dundee) 233
Linton Eliza Lynn 117
—"Girl of the Period" 117
Little Archibald and Francis 195 196
Little Mary and Maxwell 195 196
Little Dr. William 195
Liverpool 63 73 105 118 119 126 128 215 225
226 229 239
Liverpool Mercury 226
Liverpool St. / Terr. (Dover Kent) 198
Loch Luichart 12 26 218 219 227 *See also*
Kinlochluichart
Lochmaben Rd. (Dumfries) 229
Lockerbie House (Dumfriesshire) 181
Lockhart Jenny 33
London Londoners 1 7 15 18 22 31 32 45 63
70 71 76 81 105 107 112 118 138 150 162 171
178 179 181 183 185 199 202 206 210 212
222 225 226 229 231 234 236
—Ashes in the street 138
—School Board 135 136
—Streets and houses 171
London Bridge 80
London Library 137
"Lord Bacon" *See* James Spedding
Lorimer James (1779–1868) 181
Lorimer James (1818–90) 180

Lorimer Rev. Robert and Elizabeth 181
Lorne marquess of *See* John G. E. H. D.
  Sutherland Campbell
Lorraine (France) xv 54 60 73 91 93 96 97 101
  102 117 118 145
Lotharingia / Lothringen (France) 91 *See
  also* Lorraine
Lothian Lady Constance Harriet Maho-
  nesa 41
Lothian William Schomberg Robert Kerr
  Marquess of 41
Louis Napoleon *See* Napoleon III
Louis the Pious and sons 91
Louis XI ("the Prudent" king of France) 93
Louis XIV (king of France) 95 96 97
Louis XV (king of France) 95
Louis-Philippe (king of France) 182
Louisiana 95
Low Countries 93
Lowe Robert and Georgiana 18 19 178 235
Lowell Effie 211 212
Lowell Josephine Shaw and Charles Russell
  211
Lowndes William Selby 125
Loyson Charles Jean Marie 116
LÜDERS Dr. Ferdinand 34 35
Lunacy Board 151
Lutheranism 98
Lyndsay Sir David 212

MACCALL William 82 119 235
— "Penitent France" 119
M'Diarmid William Ritchie 12 16
MACFARLANE John 9
— *The Life and Times of George Lawson,
  D.D.* 9
Mackenzie *See* Stewart-Mackenzie
Macmillan's Magazine 71 129 169 235
McRaye Mrs. 17
Macedon / Macedonia 99 102 103
Mahomet / Mohammed / Muhammed 23 27
  161
Malebolge *See* Dante — *Inferno*
Manchester 130 139 142 206
Marigold *See* Mary Florence Baring
Mark Lane (London) 70
Markham Sq. (Chelsea) 234
Martin J. Royle 139 196
Martineau Harriet xix
Marylebone (London) 136
Mason & Co. (photographers) 128
Mason Robert Hindry 28

Massachusetts 71
MASSON David and Emily xix 1 7 54 55 56
  65 105 125 136 152 186 235
Masson Rosaline 54 56
Maximilian I Holy Roman Emperor 93
Maxwell Sir William Stirling and Lady Anna
  Maria 105 109 117 118 164 235
— *The Fall of Two Empires* 105 109
Mayo Richard Southwell Bourke 6th earl of
  20
Mazzini Joseph 28 154 235 238
Meadows Arthur 146
Melchet Court (Hampshire) 197 201 202 204
  205 208 214 230
Menton (Alpes-Maritimes France) 17
Menzel Friedrich Wilhelm 44
Mersey (river) 229
Metz (France) xvii 97 101
— Metz la Pucelle 97
Mid-Steeple (Dumfries) 33 47
Middlebie (Dumfriesshire) 232
Mill John Stuart and Harriet 130 235
Millais John Everett 236
Milnes Richard *See* Lord Houghton
Mirehouse (Cumbria) 113 237
Mississippi State Senate xviii 67 68
Mitchell Robert 25
Moir George 134
Molloch 86
Moltke Count Helmuth von 142
Monmouth (Wales) 102
"Monument of Mercy" 75
Moray Firth 27
Morier David Richard 178
Morier James Justinian and John Philip and
  William 178
Morier Robert Burnet David 178
Mormons 211
Morning Post 136 203
Morningside (Edinburgh) 149 233
— Asylum 149
Moxon Edward 68
Mull Isle of 224 227
Munich (Germany) 104 109 145 233
Munro Alexander and Mary and John Arthur
  Ruskin and Henry Acland 143
Muslims 23

NAESMYTH Sir John Murray 40
Nairn (Moray) 27
Nantes Edict of 94
Naples king of *See* Charles V

Napoleon Bonaparte (emperor of France) 95
   96 103 167
Napoleon III 53 93 96 98 182 212 *235*
Napoleonic wars 194
—Volunteer Corps 194
National Portrait Gallery (London) 178
Native American xviii 68
Naworth Castle (Cumbria) 224
Neaves Charles Lord 134
Nelson Lady Frances Elizabeth 202
Nether Craigenputtoch (Dumfriesshire) 4
Neuberg Joseph 111 235
New Bond St. (London) 43
New Forest (Hampshire) 201
New France 95
New South Wales (Australia) 66 195
New Year 135 193 209
—Wishes and gifts and customs 155
New York 3 202
New York Tribune 107
New Zealand 67
Newbattle Ter. (Edinburgh) 233
Newcastle Thomas Pelham-Hollis duke of
   101–2
Newspaper cuttings 117 129
Newspaper strokes on 63 157 217
Niobe 103
Nithsdale (Dumfriesshire) 46
Normandy 90
North German Federation 230
North German States 61
Northampton Charles Douglas-Compton 3d
   marquess of 46
Northern Echo 158
Northern Steamers 34 *See also* Aberdeen
   Steamers
Norton Charles Eliot 212 *236*
Norway 26 32
Norwich (Norfolk) 73
Norwood (London) 162
Nürnberg (Germany) 116
—*Nürnberg Tagblatt* 116

Oakley St. (Chelsea) 128
Oban (Argyllshire) 224 227
Ohio 70
Old Bond St. (London) 28
OLIPHANT Margaret xiv 188 192 *236*
Oliver Cromwell's Letters and Speeches
—Death mask 1
—Library edn. 1 8 13 14 34 44 70
—People's edn. 141

—Wart xv
—Wood-cut of portrait xv
On Heroes 27 110 123
Onslow Gdns. (London) 234
Onslow Sq. (London) 7
Ontario (Canada) 230
Opium 149 175 239
Orange-Nassau Elisabeth countess of 97 *See
   also* Turenne
Orford Horace Walpole 4th earl of 102
Orkney Islands 32 214 216 223
Orleans monarchy 96
Orr William Somerville 13
Orrock Agnes and Elizabeth 133
Orton Hall (Cumbria) 200
Otthenin Jean and Margaret 130 169 170 195
   196 206 *236*
Ottoman Empire 94
Owen Richard and Caroline Amelia 223

Pacific (ocean) 210
Packets (steamships) 192
Paisley (Renfrewshire) 227
Palace Gate House (Kensington) 224 234
Palatinate 97
Pall Mall Gazette 6 51 158 160
Paris (France) 6 7 8 60 77 80 82 86 87 91 102
   116 126 129 131 138 145 155 162 182 198
   208 212
—Bois de Boulogne 91 145
—Commune 182 *208*
—Printshops 8
—Siege of 77 82 86 87 91 96 99 102 132 145
   155
—Treaty of 108
Park Mr. 12
Park Walk (Chelsea) 135
PARKES Henry xvii 66
—Education 66
—Public Schools Act (Australia) 66
Parliament
—Army Reform 199 219
—Ballot boxes 122
—"Constitutional Government" 178
—Civil List pensions 141 153 170 188 *See also*
   Geraldine Jewsbury
—Elementary Education Act (1870) 154
—Emigration Commission 66–7
—House of Commons 57 219
—House of Lords 219
—Irish Land Bill 21 30
—Liberals 57 153 234 235

—Poor Law Board 57
—Royal Warrant 219
—War Office 154
—Whigs 237
Parramatta (Sydney Australia) 66
Past and Present xvii 219
—People's edn. 141
Paterson David (Erskine's sister) 233
Paterson James Erskine and Mary Jane 181
  233 236
"Patience and shuffle the cards" (Cervantes)
  83
"Patricius Walker" *See* William Allingham
Pauli Reinhold 136
Payne James Bertrand 68
Peabody George 205
Peabody Mansions (Chelsea) 205
Peebles/shire (Scottish Borders) 25 40 229
Pellegrini Carlo 55
"Penny-a-liners" 42 131 138
Pentland Firth (Scotland) 216
"People's William" *See* William Gladstone
"Père Hyacinthe" *See* Charles Jean Marie
  Loyson
Perth / Perthshire 149 181
—Asylum 149
Pharaoh 20
Philharmonic Hall (Liverpool) 73
Philip II (king of Macedon) 99 127
PHILLIPPS Catherine and family 197 236
Photographs 28 224 225
Picardy Pl. (Edinburgh) 142
Piccadilly (London) 14 128 212
Pinkerton Sir John 159
—*Modern Geography* 159
Pisa (Italy) 154
Pitt William ("the elder") *See* Chatham
Place Pigalle Montmartre (Paris) 183
Plato 158 9
Plattnauer Richard Eduard 236
Playfair Lyon 139
Plessis Armand Jean de duc de Richelieu and
  Fronsac 94 95 96
Political Economy 159
Pollock William Frederick and Juliet 192
Pomona (Roman goddess) 83
Ponsonby Sir Henry Frederick 188 190
"Poor fellow after all" (coterie speech) 27 128
Pope Alexander 158
—*Iliad* and *Odyssey* 158
—*Essay on Man* 164 207
Portobello (Edinburgh) 13

Portrush (County Antrim) 46 49
Post Office / Postal service 7 77 127 130 202
—Balloon post xvi 91 98 99
Potsdam (Germany) 182
Preston (Lancashire) 38
Prestonkirk (E. Lothian) 230
Protestants 35 66 94 95 97 98
Prussia Prussians 44 53 60 61 77 78 82 86 91
  93 99 101 102 103 112 116 119 120 130 132
  142 145 162 167 236
Prussian Diet 102
Public Advertiser 213
Public Opinion 128
"Purchase system" *See* Parliament —Army
  Reform
Puttock hawk 4

Quain Dr. Richard 44 454 207 216 236
Quàm primùm 78
Queen (steamship) 216
Queensberry Archibald 8th marquess of 181
Queensberry Charles 6th marquess of 181
Queensberry John 7th marquess of 181
Queensberry John Sholto Douglas 9th mar-
  quess of 181
Quiller Mr. (Chelsea pharmacist) 82

Railway
—Ayrshire 227
—Caledonian 55
—Glasgow & South-Western 227
—London & South-Western 204
—Travel 34 218
Ralston William Ralston Shedden 6
Ramelton (Gweedore Ireland) *See* Ballyare
Raven Rev. Wodehouse 186
Red Sea 20
Redcliffe Stratford Canning 1st Viscount
  Stratford de 162
Redwoods (trees) 210
Reed George 202
Refugees Benevolent Fund 160 *See also*
  Emily FAITHFULL
Regent St. (Portobello Edinburgh) 130
Regent Terr. (Edinburgh) 54 55 235
Regent's Park (London) 129
Reichenbach Hedwig von 120 129 173 236
Reichenbach Count Oskar von and family
  129 142 236
"Reminiscence of JWC" 217
Reminiscences xiii 4 5 9 18 24 156 169 184 185
  198 217 234 238

Republican 119
Republicanism 78
Revels Hiram Rhodes xviii 67–9
Rhine (river) 97
Rhineland Palatinate 98
Rhyader (Wales) 111
Richelieu *See* Armand Jean du Plessis
Richter Jean Paul 140
Ringhoffer Karl 112
Ringwould (Dover Kent) 197
Ripple Court (Dover Kent) 197
Ritchie Lady *See* Anne Isabella Thackeray
Robert the Bruce (king of Scotland) 35
—Statue 35
Roberts Shirley xix
Robson & Son 186
Robson Charles 1 47 48 49–50 53 *236*
—Bankruptcy 48 50 236
Rock Terr. (Claughton Birkenhead) 229
Roebuck John Arthur 170
ROGERS Charles 35 38
Roman Catholic Church 116
Roman Hill (Dumfriesshire) 38
Rome Roman 9 154
Romilly Sir John 1st Baron 52
Romsey Station (Hampshire) 204 230
Roslyn Park (Hampstead) 235
Royal Academy 207
Royal Bounty 189 *See also* Geraldine Jews-
bury —Civil List Pension
Royal Infirmary of Edinburgh xix
Royal Institution (London) 7 238
Royal Mail Steamer 224
Royal Scottish Academy Exhibition 142
Rügen Isle of 116
RUSKIN John xvi 77 80 81 82 134 141 200
213 229 *236*
—*Fors Clavigera* 134 199 200
Ruskin John James and Margaret 237
Russell Dr. James and Mary *12–13* 28 31 237
Russell John Scott 129
Russia Russians 6 108 111 142 150 238
Russian-Turk War 142
Ruthwell (Dumfriesshire) 23 24 25 168
Rutland Charles Cecil John Manners 6th
duke of 47
Rutterford James 21

Sacy A. I. Silvestre de 27
St. Andrews 178 181
St. Andrews University 139 175 *178* 181
—United College 180
St. Clair (steamship) 216

St. Fechan (Ecclefechan) 194
St. George's Hall (Langham Pl. London) 6
St. George's Hospital (London) 226
St. John's Grove (Richmond Surrey) 12
St. Luke's (Chelsea) 31 147 230
St. Magnus (steamship) 216
St. Mary's Abbey Church / Kirk (Hadding-
ton) 54 56
St. Michael 61 73
St. Pancras Rd. (London) 179 236
Salford (Lancashire) 139
Salisbury James Gascoyne-Cecil 2nd mar-
quess of and Mary Catherine marchioness
18 233
Salisbury Robert Cecil 1st earl of 19
San Francisco 211
San Gallo (Florence Italy) 212
Sandown Park (Wavertree Liverpool) 239
Sanquhar (Dumfriesshire) 46 47
Sartor Resartus 47 179 236
—Library edn. 141
—People's edn. 141 174 179 203 209
Satan 61 73
Saturday Review 51 117
Saxon Army 131
Saxony Frederick Augustus Albert crown
prince of 131
Schiller Friedrich 173
—*Wallenstein* 173
Schindler Anton 128
Schleswig and Holstein duchies of 103
Schleswig-Holstein war 103
Scotch firs 5
Scotland Scots Scottish Scotch xv 2 3 6 9 10
16 17 22 35 38 40 62 63 64 68 70 110 117
127 129 134 138 155 159 164 167 178 195
205 227
—Highlands xiv 50 217
Scotsbrig (farm Dumfriesshire) 8 17 34 76
167 222 231 232 237
Scotsman xix 105 117 118 125 129 138 178
224
Scott Jenny (Janet) (James Carlyle's da.)
William and family 31 32 76 237
Scott Sir Walter 155
—Centenary celebrations 155
Scribner Charles & Son (New York pub-
lishers) 51
Scutze-Delitzsch Herman 182
Seaforth Lodge (Devon) 230
Sedan Battle of 86 93 102 119
Seidlitz / Seydlitz Friedrich Wilhelm von 4
Sepulchre *See* Jerusalem

Seven Weeks' War *See* Austro-Prussian War
Severn Arthur 229
Severn Joan *See* Joan Agnew
Shairp John Campbell and Eliza 180 181
Shakespeare William 18
—*Hamlet* 113 211
—*Henry V* 102 150
—*Much Ado About Nothing* 104
Shankland Mr. (Ecclefechan banker) 194
Sheffield (Yorkshire) 170
Shelley Percy Bysshe 111
Shetland 32 216 223
Shirley (England) 150
"Shooting Niagara: and After?" 109
Sicily king of *See* Charles V
Signet Library (Edinburgh) 213 234
Simancas (Spain) 52
—Spanish State Papers 52
Sims Jane and Robert and family 2 3 5 11 15
  17 19 26 63 74 77 135 167 *See also* Alexan-
  der Carlyle (TC's brother)
Sinclair Sir George 162
Sinclair Sir John Tollemache 162
—*The Franco-Prussian War* 162
Skae Dr. David 149
Skye Isle of 12 219 224 227
Sloane Sq. (Chelsea) 82
Sloane St. (Chelsea) 225
Smeaton Mark 52
Smith Adam 159
—*Wealth of Nations* 159
Smith Edmund 28
Smith Sydney 10
Snipe (bird) 73
Socrates 10 158
"Sorrow on it" (coterie speech) 31
South Australia 67
South Lodge (South Pl. Knightsbridge Lon-
  don) 164 168 238
Southern Uplands 47
Southey Sir Robert 12
Spa (Germany) 183
Spain Spanish 52 93
—King of *See* Charles V
Spanish Conquest *See* Arthur Helps
Spanish Succession War of the 95 *See also*
  Louis XIV
SPEDDING James xx 61 111 113 237
SPEDDING Thomas Story and Frances
  Elizabeth xx 60 61 111 113 237
Standard 64
Stanhope Philip Henry 5th Earl 178
Stanhope St. (London) 90 107

Stanley Edward John Lord 237
Stanley Edward Lyulph 237
STANLEY Lady Henrietta Maria 160 162 165
  190 191 192 209 237
Stanley John and Susan Mary Elizabeth 225
Stanley Kate *See* Amberley
Stanley Maude 192 237
Stead William Thomas 158
Steamer Travel 27 32
Stephen Harriet 192
STEPHEN James Fitzjames and Mary
  Richenda and family 20 21 60 192 237
Stereotype plates 186
Stereotypers 71
Sterling Sir Anthony Coningham xx 63 164–5
  168 170 238
Sterling Edward and Hester 169 238
Sterling John 62 169 174 237
STERLING Capt. John Barton and Caroline
  164 165 168 170
Sterling Julia Maria and Hester Isabella 174
  238
Steuart Archibald James Edward 195
Stewart Hugh and John 238
Stewart James 5 8 238
Stewart Margaret (TC's niece) and Thomas
  and family 5 8 12 230 238
Stewart-Mackenzie James Alexander and
  Mary Elizabeth Frederica 230
Stewart-Mackenzie Keith William 225
Steyne Hotel (Worthing Sussex) 89
Stirling 35
—Stirling Castle 235
Stirling Christian (Erskine's sister) 233 238
Stirling James Hutchison 71
—*The Secret of Hegel* 71
Stirling Journal 35
Stirling School of Arts 105
Stirling Susan and James 136 142
Strachey Sir Edward 5 23
Strachey Edward and Julia 5 23 198 238
Strachey John 23
Strafford Thomas Wentworth 1st earl of 102
Strasbourg / Strasburg xvii 78 91 97
—Siege of 145
Stratford (Ontario) 8
Stratford *See* Redcliffe
Strathpeffer (Invernessshire) 46 50 218 219
  223 224
Streatham (London) 186
Stump Orators 12
Suffolk 21
Sufistic Quatrains of Omar Khayyam 122

Suleiman the Magnificent sultan 94
Sunderland 121
Surgeons' Hall Riot (Edinburgh) xix
Sussex 89
Sweden 32
Switzerland Swiss 80
Sydney (Australia) 60 67
Synod of Lothian and Tweeddale 49

TAIT Robert Scott 83 128 147 238
—A Chelsea Interior 238
Tales of Musaeus Tieck 140
Tasso Torquato 137 139
—La Gerusalemme Liberata 137
Telegrams 31 222
Telegraph xvi
Tennyson Alfred 68 111 141 170 238
Tennyson Emily Sarah 190 192 238
Tessé René de Froulay comte de 97
Teutonic 93 See also Germany
Téwodros II (emperor of Abyssinia) 20
Thackeray Anne Isabella 190 191 192
Thackeray William Makepeace and Isabella
    111 190 192
Thiers Adolphe 155 163 167 208
—Histoire du consulat et de l'empire 163
Thirty-Years' War 95
THOMPSON John Reuben xviii 67 68
Thor's hammer 74
Thornhill (Dumfriesshire) 12 13 237
Three Bishoprics 97 98 See also Metz and
    Toul and Verdun
Thrums threads 62
"Thunderer of the Times" See Edward
    Sterling
Times xiii xv xvi xvii 21 66 73 86 90 91 102 103
    104 105 106 107 108 109 110 112 117 118 120
    122 124 127 145 149 155 169 183 207 216
Tipperlinn House (Morningside Edinburgh)
    149
Tobacco box 192
Tobacco smoking cigars pipes 17 68 77 135
    146 201 202
Toronto (Canada) 192 194 230
Toul (France) 97
Tours (France) 99 155 208
Townwall St. (Dover Kent) 198
Translations from the German 140 See also
    Wilhelm Meister and Tales of Musaeus
    Tieck and Jean Paul Richter
Traquair (Peebleshire) 49
Treitzsauerwein Marx 93

Trollope Anthony 48
—Rachel Ray 48
Troqueer (Dumfriesshire) 229
Trotter Margaret Coutts 47
TUPPER Martin 140
Turenne Henri de la Tour d'Auvergne duc de
    Bouillon and vicomte de 96-7
Turenne Henri de la Tour d'Auvergne vicomte
    de 96 97
Turgenev Ivan 110 128-9 136 150 201 238
—Scènes de la russe 111
Turkey 94 108 162
Twisleton Edward Turner Boyd 213
TYNDALL John 17 73 82 135 136 141 238
—Essays on the Use and Limit of the Imagi-
    nation in Science 73
—"On the Scientific Limit of the Imagina-
    tion"73
—"On the Scientific Use of the Imagina-
    tion"73

Unitarians 235
United Kingdom 67
United Presbyterian Church 110
United States See America
Upper Belgrave Pl. (London) 143
Upper Grosvenor St. (London) 18
Upper Stenhouse (Liberton Edinburgh) 231
Usedom Count Karl Georg Guido Ludwig
    von 116
Utah 211

Vanity Fair 55
Vassy (Haute-Marne France) 236
Vatican Council 14
—Papal Infallibility 14
Venturi Emilie 154 238
Verdun (France) 97
—Treaty of 91
Verein für Volksbildung 182
Versailles 95 98 129 132 See also Franco-
    Prussian War
Viardot Pauline 111
Vichy (France) 5 16 26 105
Victoria (Australia) 66
Victoria (queen of the United Kingdom of
    Great Britain and Ireland) xiv 146 188 234
    238
Victoria Magazine 122 160
Vienna (Austria) 7 51 93 138
Villa d'Elsi (San Gallo Florence) 212
Ville Evrart (France) 131